U0920594

上海市浦东新区统计局
SHANGHAI PUDONG NEW AREA STATISTICAL BUREAU
国家统计局浦东调查队
PUDONG SURVEY TEAM OF NATIONAL STAT ISTICS BUREAU

上海浦东新区统计年鉴 2012

SHANGHAI PUDONG NEW AREA STATISTICAL YEARBOOK

(总第19期 No.19)

新区生产总值(亿元)

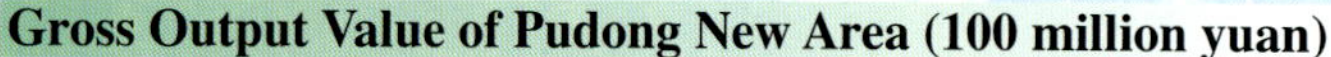
Gross Output Value of Pudong New Area (100 million yuan)

新区生产总值构成(%)

Composition of GDP of PNA (%)

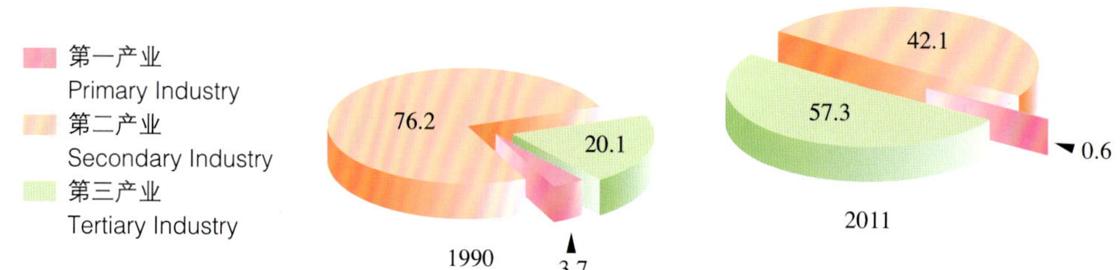

财政收入(亿元)

Financial Revenue (100 million yuan)

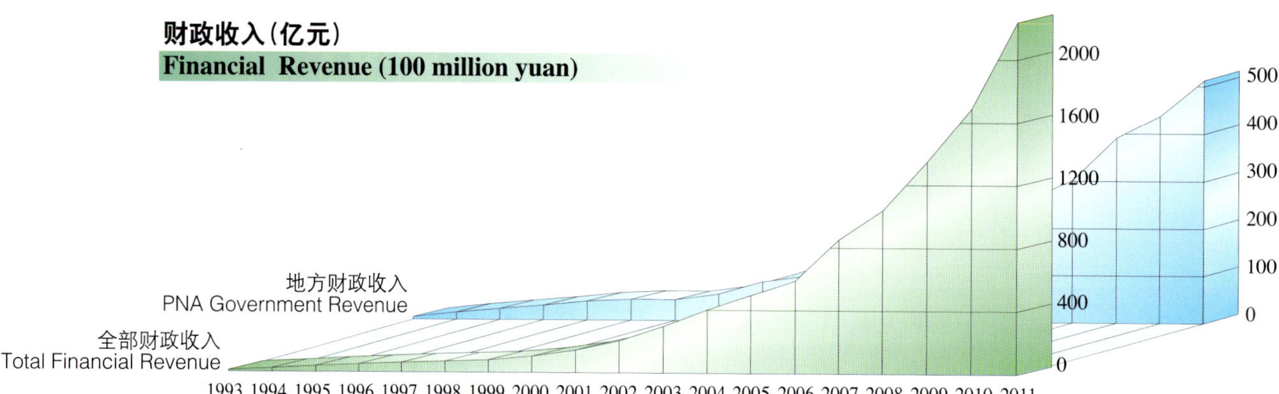

工业总产值指数(以1990年为100)

Indices of Gross Output Value of Industry (1990 as 100)

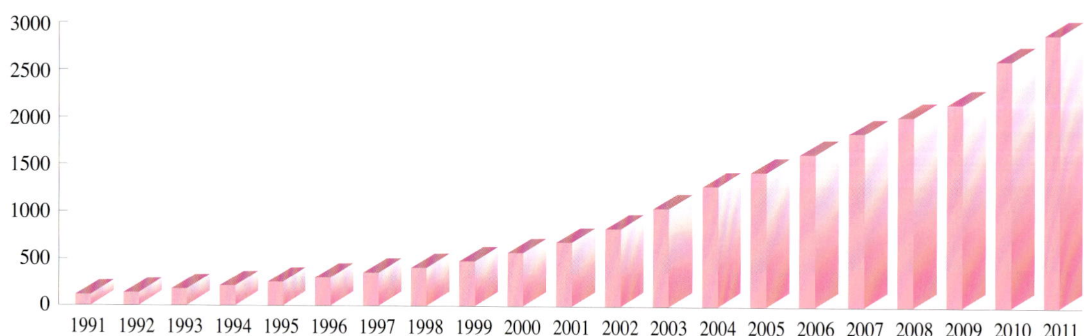

农业总产值(亿元)
Gross Output Value of Agriculture (100 million yuan)

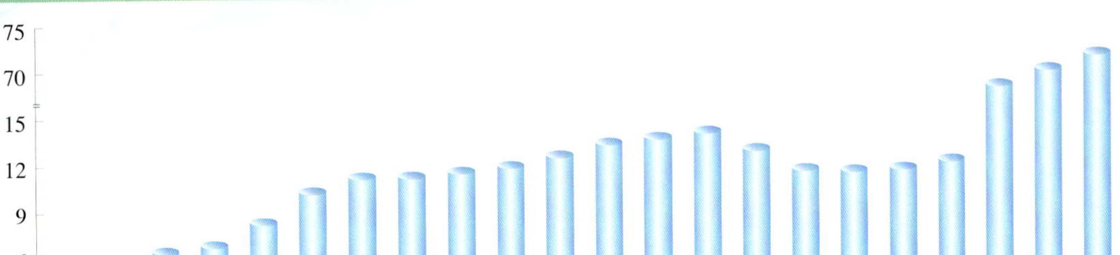

进出口货物总值(亿美元)
Total Value of Imports and Exports (USD 100 million)

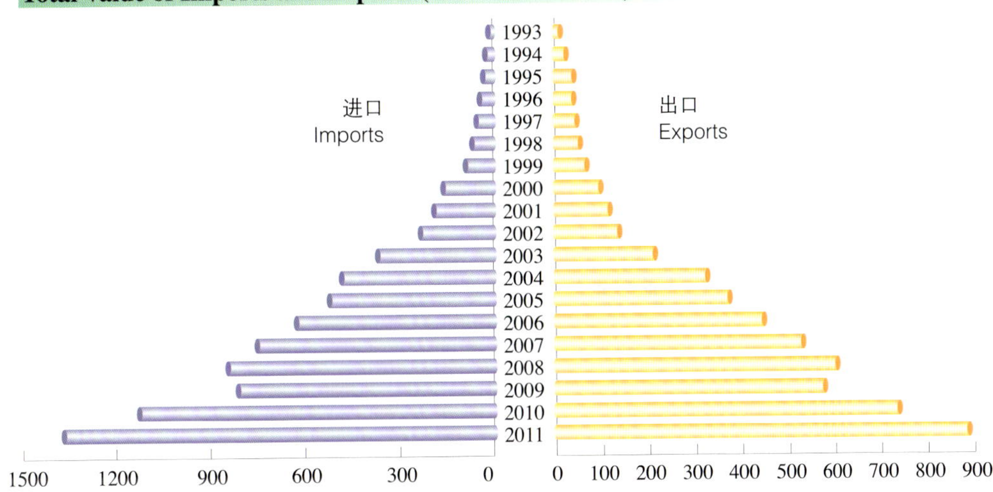

2011年六个工业重点发展行业产值构成(%)
Composition of Gross Output Value of Six Key Industries in 2011 (%)

电子信息产品制造业
Electronic Information Product Manufacturing
汽车制造业
Automobile Manufacturing
石油化工及精细化工制造业
Pertrochemical and Fine Chemical Industry
精品钢材制造业
Fine Steel and Iron Manufacturing
成套设备制造业
Equipment Complex Manufacturing
生物医药制造业
Bio-medicine Manufacturing

城市基础设施投资额构成(%)
Composition of Urban Infrastructure Investment (%)

电力建设
Electricity
运输邮电
Transportation,Post and Telecommunications
公用事业
Public Utilities
市政建设
Civic Construction

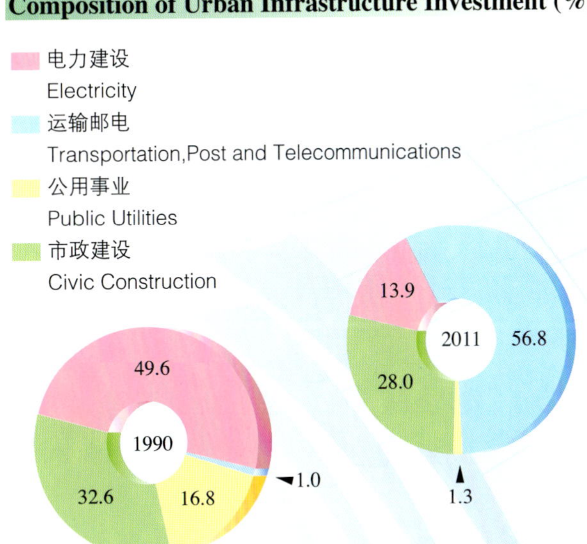

固定资产投资和城市基础设施投资(亿元)
Total Investment in Fixed Assets and Urban Infrastructure (100 million yuan)

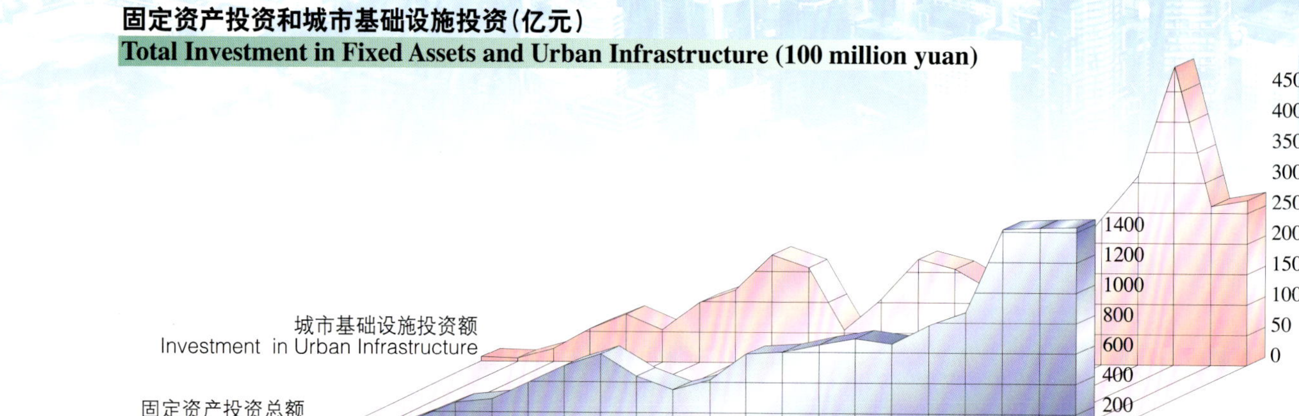

中外资银行本外币存贷款年末余额(亿元)
Balance of RMB and Foreign Currencies Deposits and Loans in Chinese and Foreign Banks (100 million yuan)

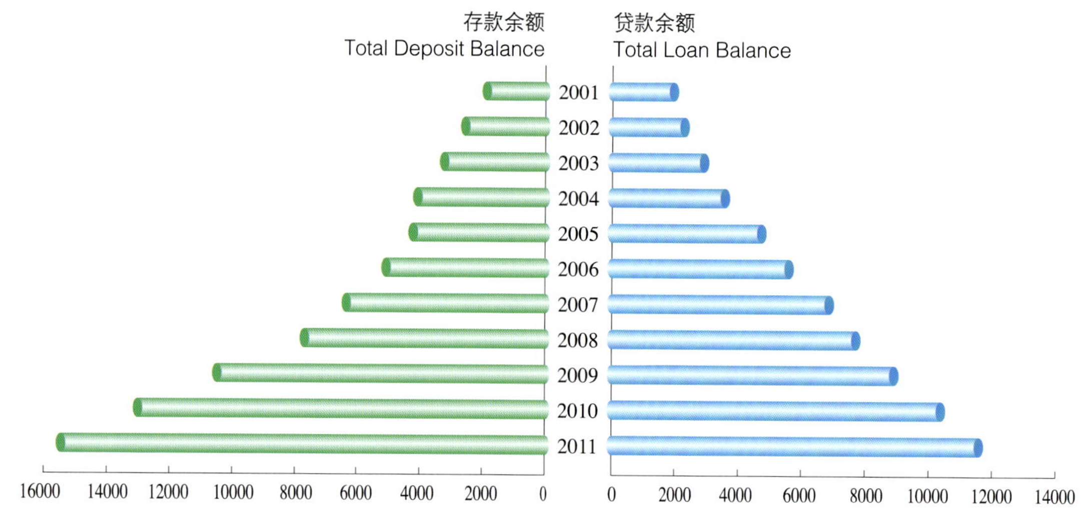

上海证券交易所市价总值(亿元)
Market Value of Shanghai Stock Exchange (100 million yuan)

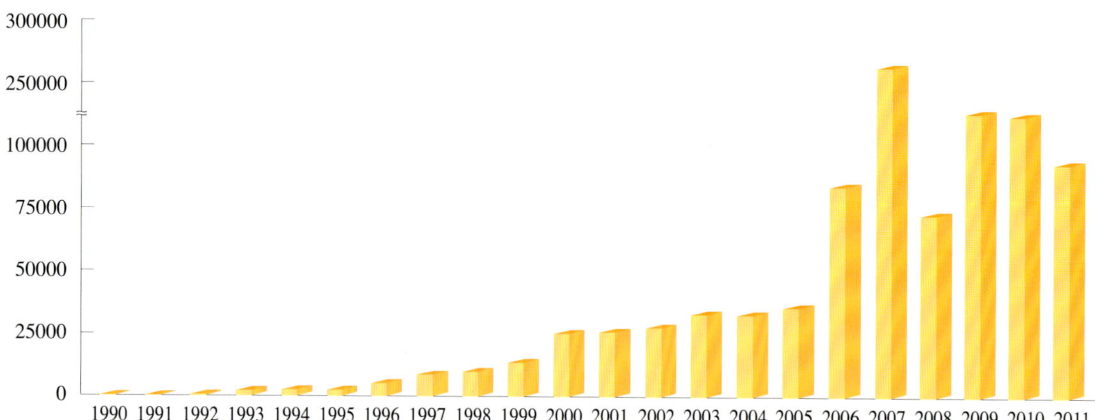

社会消费品零售总额(亿元)
Total Retail Sales of Consumer Goods (100 million yuan)

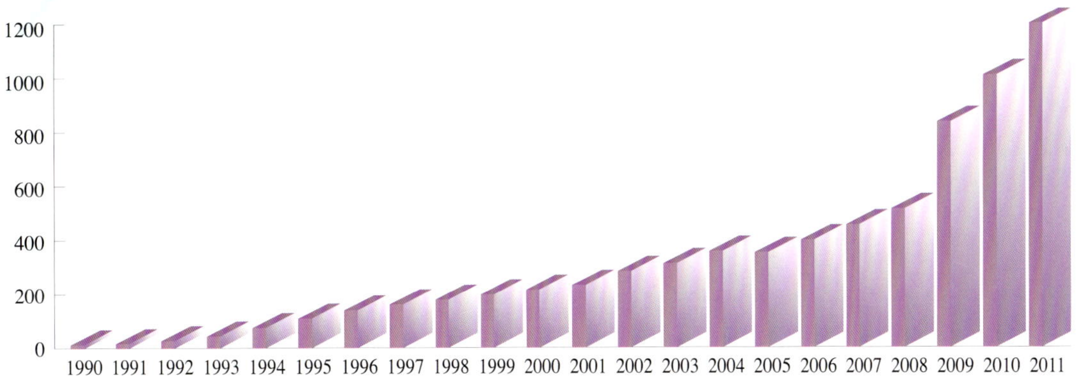

外商合同投资额的投资方式构成(%)
Composition of Contract Value of Foreign Investment by Ways of Investment (%)

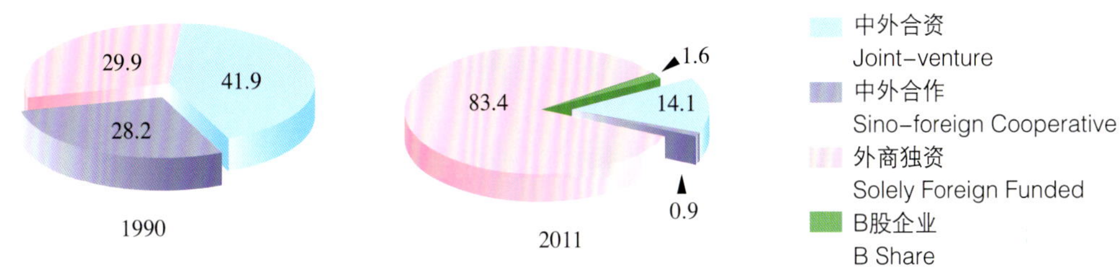

居民储蓄存款年末余额(亿元)
Resident Savings Deposit (100 million yuan)

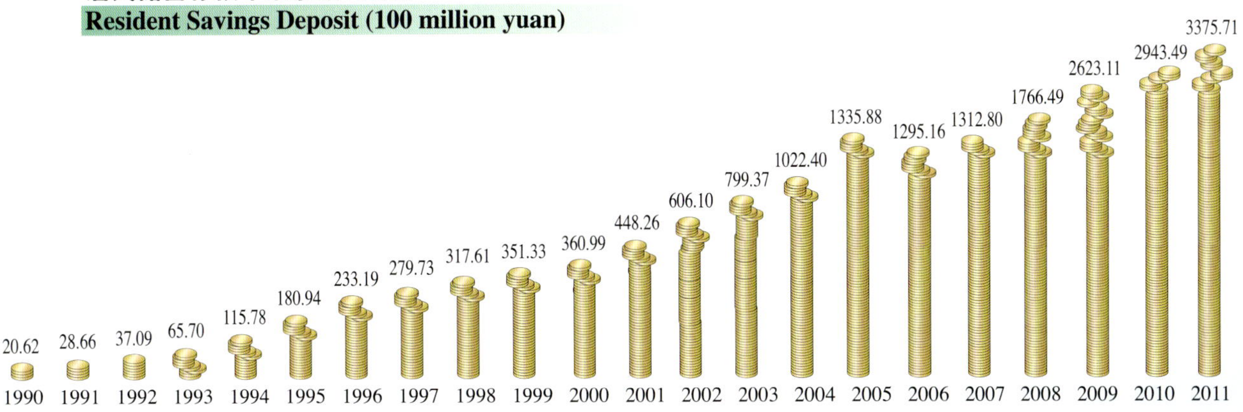

2011年城镇居民家庭消费支出构成(%)
Composition of Consumption Expenditure of Urban Families in 2011 (%)

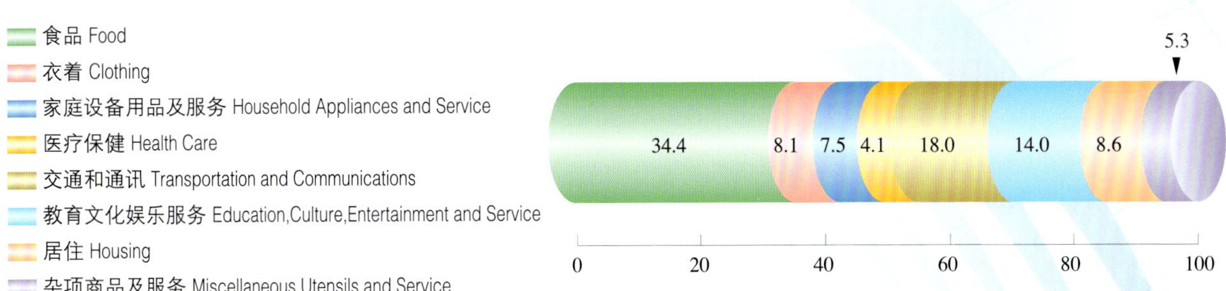

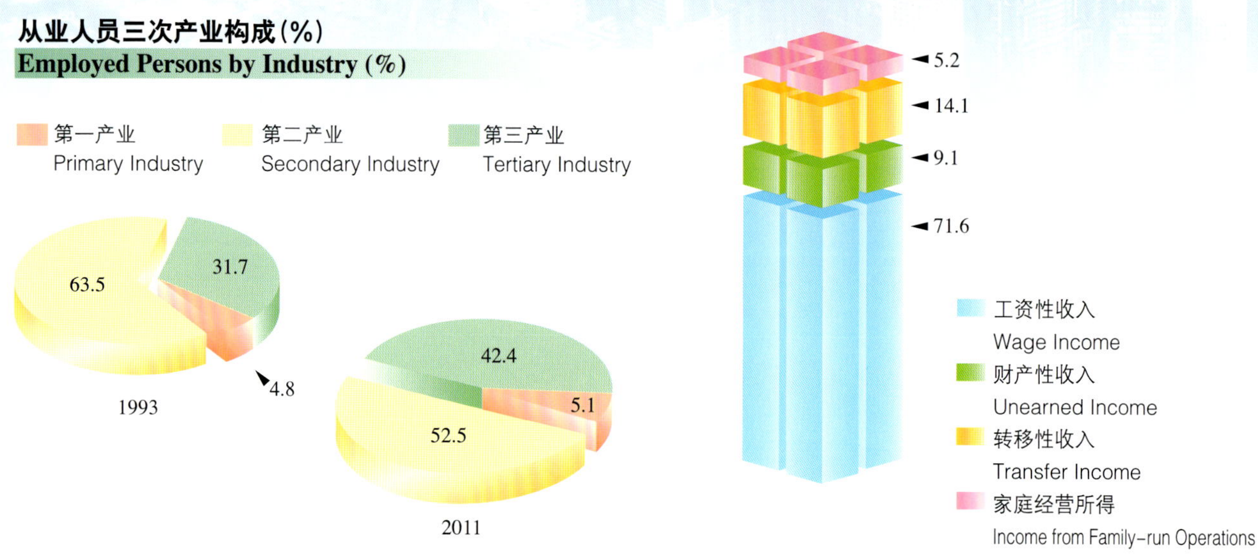
2011年郊区居民家庭收入构成(%)
Income Composition of Suburban Residents in 2011(%)
5.2
14.1
9.1
71.6
工资性收入
Wage Income
财产性收入
Unearned Income
转移性收入
Transfer Income
家庭经营所得
Income from Family-run Operations
从业人员三次产业构成(%)
Employed Persons by Industry (%)
第一产业
Primary Industry
第二产业
Secondary Industry
第三产业
Tertiary Industry
63.5
31.7
4.8
1993
42.4
5.1
52.5
2011

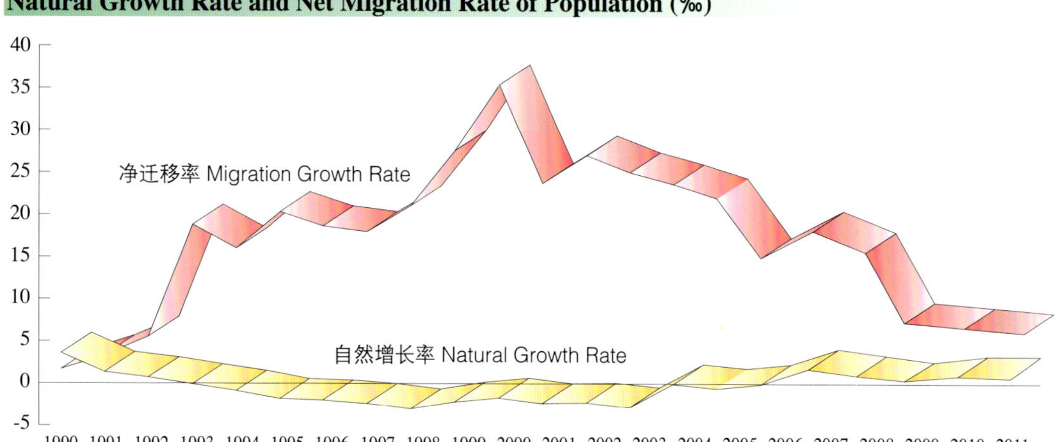
人口自然增长率和净迁移率(‰)
Natural Growth Rate and Net Migration Rate of Population (‰)
净迁移率 Migration Growth Rate
自然增长率 Natural Growth Rate
40
35
30
25
20
15
10
5
0
-5
1990 1991 1992 1993 1994 1995 1996 1997 1998 1999 2000 2001 2002 2003 2004 2005 2006 2007 2008 2009 2010 2011

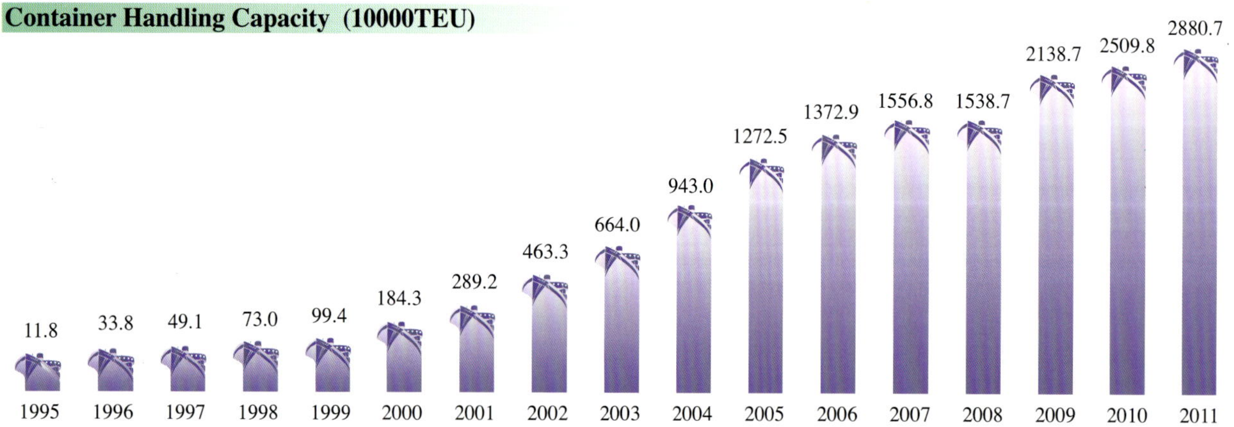
集装箱吞吐量(万标箱)
Container Handling Capacity (10000TEU)
11.8
33.8
49.1
73.0
99.4
184.3
289.2
463.3
664.0
943.0
1272.5
1372.9
1556.8
1538.7
2138.7
2509.8
2880.7
1995 1996 1997 1998 1999 2000 2001 2002 2003 2004 2005 2006 2007 2008 2009 2010 2011

人均公共绿地面积(平方米)
Public Green Space Per Capita (sq.m)

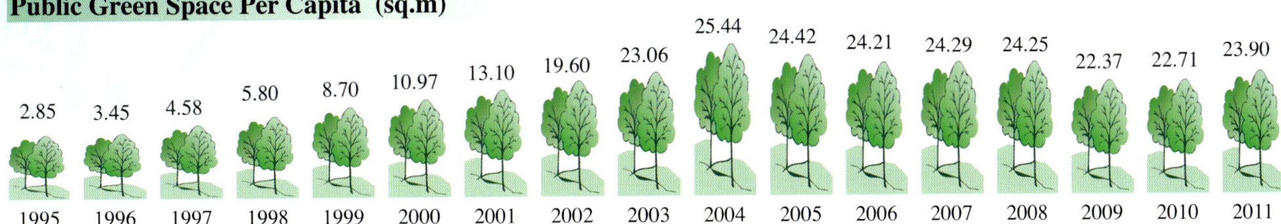

水电消耗情况
Consumption of Tap Water and Electricity

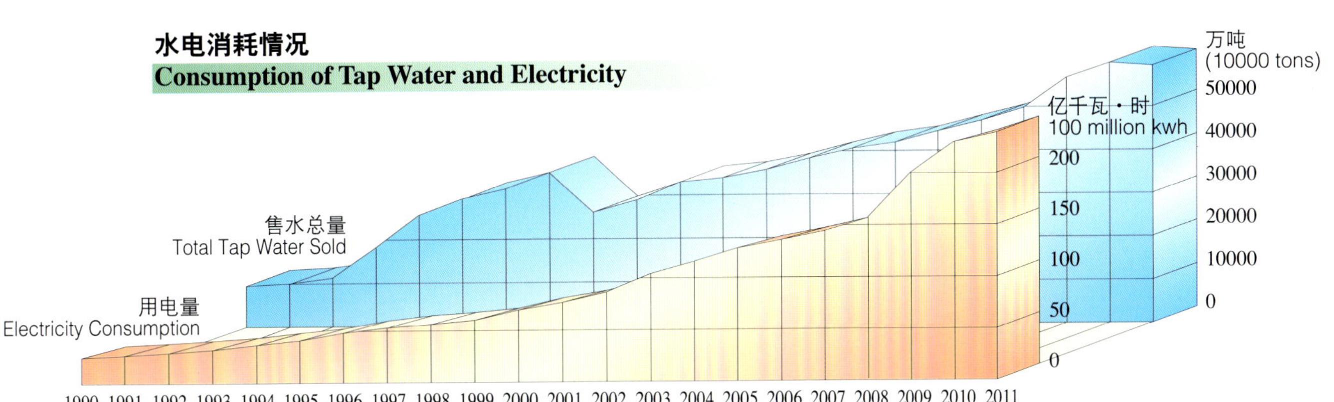

2011年前十位疾病死亡原因构成(%)
Composition of Top 10 Death-Causing Diseases in 2011 (%)

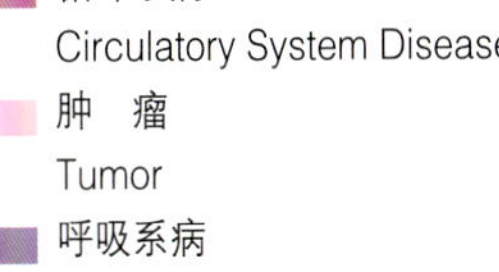

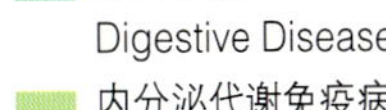

循环系病
Circulatory System Disease
肿　瘤
Tumor
呼吸系病
Respiratory Disease
损伤和中毒
Trauma & Toxicosis
消化系病
Digestive Disease
内分泌代谢免疫病
Internal Secretion, Metabolic & Immunity Diseases
传染病寄生虫病
Infectious Disease, Parasitic Disease
精神病
Mental Disease
泌尿生殖系病
Genitourinary Disease
神经系病
Neuro Disease

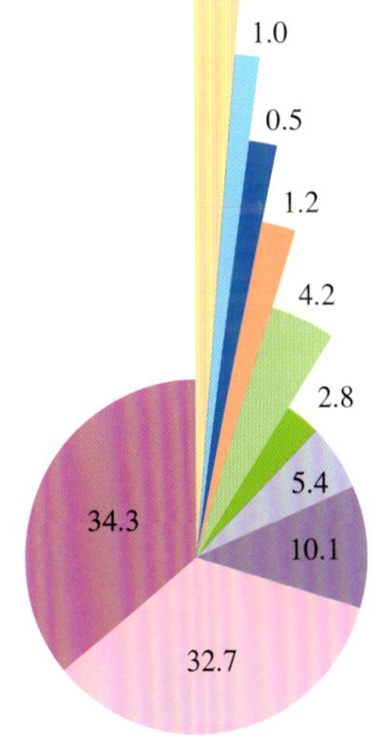

各级学校在校学生数构成(%)
Composition of Students Enrollment by Various Schools (%)

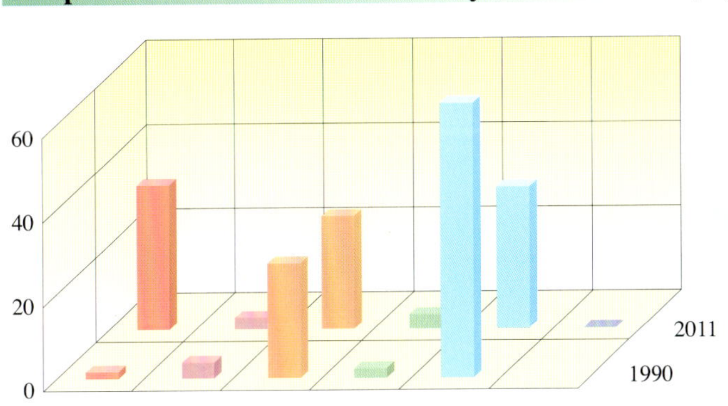

编者说明

一、《上海浦东新区统计年鉴—2012》是一部集浦东新区资料于一体的大型工具书。全书通过大量的统计数据,以中英文对照的形式记录了浦东新区开发开放以来社会经济发展的历程,全面展示了2011年浦东新区在二次创业的新阶段中,经济、社会、科技和重点开发区等各方面的发展变化。年鉴为各级领导、理论研究和实际工作者,以及国内外各界关心浦东开发开放的人士了解浦东、研究浦东、参与浦东开发建设提供了案头工具。

二、2009年,浦东新区行政体制发生重大变化。4月24日,国务院批准南汇区行政区域划入浦东新区。5月6日,上海市人民政府正式宣布两区合并。由于两区以前年度很多数据在统计方法、统计口径、统计范围等方面的不一致,数据无法简单相加,追溯存在一定难度。因此除特别注明外,本年鉴自2009年起,统计数据均为新浦东数据(即含原南汇地区),以前年度仍为原浦东数据。

三、2011年,浦东新区进行部分镇行政区划调整。10月28日上海市人民政府批准撤销川沙新镇、六灶镇建制,设立新的川沙新镇;撤销祝桥镇建制,设立新的祝桥镇,其行政区域范围作相应调整。由于调整时间较短,故今年年鉴中分镇数据除行政区划及人口数据按新的行政区域统计,其他仍用原来的行政区域统计。

四、本年鉴中平均增长速度根据每年的环比增长速度相乘再开方得到。

五、全书内容分为十九个篇目。内含:1. 综合; 2. 人口; 3. 固定资产投资; 4. 招商引资; 5. 农业; 6. 工业; 7. 建筑业; 8. 金融业及要素市场; 9. 房地产; 10. 国内外贸易; 11. 服务、旅游和住宿业; 12. 科学技术; 13. 人民生活; 14. 就业与社会保障; 15. 教育、文化、体育和卫生; 16. 法律、社会治安及其他; 17. 城市建设和环境保护; 18. 重点开发区和街镇; 19. 上海市统计资料。

六、资料中使用的度量衡单位均采用国际统一标准计量单位。

七、本年鉴部分数据总计数或相对数由于单位取舍不同,产生的计算误差均未作机械调整。

八、浦东新区在行政管理体制上于1995年11月撤乡建镇,实行镇管村体制。因此,本年鉴中有关"镇"和"镇及镇以上工业"等指标含义与全国的"乡"和"乡及乡以上工业"等指标的含义相同。

九、本年鉴中的符号使用说明:"#"表示某一指标的其中主要项;"…"表示数据不足本表最小计量单位数;"空格"表示该项统计指标数据不详或无该项数据或数据为零。

十、根据国务院和国家统计局有关我国GDP核算和数据发布制度的规定,浦东新区国内生产总值自2004年起更名为"浦东新区生产总值",简称"新区生产总值"。

十一、本年鉴中各项增加值和总产值绝对数均按当年价格计算,增长速度按可比价格计算。

十二、在使用统计资料时,凡与本年鉴有出入的,均以本年鉴为准。

十三、《上海浦东新区统计年鉴》公开出版以来，受到国内外广大读者的爱护和支持，对此我们深表谢意，并竭诚欢迎读者继续对本年鉴的不足之处给予批评和指正。

本年鉴的编制得到了上海市统计局、浦东新区各委、办、局及各开发区管委会等有关单位的大力支持，在此一并表示谢意。

EDITO′S NOTE

Ⅰ. Statistical Yearbook of Shanghai Pudong New Area (PNA)—2012 is a large, comprehensive reference book. With great amount of data and in both Chinese and English versions, it records recent years′ social and economic development in PNA. It describes the changes in economy, society, science and technology, and key development zones in PNA′s new stage of "Second Startup for Business" in 2011. It is a desktop tool-book meant for leaders at all levels, theorists, practitioners, and people at home and abroad who are interested in PNA, want to do research work on Pudong and intend to participate in its development and its construction.

Ⅱ. Great changes happened to the administrative system of Pudong New Area in 2009. On April 24, the State Council approved to add the administrative area of Nanhui District into Pudong New Area. On May 6, the Shanghai Municipal government formally announced the combination of these two districts. Because of data of previous years in these two districts can not be added simply while they had been produced with different statistical methods, approached and areas and it is hard to trace them. Unless specified, the statistical data in this Yearbook are those of new PNA (including former Nanhui District) since 2009, and the data of previous years are those of former PNA.

Ⅲ. Some towns in Pudong New Area readjusted their administrative areas in 2011. On October 28, the Government of Shanghai Municipality approved to establish Chuansha New Town by canceling the former Chuansha New Town and Liuzao Town and establish new Zhuqiao Town by canceling Zhuqiao Town, their administrative areas readjusted accordingly. As time since the readjustment is so short, data by town in this Yearbook are statistics of the former administrative areas except for the new administrative areas and population.

Ⅳ. The annual average growth rate in this Yearbook is extracted from the multiplication of the annual chain growth rates.

Ⅴ. This book falls into nineteen chapters: 1. General Survey; 2. Population; 3. Investment in Fixed Assets; 4. Business Promotion and Foreign-fund Attraction; 5. Agriculture; 6. Industry; 7. Construction; 8. Finance and Banking, and Factor Markets; 9. Real Estate; 10. Domestic and Foreign Trades; 11. Services, Tourism and Hotels; 12. Science and Technology; 13. People′s Livelihood; 14. Employment and Social Security; 15. Education, Culture, Sports and Public Health; 16. Laws, Public Order and Others; 17. Urban Construction and Environmental Protection; 18. Key Development Zones and Sub-districts and Towns; 19. Statistics of Shanghai Municipality.

Ⅵ. The units of measurement in this book are consistent with international standards.

Ⅶ. No adjustment has been made to correct the deviations of some of the figures in the Yearbook caused by different methods used in rounding.

Ⅷ. In November 1995, PNA rescinded township system and adopted town system. Villages are supervised by towns in the town system. Therefore, in this book, the meanings of "town" and "town and town-above industry" are the same as "township" and "township and township-above industry" in other Chinese statistical books.

Ⅸ. Notations used in this Yearbook:

"#" indicates the major item of a certain indicator,

"…" indicates the figure which is too small to be measured by the smallest unit in the table,

"blank" indicates the data unavailable or none in certain statistical indicator.

Ⅹ. According to relevant stipulations by the State Council and National Bureau of Statistics, GDP of Pudong New Area is to be renamed as Gross Output Value of Pudong New Area, shortened as PNA Gross Output Value starting from 2004.

Ⅺ. All added values and gross output vales in the Yearbook are listed in terms of current prices while growth rates listed in terms of comparable prices.

Ⅻ. If any statistical data from other sources conflict with the data in the present Yearbook, data in the present Yearbook shall apply.

XIII. The publication of Pudong New Area Statistical Yearbook has received great attention. Our gratitude and appreciation go to all the readers who have offered their comments. We welcome and are open to more comments and suggestions from our readers when presenting this new edition.

We appreciate the great support and efforts of Shanghai Statistics Bureau, all the commissions, offices and bureaus, and administrations of all the development zones in PNA during compilation of the present Yearbook.

目　　录
CONTENTS

综　述
ABSTRACT

第一篇　综　合
CHAPTER　1　GENERAL SURVEY

第二篇　人　口
CHAPTER 2 POPULATION

第三篇　固定资产投资
CHAPTER 3 INVESTMENT IN FIXED ASSETS

第四篇 招商引资
CHAPTER 4 BUSINESS PROMOTION AND FOREIGN-FUND ATTRACTION

第五篇 农 业
CHAPTER 5 AGRICULTURE

第六篇 工 业
CHAPTER 6 INDUSTRY

第七篇　建筑业

CHAPTER 7 CONSTRUCTION

第八篇　金融业及要素市场

CHAPTER 8 FINANCE AND BANKING, AND FACTOR MARKETS

第九篇　房地产
CHAPTER 9　REAL ESTATE

第十篇　国内外贸易
CHAPTER 10　DOMESTIC AND FOREIGN TRADES

第十一篇 服务、旅游和住宿业
CHAPTER 11 SERVICES, TOURISM AND HOTELS

第十二篇 科学技术
CHAPTER 12 SCIENCE AND TECHNOLOGY

第十三篇　人民生活
CHAPTER 13 PEOPLE'S LIVELIHOOD

第十四篇　就业与社会保障
CHAPTER　14　EMPLOYMENT AND SOCIAL SECURITY

第十五篇　教育、文化、体育、卫生
CHAPTER　15　EDUCATION, CULTURE, SPORTS AND PUBLIC HEALTH

第十六篇 法律、社会治安及其他
CHAPTER 16 LAWS, PUBLIC ORDER AND OTHERS

第十七篇　城市建设和环境保护
CHAPTER 17 URBAN CONSTRUCTIONS AND ENVIRONMENTAL PROTECTION

第十八篇　重点开发区和街镇

CHAPTER 18　KEY DEVELOPMENT ZONES AND SUB - DISTRICTS AND TOWNS

第十九篇　上海市统计资料

CHAPTER 19　STATISTICS OF SHANGHAI MUNICIPALITY

2011 年浦东新区经济和社会发展情况

2011 年是“十二五”规划的开局年，按照全市“创新驱动、转型发展”和“六个着力”的总体要求，浦东新区在区委、区政府的领导下，采取了一系列抓转型、促发展的措施，各项工作有序开展，创新驱动、转型发展成效逐步显现，经济社会发展总体呈现“经济运行平稳、转型发展加快、核心功能提升、社会建设加强、民生持续改善”的良好态势，较好地完成了年初预期目标，实现“十二五”平稳开局。

一、经济运行总体平稳，转型发展成效逐步显现

1. 经济平稳较快增长。全年经济保持两位数平稳增长，完成年初预期目标。实现地区生产总值 5484 亿元，增长 11.1%，占全市比重达到 28.6%。

2. 结构优化和效益提升进一步显现。第三产业推动经济增长的主体作用明显，占生产总值比重达到 57.3%；新型贸易业态、高技术服务业等新兴现代服务业快于服务业整体增长；完成地方财政收入 500 亿元，增长 16.7%，高于 12% 的年度目标；区属单位增加值综合能耗完成下降 4% 的目标。

3. “三大三新”产业引领工业发展。工业总产值达到 9554 亿元，增长 10.6%。其中，“三大三新”产业实现产值 5409 亿元，增长 14.6%，快于工业增速 4 个百分点。其中电子信息、新能源分别增长 22.6% 和 18.6%，民用航空增长 87.8%。商飞总装中心二期、映瑞光电等一批投资总额在 5 亿元以上的战略性新兴产业项目集中开工。

4. 内外需共同拉动作用明显。在 2010 年世博高基数基础上，社会消费品零售总额、商品销售总额仍保持较快增长，全年分别完成 1204 亿元和 10503 亿元，增长 16.1% 和 27.1%；外贸进出口总额全年达到 2260 亿美元，增长 21.1%，进口增长快于出口增长。

5. 投资强度不减、结构优化。建立企业投资推进联席会议制度，协调解决重点难点问题，全社会固定资产投资完成 1435 亿元。第三产业投资占总投资 75% 以上，战略性新兴产业投资占工业投资五成以上。

6. 招商引资总量、质量创历史最好水平。全年合同外资、实到外资分别达到 66 亿美元（不含迪士尼项目 11 亿美元）和 53 亿美元，增长 17.3% 和 37.4%。引进内资注册资本达到 808 亿元（不含约 150 亿元的增资），增长 1 倍。引入项目总体呈现第三产业项目多、大项目多、总部项目多的特点。

二、“四个中心”核心功能区建设加快推进，核心枢纽功能进一步提升

1. 金融功能建设取得新进展。陆家嘴金融城十大重点工程进展顺利，2011 年共有约 65 万平方米商办楼宇竣工，61 万平方米新开工。一批环境配套项目加快实施，上海纽约大学奠基开工，总量 2855 套的杨东青年人才公寓主体结构完工。一批功能性项目有力推进，金融城管理体制创新工作积极开展，上海股权托管交易中心建设进入最后冲刺。一批高能级金融机构入驻，新增各类监管金融机构 43 家，累计达到 692 家，引进股权投资及管理企业非监管类金融机构 337 家，新增金融专业配套服务机构 45 家。

2. 航运功能建设稳步推进。口岸枢纽功能进一步发挥，集装箱吞吐量全年完成 2881 万标箱，增长 14.8%；浦东机场货邮吞吐量完成 311 万吨，位居世界前列。航运企业和机构加快集聚，新增航运机构 300 余家，成功引进国内唯一海损理算专业机构中国贸促会理算中心，国际航运服务中心正式启用。

3. 贸易功能优势进一步凸显。期货保税交割试点等一批功能性项目有力推进，全国首个“国家进口贸易促进创新示范区”挂牌，成功举办世界自由贸易园区大会，新型贸易业态发展迅速，快钱、盛付通等 11 家企业获得第三方支付许可证，电子商务服务交易额增长迅速，电子商务商品交易额达到 3107 亿元，增长 33.6%。

4. 跨国公司地区总部加快集聚。出台新一轮总部经济扶持政策，新增跨国公司地区总部 21 家，累计达到 171 家，约占全市一半。此外，涉及金融、航运、商贸业、新兴服务业、高新技术、人才引进等“十二五”扶持政策出台。

三、国家改革示范区建设深入推进，创新功能进一步增强

1. 创新环境持续优化，创新功能继续增强。张江获批建设国家自主创新示范区，“张江创新十条”政策出台，拟与美国加州大学伯克利分校合作在张江建校。服务企业力度进一步增强，银政合作项目累计为中小企业发放贷款近70亿元，全年完成企业研发费用加计扣除额达到56亿元，增长77.3%，为企业减免税收14亿元。每百万人发明专利授权数达到393件。

2. 国家改革示范区建设深入推进，改革创新有新突破。2011年全国综改试点工作推进会、综改第三次部市合作会等高级别会议召开，国家部委支持浦东综改力度进一步增强。年度重点改革工作总体顺利，国际贸易结算中心试点拓展、融资租赁多元化发展、期货保税交割试点等多项改革试点取得重要进展。

四、社会民生持续改善，人民生活水平不断提高

1. 民生保障继续加强，人民生活进一步改善。努力降低高物价对低收入群体的影响。落实本市对四类退休人员发放“一次性补贴”及“社会救助和保障标准与物价上涨挂钩的联动机制”等保障民生新举措，惠及各类救助对象208.77万人次，累计发放各类救助帮困金6亿元。农保南北养老金标准实现统一。提前半年实现农保“三年对接到位”目标，参保者每月最低可领养老金485元。实现“新农保”制度全覆盖，“新农保”缴费人数6.3万，领取养老金人数6.7万。新型农村合作医疗进一步减轻农村居民就医负担。免挂号费，实行基本药物销售零差率，新型农村合作医疗基金筹集标准每人每年提高到900元，最高报销限额达到20.5万元，农民参保率达99.8%。贯彻实施新的社会保险法。涉及90余万从业人员的综保、镇保转储工作基本完成，新进来沪务工人员纳入城保，保障水平有较大提升。保障房建设稳步推进。新开工区级保障性住房近400万平方米，完成年初目标。临港限价房开工建设，全年市区两级累计新开工各类保障性住房666万平方米。第一批经济适用房申请家庭共计3225户通过审核、公示并摇号选房，第二批申请受理工作启动。廉租房受益家庭实现“应保尽保”。积极推动中心城区二级以下旧里（含“城中村”）和“厂中村”改造项目。启动花木龙沟10队、高桥镇西新村1队、2队等改造项目，花木龙沟三期、高桥镇南塘村等项目抓紧前期准备。居民收入较快增长。城乡居民家庭人均可支配收入分别为36815元和15861元，增长约13.9%和14.1%，转移性支付增长继续快于工资性收入增长。就业形势保持平稳。累计新增就业岗位15.40万个，增长9.6%，其中新增非农就业岗位2.32万个，超额完成全年目标；成功扶持2056人创业，完成市下达指标128.5%，带动就业7582人；城镇登记失业44848人，控制在市下达指标数内。应届毕业生就业形势较好，总体就业率91.4%，同比提高1.3个百分点，其中困难家庭应届毕业生228人，全部实现就业或安置就业。

2. 社会事业稳步发展，民生工程加快实施。社会建设投入进一步加大。以民生改善为重点的社会建设投入达到133亿元，保持两位数较快增长。各项社会事业加快发展。城乡、南北之间社会事业统筹发展力度进一步加大，多途径解决幼儿园“入园难”矛盾，教育资源公平性和均衡性进一步加强，教学质量进一步提高；一系列医改试点稳步推进，城乡整体医疗服务水平继续提升；一系列丰富多彩的文化体育活动陆续开展；一批学校、医院和文化体育设施项目加快建设。实事项目基本完成。为老服务、菜场建设等11大类39个实事项目基本完成，“走千听万”活动继续深入开展，一批百姓“急、难、愁”问题加快解决。

3. 农民增收和村庄改造计划稳步推进，“三农”重点工作取得新进展。农民增收工作的推进力度进一步加大。全面实施促进农民增收政策，落实户籍农民务农直补、承包土地流转补贴、村级组织运行费用补贴、涉农企业吸纳本区户籍农民就业补贴、农产品营销和品牌建设补贴等资金，全区近30万农民直接或间接受益，有力推动了农村居民增收，农村居民家庭人均可支配收入达到15861元，增长14.1%。村庄改造工程按计划有序推进。出台了加强村庄改造项目建设监督管理意见、资产管理意见及村庄改造长效管理实施办法。全年涉及15个镇、62个行政村、近4万户农户的村庄改造任务进展顺利。现代农业加快发展。实现农业总产值74亿元。东滩和老港、曹路等各具特色的浦东国家现代农业示范区示范基地加快规划建设，“三品”战略加快实施。社会化为农服务体系加强，新建和完善农资超市50个、农机合作社20个。农产品安全监管网络初步建成，形成1家区级检测中心、69家镇级检测点和每村1名协管员的三级监管体系。

五、城市建设和管理水平得到提升，创评创建工作顺利完成

1. 城市基础设施建设积极推进。面对严峻融资形势，积极保障轨道交通、南北对接道路，以及商飞、迪士尼和大型居住区等重大项目建设资金需求，全力以赴推进城市建设取得新成效，城市基础设施建设投资完成272亿元，增长3.9%。

2. 世博后城市长效管理取得一定成效。在城市安全管理、市容环境责任区制度落实、非法营运整治、联合执法、深化物业管理等领域取得积极成果，世博后城市运行和管理总体处于有序平稳状态。

3. 社会管理工作深入推进。全面完成71个"难点村"治理工作，加快建设沪东、潍坊等街镇的社区生活服务中心，加快推进塘桥居委会标准化建设样板试点，探索开展村民委员会自治家园建设，出台财政扶持政策促进社会组织发展。

4. 围绕创建工作积极塑造城市新形象。涉及水环境、大气环境、噪声治理与保护、固体废弃物利用与处置、工业污染防治等十大专项领域共计366个项目的第四轮环保三年行动计划顺利完成。积极开展打"黑车"、治"六小"、整网吧、推"门责"、强秩序等专项整治工作，建立健全生活垃圾"大分流"、"小分类"体系，在101个小区及"一港两村"6.8万户家庭开展厨余垃圾干湿分离。再次荣获全国文明城区称号，全国双拥模范城区"三连冠"争创成功，国家环保模范城区复检工作顺利完成，城市面貌有了新变化。

5. 智慧浦东、人文浦东建设逐步展开。一批智慧信息项目、文化事业和文化产业项目加快推进，上海云海数据中心启动，市云计算服务创新示范区落地浦东，电子商务综合创新实践区稳步推进，TD等3G网络基站建设加快，安管平台二期项目实施，上海浦东国际高新技术文化产业园区项目取得实质性进展，数字作品版权登记保护平台一期建设基本完成。

ECONOMIC AND SOCIAL DEVELOPMENT OF SHANGHAI PUDONG NEW AREA IN 2011

The year of 2011 is the first year of the "Twelfth Five-Year Planning". According to the overall demands of "Drive by innovations, develop after changes" and "Six great efforts" by the municipal government and under the leadership of Pudong New Area (PNA) Communist Party Committee and PNA Government, we have taken a series of measures that can help economic changes and prompted the development, unfolded all kinds of works orderly, and witnessed the gradual appearance of the effects from the innovative drive and changing development, so that the economic and social development presented a favorite trend of smooth economic operations, quickened development after changes, upgraded nuclear functions, strengthened social construction and continuous improvement of the people's livelihood. We have preferably completed the expected target set at the beginning of the year and realized the steady opening of the "Twelfth Five-Year Planning".

Ⅰ. Generally smooth economic operations, effects of development after changes gradually appeared

1. Economic operations keeping moderately fast growth. The economic data kept a steady two-digital grow in the whole year, achieving the expected target set at the beginning of the year. The total regional output value reached 548. 4 billion yuan, an increase of 11. 1% over the previous year, occupying 28. 6% of that of the municipality.

2. Optimized structure and upgraded effects further appeared. The primary functions that the third industry has boosted the economic growth were obvious, and the output value of the third industry reached 57. 3% of the total value. Some newly emerging modern services such as new types of trading operations and high-tech services have developed more rapid than the pace of the whole service trades. The local fiscal revenue achieved 50 billion yuan, an increase of 16. 7% over the previous year, which is 12% higher than that of the target of the year. The comprehensive power consumption of added value of the PNA organizations achieved the target of 4%-decrease.

3. "Three Big, Three New" industries taking the lead in the industrial development. The total industrial output value achieved 955. 4 billion yuan, increased by 10. 6% over the previous year, in which the "Three Big, Three New" industries achieved an output value of 540. 9 billion yuan, an increase of 14. 6%, 4 percent faster than that of the whole industry. The output value of electronic information and that of new resources increased by 22. 6% and 18. 6%, respectively, and that of civil aviation, 87. 8%. Some strategically new emerging industrial projects with the investment amount of more than 500 million yuan such as the second phase of general assembly center for commercial planes and Enraytek Optoelectronics have started their construction.

4. Effects of both domestic and foreign demands obvious. Under the high base of the World Expo 2010, the retail amount of social consumer goods and sales amount of commercial goods kept a fast growth, which achieved 120. 4 billion yuan and 1050. 3 billion yuan in 2011, respectively, increased by 16. 1% and 27. 1%. The total amount of foreign trade achieved USD 226 billion, an increase of 21. 1%, and the growth of imports was faster than that of exports.

5. Without decreasing the investment intensity, the economic structure optimized. The joint conference system for business investment promotion was established so as to solve the important and difficult problems by coordination. The total investment of fixed assets finished 143. 5 billion yuan, in which the investment of the third industry was more than 75% of the total investment, and that of strategically new emerging industries was more than 50% of that of the industry investment.

6. The number and quality of capital attraction achieved the highest level in history. The contracted foreign investment and actual paid foreign capital achieved USD 6.6 billion (excluding the Disney Project) and USD 5.3 billion, respectively, increased by 17.3% and 37.4%. The registered capital of introduced domestic investment achieved 80.8 billion yuan (excluding the increased capital of about 15 billion yuan), increased by 100%. The introduced projects were characterized with more third industry projects, more big projects and more headquarters projects.

Ⅱ. Construction of "Four Centers" nuclear functional areas quickened to promote, the function of nuclear pivot further advanced

1. Construction of financial function achieved new progress. Ten key projects for the financial city in Lujiazui Financial and Trade Zone advanced smoothly. In 2011, we completed the construction of commercial office buildings with a floor space of about 650,000 sq. m, and started the construction of about 610,000 sq. m. Some supporting projects near these office buildings quickened to start their construction. We lay the foundation and started to construct the Shanghai-New York University, finished the main body of Yangdong apartment with 2855 suites for young talents. Some functional projects were strongly promoted, innovative works for the managing system of the financial city were actively launched, and the construction of Shanghai Equity Exchange came to its completion. Some high-leveled financial institutions got settled down in Lujiazui, 43 supervisory financial institutions of all kinds were newly increased. The number of supervisory financial institutions was added to 692. We have introduced 337 non supervisory financial institutions for equity investment and managing business and increased 45 supporting service agencies for financial business.

2. Construction of air transportation and ocean shipping steadily advanced. With further play of the function of port pivot, the container handling capacity achieved 28.81 million TEUs in the whole year, an increase of 14.8%. The handling capacity of goods and mails in Pudong International Airport achieved 3.11 million tons, ranking the first of the airports all over the world. As the enterprises and institutions engaged in air transportation and ocean shipping quickened their pace to settle down in Pudong, more than 300 air transportation and ocean shipping institutions were established, the Average Adjustment Center of China Trade Promotion Committee, the only professional average adjustment agency in our country, was successfully introduced, and the international air transportation and ocean shipping service center formally started its business.

3. Advantages of trade function further highlighted. With the powerful advance of some functional projects such as the trial of futures bonded delivery, the national innovation and demonstration zone for import trade promotion, the first throughout the country, put into practice and successfully hosted the world free trade zones conference. New types of trade developed rapidly. Eleven enterprises, such as 99Bill and Shengpay, have got the license for the third part payment services. The transaction volume of E-business and services developed rapidly. The trading amount of E-business goods reached 310.7 billion yuan, increased by 33.6% over the previous year.

4. Regional headquarters of transnational corporations quickened to converge. A patch of new supporting policies for the headquarters economy has appeared publicly. The number of regional headquarters of transnational corporations in Pudong has added to 171 with the entrance of another 21 headquarters, which is about half of that of the municipality. On the other hand, some "Twelfth Five-Year Planning" supporting policies has also appeared publicly, which are related to the finance, air aviation and ocean shipping, commerce and trade, newly-emerging services, high and new technology, and talents attraction.

Ⅲ. Construction of national reforms and demonstration zone deeply advanced, innovative function further enhanced

1. Environment for innovations continuously optimized and functions of innovations continuously strengthened. Zhangjiang was approved to establish the national independent innovation demonstration zone, the policy of "Ten Clauses of Zhangjiang Innovations" appeared publicly, and we are planning to establish a university with University of California, Berkeley in Zhangjiang. The efforts to serve the enterprises further strengthened. The cooperation pro-

jects between banks and the government have made loans of almost 7 billion yuan for middle and small businesses, research and development expenditure and total deductions for the enterprises reached 5.6 billion yuan last year, increased by 77.3%, and the tax relief for the enterprises reached 1.4 billion yuan. The number of invention and patent licenses per 1 million persons reached 393.

2. Construction of national reforms and demonstration zone deeply advanced, reforms and innovations made new breakthroughs. In 2011, high-leveled conferences were held such as the national promotion conference for comprehensive reforms and experiments, and the third cooperation conference between the ministries and the cities for the comprehensive reforms. Leaders of national ministries and commissions supported Pudong to further strengthen the comprehensive reforms. The annual key reforming works got along smoothly. Many reforms and experiments made great progress, such as the experimental expansion of international trade settlement center, diversified development of financing and leasing, and the trial of futures bonded delivery.

Ⅳ. Social welfare steadily improved, people's living standard continuously increasing

1. Welfare guarantee continuously strengthened, the people's living further improved. We tried hard to eliminate the influence that high prices imposed on the low income groups. We carried out the new measures to guarantee the social welfare such as granting four kinds of retirees with one-off subsidies and the interlocking mechanism among the social assistance, guarantee standards and the rising prices. There were 2087,700 persons who had been benefited from these measures, and the number of the assistance money of all kinds that has been granted was accumulated to 600 million yuan. The pension standard between citizens living the north and south part of Pudong New Area with rural insurance has been unified. We achieved the target of unified standard within three years, half a year earlier than expected. The insurance beneficiary can draw at least 485 yuan from his/her pension account every month. We have completely covered the rural people with the new rural insurance system. The participants of the new rural insurance achieved 63,000, and 67,000 retirees could draw their pensions. The new rural cooperative medical service further eliminated the medical burdens for the rural residents. Medical registration is free of charge and we carried out the policy of zero rate for the sale of basic medicine. The raising standard of new rural cooperative medical funds per capita increased to 900 yuan every year, and the maximum reimbursement allowance reached 205,000 yuan. The insurance rate of the farmers achieved 99.8%. New social insurance laws were carried out. We have almost finished the work of turning comprehensive insurance and town insurance participants of more than 900,000 people into the urban insurance coverage. New migrants have been covered with the rural insurance, and the guarantee level was greatly improved. The construction of public housing was steadily advanced. The new start of buildings for public housing in PNA had a floor space of nearly 4 million square meters, which achieved the target set at the beginning of the year. Buildings with limited prices by the government started construction in Lingang New City. We have started all kinds of public buildings of both the municipal and PNA levels, with a floor space of 6.66 million square meters in Pudong. The first patch of families applied for the affordable houses, and among them 3225 families have been approved, made public and chosen their houses by lottery numbers. And the acceptance work for the second patch has commenced. Every family who would benefit from the low-rent house has been achieved the coverage. We have actively promoted the reconstruction projects in old lanes (including "Villages inside the town") and "Villages inside the factory" of Level-II and below in central urban area. We started the reconstruction projects such as the Tenth Team of Longgou Village in Huamu Town, the first team and the second team of Xixin Village in Gaoqiao Town. We got ready for the projects such as the third phase of Longgou Village in Huamu Town and Nantang Village in Gaoqiao Town. The income of residents increased rapidly. The disposable incomes of urban and suburban residents per capita were 36,815 yuan and 15,861 yuan, respectively, increased by about 13.9% and 14.1%. The transfer payment continued to grow faster than that of salary income. The employment prospects kept stable. The number of new jobs was 154,000, increased by 9.6%, in which the number of new non-agricultural jobs was 23,200, fulfilling the target set at the beginning of the year. We successfully supported 2056 persons to create their own business, fulfilling the target set by the municipality of 128.5%, which took over 7852 employees. The number of registered unemploy-

ment was 44,848, which was under the guideline of the municipality. The employment prospects were favorite for new college graduates, with an overall employment rate of 91.4%, an increase of 1.3% over that of the previous year. The number of new college graduates from poor families was 228, who have all been employed or settled for the employment by the government.

2. Social undertakings steadily developed, people's livelihood projects quickened to carry out. The investment on social construction was increased. We put the amount of 13.3 billion yuan on the social construction with the key of improving the people's livelihood, and the investment kept a two-digital growth rate. All kinds of social undertakings quickened to develop. We further planned the social undertakings between the towns and suburban areas and between the northern part and southern part of PNA, solved the problem that it is difficult for children to be enrolled by the kindergartens with several efficient methods, further made the educational resources more fair and balanced, and further improved the teaching quality. We steadily promoted the experiment on a series of medical reforms, continued to increase the overall medical service level in the urban and suburban areas. We developed a series of colorful cultural and sports activities in succession and quickened the construction of a series of projects for schools, hospitals, cultural and sports facilities. Practical projects have been finished on the whole. We have basically completed 39 practical projects from 11 kinds such as the service for the old and the construction of food markets, continued to develop the activity of "Visiting a thousand families and listening to ten thousand persons' stories", and quickened to solve many "urgent, difficult and worried" problems that the common people were facing with.

3. Program of increasing farmers' income and reconstructing the village steadily advanced, key "Three Agriculturals" work made new progress. More efforts were put on the work of increasing farmers' income. We have completely realized the policy of raising farmers' income, carried out direct subsidies for the farming by local registered farmers, for the circulation of contracted rural land, for the operation of village-leveled organizations, for the employment of agriculture-related enterprises admitting local registered farmers, for the marketing of agricultural products and the establishment of brands. Nearly 300,000 farmers in PNA were directly or indirectly benefited from the capital, which strongly promoted the income rise of rural residents. The disposal income per capita of rural resident families reached 15,861 yuan in 2011, increased by 14.1%. The reconstruction project for the village was orderly advanced according to the plan. We have appeared publicly some suggestions of the supervision and management for strengthening the construction projects of villages, opinions on assets management, and long-term implementation methods for the reconstruction of villages. The task of reconstructing villages relating to 62 administrative villages of 15 towns and near 40,000 households was developed smoothly in 2011. Modern agriculture was quickened to develop. We completed the total output value of agriculture worthy of 7.4 billion yuan. We planned to quickly construct Pudong-characterized national modern agricultural demonstration area bases such East Shoal, Laogang and Caolu. The "Three Brands" strategy quickened to implement. We have strengthened the social service system for the agriculture, constructed and made perfect 50 agricultural materials supermarkets and 20 rural cooperatives. We have primarily constructed the supervision and management network for the safety of agricultural products and formed a three-leveled system of supervision and management which consisted of one PNA-leveled testing center, 69 town-leveled testing points and one assistant every village.

V. Urban construction and management level advanced, work of creation and establishment smoothly finished.

1. Construction of urban infrastructure actively proceeded. Faced with the austere financing situations, we actively guaranteed the demands for the capital of key projects such as constructing railways, linking the roads between the northern part and the southern part within PNA, constructing commercial planes, Disney Park and some large residential quarters. We whole-heartedly advanced the urban construction to make new progress. The investment on the urban infrastructure completed 27.2 billion yuan, an increase of 3.9% over the previous year.

2. Long-term city administration after World Expo achieved favorable effects. We have obtained positive effects on fields such as the safe administration of the city, the implementation of the responsibility area system for city ap-

pearance and environment, the control of illegal transportations, activities of joint law enforcement, and in-depth property management, so that the operation of the city and its administration after the end of the World Expo 2010 has been in a stable and orderly condition in a whole.

3. Social management deeply advanced. We have finished the task of putting 71 "difficult villages" in order, quickened to construct community life and service centers in sub-districts such as Hudong and Weifang, quickened to advance the sample experiments on the standardization construction of Tangqiao Residential Committee, explored to conduct the construction of self-managing homeland in village committees, and come out financially supporting policies to facilitate the development of social organizations.

4. Conducting the work for civilized city, actively shaping new city images. We have successfully finished the fourth round of "Three-year Action" for the environmental protection related to 366 projects in ten special fields such as water environment, atmospheric environment, noise control and protection, utilization and disposal of solid wastes, and prevention and control of industrial pollution. We have actively conducted special controls on problems such as illegal transportation, six kinds of illegal small businesses, illegal internet bars, disorder in front of store doors, and other disordered situations. We have established and made perfect the system of sorting wastes according to their sizes for life garbage. We divided the dry kitchen waste from the wet one in 101 residential quarters and "One harbor and two villages", which are related to 68,000 households. Pudong has again been obtained the title of national civilized city. We managed to obtain the title of national double-support model city for the third time successively, and successfully finished the reexamination work for the national environmental protection civilized city. The city appearance had a new change.

5. Construction for a wise and humanistic Pudong gradually deployed. We have quickened to advance some projects of intelligence information, cultural undertakings and industries. The project of Shanghai Cloud Sea Data Center commenced, the municipal cloud computation service and innovation demonstration zone was settled in Pudong, comprehensive innovation and practice zone for e-commerce was steadily advanced, 3G network base stations such as TD were quickened to be constructed, and the second phase of Security Operation Center project were implemented. The project of Shanghai Pudong International High and New Technology Cultural Industrial Park has made substantial progress, and the construction of the first phase of Copyright Registration and Protection Platform for Digital Works project was near to be accomplished.

第一篇

Chapter 1

综合

GENERAL SURVEY

表 1-1　气象概况
Climate
(2011)

月　份 Month		气　温(℃) Temperature(℃) 平均气温 Average Temperature	平均最高气温 Average Highest Temperature	平均最低气温 Average Lowest Temperature	35℃以上高温日数(天) >35℃(day)	0℃以下低温日数(天) <0℃(day)
年平均	**Annual Average**	**16.7**	**20.9**	**13.4**	**12**	**35**
1　月	January	1.6	4.8	-1.2		22
2　月	February	5.9	10.6	2.5		7
3　月	March	8.9	13.6	4.5		
4　月	April	15.6	21.3	10.6		
5　月	May	21.1	26.2	16.8		
6　月	June	24.0	27.5	21.4	1	
7　月	July	29.6	33.9	26.8	8	
8　月	August	27.9	31.3	25.3	3	
9　月	September	24.3	28.3	21.3		
10　月	October	18.9	22.4	15.6		
11　月	November	16.5	20.1	13.2		
12　月	December	6.4	10.3	3.4		6

表 1-1　续表　Continued

月　份 Month		日　照(小时) Sunshine(hour)	降　水 Rainfall 雨　量(毫米) Rainfall(mm)	雨　日(天) Rainy Day(day)	蒸发量(毫米) Evaporation(mm)	平均相对湿度(%) Relative Humidity(%)
全年总计	**Annual Total**	**1 841.5**	**926.9**	**171**	**1 249.3**	**69.8**
1　月	January	114.9	17.3	11	49.8	63
2　月	February	114.9	15.9	7	51.4	72
3　月	March	194.8	36.1	10	94.7	61
4　月	April	207.7	30.2	11	133.6	63
5　月	May	196.4	28.3	12	170.8	63
6　月	June	102.1	290.8	25	92.6	80
7　月	July	185.3	52.7	19	180.2	72
8　月	August	135.6	247.5	27	119.5	78
9　月	September	195.5	33.0	13	142.1	71
10　月	October	143.3	73.0	15	106.7	70
11　月	November	113.3	67.0	15	57.3	77
12　月	December	137.7	35.1	6	50.6	68

注：2011 年极端最高气温 38.1℃，出现在 7 月 3 日；极端最低气温 -4.7℃，出现在 1 月 13 日；初霜日 11 月 26 日，终霜日 3 月 30 日，无霜期 238 天。

Note: The utmost highest temperature amounted to 38.1℃ on July 3rd and the utmost lowest temperature came to -4.7℃ on January 13 in 2011. The frost season started on November 26 and ended on March 30. There were 238 frost-free days in 2011.

表1-2 行政区划
Administrative Regions
(2011)

单位:个 (unit)

地 区 Subdistrict/Town		居民委员会 Neighborhood Committee	村民委员会 Village Committee	地 区 Subdistrict/Town		居民委员会 Neighborhood Committee	村民委员会 Village Committee
街镇总计(37个)	**Total**	**783**	**374**				
街 道(13个)	**Subdistricts (13)**	**405**					
潍坊新村街道	Weifangxincun Subdistrict	27		金杨新村街道	Jinyangxincun Subdistrict	48	
陆家嘴街道	Lujiazui Subdistrict	30		洋泾街道	Yangjing Subdistrict	38	
周家渡街道	Zhoujiadu Subdistrict	32		浦兴路街道	Puxinglu Subdistrict	40	
塘桥街道	Tangqiao Subdistrict	23		东明路街道	Dongminglu Subdistrict	37	
上钢新村街道	Shanggang xincun Subdistrict	23		花木街道	Huamu Subdistrict	41	
南码头路街道	Nanmatoulu Subdistrict	27		申港街道	Shengang Subdistrict	6	
沪东新村街道	Hudongxincun Subdistrict	33					
镇(24个)	**Towns (24)**	**378**	**374**				
川沙新镇	Chuansha New Town	34	43	周浦镇	Zhoupu Town	15	12
高桥镇	Gaoqiao Town	27	14	新场镇	Xinchang Town	5	13
北蔡镇	Beicai Town	46	9	大团镇	Datuan Town	4	16
合庆镇	Heqing Town	6	29	芦潮港镇	Luchaogang Town	7	1
唐 镇	Tangzhen Town	10	17	康桥镇	Kangqiao Town	28	12
曹路镇	Caolu Town	13	32	航头镇	Hangtou Town	7	13
金桥镇	Jinqiao Town	9	3	祝桥镇	Zhuqiao Town	22	40
高行镇	Gaohang Town	28	4	泥城镇	Nicheng Town	9	11
高东镇	Gaodong Town	12	12	宣桥镇	Xuanqiao Town	5	12
张江镇	Zhangjiang Town	21	9	书院镇	Shuyuan Town	5	13
三林镇	Sanlin Town	39	16	万祥镇	Wanxiang Town	3	7
惠南镇	Huinan Town	21	29	老港镇	Laogang Town	2	7

注：2011年六灶镇并入川沙新镇，川沙新镇内的原机场镇划入祝桥镇。

Note: In 2011, Liuzao Town was incorporated into Chuansha New Town and the former Jichang Town inside Chuanshan New was incorporated into Zhuqiao Town.

表1-3　主要年份经济发展主要指标
Major Indicators of Economic Development in Main Years

指　标	Indicators	1993	2000	2005	2010	2011
新区生产总值(亿元)	**Gross Domestic Product of PNA(100 million yuan)**	**164.00**	**923.51**	**2 108.79**	**4 707.52**	**5 484.35**
第一产业	Primary Industry	2.12	5.72	6.09	31.47	34.46
第二产业	Secondary Industry	114.45	488.60	1 070.96	2 036.58	2 306.32
第三产业	Tertiary Industry	47.43	429.19	1 031.74	2 639.47	3 143.57
财　政	**Finance**					
财政收入(亿元)	Financial Revenue(100 million yuan)	11.15	103.21	494.94	2 046.17	2 256.13
#地方财政收入	Local Financial Revenue	5.53	56.40	155.31	428.82	500.26
地方财政支出(亿元)	Local Financial Expenditure (100 million yuan)	9.53	69.60	198.79	524.06	615.24
固定资产投资总额(亿元)	**Total Investment in Fixed Assets (100 million yuan)**	**164.56**	**351.06**	**693.61**	**1 432.30**	**1 435.39**
#房地产开发投资	Investment in Real Estate Development		110.74	287.92	555.74	589.45
#城市基础设施投资额	Investment in Urban Infrastructure	54.73	54.51	125.95	261.92	272.02
招商引资	**Business Promotion and Foreign-Fund Attraction**					
外商直接投资合同项目(项)	Projects of Foreigin Direct Investment((unit)	924	693	1734	906	995
外商直接投资合同金额(亿美元)	Project Amount of Foreign Direct Investment (USD 100 million)	17.57	28.84	56.54	56.25	65.97
期末内资企业注册数(个)	Number of Registered Domestically-Funded Enterprises at End of Term (unit)				10 961	10 636
科技创新	**Technological Innovations**					
研发机构数(个)	Number of R&D Institutions (unit)			161	393	393
申请专利数(项)	Patent Claiming(item)		718	3 141	17 587	18 819
授权专利数(项)	Number of Authorized Patents (Piece)			1 204	12 764	12 685

注：1. 2005 年至 2008 年，"港口货物吞吐量"和"集装箱吞吐量"为外高桥港区数据；2009 年起"港口货物吞吐量"和"集装箱吞吐量"为外高桥港区和洋山深水港区数据。
2. "中外资保险机构原保费收入"与历年年鉴中的"保费收入"统计口径相同，下同。

Note: 1. The items of "Volume of Cargo Handled at Port" and "Container Handling Capacity" are the data at Waigaoqiao Port from 2005 to 2008. These two items are the data at Waigaoqiao Port and Yangshan Deepwater Port since 2009.
2. The item of "Former premium income of insurances by Chinese and foreign insurance institutions" has the same statistical approach with that of "Premium income" of previous years. The below are the same.

表1-3 续表 Continued

指 标 Indicators		1993	2000	2005	2010	2011
工业总产值(亿元)	**Gross Output Value of Industry (100 million yuan)**	**604.40**	**1 625.77**	**4 242.47**	**8 591.50**	**9 553.79**
#高技术工业	Industrial Output of High Technologies			1 190.72	2 259.08	2 704.33
国内外贸易	**Domestic and Foreign Trades**					
商品销售总额(亿元)	Aggregate Sales of Commodities (100 million yuan)		752.94	2 807.47	8 263.56	10 502.98
社会消费品零售总额(亿元)	Total Retail Sales of Consumer Goods (100 million yuan)	41.92	215.17	353.69	1 036.88	1 204.04
外贸进出口总额(亿美元)	Total Imports and Exports (USD 100 million)	25.92	254.86	894.75	1 865.62	2 260.00
出口总额	Total Exports	12.02	95.80	372.12	738.79	888.98
进口总额	Total Imports	13.90	159.06	522.63	1 126.83	1 371.02
功能开发	**Functional Development**					
中外资金融机构数(个)	Number of Chinese and Foreign Financial Institutions (unit)			369	649	692
中外资银行本外币存款余额(亿元)	Balance of RMB and Foreign Currencies Deposits in Chinese and Foreign Banks (100 million yuan)			4 244	13 079	15 553
中外资银行本外币贷款余额(亿元)	Balance of RMB and Foreign Currencies Loans in Chinese and Foreign Banks (100 million yuan)			4 668	10 436	11 672
期末认定跨国公司地区总部入驻数(户)	Settled Headquarters of Transnational Companies at End of Term (in number)			64	150	171
举办展览(博览)(次)	Number of Exhibitions Hosted (time)			114	120	156
举办国际性会议(次)	Number of International Conferences Hosted (time)			199	26	1 949
接待国内外游客总数(万人次)	Foreign and Domestic Tourists Received (10 000 person-times)		1 133	1 660	3 215	3 133
浦东国际机场旅客吞吐量(万人次)	Passenger Capacity at Pudong International Airport (10 000 person-times)			2 358	4 041	4 144
浦东国际机场货邮吞吐量(万吨)	Volume of Cargo Handled at Pudong International Airport (10 000 tons)			185	322	311
港口货物吞吐量(万吨)	Volume of Cargo Handled at Port (10 000 tons)	9 017	4 990	10 646	22 470	26 332
集装箱吞吐量(万标箱)	Container Handling Capacity (10 000 TEUs)		184.3	1 272.5	2 509.8	2 880.7

表 1-4 主要年份社会发展主要指标
Major Indicators of Social Development in Main Years

指 标	Indicators	1993	2000	2005	2010	2011
人 口	**Population**					
年末常住人口(万人)	Permanent Population at Year-end (10 000 persons)		240.23	279.19	504.44	517.50
年末户籍总人口(万人)	Registered Population at Year-end (10 000 persons)	143.73	164.87	184.81	275.80	278.53
年末总户数(万户)	Total Households at Year-end(10 000 households)	48.63	60.52	68.95	106.08	107.32
自然增长率(‰)	Natural Growth Rate(‰)	-0.08	-1.71	-0.58	1.06	0.77
劳动就业	**Labor and New Jobs**					
从业人员(万人)	Employed Persons (10 000 persons)	104.40	104.04	144.08	235.11	280.68
第一产业	Primary Industry	4.98	4.25	1.99	14.78	14.37
第二产业	Secondary Industry	66.37	48.06	57.07	123.90	147.36
第三产业	Tertiary Industry	33.05	51.73	85.02	96.43	118.95
职工人数(万人)	Staff and Workers(10 000 persons)	78.88	67.75	70.16	85.02	138.53
新增就业岗位(万人)	Number of New Jobs (10 000 persons)			11.50	14.04	15.40
期末城镇登记失业人数(万人)	Number of Registered Unemployed Persons in Towns at End of Term (10 000 persons)			4.29	4.35	4.48
人民生活	**People's Livelihood**					
城镇居民人均年可支配收入(元)	Annual Disposable Income Per Capita of Urban Residents (yuan)			19 089	32 330	36 815
郊区居民人均年可支配收入(元)	Annual Disposable Income Per Capita of Rural Residents (yuan)			9 779	13 898	15 861
职工工资总额(亿元)	Total Wages of Staff and Workers (100 million yuan)	47.26	120.59	235.03	765.95	1 243.20
职工年平均工资(元)	Average Annual Wages of Staff and Workers (yuan)	5 999	17 607	33 186	89 424	90 721
城镇居民人均住宅建筑面积(平方米)	Floor Space of Urban Residents Per Capita (sq·m)			32.73	39.26	36.30
平均期望寿命(岁)	Life Expectancy (year)	76.10	78.01	80.85	82.57	82.62

表 1-4 续表 Continued

指 标	Indicators	1993	2000	2005	2010	2011
教 育	**Education**					
高等学校在校学生数(人)	Student Enrollment of Higher Education (person)	3 776	11 940	41 034	167 746	184 831
中等学校在校学生数(人)	Student Enrollment at High Schools(person)	79 751	138 941	149 407	171 968	172 446
小学在校学生数(人)	Student Enrollment at Primary Schools (person)	131 204	110 573	92 062	165 009	176 328
市实验性、示范性高中和区重点高中就读学生比例(%)	Rate of Students Enrolled in Municipal Experimental and Demonstration High Schools and District-Key High Schools(%)				73.2	74.3
学龄儿童入学率(%)	Rate of School-age Child Enrollment (%)	99.2	99.5	100.0	100.0	100.0
幼儿园幼儿数(人)	Young Child Enrollment at Kindergartens (person)	42 378	34 030	44 554	83 313	94 727
卫 生	**Health**					
医疗机构数(个)	Healthcare Institutions (unit)	378	586	630	1 057	1 074
#医 院	Hospitals	47	48	57	56	59
医院病床(张)	Hospital Bed (bed)	4 840	6 947	6 520	15 164	17 731
卫生技术人员(人)	Healthcare Professionals (person)	7 717	8 810	9 794	18 925	23 099
#执业医生	Medical Practitioners	4 102	4 552	4 726	7 644	8 864
注册护士	Registered Nurses	2 179	2 739	3 390	7 448	9 631
城市建设、环境保护	**Urban Construction and Environmental Protection**					
建成区绿化覆盖率(%)	Coverage of Urban Green Areas in PNA (%)		30.2	37.8	36.1	36.1
城镇污水纳管率(%)	Rate of Sewage Pipe in Towns(%)			70.4	81.9	82.5
空气质量优良率(%)	Rate of Fine Air Quality (%)			89.3	92.6	94.2
人均公共绿地(平方米)	Public Green Space Per Capita (sq·m)	3.40	11.00	24.42	22.71	23.94

表1-5 历年社会经济主要指标增长率(以上年为基期)

(1993～2011)

单位:%

指 标	Indicators	1993	1994	1995	1996	1997	1998
年末总户数	Total Households at Year-end		2.6	3.1	3.1	2.8	3.4
年末户籍总人口	Registered Population at Year-end	2.2	1.7	1.7	1.7	1.5	1.8
男	Male	2.3	1.9	1.8	1.8	1.5	2.0
女	Female	2.0	1.6	1.5	1.6	1.5	1.7
年末常住人口	Permanent Population at Year-end						
新区生产总值	Gross Output Value of PNA	30.2	28.6	22.0	20.2	18.3	16.8
第一产业	Primary Industry	-8.5	5.1	14.2	1.9	5.3	5.9
第二产业	Secondary Industry	22.0	21.6	21.9	17.4	16.3	14.0
第三产业	Tertiary Industry	46.6	42.8	22.6	30.0	24.3	24.2
工业总产值	Gross Domestic Product of Industry	28.7	20.1	19.3	18.2	18.4	15.1
财政收入	Financial Revenue		1.2倍(times)	62.9	30.5	21.4	13.0
#地方财政收入	Local Financial Revenue		1.8倍(times)	51.6	32.1	30.0	10.2
地方财政支出	Local Financial Expenditure		1.1倍(times)	93.9	10.1	18.2	10.8
固定资产投资总额	Total Investment in Fixed Assets	1.2倍(times)	58.7	9.2	38.6	27.7	15.6
#房地产开发投资	Investment in Real Estate Development						
城市基础设施投资额	Investment in Urban Infrastructure	1.5倍(times)	43.9	-32.2	84.7	20.9	48.5
商品销售总额	Aggregate Sales of Commodities			16.7	21.2	28.3	-1.6
社会消费品零售总额	Total Retail Sales of Consumer Goods	48.5	97.4	32.9	27.5	15.7	10.3
外贸进出口总额	Total Imporst and Exports		82.7	52.0	12.2	22.6	21.0
出口总额	Total Exports		93.1	70.8	-2.2	18.3	15.1
进口总额	Total Imports		73.7	33.9	30.0	26.5	26.1

注：凡财政指标均为2004年财税体制改革后的同口径对比数,后续相关指标口径相同。
Note：Every financial indicator is the comparative number with the same approach after reforms of finance and taxation system in 2004. Hereinafter are the same.

Growth Rate of Major Indicators of Social Economy in Main Years (the Previous Year as Base)

(%)

1999	2000	2001	2002	2003	2004	2005	2006	2007	2008	2009	2010	2011
3.1	4.1	2.3	2.4	2.6	2.3	3.3	1.7	1.8	1.3	1.3	2.6	1.2
2.5	3.0	2.2	2.6	2.2	2.4	2.2	1.5	1.9	1.6	1.4	1.3	1.0
2.6	3.2	2.3	2.7	2.4	2.4	2.1	1.4	1.8	1.4	1.3	1.2	0.9
2.4	2.8	2.0	2.5	2.1	2.3	2.2	1.5	2.1	1.9	1.4	1.4	1.0
		3.1	3.0	3.0	3.1	3.1	2.2	7.0	0.1	1.7	20.4	2.6
16.1	16.5	16.1	16.7	17.5	16.4	12.1	13.4	15.2	11.6	10.5	12.4	11.1
3.8	4.9	6.1	4.9	1.6	-7.3	-4.0	-5.1	-5.4	-5.8	-2.7	-2.7	-0.9
13.5	15.2	16.3	16.4	19.3	17.2	10.5	12.1	10.1	9.1	6.3	15.3	9.5
22.5	19.6	16.1	17.1	15.8	15.7	14.0	15.0	20.4	14.0	14.5	10.3	12.4
17.3	18.9	20.1	21.0	26.4	22.4	11.8	13.3	14.3	9.4	6.7	21.1	11.2
13.2	30.1	39.1	41.2	46.1	25.7	10.5	18.7	45.4	22.0	5.8	25.4	10.3
-0.5	27.6	47.2	14.6	41.6	20.9	13.0	14.8	46.3	16.0	9.1	12.0	16.7
4.8	19.1	26.9	36.9	32.6	20.7	2.7	12.0	29.1	28.9	7.1	10.2	17.4
-24.9	-19.9	18.5	41.1	2.5	8.3	6.4	-4.8	18.8	11.3	16.2	0.8	0.2
	6.6	6.5	93.6	13.9	13.7	3.0	-10.5	-4.0	13.1	6.2	28.8	6.1
-11.7	-65.2	93.3	62.6	-9.2	-22.1	3.9	23.9	50.3	32.7	33.3	-46.6	3.9
93.8	26.9	33.5	77.9	35.5	21.0	-4.3	4.9	22.7	28.6	13.7	39.9	27.1
10.8	8.5	8.3	22.0	10.2	14.4	13.2	13.1	14.0	15.5	14.4	20.6	16.1
28.2	65.9	16.9	21.9	57.5	39.0	10.7	19.9	19.3	13.2	-12.9	34.2	21.1
26.3	43.7	15.0	18.2	55.8	52.8	14.9	19.5	18.8	14.4	-16.9	28.2	20.3
29.8	82.9	17.9	24.2	58.6	31.1	7.9	20.2	19.7	12.4	-9.8	38.5	21.7

单位:%

表 1-5 续表 Continued

指 标	Indicators	1993	1994	1995	1996	1997	1998
浦东国际机场旅客吞吐量	Passenger Capacity at Pudong International Airport						
浦东国际机场货邮吞吐量	Volume of Cargo Handled at Pudong International Airport						
港口货物吞吐量	Volume of Cargo Handled at Port	21.8	-7.8	-27.6	19.7	2.9	-5.8
集装箱吞吐量	Container Handling Capacity				1.9 倍 (times)	45.3	48.7
外商直接投资合同项目	Projects of Foreign Direct Investment	63.0	12.0	-19.0	-4.3	-23.2	-9.9
外商直接投资合同金额	Actual Paid Amount of Foreign Direct Investment	29.9	47.6	25.6	-44.4	-0.5	55.0
中外资银行本外币存款余额	Balance of RMB and Foreign Currencies Deposits in Chinese and Foreign Banks						
中外资银行本外币贷款余额	Balance of RMB and Foreign Currencies Loans in Chinese and Foreign Banks						
城镇居民人均年可支配收入	Annual Disposable Income Per Capita of Urban Residents						
农村居民人均年可支配收入	Annual Disposable Income Per Capita of Rural Residents						
居民储蓄存款年末余额	Residents' Savings Deposit Balance (Year End)	77.1	76.2	56.3	28.9	20.0	13.5
高等学校在校学生数	Student Enrollment of Higher Education	26.4	11.3	13.0	6.6	11.9	29.0
中等学校在校学生数	Student Enrollment at High Schools	9.6	17.1	15.6	8.2	5.0	5.9
小学在校学生数	Student Enrollment at Primary Schools	7.7	0.2	-1.8	-0.1	1.3	-2.7
幼儿园幼儿数	Young Child Enrollment at Kindergartens		-12.0	-3.5	-9.0	0.5	-0.5
医院病床	Hospital Beds	3.1	3.7	4.8	2.8	-1.2	3.4
卫生技术人员	Healthcare Professionals	3.4	4.0	2.3	4.4	5.2	3.1
#执业医生	Medical Practitioners	6.6	5.1	3.0	6.4	4.5	2.6
注册护士	Registered Nurses	3.7	4.9	2.6	3.7	7.6	5.1
期末认定跨国公司地区总部入驻数	Settled Headquarters of Transnational Companies at End of Term						

(%)

1999	2000	2001	2002	2003	2004	2005	2006	2007	2008	2009	2010	2011
			64.9	36.3	39.7	12.1	13.1	8.6	-2.8	13.4	26.2	2.5
			79.5	81.8	38.5	-1.1	16.8	16.2	4.8	-2.4	26.8	-3.4
-1.3	10.1	20.9	36.9	16.5	36.0	33.2	6.6	15.3	0.4	-4.9	14.3	17.2
36.2	85.4	56.9	60.2	43.3	42.0	34.9	7.9	13.4	-1.2	-9.7	17.4	14.8
-15.2	47.4	27.0	9.5	73.4	1.0	2.7	-16.6	-13.3	-36.0	-12.1	16.2	9.8
-61.5	1.7倍 (times)	-30.6	33.3	7.8	12.1	75.4	-14.4	2.2	0.9	0.3	1.7	17.3
						25.3	18.8	25.0	22.2	22.9	24.2	18.9
						21.4	20.2	23.8	12.0	7.6	16.9	11.8
						12.4	12.4	13.2	14.5	9.3	11.0	13.9
						11.4	11.6	12.2	12.5	9.2	12.1	14.1
10.6	2.7	24.2	35.2	31.9	27.9	30.7	17.1	1.4	34.6	18.2	12.2	14.7
21.7	34.4	28.0	86.2	21.3	9.6	8.5	5.9	8.2	19.0	4.7	29.5	10.2
6.2	0.8	-1.0	0.2	-1.5	12.3	-2.0	-4.1	-3.8	-3.0	-0.5	-0.7	0.3
-6.7	-6.7	-6.3	-2.3	-0.6	-11.4	3.3	3.5	3.3	3.1	17.3	3.2	6.9
1.0	3.0	-1.9	11.0	6.4	7.3	5.4	4.2	9.9	5.5	9.1	10.6	13.7
9.8	2.2	5.3	6.0	4.6	-0.6	-5.4	17.4	5.6	2.7	2.5	7.8	16.9
1.2	1.4	0.9	-1.3	-0.1	12.3	0.1	6.5	19.6	10.5	3.2	-1.8	22.1
1.6	1.5	0.5	-8.4	-0.2	3.7	-0.1	1.4	9.9	9.6	1.8	2.8	10.9
2.7	2.6	3.9	9.9	0.6	7.4	1.6	18.0	18.2	8.4	8.9	4.4	29.3
							29.7	15.7	19.8	17.4	11.1	14.0

表1-6 社会经济主要指标年均增长速度

Average Annual Growth Rate of Main Social Economic Indicators

单位:% (%)

指 标	Indicators	平均每年增长 Annual Growth Rate 1993~2011	1991~1995	1996~2000	2001~2005	2006~2010
年末户籍总人口	Registered Population at Year-end	1.9	2.1	2.1	2.3	1.5
新区生产总值	Gross Domestic Product in PNA	16.8	23.0	17.6	15.7	13.1
第一产业	Primary Industry	0.4	2.4	4.4	0.1	0.5
第二产业	Secondary Industry	14.9	20.0	15.3	15.9	11.6
第三产业	Tertiary Industry	20.6	29.8	24.1	15.7	14.9
工业总产值	Gross Output Value of Industry	17.4	20.3	17.6	20.3	14.9
*财政收入	Financial Revenue	30.2		21.4	36.8	22.8
* #地方财政收入	Local Financial Revenue	28.6		19.2	22.5	18.9
*地方财政支出	Local Financial Expenditure	24.8		12.5	23.4	17.1
社会消费品零售总额	Total Retail Sales of Consumer Goods	20.4	50.4	14.4	14.0	16.7
*外贸进出口总额	Total Imports and Exports	27.4		28.8	28.6	15.8
* #出口总额	Total Exports	25.7		19.3	31.2	14.7
* #进口总额	Total Imports	28.6		37.5	26.9	16.6
中外资银行本外币存款余额	Balance of RMB and Foreign Currencies Deposits in Chinese and Foreign Banks					20.8
中外资银行本外币贷款余额	Balance of RMB and Foreign Currencies Loans in Chinese and Foreign Banks					19.2
居民储蓄存款年末余额	Balance of Residents' Savings Deposits at Year-end	26.5	54.4	14.8	29.9	21.6

注：1. 带"*"指标宾栏第一栏年均增长速度的年份为"1994~2011"。
2. 带"*"指标宾栏第二栏因仅有二年增长速度,故不再计算该指标的年均增长速度。

Note: 1. The year with the annual growth rate in the first horizontal column that is indicated with the symbol of "*" is from 1994 to 2011.
2. Because the second column in the field of indicators with the sign of "*" only have the growth rate of the recent two years, we will not calculate the annual growth rate of this indicator.

表1-7 社会经济结构主要指标
Main Indicators of Economic and Social Structures

单位:% (%)

指 标	Indicators	2005	2009	2010	2011
第三产业增加值占GDP比重	Ratio of Added Value of the Tertiary Industry in GDP	48.9	56.6	56.1	57.3
新区财政收入相当于GDP比例	Ratio of PNA Financial Revenue in GDP	23.5	33.9	36.1	41.1
地方财政收入相当于GDP比例	Ratio of Local Financial Revenue in GDP	7.4	9.5	9.0	9.1
固定资产投资相当于GDP比例	Ratio of Fixed Capital Investment in GDP	32.9	35.5	30.4	26.2
外贸进出口总额相当于GDP比例	Ratio of Total Volume of Foreign Trade in GDP	342.4	237.2	262.5	259.6
外贸出口总额相当于GDP比例	Ratio of Total Exports of Foreign Trade in GDP	142.4	98.4	103.9	102.1
社会消费品零售总额相当于GDP比例	Ratio of Total Volume of Retail Sales for Social Consumer Goods in GDP	16.8	21.5	22.0	22.0
六个重点发展行业总产值占工业总产值比重	Ratio of Total Output Value of Six Key Industries in Total Value of Industrial Output	68.1	68.2	70.0	70.6
高技术产业工业总产值占工业总产值比重	Ratio of Total Output Value of Hi-tech Industries in Total Value of Industrial Output		24.8	26.3	28.3
城市基础设施投资占固定资产投资总额比重	Ratio of Investment for Urban Infrastructure in Gross Investment in Fixed Assets	18.2	34.5	18.3	19.0
房地产开发投资占固定资产投资总额比重	Ratio of Investment for Real Estate Development in Gross Investment in Fixed Assets	41.5	30.4	38.8	41.1
机电产品出口占外贸出口商品总额比重	Ratio of Exports of Machinery and Electrical Equipment in Total Exports of Foreign Trade	61.0	66.0	66.4	65.5
高新技术产品出口占外贸出口商品总额比重	Ratio of Export of High and New Technological Products in Total Export of Foreign Trade	33.4	33.3	36.6	38.4
第三产业实到外资占新区实到外资金额比重	Ratio of Foreign Investment in Place for the Tertiary Industry in Total of Foreign Investment in Place in PNA	71.8	75.1	86.8	90.6
发明专利申请量占专利申请量比重	Ratio of the Number of Applications for Invention Patents in the Volume of Patent Applications	57.1	36.7	37.4	49.0
城镇居民家庭人均食品支出占人均消费支出比重	Ratio of Expenses for Food per Capita of Urban Families in Consumption Expenditure Per Capita	36.2	34.7	34.9	34.5
城镇居民家庭人均服务性消费支出占人均消费支出比重	Ratio of Expenses for Service Consumptions Per Capita of Urban Families in Consumption Expenditure Per Capita	32.7	32.9	31.0	30.1

表 1-8 主要年份社会经济部分指标平均每天水平
Daily Average Level of Major Economic and Social Indicators in Main Years

指 标	Indicators	单 位 Unit	2000	2005	2010	2011
新区生产总值	Gross Output Value in PNA	万元 10 000 yuan	25 223	57 775	128 973	150 256
工业总产值	Gross Output Value of Industry	万元 10 000 yuan	44 542	116 232	235 384	261 748
财政收入	Financial Revenue	万元 10 000 yuan	2 828	13 560	56 059	61 812
#地方财政收入	Local Financial Revenue	万元 10 000 yuan	1 545	4 255	11 748	13 706
固定资产投资额	Total Investment in Fixed Assets	万元 10 000 yuan	9 618	19 003	39 241	39 326
新增固定资产	Newly Acquired Fixed Assets	万元 10 000 yuan	10 400	10 409	17 066	21 637
商品销售总额	Total Sales of Commodities	万元 10 000 yuan	20 628	76 917	226 399	287 753
社会消费品零售额	Retail Sales of Consumer Goods	万元 10 000 yuan	5 895	11 370	28 408	32 987
外贸出口货物总额	Total Exports Value of Commodities in Foreign Trade	万美元 USD 10 000	2 625	10 195	20 241	24 356
外商直接投资合同项目	Projects of Foreigin Direct Investment	个 unit	1.90	4.75	2.48	2.73
外商直接投资合同金额	Project Amount of Foreign Direct Investment	万美元 USD 10 000	790	1 549	1 541	1 807
港口货物吞吐量	Volume of Cargo Handled at Port	万吨 10 000 tons	13.67	29.17	61.56	72.14
函 件	Mails	万份 10 000 pieces	12.37	14.82	41.40	55.35
自来水售水量	Sales of Tap Water	万立方米 10 000 cu. m	90.45	114.87	164.62	162.79
售电量	Electricity Sales	万千瓦·时 10 000 kwh	1 911	3 512	6 293	6 548
管道燃气售气量	Sales of Pipelined Gas	万立方米 10 000 cu·m	30.43	121.37	175.89	183.01
公交车辆乘客人数	Passengers Carried by Public Vehicles	万人次 10 000 person-times	136.70	173.12	206.02	218.75
医院诊疗人数	Outpatients Treated	万人次 10 000 person-times	2.53	3.49	8.12	9.56
出生人数	Birth	人 person	23	34	61	61
死亡人数	Death	人 person	30	37	53	55

表1-9 主要年份社会经济人均指标
Annual Average Level of Major Social and Economical Indicators Per Capita in Main Years

指标	Indicators	单位 Unit	2000	2005	2010	2011
工业总产值	Gross Output Value of Industry	元 yuan	68 598	154 244	186 066	186 974
财政收入	Financial Revenue	元 yuan	4 355	17 995	44314	44 154
#地方财政收入	Local Financial Revence	元 yuan	2 380	5 647	9 287	9 790
固定资产投资额	Total Investment in Fixed Assets	元 yuan	14 813	25 218	31 019	28 091
新增固定资产	Newly Acquired Fixed Assets	元 yuan	16 017	13 813	13 490	15 456
社会消费品零售额	Total Retail Sales of Consumer Goods	元 yuan	9 079	12 859	22 456	23 564
外贸出口总额	Total Exports Value of Foreign Trade	美元 USD	4 042	13 529	16 000	17 398
外贸进口总额	Total Imports Value of Foreign Trade	美元 USD	6 711	19 001	24 404	26 832
居民年末储蓄存款余额	Balance of Savings Deposits at Year-end	元 yuan	15 232	40 209	63 747	66 065
职工年平均工资	Annual Average Wage of Staff and Workers	元 yuan	17 607	33 186	89 424	90 721
城镇居民年人均可支配收入	Annual Disposable Income Per Capita of Urban Residents	元 yuan		19 089	32 330	36 815
农村居民年人均可支配收入	Annual Disposable Income Per Capita of Suburban Residents	元 yuan		9 779	13 898	15 861
公共绿地占有面积	Public Green Area	平方米 sq · m	11.00	24.42	22.71	23.94
邮政订销报刊数	Total Circulation of Newspapers and Magazines	份 in number	53	43	16	35
城镇居民人均住房建筑面积	Building Area of Housing Per Capita	平方米 sq · m		32.73	39.26	36.30
每万人拥有病床数	Number of Sick-beds per 10 000 Persons	张 bed		23.35	32.84	34.70
每万名中小学生拥有教职员工数	Number of Teaching Staff per 10 000 Primary and Middle School Students	人 person		882	821	796
实有人口万人发案率	Ratio of Criminal Cases per 10 000 Persons	起/万人 in number /10 000 persons		61.76	50.93	51.02
每万人拥有律师数	Number of Lawyers per 10 000 Persons	人 person		5.4	6.4	6.4

注：1. 上述指标除特别注明外，人均水平均采用常住人口计算。
2. 居民年人均可支配收入为住户调查资料。

Note：1. The average level per capita has been calculated in the permanent population except the above-mentioned indicators are otherwise specified.
2. The data of annual disposable income per capita are surveyed from household residents.

表1-10 历年新区生产总值

Gross Domestic Product in PNA in Main Years (1990～2011)

单位:亿元 (100 million yuan)

年 份 Year	新区生产总值 Gross Domestic Product of PNA	第一产业 Primary Industry	第二产业 Secondary Industry	#工 业 Industry	第三产业 Tertiary Industry	#金 融 Banking	房地产 Real Estate
1990	60.24	2.22	45.89	43.13	12.13	3.07	
1991	71.54	2.41	53.45	50.46	15.68	4.46	
1992	101.49	1.89	73.72	70.25	25.88	6.96	
1993	164.00	2.12	114.45	108.16	47.43	16.40	
1994	291.20	3.19	197.13	177.45	90.88	23.73	
1995	414.65	4.22	283.92	260.07	126.51	28.59	36.52
1996	496.47	4.57	320.31	286.32	171.59	39.08	40.61
1997	608.22	4.95	376.87	325.38	226.40	69.10	46.20
1998	704.27	5.30	412.82	349.97	286.15	101.31	52.68
1999	801.36	5.47	435.66	388.88	360.23	138.35	47.26
2000	923.51	5.72	488.60	445.43	429.19	159.88	55.36
2001	1 087.53	6.06	560.29	508.62	521.18	170.12	70.39
2002	1 244.00	6.38	635.54	579.86	602.08	166.04	100.51
2003	1 510.32	6.67	767.53	708.98	736.12	183.48	129.12
2004	1 850.13	6.00	952.25	894.13	891.88	218.13	168.25
2005	2 108.79	6.09	1 070.96	1 009.47	1 031.74	249.69	174.48
2006	2 365.33	5.88	1 194.47	1 133.76	1 164.98	313.98	169.24
2007	2 793.39	6.06	1 306.49	1 237.36	1 480.84	474.83	185.38
2008	3 150.99	5.88	1 430.25	1 351.44	1 714.86	553.46	181.49
2009	4 001.39	30.61	1 706.29	1 581.82	2 264.49	708.28	258.94
2010	4 707.52	31.47	2 036.58	1 899.04	2 639.47	825.78	250.08
2011	5 484.35	34.46	2 306.32	2 154.27	3 143.57	991.61	229.71

表1-11 历年新区生产总值结构

Structure of Total Gross Domestic Product in PNA in Main Years (1990~2011)

单位:% (%)

年 份 Year	新区生产总值 Gross Domestic Product of PNA	第一产业 Primary Industry	第二产业 Secondary Industry	#工 业 Industry	第三产业 Tertiary Industry	#金 融 Banking	房地产 Real Estate
1990	100.0	3.7	76.2	71.6	20.1	5.1	
1991	100.0	3.4	74.7	70.5	21.9	6.2	
1992	100.0	1.9	72.6	69.2	25.5	6.9	
1993	100.0	1.3	69.8	66.0	28.9	10.0	
1994	100.0	1.1	67.7	60.9	31.2	8.1	
1995	100.0	1.0	68.5	62.7	30.5	6.9	8.8
1996	100.0	0.9	64.5	57.7	34.6	7.9	8.2
1997	100.0	0.8	62.0	53.5	37.2	11.4	7.6
1998	100.0	0.7	58.6	49.7	40.7	14.4	7.5
1999	100.0	0.7	54.4	48.6	44.9	17.3	5.9
2000	100.0	0.6	52.9	48.2	46.5	17.3	6.0
2001	100.0	0.6	51.5	46.8	47.9	15.6	6.5
2002	100.0	0.5	51.1	46.6	48.4	13.4	8.1
2003	100.0	0.5	50.8	46.9	48.7	12.1	8.6
2004	100.0	0.3	51.5	48.3	48.2	11.8	9.1
2005	100.0	0.3	50.8	47.9	48.9	11.8	8.3
2006	100.0	0.2	50.5	47.9	49.3	13.3	7.2
2007	100.0	0.2	46.8	44.3	53.0	17.0	6.6
2008	100.0	0.2	45.4	42.9	54.4	17.6	5.7
2009	100.0	0.8	42.6	39.5	56.6	17.7	6.5
2010	100.0	0.7	43.2	40.3	56.1	17.5	5.3
2011	100.0	0.6	42.1	39.3	57.3	18.1	4.2

表1-12 主要年份新区生产总值(新行业分类)
Gross Domestic Product in Main Years(Grouped by New Sectors)

单位:亿元 (100 million yuan)

指 标	Indicators	2000	2005	2010	2011
新区生产总值	**Gross Gross Domestic Production of PNA**	**923.51**	**2 108.79**	**4 707.52**	**5 484.35**
第一产业	Primary Industry	5.72	6.09	31.47	34.46
第二产业	Secondary Industry	488.60	1 070.96	2 036.58	2 306.32
工 业	Industry	445.43	1 009.47	1 899.04	2 154.27
建筑业	Construction	43.17	61.49	137.54	152.05
第三产业	Tertiary Industry	429.19	1031.74	2639.47	3143.57
交通运输、仓储业、邮政业	Transportation, Warehousing and Post Service	23.38	88.88	170.97	196.27
信息传输、计算机服务和软件业	Information Transmission, Computer Service and Computer Software	15.60	73.34	233.07	294.47
批发和零售业	Wholesale and Retail	109.61	212.05	608.27	762.72
住宿和餐饮业	Hotel and Catering	10.39	28.13	53.03	58.33
金融业	Banking	159.88	249.69	825.78	991.61
房地产业	Real Estate	55.36	174.48	250.08	229.71
其他服务业	Other Services	54.97	205.17	498.27	610.46
构 成(%)	**Composition (%)**	**100.0**	**100.0**	**100.0**	**100.0**
第一产业	Primary Industry	0.6	0.3	0.7	0.6
第二产业	Secondary Industry	52.9	50.8	43.2	42.1
工 业	Industry	48.2	47.9	40.3	39.3
建筑业	Construction	4.7	2.9	2.9	2.8
第三产业	Tertiary Industry	46.5	48.9	56.1	57.3
交通运输、仓储业、邮政业	Transportation, Warehousing and Post Service	2.5	4.2	3.6	3.6
信息传输、计算机服务和软件业	Information Transmission, Computer Service and Computer Software	1.7	3.5	5.0	5.4
批发和零售业	Wholesale and Retail	11.9	10.1	12.9	13.9
住宿和餐饮业	Hotel and Catering	1.1	1.3	1.2	1.0
金融业	Banking	17.3	11.8	17.5	18.1
房地产业	Real Estate	6.0	8.3	5.3	4.2
其他服务业	Other Services	6.0	9.7	10.6	11.1

表 1-13 历年新区生产总值指数
Gross Domestic Product Indexes of PNA in Main Years
(1991 ~2011)

(以 1990 年为 100) (Taking1990 as 100)

年 份 Year	新区生产总值 Gross Domestic Product of PNA	第一产业 Primary Industry	第二产业 Secondary Industry	#工 业 Industry	第三产业 Tertiary Industry	#金 融 Banking	房地产 Real Estate
1991	113.9	101.2	113.1		119.5	141.0	
1992	138.0	102.3	137.6		143.8	179.1	
1993	179.7	93.6	167.9	121.9	210.7	332.7	
1994	231.1	98.4	204.2	148.0	301.0	408.5	
1995	282.0	112.4	248.9	172.1	369.0	440.0	105.2
1996	339.0	114.5	292.2	199.8	479.7	576.9	111.6
1997	401.0	120.6	339.9	227.4	596.2	856.7	120.8
1998	468.3	127.7	387.4	256.7	740.5	1 210.5	132.1
1999	543.8	132.6	439.7	301.4	907.1	1 571.2	105.4
2000	633.5	139.1	506.5	352.9	1 084.9	1 850.9	127.7
2001	735.5	147.6	589.1	406.2	1 259.6	1 937.9	157.4
2002	858.3	154.8	685.7	473.3	1 475.0	1 941.7	214.3
2003	1 008.5	157.3	818.0	570.3	1 708.1	2 145.6	250.3
2004	1 173.9	145.8	958.7	678.1	1 976.3	2 488.9	276.5
2005	1 315.9	140.0	1 059.4	752.0	2 253.0	2 854.8	273.5
2006	1 492.2	132.9	1 187.6	849.0	2 591.0	3 565.6	261.7
2007	1 719.0	125.7	1 307.5	935.6	3 119.5	4 963.3	267.7
2008	1 918.5	118.3	1 426.7	1 019.8	3 555.9	5 712.8	257.0
2009	2 119.9	115.1	1 516.6	1 080.9	4 071.6	7 369.5	314.1
2010	2 382.8	112.0	1 748.6	1 253.8	4 491.0	7 819.0	282.7
2011	2 647.3	111.0	1 914.7	1 381.8	5 047.8	8 663.5	257.5

注：工业增加值以 1992 年为 100，房地产增加值以 1994 年为 100。
Note: The added industrial value takes the data of 1992 as 100, and the added real estate value takes the data of 1994 as 100.

表1-14 历年新区生产总值指数

Gross Domestic Product Indexes of PNA in Main Years

(1991~2011)

（以上年为环比基期） (Previous Year as Chain Base)

年 份 Year	新区生产总值 Gross Domestic Product of PNA	第一产业 Primary Industry	第二产业 Secondary Industry	#工 业 Industry	第三产业 Tertiary Industry	#金 融 Banking	房地产 Real Estate
1991	113.9	101.2	113.1	113.8	119.5	141.0	
1992	121.2	101.1	121.7	120.1	120.3	127.0	
1993	130.2	91.5	122.0	121.9	146.6	185.8	
1994	128.6	105.1	121.6	121.4	142.8	122.8	
1995	122.0	114.2	121.9	116.3	122.6	107.7	105.2
1996	120.2	101.9	117.4	116.1	130.0	131.1	106.1
1997	118.3	105.3	116.3	113.8	124.3	148.5	108.2
1998	116.8	105.9	114.0	112.9	124.2	141.3	109.4
1999	116.1	103.8	113.5	117.4	122.5	129.8	79.8
2000	116.5	104.9	115.2	117.1	119.6	117.8	121.1
2001	116.1	106.1	116.3	115.1	116.1	104.7	123.3
2002	116.7	104.9	116.4	116.5	117.1	100.2	136.1
2003	117.5	101.6	119.3	120.5	115.8	110.5	116.8
2004	116.4	92.7	117.2	118.9	115.7	116.0	110.5
2005	112.1	96.0	110.5	110.9	114.0	114.7	98.9
2006	113.4	94.9	112.1	112.9	115.0	124.9	95.7
2007	115.2	94.6	110.1	110.2	120.4	139.2	102.3
2008	111.6	94.2	109.1	109.0	114.0	115.1	96.0
2009	110.5	97.3	106.3	106.0	114.5	129.0	122.2
2010	112.4	97.3	115.3	116.0	110.3	106.1	90.0
2011	111.1	99.1	109.5	110.2	112.4	110.8	91.1

表1-15 历年第三产业增加值指数(旧行业分类)
Indexes of Value Added in Tertiary Industry in Main Years (Grouped By Old Sectors) (1991~2000)

(以上年为环比基期) (Previous Year as Chain Base)

年 份 Year	第三产业增加值 Value Added in Tertiary Industry	#交通、运输、仓储、邮电通讯业 Transportation, Warehousing, Post and Telecommunications	批发和零售贸易、餐饮业 Wholesale, Retail and Catering	金融保险 Banking and Insurance	房地产 Real Estate
1991	119.5	108.8	108.1	141.0	
1992	120.3			127.0	
1993	146.6	137.3	124.8	185.8	
1994	142.8	105.4	154.1	122.8	
1995	122.6	115.2	172.8	107.7	105.2
1996	130.0	128.4	158.9	131.1	106.1
1997	124.3	112.2	118.5	148.5	108.2
1998	124.2	117.0	118.3	141.3	109.4
1999	122.5	122.1	129.1	129.8	79.8
2000	119.6	117.9	119.1	117.8	121.1

表1-16 历年第三产业增加值指数(新行业分类)
Index of Value Added in Tertiary Industry in Main Years(Grouped by New Sectors) (2001~2011)

(以上年为环比基期) (Previous Year as Chain Base)

年 份 Year	第三产业增加值 Value Added in Tertiary Industry	#交通运输、仓储业、邮政业 Transportation, Warehousing and Post Service	信息传输、计算机服务和软件业 Information Transmission, Computer Service and Computer Software	批发和零售业 Wholesale and Retail	金融业 Banking	房地产业 Real Estate
2001	116.1	127.5	109.4	121.6	104.7	123.3
2002	117.1	127.1	109.7	116.9	100.2	136.1
2003	115.8	115.8	164.3	113.6	110.5	116.8
2004	115.7	122.2	121.4	112.6	116.0	110.5
2005	114.0	118.6	118.3	114.8	114.7	98.9
2006	115.0	115.2	119.1	112.9	124.9	95.7
2007	120.4	115.7	116.4	114.7	139.2	102.3
2008	114.0	110.9	120.3	115.4	115.1	96.0
2009	114.5	94.7	105.4	114.3	129.0	122.2
2010	110.3	116.5	110.9	120.1	106.1	90.0
2011	112.4	112.3	118.4	116.6	110.8	91.1

表1-17 社会经济主要指标占全市比重
The Proportion of Major Economic and Social Indicators in Shanghai

指标	Indicators	2010 浦东新区 PNA	2010 全市 Shanghai	2010 浦东新区占全市比重(%) Proportion of PNA in Shanghai(%)	2011 浦东新区 PNA	2011 全市 Shanghai	2011 浦东新区占全市比重(%) Proportion of PNA in Shanghai(%)
土地面积(平方公里)	Land Area (sq・km)	1 290.63	6 340.50	20.4	1 291.64	6 340.50	20.4
年末常住人口(万人)	Permanent Population at Year-end (10 000 persons)	504.44	2 302.66	21.9	517.50	2 347.46	22.0
年末户籍总人口(万人)	Registered Population at Year-end (10 000 persons)	275.80	1 412.32	19.5	278.53	1 419.36	19.6
从业人员(万人)	Employment (10 000 persons)	235.11	1 090.76	21.6	280.68	1 104.33	25.4
职工人数(万人)	Staff and Workers(10 000 persons)	85.02	648.49	13.1	138.53	868.42	16.0
生产总值(亿元)	Gross Domestic Product (100 million yuan)	4 707.52	17 165.98	27.4	5 484.35	19 195.69	28.6
第一产业	Primary Industry	31.47	114.15	27.6	34.46	124.94	27.6
第二产业	Secondary Industry	2 036.58	7 218.32	28.2	2 306.32	7 927.89	29.1
#工 业	Industry	1 899.04	6 536.21	29.1	2 154.27	7 208.59	29.9
第三产业	Tertiary Industry	2 639.47	9 833.51	26.8	3 143.57	11 142.86	28.2
#金 融	Banking	825.78	1 950.96	42.3	991.61	2 277.40	43.5
房地产	Real Estate	250.08	1 002.50	24.9	229.71	1 019.68	22.5
工业总产值(亿元)	Gross Output Value of Industry (100 million yuan)	8 591.50	31 038.57	27.7	9 553.79	33 834.44	28.2
固定资产投资总额(亿元)	Total Investment in Fixed Assets (100 million yuan)	1 432.30	5 317.67	26.9	1 435.39	5067.09	28.3
城市基础设施投资额(亿元)	Investment in Urban Infrastructure (100 million yuan)	261.92	1 497.46	17.5	272.02	1 157.34	23.5
地方财政收入(亿元)	Local Government Revenue (100 million yuan)	428.82	2 873.58	14.9	500.26	3 429.83	14.6
地方财政支出(亿元)	Local Government Expenditure (100 million yuan)	524.06	3 302.89	15.9	615.24	3 914.88	15.7

表1-17 续表 Continued

指 标 Indicators		2010 浦东新区 PNA	2010 全市 Shanghai	2010 浦东新区占全市比重(%) Proportion of PNA in Shanghai(%)	2011 浦东新区 PNA	2011 全市 Shanghai	2011 浦东新区占全市比重(%) Proportion of PNA in Shanghai(%)
商品销售总额(亿元)	Aggregate Sales of Commodities (100 million yuan)	8 263.56	37 383.25	22.1	10 502.98	46 075.87	22.8
社会消费品零售总额(亿元)	Retail Sales of Consumer Goods (100 million yuan)	1 036.88	6 070.50	17.1	1 204.04	6 814.80	17.7
年末居民储蓄存款余额(亿元)	Savings Deposit Balance of Rural and Urban Residents (100 million yuan)	2 943.49	16 249.29	18.1	3 375.71	17 958.22	18.8
外贸进出口商品总额(亿美元)	Total Value of Imports and Exports (USD 100 million)	1 865.62	3 688.69	50.6	2 260.00	4 374.36	51.7
#出口总额	Value of Exports	738.79	1807.84	40.9	888.98	2 097.89	42.4
外商直接投资合同项目(个)	Projects of Foreigin Direct Investment (unit)	906	3 906	23.2	995	4 329	23.0
外商直接投资合同金额(亿美元)	Project Amount of Foreign Direct Investment (USD 100 million)	56.25	153.07	36.7	65.97	201.03	32.8
外商直接投资实际到位金额(亿美元)	Foreign Direct Investment Actually Absorbed (USD 100 million)	38.56	111.21	34.7	52.97	126.01	42.0
国际机场旅客吞吐量(万人次)	Passenger Capacity in Pudong International Airport (10 000 person-times)	4 040.57	7 170.09	56.4	4 144.23	7 406.01	56.0
港口货物吞吐量(万吨)	Volume of Cargo Handled at Port (10 000 tons)	22 470	65 300	34.4	26 332	72 758	36.2
集装箱吞吐量(万标箱)	Container Handling Capacity (10 000 TEUs)	2 509.8	2 906.9	86.3	2 880.7	3 173.9	90.8
各级各类学校在校学生数(万人)	Student Enrollment by Level and Type of Schools (10 000 persons)	50.56	196.62	25.7	53.44	197.64	27.0
医院病床(张)	Number of Hospital Beds (bed)	15 164	105 083	14.4	17 731	107 130	16.6
专业卫生技术人员(万人)	Medical Technical Personnel (10 000 persons)	1.89	13.54	14.0	2.31	13.91	16.6
#执业医生	Medical Practitioners	0.76	5.13	14.8	0.86	5.21	16.5
申请专利(项)	Patent Claiming (item)	17 587	71 196	24.7	18 819	80 215	23.5

表 1-18 财政收支

Financial Revenue and Expenditure

单位:万元 (10 000 yuan)

指 标	Indicators	2000	2005	2010	2011
全部财政收入	**Total Financial Revenue**	**1 032 077**	**4 949 366**	**20 461 744**	**22 561 309**
地方财政收入	**PNA Government Revenue**	**564 020**	**1 553 141**	**4 288 216**	**5 002 592**
区级财政收入	**PNA Financial Revenue**	**355 863**	**1 553 141**	**6 866 283**	**6 933 355**
#增值税	Value Added Tax	44 293	275 873	695 060	695 307
营业税	Business Income Tax	122 200	528 808	1 478 656	1 512 511
企业所得税	Enterprise Tax	72 712	251 733	911 281	1 119 566
个人所得税	Individual Income Tax	77 662	199 439	447 612	541 489
城市维护建设税	Tax on Urban Construction and Maintenance	11 603	24 329	64 066	98 026
房产税	Tax on Real Estate	13 418	35 192	78 264	99 360
印花税	Stamp Tax	3 588	22 007	124 409	150 480
契 税	Contract Tax	7 107	202 445	315 205	323 867
地方财政支出	**PNA Government Expenditure**	**695 999**	**1 987 939**	**5 240 626**	**6 152 362**
#一般公共服务	Ordinary Community Services			337 484	372 136
公共安全	Public Security			217 982	231 784
教 育	Education			493 988	692 047
科学技术	Technology			239 029	326 331
文化体育与传媒	Culture, Sports and Media			55 135	91 315
社会保障和就业	Social Security and Employment			456 319	510 653
医疗卫生	Healthcare			260 061	286 751
节能环保	Lower Power Consumption and Environment Protection			61 191	33 877
城乡社区事务	Urban and Suburban Community Affairs			1 475 828	1 802 289
农林水事务	Agricultural, Forest and Water Affairs			285 049	294 139
交通运输	Traffic and Transportation			153 107	133 429
资源勘探电力信息等事物	Resource Exploration and Electric Power Information, etc			879 267	1 099 532
商业服务业等事物	Business Services, etc			63 436	39 206
金融监管等事物支出	Expenditure such as Supervision on Financial Affaires			88 000	58 400

注: 1. 2007 年财政部进行财税体制改革,起用新科目,2000 及 2005 年口径数据无法提供。
2. 2010、2011 年财政收入数按“十二五”市财税体制改革确定的新体制口径填列。

Note: 1. This table is provided by PNA Financial Bureau. The Financial Department has started the reform of the finance and taxation system since 2007, which began to use the new subject. Data approached in 2000 and those in 2005 are not available.
2. The number of financial revenue in 2010 and that of 2011 are filled in according to the new ssytem approach determined by the municipal finance-and system reforms during the “Twelfth-Five-Year Planning”

主要统计指标解释

气　温

气温是指空气的温度,一般以摄氏度(℃)为单位表示。气象观测的温度表是放在离地面约1.5米处通风良好的百叶箱里测量的,因此,通常说的气温指的是离地面1.5米处百叶箱中的温度。其统计计算方法为:

月平均气温是将全月各日的平均气温相加,除以该月的天数而得。

年平均气温是将12个月的月平均气温累加后除以12而得。

降水量

降水量是指从天空降落到地面的液态或固态(经融化后)水,未经蒸发、渗透、流失而在地面上积聚的深度。其统计计算方法为:

月降水量是将全月各日的降水量累加而得。

年降水量是将12个月的月降水量累加而得。

日照时数

日照时数是指太阳实际照射地面的时间。其统计方法与降水量相同。

生产总值(原国内生产总值)

国内生产总值是指按市场价格计算的一个地区所有常住(驻)单位在一定时期内生产活动的最终成果。生产总值有三种表现形态,即价值形态、收入形态和产品形态。从价值形态看,它是所有常驻单位在一定时期内所生产的全部货物和服务价值超过同期投入的全部非固定资产货物和服务价值的差额,即所有常住(驻)单位的增加值之和;从收入形态看,它是所有常住(驻)单位在一定时期内所创造并分配给常住(驻)单位和非常住(驻)单位的初次(分配)收入之和;从产品形态看,它是所有常住单位在一定时期内最终使用的货物和服务减去进口货物和服务。在实际核算中,生产总值有三种计算方法(其三种表现形态体现为三种计算方法),即生产法、收入法和支出法。三种方法分别从不同的方面反映生产总值及其构成。根据国务院和国家统计局有关我国GDP核算和数据发布制度的规定,浦东新区国内生产总值自2004年起更名为"浦东新区生产总值",简称"浦东新区GDP"。

三次产业

根据社会生产活动历史发展的顺序对产业结构的划分,产品直接取自自然界的部门称为第一产业,对初级产品进行再加工的部门称为第二产业,为生产和消费提供各种服务的部门称为第三产业。

第一产业:农林牧渔业(包括农业、林业、畜牧业、渔业和农林牧渔服务业)。

第二产业:包括采矿业、制造业、电力、燃气及水的生产和供应业与建筑业。

第三产业:除第一、第二产业以外的其他各业。

指　数

指数是一种表明社会经济现象动态的相对数。运用指数可以测定不能直接相加和直接对比的社会经济现象的总动态;可以分析社会经济现象总变动中各因素变动的影响程度;可以研究总平均指标变动中各组标志水平和总体结构变动的作用。它是在把各个年份的产值换算成可比价格的基础上,根据定基数等于相应各个环比指数的连乘积这个换算关系计算出来的。

平均每年增长速度

在我国计算平均增长速度有两种方法,一种是习惯上经常使用的"水平法",又称几何平均法,是各以间隔期最后一年的水平同基期水平对比来计算平均每年增长(或下降)速度。另一种是"累计法",又称代数平均法或方程法,是以间隔期内各年水平的总和同基期水平对比来计算平均每年增长(或下降)速度。

在一般正常情况下,两种方法计算的平均每年增长速度比较接近,但在经济发展不平衡,出现大起大落时,两种方法计算的结果差别较大。

本年鉴内所列的平均每年增长速度,除固定资产投资、直接吸收外资是用"累计法"计算以外,其余均用"水平法"计算。

财政收入

指国家财政参与社会产品分配所取得的收入,是实现国家职能的财力保证。财政收入所包括的内容几经变化,目前主要包括:

(1)各项税收:包括增值税、营业税、消费税、土地增值税、城市维护建设税、资源税、城市土地使用税、企业所得税、个人所得税、关税、证券交易印花税、车辆购置税、农牧业税和耕地占用税等。

(2)专项收入:包括排污费收入、城市水资源费收入、矿产资源补偿费收入、教育费附加收入等。

(3)其他收入:包括利息收入、基本建设贷款归还收入、基本建设收入、捐赠收入等。

(4)国有企业亏损补贴:此项为负收入,冲减财政收入。主要包括对工业企业、商业企业、粮食企业的补贴。

中央财政收入和地方财政收入

指按现行分税制财政体制划分的中央本级收入和地方本级收入。1994 年实行分税制财政体制以后,属于中央财政的收入包括关税、海关代征消费税和增值税,消费税,中央企业所得税,地方银行和外资银行及非银行金融企业所得税,铁道部门、各银行总行、各保险总公司等集中缴纳的营业税、利润和城市维护建设税,车辆购置税,船舶吨税,增值税的 75% 部分,证券交易税(印花税)94% 部分,个人所得税中的利息所得税,利息所得税之外的个人所得税中央分享的部分,海洋石油资源税。属于地方财政的收入包括营业税,地方企业所得税,利息所得税之外的个人所得税地方分享的部分,城镇土地使用税,固定资产投资方向调节税,城镇维护建设税,房产税,车船使用税,印花税,屠宰税,农牧业税,农业特产税,耕地占用税,契税,土地增值税、国有土地有偿使用收入,增值税 25% 部分,证券交易税(印花税)6% 部分和除海洋石油资源税以外的其他资源税。

地方财政支出

地方财政支出指根据政府在经济和社会活动中,按照政府的责权划分确定的支出。地方财政支出主要包括地方行政管理和各项事业费,地方统筹的基本建设、技术改造支出,支援农村生产支出,城市维护和建设经费,价格补贴支出等。

港口货物吞吐量

指经水运进出港区范围,并经过装卸的货物数量,包括邮件及办理托运手续的行李、包裹以及补给运输船舶的燃、物料和淡水。货物吞吐量按货物流向分为进口、出口吞吐量,按货物交流性质分为外贸货物吞吐量和国内贸易货物吞吐量。货物吞吐量的货类构成及其流向,是衡量港口生产能力大小的重要指标。

国际标准集装箱吞吐量

凡经过水运进、出港区范围,并经过装卸的集装箱箱数和重量(含集装箱自重),通常是按进港和出港分别统计。

TEU 是"折合 20 英尺标准箱"的英文缩写。它是指各种尺寸的国际标准集装箱的自然箱数,按各自的换算比例,折算为 20 英尺标准箱的换算箱数。其换算比例为:40 英尺箱 1 : 2;35 英尺箱 1 : 1.75;20 英尺箱 1 : 1;10 英尺箱 1 : 0.5。

EXPLANATORY NOTES TO MAJOR STATISTICAL INDICATORS

Temperature

Temperature refers to the air temperature. It often uses centigrade as the unit. The thermometry used for weather observation is put in a breezy shutter, which is 1.5 meters high from the ground. Therefore, the commonly used temperature refers to the temperature in the breezy shutter 1.5 meters away from the ground. The calculation method is as follows:

Monthly average temperature is the summation of average daily temperature of one month divided by the actual days of that particular month.

Annual average temperature is the summation of monthly average of a year divided by 12 months.

Volume of Precipitation

Volume of Precipitation refers to the deepness of liquid state or solid state (thawed) water falling from the sky to the ground that has not been evaporated, infiltrated or run off. The calculation method is as follows:

Monthly precipitation is the summation of daily precipitation of a month.

Annual precipitation is the summation of 12 months precipitation of a year.

Sunshine Hours

Sunshine Hours refer to the actual hours of sun irradiating the earth. The calculation method is the same as that of the precipitation.

Gross Domespic Product

Gross Domespic Product refers to the final products at market prices by (of) all resident units of a region during a certain period of time. Gross product is expressed in three different forms, i. e value, income, and products respectively. The form of value added refers to the total value of all products and services produced by all resident units during a certain period of time minus the total value of inputs of non fixed-assets products and services or the summation of the value added of all resident units; the form of income includes all the income items produced by all resident units and distributed primarily to all resident and non-resident units; the form of product refers to all final goods and services minus imports of goods and services. In the practice of national accounting, it is calculated by three approaches, i. e. product approach, income approach, and expenditure approach, respectively, to reflect Gross Product and its composition of different aspects. According to the regulations of GDP national accounting and data release issued by the State Council and National Bureau of Statistics, since 2004 Pudong New Area Gross Domestic Product has been renamed as Pudong New Area Gross Product Value, for short PNA GDP.

Three Industries

Three Industries have been classified according to the historical sequence of development. Primary industry refers to extraction of natural resources; secondary industry involves processing of primary products; and tertiary industry provides services of various kinds for production and consumption.

Primary industry: Agriculture, forestry, animal husbandry and fishery. (including farming, forestry, animal husbandry, fishery industry and service industry for farming, forestry, animal husbandry and fishery).

Secondary industry: Mining, manufacturing, power, steam and water production and supply and construction.

Tertiary industry: All other industries not included in primary or secondary industries.

Index

Index refers to the relative figures indicating social and economic phenomena and developments. Index is used to evaluate the overall development of social and economic phenomena which can not be determined by simple addition or direct comparison. It is also used to analyze the outcome of various changes in the general phenomenon movement of social and economic development, and to study the level of each sub-index in the changes of general average index and the role of the changes of the overall structure. It is calculated at the comparable prices conversed from the output value of each year, using the formula of index number with fixed base period equal to the continuous product of its relative chain index.

Average Annual Growth Rate

Two methods for calculating Average Annual Growth Rate are applied in China, one is often called "level approach" or geometry average, which is derived by comparing the growth rate for the last year of the interval with that of the beginning year; the other is called "accumulating approach" or algebraic average or equation method, which is calculated by comparing the total growth rate of each year for the interval with that of base year.

Usually the results calculated by the two methods are fairly close, but they differ sharply when imbalance occurred in economic development with striking fluctuations in growth.

The Average Annual Growth Rates listed in this statistical yearbook are calculated by "level approach" except for the growth rate of investment in fixed assets and foreign capital absorbed.

Government Revenue

Government Revenue refers to the revenue of the government finance by means of participating in the distribution of the social products, which is the financial resources for ensuring the government to function. The contents of government revenue have been changed several times. Now it includes the following main items:

(1) Various tax revenues, including value added tax, business tax, consumption tax, land value added tax, tax on city maintenance and construction, resources tax, tax on use of urban land, enterprise income tax, personal income tax, tariff, stamp tax on security transactions, tax on purchase of motor vehicles, tax on agriculture and animal husbandry and tax on occupancy of cultivated land, etc.

(2) Special revenues, including revenues from the fee on sewage treatment, fee on urban water resources, fee for the compensation of mineral resources and extra-charges for education, etc.

(3) Other revenues, including revenue from interest, revenue from the repayment of capital construction loan, revenue from capital construction projects, and donations and grants.

(4) Subsidies for the losses of the state-owned enterprises. This is an item of negative revenue, consisting of subsidies to industrial, commercial and grain purchasing and supply enterprises.

Revenue of the Central Government and Revenue of the Local Government

Revenue of the central government and revenue of the local governments: refers to the revenue of the central government and that of the local governments as defined by the decentralized taxation system starting from 1994. In accordance with this system, the revenue of the central government includes tariff, consumption tax and value added tax levied by the customs, consumption tax, income tax of the enterprises subordinate to the central government, income taxes of the local banks, foreign-funded banks and non-bank financial institutions, business tax and profits of railways, head offices of banks, head office of insurance company , which are handed over to the government in a centralized way, tax on city maintenance and construction, tax on purchasing motor vehicles, tonnage tax of ships, 75% of the value added tax, 94% of the tax on stock dealing (stamp tax), interest income tax in the personal income tax, proportion of the personal income tax (other that interest income tax) to be shared by the central government, and tax on ocean petroleum resources. The revenue of the local governments includes business tax, income tax of the enterprises subordinate to the local government, proportion of the personal income tax (other that interest income tax) to be shared by the central government, tax on the use of urban land, tax on the adjustment of the investment in fixed assets, tax on town maintenance and construction, tax on real estates, tax on the use of vehicles and ships, stamp tax, slaughter tax, tax on agriculture and animal husbandry, tax on special agricultural products, tax on the occupancy of cultivated land, contract tax, value-added tax on land, income from charges on use of state-owned land, 25% of the value added tax, 6% of the tax on stock dealing (stamp tax) and tax on resources other than the ocean petroleum resources.

Expenditure of the Local Government

Expenditure of the local government includes mainly the administrative expenses and various operating expenses at the level of local governments, the expenditure for capital construction and technological innovation with the funds raised by the local government, expenditure for supporting rural production, expenditure for city maintenance and construction and expenditure for price subsidies, etc.

Volume of Freight Handled in Ports

Volume of Freight Handled in Ports refers to the volume of cargo passing in and out the harbor area of the ports and having been loaded and unloaded. The volume includes that of the postal matters, registered luggage and fuels, materials and fresh water as supplies of the ships. The volume of freight handled may be classified by direction of flow as freight for import and freight for export, or by nature of cargo as freight for domestic trade and freight for foreign trade. As an important indicator, the volume of freight handled by type of cargo and by main flow direction reflects the production capacity of ports.

International Container Throughput Capacity

International Container Throughput Capacity refers to number and weight of containers which are loaded or unloaded within port area via water carriage. It is often calculated by entering and leaving port, respectively. TEU was the abbreviation of twenty foot equivalent unit, which refers to converted number of all kinds of containers. The conversion method is based on respective conversion ratio and the number of all kinds of container is converted to the standard number of twenty foot equivalent unit. The conversion ratio is: 40 feet container 1 : 2, 35 feet container 1 : 1.75, 20 feet container 1 : 1, 10 feet container 1 : 0.5.

第二篇

Chapter 2

人口

POPULATION

SHANGHAI PUDONG NEW AREA STATISTICAL YEARBOOK

表2-1 历年常住人口、户籍人口、流动人口情况
(1990~2011)

单位:万人

年 份 Year	年末常住人口 Permanent Population at year-end	常住人口密度(人/平方公里) Density of Permanent Population (Persons/sq·km)	年末户籍人口 Registered Population at Year-end	按户籍 Grouped by Types of
				非农业 Non-agriculture
1990			133.94	81.67
1991			137.34	85.45
1992			140.67	89.65
1993			143.73	97.78
1994			146.20	104.63
1995			148.63	109.73
1996			151.11	113.84
1997			153.40	119.20
1998			156.18	123.70
1999			160.08	128.51
2000	240.23	4 503	164.87	134.57
2001	247.56	4 641	168.45	139.85
2002	255.11	4 782	172.82	146.25
2003	262.89	4 616	176.69	153.46
2004	270.91	4 756	180.90	160.13
2005	279.19	4 902	184.81	170.17
2006	285.30	5 009	187.56	175.24
2007	305.35	5 361	191.16	179.90
2008	305.70	5 367	194.29	183.62
2009	419.05	3 462	272.28	240.32
2010	504.44	3 908	275.80	245.06
2011	517.50	4 007	278.53	248.63

Permanent Population, Household Registered Population and Migrating Population in Main Years

(10 000 Persons)

性质分 Residence Registration	按性别分 Grouped by Sex		户籍人口密度（人/平方公里）Population Density (persons/sq · km)	期末登记流动人口数 Number of Registered Migrating Population
农 业 Agriculture	男 Male	女 Female		
52.27	66.41	67.53	2 584	
51.89	68.22	69.12	2 650	
51.02	69.96	70.71	2 714	
45.95	71.59	72.14	2 749	
41.57	72.92	73.28	2 797	
38.90	74.23	74.40	2 843	
37.27	75.53	75.58	2 891	
34.20	76.70	76.70	2 934	
32.48	78.21	77.97	2 988	
31.57	80.22	79.86	3 001	
30.30	82.75	82.12	3 091	
28.60	84.66	83.79	3 158	
26.57	86.97	85.85	3 240	67.94
23.23	89.03	87.66	3 102	80.16
20.77	91.20	89.70	3 176	82.58
14.64	93.12	91.69	3 245	93.73
12.32	94.45	93.11	3 293	119.75
11.26	96.13	95.03	3 356	130.97
10.67	97.48	96.81	3 411	127.30
31.96	136.00	136.28	2 249	169.53
30.74	137.60	138.20	2 137	218.33
29.90	138.87	139.65	2 156	206.50

表2-2 土地面积、户数、人口、人口密度及人口迁移情况
(2011 年底)

单位:人

地 区 Subdistrict/Town		土地面积(平方公里) Land Area (sq. km)	户 数(户) Household (household)	年末人口 Year-end Population	按户籍性质分 Grouped by Types of Residence Registration	
					非农业 Non-agriculture	农 业 Agriculture
总 计	**Total**	**1 290.63**	**1 073 227**	**2 785 271**	**2 486 253**	**299 018**
街道小计	**Subdistrict Tot**	**106.64**	**436 366**	**1 162 231**	**1 162 174**	**57**
潍坊新村街道	Weifangxincun Subdistrict	3.74	31 863	91 472	91 472	
陆家嘴街道	Lujiazui Subdistrict	6.89	38 184	119 102	119 101	1
周家渡街道	Zhoujiadu Subdistrict	5.52	43 940	115 536	115 536	
塘桥街道	Tangqiao Subdistrict	3.86	21 873	57 922	57 918	4
上钢新村街道	Shanggangxincun Subdistrict	7.54	37 681	105 190	105 190	
南码头路街道	Nanmatoulu Subdistrict	4.25	30 234	81 490	81 489	1
沪东新村街道	Hudongxincun Subdistrict	5.39	28 649	72 090	72 090	
金杨新村街道	Jinyangxincun Subdistrict	8.02	52 702	130 182	130 182	
洋泾街道	Yangjing Subdistrict	7.38	38 822	106 026	106 026	
浦兴路街道	Puxinglu Subdistrict	6.25	41 017	98 407	98 407	
东明路街道	Dongminglu Subdistrict	4.90	26 593	63 066	63 024	42
花木街道	Huamu Subdistrict	20.90	44 136	107 277	107 268	9
申港街道	Shengang Subdistrict	22.00	672	14 471	14 471	
镇小计	**Town Tot**	**1 183.99**	**636 861**	**1 623 040**	**1 324 079**	**298 961**
川沙新镇	Chuansha New Town	96.70	51 874	139 893	102 262	37 631
高 桥 镇	Gaoqiao Town	39.02	34 175	87 575	81 795	5 780
北 蔡 镇	Beicai Town	23.71	48 482	123 776	120 107	3 669
合 庆 镇	Heqing Town	41.86	21 979	55 791	35 015	20776
唐 镇	Tangzhen Town	32.32	15 325	39 964	37 015	2 949
曹 路 镇	Caolu Town	45.48	23 922	71 672	58 661	13 011
金 桥 镇	Jinqiao Town	25.28	10 566	29 166	28 619	547
高 行 镇	Gaohang Town	22.85	19 567	49 823	49 769	54
高 东 镇	Gaodong Town	35.16	13 591	36 261	31 981	4 280
张 江 镇	Zhangjiang Town	45.02	24 989	72 611	72 594	17
三 林 镇	Sanlin Town	34.19	47 378	117 778	110 687	7 091
惠 南 镇	Huinan Town	59.08	45 622	114 800	99 954	14 846
周 浦 镇	Zhoupu Town	43.23	29 787	73 475	66 231	7244
新 场 镇	Xinchang Town	53.45	21 088	51 254	31 615	19 639
大 团 镇	Datuan Town	50.58	28 694	66 810	34 254	32 556
芦潮港镇	Luchaogang Town	47.97	7 441	16 373	16 368	5
康 桥 镇	Kangqiao Town	41.04	23 969	62 235	60 944	1 291
航 头 镇	Hangtou Town	59.96	24 065	58 200	41 768	16 432
祝 桥 镇	Zhuqiao Town	152.99	56 254	145 108	106 690	38 418
泥 城 镇	Nicheng Town	59.49	24 577	57 759	42 690	15 069
宣 桥 镇	Xuanqiao Town	45.73	18 323	42 300	33 513	8 787
书 院 镇	Shuyuan Town	66.91	21 941	51 593	26 668	24 925
万 祥 镇	Wanxiang Town	23.07	9 911	24 973	16 502	8 471
老 港 镇	Laogang Town	38.90	13 341	33 850	18 377	15 473

注：申港街道集体户口居多,因此不计算他的户规模。

Note: As the number of collective households in Shengang Subdistrict is much more than that of urban households, we do not calculate the scale of one certain household.

Land Area, Households, Population, Density of Population and Migration of Population (End of 2011)

(person)

按性别分 Grouped by Sex		平均每户人口 Average Persons Per Household	人口密度（人/平方公里）Population Density (persons/sq·km)	人口迁移情况 Population Mobility		
男 Male	女 Female			迁入 Population Moved-in	迁出 Population Moved-out	净迁入 Net Mobility
1 388 737	**1 396 534**	**2.60**	**2 158**	**26 596**	**9 816**	**16 780**
582 844	**579 387**	**2.66**	**10 899**	**14 595**	**4 670**	**9 925**
45 183	46 289	2.87	24 458	387	51	336
58 885	60 217	3.12	17 286	1 277	395	882
57 482	58 054	2.63	20 930	1 319	82	1 237
28 731	29 191	2.65	15 006	324	52	272
52 443	52 747	2.79	13 951	553	46	507
40 251	41 239	2.70	19 174	381	32	349
36 990	35 100	2.52	13 375	707	72	635
65 279	64 903	2.47	16 232	829	97	732
53 729	52 297	2.73	14 367	2 525	648	1 877
50 369	48 038	2.40	15 745	1 064	114	950
32 133	30 933	2.37	12 871	565	66	499
53 426	53 851	2.43	5 133	982	102	880
7 943	6 528		658	3 682	2 913	769
805 893	**817 147**	**2.55**	**1 371**	**12 001**	**5 146**	**6 855**
69 350	70 543	2.70	1 447	614	81	533
43 708	43 867	2.56	2 244	437	77	360
62 302	61 474	2.55	5 220	1 129	239	890
27 481	28 310	2.54	1 333	207	22	185
19 678	20 286	2.61	1 237	192	126	66
35 640	36 032	3.00	1 576	2 275	1 400	875
14 904	14 262	2.76	1 154	280	34	246
25 148	24 675	2.55	2 180	558	63	495
18 016	18 245	2.67	1 031	289	24	265
36 656	35 955	2.91	1 613	1 713	990	723
58 463	59 315	2.49	3 445	711	63	648
56 370	58 430	2.52	1 943	576	819	-243
36 119	37 356	2.47	1 700	579	277	302
25 235	26 019	2.43	959	97	25	72
33 282	33 528	2.33	1 321	132	32	100
8 119	8 254	2.20	341	32	8	24
31 039	31 196	2.60	1 516	1 215	682	533
28 676	29 524	2.42	971	207	23	184
71 634	73 474	2.58	948	293	58	235
28 460	29 299	2.35	971	107	35	72
20 879	21 421	2.31	925	127	8	119
25 550	26 043	2.35	771	112	24	88
12 379	12 594	2.52	1 082	45	16	29
16 805	17 045	2.54	870	74	20	54

表2-3 各街镇户籍人口自然变动

Natural Change of Registered Population in Subdistricts and Towns (2011)

单位：人 (person)

指 标	Indication	出生人口 Birth Population			死亡人口 Death Population			自然增加人口 Natural Growth		
		合 计 Total	男 Man	女 Female	合 计 Total	男 Man	女 Female	合 计 Total	男 Man	女 Female
总 计	**Total**	**22 336**	**11 469**	**10 867**	**20 202**	**10 742**	**9 460**	**2 134**	**727**	**1 407**
街道小计	**Subdistrict Tot**	**9 420**	**4 820**	**4 600**	**9 041**	**4 752**	**4 289**	**379**	**68**	**311**
潍坊新村街道	Weifangxincun Subdistrict	660	338	322	787	401	386	-127	-63	-64
陆家嘴街道	Lujiazui Subdistrict	938	474	464	963	515	448	-25	-41	16
周家渡街道	Zhoujiadu Subdistrict	709	367	342	1034	541	493	-325	-174	-151
塘桥街道	Tangqiao Subdistrict	463	233	230	434	235	199	29	-2	31
上钢新村街道	Shanggangxincun Subdistrict	657	342	315	1001	539	462	-344	-197	-147
南码头路街道	Nanmatoulu Subdistrict	535	290	245	723	376	347	-188	-86	-102
沪东新村街道	Hudongxincun Subdistrict	590	286	304	579	305	274	11	-19	30
金杨新村街道	Jinyangxincun Subdistrict	911	481	430	956	517	439	-45	-36	-9
洋泾街道	Yangjing Subdistrict	1 024	522	502	672	347	325	352	175	177
浦兴路街道	Puxinglu Subdistrict	998	496	502	727	385	342	271	111	160
东明路街道	Dongminglu Subdistrict	599	315	284	585	299	286	14	16	-2
花木街道	Huamu Subdistrict	1 277	651	626	577	289	288	700	362	338
申港街道	Shengang Subdistrict	59	25	34	3	3	0	56	22	34
镇小计	**Town Tot**	**12 916**	**6 649**	**6 267**	**11 161**	**5 990**	**5 171**	**1 755**	**659**	**1 096**
川沙新镇	Chuansha New Town	1 177	604	573	901	504	397	276	100	176
高桥镇	Gaoqiao Town	634	316	318	616	354	262	18	-38	56
北蔡镇	Beicai Town	1 040	575	465	971	524	447	69	51	18
合庆镇	Heqing Town	345	186	159	431	230	201	-86	-44	-42
唐镇	Tangzhen Town	363	186	177	309	178	131	54	8	46
曹路镇	Caolu Town	519	256	263	443	235	208	76	21	55
金桥镇	Jinqiao Town	271	145	126	184	97	87	87	48	39
高行镇	Gaohang Town	549	285	264	315	161	154	234	124	110
高东镇	Gaodong Town	205	98	107	266	135	131	-61	-37	-24
张江镇	Zhangjiang Town	888	443	445	377	197	180	511	246	265
三林镇	Sanlin Town	1 092	549	543	813	413	400	279	136	143
惠南镇	Huinan Town	855	438	417	718	371	347	137	67	70
周浦镇	Zhoupu Town	569	297	272	505	267	238	64	30	34
新场镇	Xinchang Town	378	201	177	388	227	161	-10	-26	16
大团镇	Datuan Town	392	192	200	505	260	245	-113	-68	-45
芦潮港镇	Luchaogang Town	98	41	57	87	47	40	11	-6	17
康桥镇	Kangqiao Town	722	396	326	408	213	195	314	183	131
航头镇	Hangtou Town	448	234	214	416	230	186	32	4	28
祝桥镇	Zhuqiao Town	920	489	431	1091	600	491	-171	-111	-60
泥城镇	Nicheng Town	376	187	189	375	192	183	1	-5	6
宣桥镇	Xuanqiao Town	333	173	160	290	158	132	43	15	28
书院镇	Shuyuan Town	355	166	189	323	175	148	32	-9	41
万祥镇	Wanxiang Town	172	83	89	179	97	82	-7	-14	7
老港镇	Laogang Town	215	109	106	250	125	125	-35	-16	-19

表2-4　主要年份户籍人口变动
Change of Registered Population in Main Years

单位：人　　(person)

指　标	Indicators	1990	1993	1995	2000	2005	2010	2011
人口自然变动	**Natural Changes in Population**							
出生人口	Birth	13 459	9 785	7 877	8 229	12 363	22 337	22 336
出生率(‰)	Birth Rate (‰)	10.20	6.88	5.34	5.07	6.76	8.10	8.02
死亡人口	Death	8 711	9 899	10 538	11 007	13 423	19 415	20 202
死亡率(‰)	Death Rate (‰)	6.60	6.96	7.15	6.78	7.34	7.04	7.25
自然增长人口	Natural Growth	4 748	-114	-2 661	-2 778	-1 060	2 922	2 134
自然增长率(‰)	Natural Growth Rate (‰)	3.60	-0.08	-1.81	-1.71	-0.58	1.06	0.77
人口迁移变动	**Population Mobility**							
迁入人口	Population Moved-in	18 079	59 214	54 560	160 975	128 476	27 440	26 596
#市外迁入	Non-Shanghai Population Moved-in	8 102	10 469	10 419	18 522	18 346	26 845	25 907
迁入率(‰)	Rate of Population Moved-in (‰)	13.50	41.20	37.01	99.10	70.26	9.95	9.54
迁出人口	Population Moved-out	15 820	32 457	24 600	103 486	88 315	9 119	9 816
#迁出市外	Population Moved Out of Shanghai	5 843	3 356	3 836	5 734	2 612	8 434	9 239
迁出率(‰)	Rate of Population Moved-out (‰)	11.81	22.58	16.69	63.70	48.30	3.31	3.52
迁移增长人口	Growth of Population Mobility	2 259	26 757	29 960	57 489	40 161	18 321	16 780
#市外迁移增长	Growth of Inward Mobility	2 259	7 113	6 583	12 788	15 734	18 411	16 668
净迁移率(‰)	Rate of Net Mobility (‰)	1.69	18.62	20.32	35.40	21.96	6.64	6.02

表2-5 年末流动人口登记情况
Registered Migrating Population at Year End

单位:人　　(person)

指 标	Indicators	2005	2008	2009	2010	2011
总 计	**Total**	**937 331**	**1 272 983**	**1 695 349**	**2 183 277**	**2 064 975**
潍坊新村街道	Weifangxincun Subdistrict	10 975	17 525	21 608	30 057	30 314
陆家嘴街道	Lujiazui Subdistrict	17 538	23 476	29 680	53 091	45 802
周家渡街道	Zhoujiadu Subdistrict	13 614	16 705	21 291	28 984	22 985
塘桥街道	Tangqiao Subdistrict	7 319	11 458	13 763	19 797	20 280
上钢新村街道	Shanggangxincun Subdistrict	9 998	13 356	14 886	17 907	15 551
南码头路街道	Nanmantoulu Subdistrict	9 295	16 395	18 356	19 957	24 170
沪东新村街道	Hudongxincun Subdistrict	11 559	17 102	21 045	23 289	23 218
金杨新村街道	Jinyangxincun Subdistrict	27 016	35 981	39 864	42 152	46 409
洋泾街道	Yangjing Subdistrict	19 041	25 734	40 767	50 032	38 520
浦兴路街道	Puxinglu Subdistrict	15 898	27 283	33 187	38 169	41 471
东明路街道	Dongminglu Subdistrict	14 981	17 520	23 812	26 787	25 946
花木街道	Huamu Subdistrict	36 626	37 006	50 779	60 266	56 620
申港街道	Shengang Subdistrict			5 937	11 759	5 975
水上派出所	Boat Police Station	333	270			
世博治安派出所	Shibo Public Security and Police Station		5 332	16 811	14	4
外高桥保税区	Waigaoqiao Free Trade Zone	3 036	502	872	3 443	3 476
川沙新镇	Chuansha New Town	123 566	150 520	140 691	173 882	122 999
高 桥 镇	Gaoqiao Town	51 477	69 671	66 805	84 918	83 285
北 蔡 镇	Beicai Town	75 586	126 057	123 182	140 747	127 392
合 庆 镇	Heqing Town	40 144	54 109	60 093	72 050	76 309
唐　 镇	Tangzhen Town	49 296	61 186	66 496	79 778	84 491
曹 路 镇	Caolu Town	55 245	72 600	66 823	96 229	103 834
金 桥 镇	Jinqiao Town	69 312	76 449	57 515	65 756	41 661
高 行 镇	Gaohang Town	45 035	50 390	57 153	63 057	61 755
高 东 镇	Gaodong Town	59 380	67 661	60 210	71 851	68 811
张 江 镇	Zhangjiang Town	51 157	75 670	66 465	124 278	106 880
三 林 镇	Sanlin Town	119 904	203 025	167 460	196 584	165 690
惠 南 镇	Huinan Town			44 213	92 325	89 293
周 浦 镇	Zhoupu Town			45 682	67 239	73 402
新 场 镇	Xinchang Town			32 488	42 297	36 330
大 团 镇	Datuan Town			11 403	13 800	12 340
芦潮港镇	Luchaogang Town			7 194	12 406	13 026
康 桥 镇	Kangqiao Town			122 636	152 304	159 611
航 头 镇	Hangtou Town			45 655	59 749	56 417
六 灶 镇	Liuzao Town			15 901	18 292	
祝 桥 镇	Zhuqiao Town			31 839	46 462	105 148
泥 城 镇	Nicheng Town			11 793	21 397	19 137
宣 桥 镇	Xuanqiao Town			15 846	26 775	23 983
书 院 镇	Shuyuan Town			14 322	19 569	17 410
万 祥 镇	Wanxiang Town			2 520	3 440	4 456
老 港 镇	Laogang Town			8 306	12 388	10 574

表2-6 主要年份婚姻登记和计划生育情况
Marriage Registration and Family Planning in Main Years

单位:人 (person)

指标	Indicators	1993	1995	2000	2005	2009	2010	2011
婚姻登记	**Marriage Registration**							
准予登记结婚(对)	Registered Marriage (couple)	7 362	8 968	11 083	14 602	28 515	23 831	28 976
离婚登记(对)	Registered Divorce (couple)	489	1 049	2 102	4 402	7 398	7 511	8 146
计划生育	**Planned Birth**							
出 生	**Birth**							
出生人数	Number of Birth	9 785	7 877	9 958	12 363	20 379	22 337	22 336
第一孩	First Child	9 309	7 560	9 669	11 928	19 359	20 893	20 674
第二孩	Second Child	471	157	285	424	1 013	1 423	1 635
多 孩	≥ Third Child	5		4	11	7	21	27
符合计划生育人数	Planned Parenthood	9 760	7 519	9 903	12 323	20 281	22 273	22 284
计划生育率(%)	Rate of Planned Birth (%)	99.74	95.46	99.45	99.68	99.52	99.71	99.80
节 育	**Birth Control**							
已婚育龄妇女人数(万人)	Married Women at Child-bearing Age (10 000 persons)	31.69	31.73	32.34	29.33	44.88	45.08	45.51
已领独生子女证人数(万人)	Persons Who Have Applied for One-child Certificate (10 000 persons)	22.66	22.95	15.48	10.84	14.90	13.80	15.10
独生子女领证率(%)	Rate of One-child Certificate (%)	71.50	72.34	47.86	36.98	33.21	30.60	33.20
晚 婚	**Late Marriage**							
女性初婚人数	Number of First Marriage of Female	5 712	7 736	7 564	11 594	14 291	12 054	15 101
#23岁以上	≥ 23 Years Old	2 115	3 833	4 217	8 941	12 029	10 289	13 467
晚婚率(%)	Rate of Belated Marriage (%)	37.03	49.55	55.75	77.12	84.17	85.36	89.18

主要统计指标解释

人口数

为每年12月31日的年末总人口。根据统计口径的不同,分为户籍人口和常住人口。户籍人口是指在公安部门办理了户籍登记的人口。常住人口是指实际上经常居住在一个地方(住所)的人口,一般都以在其住所居住半年以上者为常住人口。年鉴中除特别注明是常住人口、实有人口等统计口径外,其他均为户籍人口数。

农业人口、非农业人口

是人口按经济特征分组的主要指标。农业人口指依靠从事农业(包括种植业、林业、牧业、渔业)维持生活的全部人口,即包括从事农、林、牧、渔业生产的人口以及由他们抚养的人口。非农业人口指依靠从事农业以外职业的人口以及由他们抚养的人口。但长期来在户籍管理上,往往把在农村中就业并按工资形式获得劳动报酬及由其抚养的人口统计为非农业人口;在农村劳动并参加农村合作经济收益分配的人,及由其抚养的人口作为农业人口统计。

出生率(又称粗出生率)

指在一定时期内(通常为一年)一定地区的出生人数与同期平均人数(或期中人数)之比,一般用千分率表示。计算公式:

$$出生率 = \frac{年出生人数}{年平均人数} \times 1000‰$$

出生人数是指活产婴儿,即胎儿脱离母体时(不管怀孕月数),有过呼吸或其他生命现象。年平均人数是年初、年底人口数的平均数,也可用年中人口数代替。

死亡率(又称粗死亡率)

指在一定时期内(通常为一年)一定地区的死亡人数与同期平均人数(或期中人数)之比,一般用千分率表示。计算公式:

$$死亡率 = \frac{年死亡人数}{年平均人数} \times 1000‰$$

人口自然增长率

指在一定时期内(通常为一年)人口自然增加数(出生人数减死亡人数)与该时期内平均人数(或期中人数)之比,一般用千分率表示。计算公式:

$$人口自然增长率 = \frac{本年出生人数 - 本年死亡人数}{年平均人数} \times 1000‰$$

人口自然增长率 = 人口出生率 - 人口死亡率

EXPLANATORY NOTES TO MAJOR STATISTICAL INDICATORS

Population

Population refers to the total population by December 31 every year. According to different statistical approaches, there are two definitions of population named as population with registered residence and population with permanent residence. The former refers to the population with registration in the police while the latter refers to the population that actually reside in a place (residence) permanently ,usually longer than half a year. Unless the statistical approaches are specified as permanent population and present population, the others are the number of registered population in this Yearbook.

Agricultural Population, Non-agricultural Population

Agricultural Population, Non-agricultural Population are main indicators of population grouped by economic features. Agricultural Population refers to the total number of people who live on agriculture, including farming, forestry, husbandry and fishery, and their dependents. Non-agricultural Population refers to the number of people who live on non-agricultural jobs and their dependents. According to the resident registering control system, however, the people who are employed in rural area, receive income, and their dependents are actually registered as non-agricultural population. The people who work in rural area and receive their income from agricultural collective units and their dependents are statistically defined as agricultural population.

Birth Rate

Birth Rate (or gross birth rate) means the ratio of the number of births in a certain period (usually a year) to the average population in the same period (or mid-year figure). It is usually calculated in terms of permillage and its calculating formula is:

$$\text{Birth Rate} = \frac{\text{Number of Births}}{\text{Average Number of Popualtion}} \times 1000‰$$

Number of Births refers to live births, when babies have showed any vital phenomena regardless of the length of pregnancy.

Average Number of Population is the average of the number of population at the beginning of the year and, at the end of the year and sometimes is substituted for with mid-year population.

Death Rate

Death Rate (or Gross Death Rate) refers to the ratio of number of deaths to the average population (or mid-year population) during a certain period of time (usually a year), which is often presented as permillage. Its calculating formula is :

$$\text{Death Rate} = \frac{\text{Number of Deaths}}{\text{Average Number of Population}} \times 1000‰$$

Natural Growth Rate of Population

Natural Growth Rate of Population refers to the ratio of natural increase in population (number of births minus number of deaths) in a certain period of time (usually a year) to the average population (or mid-year population) of the same period, which is often presented as permillage. The following formula are applied:

$$\text{Natural Growth Rate of Population} = \frac{\text{Number of Births-Number of Deaths}}{\text{Average Number of Population}} \times 1000‰$$

Natural Growth Rate of Population = Birth Rate-Death Rate

第三篇

Chapter 3

固定资产投资

INVESTMENT IN FIXED ASSETS

表3-1　固定资产投资主要指标
(2011)

单位:万元

指　标	Indicators	合　计 Total	内　资 Domestic Investment	国　有 State-owned	集　体 Collective-owned	股份合作 Share Holding
本年完成投资额(万元)	**Completed Investment in This Year (10 000 yuan)**	**14 353 877**	**11 618 508**	**4 144 053**	**110 881**	**9 685**
按构成分	**By Use of Funds**					
建筑安装工程	Construction and Installation	8 086 252	6 906 294	2 707 077	95 068	649
设备工具器具购置	Purchase of Equipment and Instrument	2 616 729	1 669 566	282 131	4 312	7 958
其他费用	Others	3 650 896	3 042 648	1 154 845	11 501	1 078
按建设性质分	**By Type of Construction**					
#新　建	New Construction	5 169 388	4 543 751	2 442 546	37 800	
改　建	Reconstruction	1 547 273	1 101 519	463 543	7 859	8 219
扩　建	Expansion	580 774	412 041	107 374	13 071	
按三次产业分	**By Industry**					
第一产业	Primary Industry	92 129	92 129	854	11 505	
第二产业	Secondary Industry	3 610 786	2 283 471	461 211	4 279	6 339
第三产业	Tertiary Industry	10 650 962	9 242 908	3 681 988	95 097	3 346
按主要行业分	**By Main Sector**					
#工　业	Industry	3 610 286	2 282 971	461 211	4 279	6 339
交通运输、仓储和邮政业	Transportation, Warehousing and Post Service	1 586 788	1 466 999	987 460	1 687	
信息传输、计算机服务和软件业	Information Transmission, Computer Service and Computer Software	112 970	101 625	39 303		
批发和零售业	Wholesale and Retail	209 973	162 658	13 681		
住宿和餐饮业	Hotel and Catering	222 118	214 344	46 268		
金融业	Banking	215 530	215 530	88 635		
新增固定资产	**Investment in Newly Increased Fixed Assets**	**7 897 436**	**5 791 819**	**2 618 891**	**38 602**	**3 558**
固定资产交付使用率(%)	Rate of Fixed Assets Put into Use(%)	55.0	49.8	63.2	34.8	36.7
房屋建筑面积(万平方米)	**Floor Area of Buildings (10 000 sq·m)**					
施工面积	Floor Area Under Construction	4 558.16	3 984.79	1 084.20	50.04	
#住　宅	Residential Housing	2 296.52	2 165.33	492.24	37.01	
竣工面积	Floor Area Completed	692.94	620.15	105.43	2.21	
#住　宅	Residential Housing	286.14	280.43	5.25		

Major Indicators of Investment in Fixed Assets

(10 000 yuan)

联 营 Jointly Operated	有限责任公司 Companies with Limited Liability	股份有限公司 Companies Limited by Shares	私营及个 体 Private/ Individual	其 他 Others	港澳台商投资 Hong Kong/ Macao/Taiwan Funded	#独资企业 Solely Foreigner Funded Enterprises	外商投资 FIE	#独资企业 Solely Foreigner Funded Enterprises
76 667	**4 048 063**	**562 461**	**2 596 943**	**69 755**	**784 647**	**140 279**	**1 950 722**	**762 304**
45 353	2 307 862	148 558	1 570 181	31 546	402 758	54 882	777 200	335 564
2 407	671 546	334 950	364 887	1 375	135 638	64 886	811 525	388 906
28 907	1 068 655	78 953	661 875	36 834	246 251	20 511	361 997	37 834
46 828	1 232 549	232 168	549 769	2 091	111 738	52 654	513 899	317 269
9 242	482 293	6 202	122 246	1 915	104 635	61 338	341 119	158 281
13 274	72 736	49 006	153 921	2 659	20 279	19 479	148 454	87 577
7 880	7 980		59 981	3 929				
	1 088 506	174 400	547 736	1 000	206 187	99 564	1 121 128	680 415
68 787	2 951 577	388 061	1 989 226	64 826	578 460	40 715	829 594	81 889
	1 088 506	174 400	547 236	1 000	206 187	99 564	1 121 128	680 415
13 274	38 212	262 190	164 176		29 091	9 470	90 698	12 026
	27 861	2 972	5 669	25 820	10 697	10 697	648	
9	82 318	204	65 531	915	29 408		17 907	17 907
7 615	82 503		77 958				7 774	2 660
	14 508	112 387						
175 957	**1 923 880**	**201 785**	**822 886**	**6 260**	**785 659**	**48 272**	**1 319 958**	**902 275**
229.5	47.5	35.9	31.7	9.0	100.1	34.4	67.7	118.4
61.54	1575.81	78.65	1066.96	67.59	294.96	21.67	278.41	79.26
35.85	1051.15		495.12	53.96	78.25		52.94	
20.61	233.63		256.22	2.05	59.88	1.89	12.91	8.75
4.80	143.22		127.16		2.75		2.96	

表3-2 历年固定资产投资总额
Total Investment in Fixed Assets in Main Years
(1990~2011)

单位:亿元 (100 million yuan)

年 份 Year	投资总额 Total Investment	#城市基础设施 Investment in Urban Infrastructure	#房地产开发 Real Estate Development	#工 业 Industry
1990	14.15	7.50		
1991	28.95	5.42		
1992	75.00	21.84		
1993	164.56	54.73		
1994	261.13	78.76		
1995	285.07	53.42	18.26	
1996	395.04	98.68	95.45	112.55
1997	504.36	119.32	125.00	140.95
1998	583.22	177.24	134.87	209.11
1999	438.20	156.54	103.88	135.50
2000	351.06	54.51	110.74	140.65
2001	416.18	105.36	111.66	161.48
2002	587.20	147.00	215.80	192.87
2003	602.16	155.63	245.81	191.00
2004	651.94	121.21	279.49	200.29
2005	693.61	125.95	287.92	144.61
2006	659.97	156.04	257.81	139.56
2007	784.10	234.54	247.46	224.59
2008	872.68	311.30	279.97	158.59
2009	1 420.77	490.77	431.36	298.71
2010	1 432.30	261.92	555.74	336.72
2011	1 435.39	272.02	589.45	361.03
1990~2011年累计 Accumulated from 1990 to 2011	12 657.04	3 209.70	4 090.67	3 148.21

表3-3 各行业固定资产投资情况
Investment in Fixed Assets by Sector
(2011)

指 标	Indicators	施工项目(个) Projects Under Construction (unit)	竣工项目(个) Projects Completed (unit)	本年完成投资额(万元) Investment (10 000 yuan)	新增固定资产(万元) Newly Increased Fixed Assets (10 000 yuan)
总 计	**Total**	**1 154**	**347**	**14 353 877**	**7 897 436**
农 业	Agriculture	65	40	92 129	53 378
工 业	Industry	481	160	3 610 286	2 146 664
#制造业	Manufacturing	447	142	3 192 736	2 025 654
电力煤气及水的生产和供应	Production and Supply of Electricity, Gas and Water	34	18	417 550	121 010
建筑业	Construction	1		500	
交通运输、仓储及邮政业	Transportation, Warehousing and Postal Service	51	14	1 586 788	1 255 828
信息传输、计算机服务和软件业	Information Transmission, Computer Services and Software	17	2	112 970	82 139
批发和零售业	Wholesale and Retailing	39	14	209 973	101 631
住宿和餐饮业	Accommodations and Restaurants	30	12	222 118	155 015
金融业	Banking	12	2	215 530	175 545
房地产业	Real Estate	33	2	6 224 284	3 101 452
租赁和商务服务业	Leasing and Commercial Services	32	7	194 793	71 543
科学研究、技术服务和地质勘察业	Scientific Researches, Technology Services and Geologic Prospecting	48	11	282 580	185 227
水利、环境和公共设施管理业	Water Conservancy, Environment and Public Facility Management	170	40	879 976	319 225
居民服务和其他服务业	Resident Service and Other Services	5	1	19 936	4 700
教 育	Education	68	15	169 581	94 506
卫生、社会保障和社会福利业	Public Health, Social Guarantee and Social Welfare	40	15	285 505	57 624
文化、体育和娱乐业	Culture, Sports and Entertainment	17	6	137 013	15 342
公共管理和社会组织	Public Administration and Social Organizations	45	6	109 915	77 617

表3-4　固定资产投资房屋建筑面积
Floor Space of Housing and Buildings in Fixed Assets Investment

单位:万平方米　　(10 000 sq · m)

指　标	Indicators	2005	2009	2010	2011	1990~2011 年累计 Accumulated Investment (1990~2011)
房屋施工面积	**Floor Area Under Construction**					
合　计	**Total**	**2 483.56**	**4 035.74**	**4 322.59**	**4 558.16**	
住　宅	Residential Housing	1 510.04	1 795.27	2 086.26	2 296.52	
厂房仓库	Factory Building and Warehouse	120.52	306.50	308.28	312.56	
商业营业用房	Commerce	276.76	458.69	491.29	518.07	
办公室	Office	196.68	579.93	601.15	621.46	
教育用房	Education	20.35	45.15	48.36	49.82	
医疗用房	Healthcare	7.39	15.13	9.20	11.82	
其　他	Others	351.82	835.07	778.05	747.91	
房屋竣工面积	**Floor Area Completed**					
合　计	**Total**	**615.37**	**979.63**	**646.98**	**692.94**	**11 970.38**
住　宅	Residential Housing	408.44	508.10	297.89	286.14	7 230.71
厂房仓库	Factory Building and Warehouse	43.89	84.04	55.50	59.44	1 333.20
商业营业用房	Commerce	85.64	93.62	61.83	72.35	796.21
办公室	Office	54.08	142.05	93.82	130.48	1 074.38
教育用房	Education	8.37	15.23	10.06	12.77	227.38
医疗用房	Healthcare		6.91	4.56	4.89	71.29
其　他	Others	14.95	129.68	123.32	126.87	1 237.21

表3-5 历年新增固定资产
Newly Increased Fixed Assets In Main Years
(1994～2011)

指 标	Indicators	1994	1995	1996	1997	1998	1999	2000	2001	2002
新增固定资产（亿元）	Newly Increased Fixed Assets(100 million yuan)	141.03	150.76	260.75	329.84	331.79	396.22	379.60	261.82	279.79
固定资产交付使用率(%)	Rate of Fixed Assets Transferred in Use (%)	54.0	52.9	66.8	65.4	56.9	90.4	108.1	62.9	47.6

表3-5 续表 Continued

指 标	Indicators	2003	2004	2005	2006	2007	2008	2009	2010	2011
新增固定资产（亿元）	Newly Increased Fixed Assets (100 million yuan)	407.66	633.37	379.92	522.56	380.96	638.70	656.15	622.89	789.74
固定资产交付使用率(%)	Rate of Fixed Assets Transferred in Use(%)	67.7	97.2	54.8	79.2	48.6	73.2	46.2	43.5	55.0

表3-6 主要年份固定资产投资资金来源
Capital Resources of Investment in Fixed Assets in Main Years

单位:亿元 (100 million yuan)

指 标	Indicators	2005	2010	2011
资金来源合计	**Total Capital Resources**	**1 057.43**	**2 045.60**	**2 050.04**
上年末结余资金	Balance at End of Previous Year	170.99	363.69	428.89
本年资金来源小计	Sub-total Capital Resources of this Year	886.44	1 681.91	1 621.15
国家预算内资金	State Budgetary Funds	16.05	23.97	22.10
国内贷款	Domestic Loans	166.05	381.47	342.15
债 券	Bonds		8.00	3.47
利用外资	Foreign Investment	61.96	79.00	54.70
#外商直接投资	Foreign Direct Investment	40.36	42.14	47.60
自筹资金	Self-Financed Capital	395.39	872.50	859.18
#市自筹	Self-Financed by Municipal Government	36.95	34.50	26.05
企事业自有资金	Self-Financed by Enterprises and Institutions	311.07	515.87	552.39
其他资金	Other Capitals	246.99	316.97	339.55
#集 资	Raised Funds	0.42	2.86	0.50
本年各项应付投资款	Investment Due to Pay This Year	108.32	196.79	218.89
#工程款	Project Funds	57.76	85.70	82.05

表3-7　城市基础设施投资额
Investment in Urban Infrastructure

指　标	Indicators	2005	2010	2011	1990～2011年累计 Accumulated Investment (1990～2011)
投资额总计(万元)	**Total Investment(10 000 yuan)**	**1 259 548**	**2 619 188**	**2 720 196**	**32 340 653**
电力建设	Electricity	75 089	243 807	378 335	3 705 336
运输邮电	Transportation, Post and Telecommunications	800 236	1 168 456	1 545 203	14 897 377
#市内公共交通	Urban Public Transportation	188 595	314 772	578 766	4 643 392
公用设施	Public Facilities	384 223	1 206 925	796 658	13 737 940
公用事业	Public Utilities	42 376	38 458	36 241	1 434 907
自来水	Tap Water	30 627	25 553	20 782	714 962
燃　气	Gas	11 749	12 905	15 459	719 945
市政建设	Civic Construction	341 847	1 168 467	760 417	12 303 033
市政工程	Civic Projects	323 614	1 005 061	668 366	11 393 738
园林绿化	Garden/Park	18 046	140 780	82 848	628 305
环境卫生	Environmental Sanitation	187	20 967	8 903	272 089
其　他	Others		1 659	300	8 901
构　成(%)	**Composition(%)**				
投资额总计	**Total Investment**	**100.0**	**100.0**	**100.0**	**100.0**
电力建设	Electricity	6.0	9.3	13.9	11.5
运输邮电	Transportation, Post and Telecommunications	63.5	44.6	56.8	46.1
#市内公共交通	Urban Public Transportation	15.0	12.0	21.3	14.4
公用设施	Public Facilities	30.5	46.1	29.3	42.4
公用事业	Public Utilities	3.4	1.5	1.3	4.4
自来水	Tap Water	2.5	1.0	0.7	2.2
燃　气	Gas	0.9	0.5	0.6	2.2
市政建设	Civic Construction	27.1	44.6	28.0	38.0
市政工程	Civic Projects	25.7	38.3	24.6	35.2
园林绿化	Garden/Park	1.4	5.4	3.0	1.9
环境卫生	Environmental Sanitation		0.8	0.3	0.8
其　他	Others		0.1	0.1	0.1

表3-8 工业各行业投资主要指标

Main Indicators of Investment By Industrial Sectors

(2011)

指 标	Indicators	施工项目（个）Projects Under Construction (unit)	全部建成投产项目（个）Projects Completed and Put into Production (unit)	建成投产率（%）Rate of Projects Completed and Put into Use(%)	工业本年完成投资额（万元）Completed Investment in Industry in This Year (10 000 yuan)
总 计	**Total**	**481**	**160**	**33.3**	**3 610 286**
#制造业	**Manufacturing**	**447**	**142**	**31.8**	**3 192 736**
农副食品加工业	Processing of Agricultural Side-line Food	5	2	40.0	12 625
食品制造业	Food Manufacturing	6	1	16.7	19 024
饮料制造业	Beverage Manufacturing	1			2 227
烟草制品业	Tobacco Manufacturing	4	1	25.0	16 452
纺织业	Textile Industry	2	1	50.0	2 139
纺织服装、鞋、帽制造业	Textile Products, Clothes, Shoes and Hats	10	3	30.0	23 857
皮革、毛皮、羽毛(绒)及其他制品业	Leather, Furs, Down and Related Products	1			1 037
木材加工及木、竹、藤、棕、草制品业	Timber Processing, Bamboo, Cane, Palm, Fiber and Straw Products	2	1	50.0	1 763
家具制造业	Furniture Manufacturing	5	2	40.0	5 535
造纸及纸制品业	Paper-making and Paper Products	7	2	28.6	8 036
印刷业和记录媒介的复制	Printing and Record Medium Reproduction	11	4	36.4	24 997
文教体育用品制造业	Stationery, Educational and Sports Goods				
石油加工、炼焦及核燃料加工业	Petroleum Processing, Coking and Processing of Nuclear Fuels	16	8	50.0	44 504
化学原料及化学制品制造业	Chemical Materials and Chemical Products	36	15	41.7	63 310
医药制造业	Medicine Manufacturing	24	3	12.5	155 375
化学纤维制造业	Chemical Fiber Manufacturing				
橡胶制品业	Rubber Products	1			691
塑料制品业	Plastic Products	11	5	45.5	21 386
非金属矿物制品业	Non-metal Mineral Products	5			61 084
黑色金属冶炼及压延加工业	Smelting and Processing of Ferrous Metals	1			13 588
有色金属冶炼及压延加工业	Smelting and Processing of Non-ferrous Metals	2	1	50.0	71 747
金属制品业	Metal Products	21	9	42.9	41 802
通用设备制造业	Equipment Manufacturing for General Use	33	12	36.4	156 195
专用设备制造业	Equipment Manufacturing for Special Purpose	29	8	27.6	167 078
交通运输设备制造业	Manufacturing of Transportation Equipment	58	18	31.0	483 201
电气机械及器材制造业	Manufacturing of Electric Machinery and Apparatus	35	9	25.7	165 354
通信设备、计算机及其他电子设备制造业	Manufacturing of Telecommunications, Computer and Other Electronic Equipment	63	20	31.7	1 229 851
仪器仪表及文化、办公用机械制造业	Manufacturing of Instrument, Meter, Culture and Office Machinery	6	3	50.0	22 644
工艺品及其他制造业	Manufacturingof Handcrafts and Other Productions	52	14	26.9	377 234
电力、燃气及水的生产和供应业	**Production and Supply of Electricity, Gas and Water**	**34**	**18**	**52.9**	**417 550**
电力、热力的生产和供应业	Production and Supply of Electricity and Heating Power	25	15	60.0	376 239
燃气生产和供应业	Production and Supply of Gas	9	3	33.3	41 311
水的生产和供应业	Production and Supply of Tap Water				

表3-9　主要年份建设改造投资主要指标
Major Indicators of Investment on Constructions and Transformations

指　标	Indicators	单位　unit	2010	2011
投资总额	**Total Investment**	**万元 10 000 yuan**	**8 765 632**	**8 459 391**
按建设性质分	**Grouped by Type of Construction**			
#新　建	New Construction	万元 10 000 yuan	5 896 736	5 169 388
改建和技改	Reconstruction	万元 10 000 yuan	1 515 554	1 547 273
扩　建	Expansion	万元 10 000 yuan	432 134	580 774
按产业分	**Grouped by Type of Industry**			
第一产业	Primary Industry	万元 10 000 yuan	94 209	92 129
第二产业	Secondary Industry	万元 10 000 yuan	3 368 008	3 610 786
第三产业	Tertiary Industry	万元 10 000 yuan	5 303 415	4 756 476
按行业分	**Grouped by Sectors**			
农林牧渔业	Farming, Forestry, Animal Husbandry and Fishery	万元 10 000 yuan	94 209	92 129
工　业	Industry	万元 10 000 yuan	3 367 198	3 610 286
建筑业	Construction	万元 10 000 yuan	810	500
交通运输、仓储和邮政业	Transportation, Storage and Post Service	万元 10 000 yuan	1 337 102	1 586 788
信息传输、计算机服务和软件业	Information Transmission, Computer Servcie and Software	万元 10 000 yuan	65 448	112 970
批发和零售业	Retail and Wholesale	万元 10 000 yuan	232 060	209 973
住宿和餐饮业	Hotel and Catering	万元 10 000 yuan	129 663	222 118
金融业	Financial Industry	万元 10 000 yuan	223 122	215 530
房地产业	Real Estate Industry	万元 10 000 yuan	914 799	329 798
租赁和商务服务业	Leasing and Business Service	万元 10 000 yuan	278 118	194 793
科学研究、技术服务和地质勘查业	Scientific Research, Technology Service and Geological Prospecting	万元 10 000 yuan	367 695	282 580
水利、环境和公共设施管理业	Water Conservancy, Environment and Public Facility Management	万元 10 000 yuan	1 333 650	879 976
居民服务和其他服务业	Resident Service and Other Services	万元 10 000 yuan	5 529	19 936
教　育	Education	万元 10 000 yuan	161 912	169 581
卫生、社会保障和社会福利业	Public Health, Social Guarantee and Social Welfare	万元 10 000 yuan	85 896	285 505
文化、体育和娱乐业	Culture, Sports and Entertainment	万元 10 000 yuan	121 595	137 013
公共管理和社会组织	Public Administration and Social Organizations	万元 10 000 yuan	46 826	109 915
新增固定资产	**Newly Increased Fixed Assets**			
固定资产交付使用率	Rate of Fixed Assets Transfered in Use	%	43.5	56.2
房屋建筑面积	**Floor Space of Buildings**			
施工面积	Floor Space Under Construction	万平方米 10 000 sq·m	1 089.55	1 046.01
#住　宅	Residential Housing	万平方米 10 000 sq·m	1.19	…
竣工面积	Floor Space Completed	万平方米 10 000 sq·m	222.09	204.79
#住　宅	Residential Housing	万平方米 10 000 sq·m	1.19	…

表3-10 主要年份住宅投资(按经济类型分)
Investment in Residential Housing by Ownership in Main Years

单位:万元 (10 000 yuan)

指 标	Indicators	2005	2010	2011
住宅投资额总计	**Total Investment in Residential Housing**	**2 013 328**	**3 435 706**	**4 045 980**
占固定资产投资额比重(%)	Percentage of Investment in Fixed Assets (%)	29	24	28
内 资	Domestic Investment	1 625 348	3 093 192	3 419 821
国 有	State-owned	364 095	486 901	796 911
集 体	Collective-owned	35 100	300 590	45 011
股份合作	Share-holding	11 010		
联 营	Jointly-operated	43 162	263 083	6 040
有限责任公司	Companies with Limited Liability	547 107	1 154 547	1 658 304
股份有限公司	Companies Limited by Shares	10 823	9 246	
私 营	Private	612 798	878 825	861 104
其 他	Others	1 253		52 451
港澳台商投资	Hong Kong/Macao/Taiwan Invested	122 652	121 618	308 517
#港澳台商独资	Solely Hong Kong/Macao/Taiwan Funded	60 196	61 767	
外商投资	FIE	265 328	220 896	317 642
#外商独资	Solely Foreigner Funded	129 903	213 689	

表3-11 主要重大项目(浦东部分)投资完成额

Amount of Completed Investment in Key Civic Projects in PNA

(2011)

单位:亿元 (100 million yuan)

序号 No.	指 标	Indication	计划总投资 Total Planned Investment	累计完成投资 Accumulated Investment	#2011 年完成投资 Investment Completed in 2011
	合 计	**Total**	**1 160.35**	**710.98**	**184.64**
1	上海华力微电子“909”工程升级改造 12 英寸集成电路芯片项目	Project of Upgrading and Renovating 12 inch IC Chips for 909 Project of Shanghai Huali Microelectronics Corporation	145.00	94.63	32.49
2	轨道交通十一号线南段工程	Southern Part Project of L11	194.79	82.64	55.00
3	东西通道	Project of East-to-west Passageway	71.95	48.58	0.68
4	外高桥港区六期工程	Project of Phase VI at Waigaoqiao Port	47.91	43.84	7.45
5	申能临港电厂一期工程建设项目	Constrcution Building Project of Phase I at Shenneng Lingang Power Plant	46.67	39.21	18.06
6	大芦线航道整治工程(临港新城)	Project of Waterway Improvement for Dalu Line (Lingang New City)	41.05	37.39	3.07
7	浦东新区环城绿带开天窗补绿工程	Project of Green Supplement in Green-belt Around PNA	64.50	36.03	1.10
8	上海通用汽车增资生产新一代中级、中高级轿车项目	Project of Production of New Generation Cars with Medium and Medium-High Grades Newly Invested by Shanghai GM	52.00	32.86	1.86
9	日月光半导体一期厂房工程及增资项目	Project of Phase I Workshop and Newly Investment by Advanced Semiconductor Engineering Incorporated	29.80	29.55	0.08
10	浦东软件园软件出口基地三期工程	Phase III Project of Pudong Software Park Exports Base	27.58	27.69	2.60
11	上海汽车临港基地自主品牌新产品技术改造项目	Project of Technical Innovation for Self-branded New Products at Lingang Base of SAIC	36.72	26.87	4.79
12	上海飞机制造有限公司 C919 大型客机研制保障条件能力建设项目	Development and Guarantee Capacity Construction Project for C919 Large-scale Airliner of Shanghai Aircraft Manufacturing Co., Ltd.	69.85	26.83	10.46
13	申江南路(沪南公路—浦东区界)	Shenjiangnan Road Project (Hunan Highway-Pudong)	22.44	21.80	4.19
14	上海外高桥粮食储备库及码头设施项目	Project of Grain Reserve and Terminal Facilities in Waigaoqiao Port	25.49	21.10	0.21
15	浦东生态专项工程	Specialized Ecological Project in PNA	34.00	20.00	4.00
16	上海通用汽车新一代大型直立四缸发动机项目	New Geneartion Large Upright Four Cylinder Engine Project of Shanghai GM	26.93	15.00	1.60
17	招商银行信用卡中心	Credit Card Center of China Merchants Bank	18.90	13.19	3.60
18	上海飞机设计研究院大型客机研保条件建设项目	Large-scale Airliner Development Condition Constrcution Project of Shanghai Aircraft Design and Research Institute	15.19	12.56	4.85
19	招商银行上海大厦	Shanghai Mansion of China Merchants Bank	11.33	12.49	1.99
20	临港大道	Lingang Avenue	14.55	12.22	0.60
21	日月光封装测试(上海)有限公司设备购置及配套技改工程	Equipment Purchuse and Supporting Technical Reforms Project of ASE Test Packaging (Shanghai) Co., Ltd.	7.64	12.04	3.93
22	上海集成电路研发中心开放式集成电路中试线建设和关键工艺技术开发	Open IC Test Line Construction and Key Process Development of Shanghai IC R&D Center	11.50	11.71	4.09
23	临港新城皇冠假日酒店	Crowne Plaza Hotel of Lingang New City	11.31	11.31	3.71
24	中环线浦东段(军工路隧道-高科中路)	Pudong Section of Mid-ring Route (Jungong Road Tunnel-Gaokezhong Road)	122.55	10.77	10.77
25	上海振华重工(集团)公司总部	Headquarters of Shaghai Zhenhua Heavy Industries (Group) Company	10.70	10.70	3.47

表3-12 当年建成部分大项目一览表
Major Projects Completed in Current Year
(2011)

单位:万元 (10 000 yuan)

序号 No.	指 标	Indication	计 划 总投资 Total Planned Investment	累计完成投资 Accumulated Investment	#2011年完成投资 Investment Completed in 2011
1	上海浦东嘉里中心	Shanghai Pudong Kerry Center	391 683	359 031	20 257
2	浦东星河湾一期	Phase I of Pudong Xinghewan Residential Quarter	390 000	387 500	1 035
3	上海浦东软件园出口基地三期工程	Phase III Project of Shanghai Pudong Software Park Export Base	275 811	276 906	25 950
4	上海保利广场	Shanghai Poly Plaza	211 527	205 066	7 700
5	南郊中华园	Nanjiao Zhonghua Yuan Residential Quarter	180 000	145 780	17 855
6	天和湖滨家园	Tianhe Hubing Garden Residential Quarter	158 600	140 448	24 025
7	绿地康林公寓	Lude Kanglin Apartment Residential Quarter	157 265	157 265	13 593
8	上海期货交易所衍生品开发与数据处理中心	Derivative Development and Data Processing Center of Shanghai Futures Exchange	118 000	105 037	20 884
9	上海集成电路研发中心有限公司开放式集成电路中试线建设和关键工艺技术开发	Open IC Test Line Construction and Key Process Development of Shanghai IC R&D Center	115 000	117 105	40 912
10	临港新城皇冠假日酒店	Crowne Plaza Hotel of Lingang New City	113 077	113 075	37 081
11	印象春城三、四街区	Third, Fourth Block of Impression Spring Town Residential Quarter	117 371	117 170	38 192
12	上海振华重工(集团)股份有限公司总部大楼	Headquarters Building of Shanghai Zhenhua Heavy Industries(Group)Company	107 000	107 000	34 708
13	金谊河畔三期	Phase III of Jinyi Riverside Residential Quarter	99 166	99 166	11 811
14	蓝山小城三期	Phase III of Lanshan Town Residential Quarter	97 648	79 939	27 710
15	由由世纪广场	Youyou Centurial Plaza	94 000	79 804	31 075
16	宜家家居上海北蔡商场项目	Shanghai Beicai Marketplace Project of IKEA Furniture	92 000	69 419	16 932
17	曹路基地5号地块(中虹家园)	No. 5 Block of Caolu Base(Zhonghong Jiayuan)	90 000	82 940	21 630
18	上海金陵股份有限公司金桥园区建设	Jinqiao Park Construcition of Shanghai Jinling Co., Ltd.	84 690	86 489	37 858
19	上海高桥石化80万吨/年连续重整-苯抽提装置	800 000-ton/year CCR Benzene Extraction Unit of Shanghai Gaoqiao Petrochemical Co., Ltd.	84 120	84 120	19 120
20	中芯国际集成电路制造有限公司购置设备及安装工程	Project of Equipment Purchase and Installation of SMIC	80 000	76 090	76 090
21	香梅花园五期	Phase V of Xiangmei Garden Residential Quarter	72 000	70 200	12 799
22	锦绣14#地块一期	Phase I of No. 14 Block of Jinxiu Residential Quarter	70 000	68 568	23 488
23	曹路2号地块配套商品房	No. 2 Block Supporting Commerical Building in Caolu Base	66 583	63 346	24 315
24	张江高科苑	Gaoke Yuan Residential Quarter in Zhangjiang	64 610	58 392	6 679
25	上海市银行卡产业园开发有限公司业务流程外包孵化中心1-2期	Phase I and II of Business Process Outsourcing and Incubation Center for Shanghai Bank Card Industry Park Development Co., Ltd.	57 500	55 508	14 133

主要统计指标解释

全社会固定资产投资

固定资产投资是国民经济再生产活动的一个重要部分。固定资产投资额是以货币形式表现的在一定时期内建造和购置固定资产的工作量以及与此有关的费用总称。它是反映固定资产投资规模、结构和发展速度的综合性指标。按照现行国家统计制度,全社会固定资产投资包括城镇建设项目投资、房地产开发、农村非农户建设项目投资。

从2011年起,固定资产投资统计起点为500万元(含500万元)以上项目。

房地产开发投资

指各种登记注册类型的房地产开发公司统一开发的包括统代建、拆迁还建的住宅、厂房、仓库、饭店、宾馆、度假村、写字楼、办公楼等房屋建筑物和配套的服务设施,土地开发工程(如道路、给水、排水、供电、供热、通讯、平整场地等基础设施工程)的投资;不包括单纯的房地产管理、代理与经纪的企业。

固定资产投资按国民经济行业分

固定资产投资按国民经济行业分是根据建设项目建成投产后的主要产品或主要用途及社会经济活动性质来确定国民经济行业。一般情况下,一个建设项目或一个企业、事业单位只能属于一种国民经济行业。

固定资产投资按构成分

固定资产投资按构成分是按其工程内容和实现方式来划分的,主要分为建筑工程,安装工程,设备、工具、器具购置,其他费用四个部分。

(1)建筑工程(建筑工作量):指各种房屋、建筑物的建造工程,又称建筑工程。包括:①各种房屋。如厂房、仓库、办公室、住宅、商店、学校、医院、俱乐部、食堂、招待所等工程,包括列入房屋工程预算内的暖气、卫生、通风、照明、煤气等设备的价值及装饰油饰工程,列入建筑工程预算内的各种管道(如蒸汽、压缩空气、石油、给排水等管道)、电力、电讯电缆导线的敷设工程。②设备基础、支柱、操作平台、梯子、烟囱、凉水塔、水池、灰塔等建筑工程;炼焦炉、蒸汽炉等窑炉的砌筑工程及金属结构工程。③为施工而进行的建筑场地的布置、工程地质勘探,原有建筑物和障碍物的拆除,平整土地、施工临时用水、电、气、道路工程,以及完工后建筑场地的清理、环境绿化美化工作等。④矿井的开凿,井巷掘进延伸,露天矿的剥离,石油、天然气钻井工程和铁路、公路、港口、桥梁等工程。⑤水利工程,如水库、堤坝、灌溉以及河道整治等工程。⑥防空、地下建筑等特殊工程。房地产开发单位进行的商品房屋开发建设工程、土地开发工程。

(2)安装工程(安装工作量):①生产、动力、起重、运输、传动和医疗、实验等各种需要安装设备的装配和安装,与设备相连的工作台、梯子、栏杆等装设工程,附属于被安装设备的管线敷设工程,被安装设备的绝缘、防腐、保温、油漆等工作。②为测定安装工程质量,对单个设备、系统设备进行单机试运,系统联动无负荷试运工作(投料试运工作不包括在内)。在安装工程中,不包括被安装设备本身的价值。

(3)设备、工具、器具购置:是指把工业生产的产品转为固定资产的购置活动。包括:建设单位或在企、事业单位购置或自制达到固定资产标准的设备、工具、器具的价值。固定资产的标准按财务部门规定。新建单位及扩建单位的新建车间,按照设计和计划要求购置或自制的全部设备、工具、器具,不论是否达到固定资产标准均计入"设备、工具、器具购置"中。

(4)其他费用:指不属于上述几项的投资完成额。包括计入固定资产的费用(如农林建设单位牲畜购置费、各种经济林木营造费、办公和生活用家具、器具购置费、建设单位管理费、土地、青苗补偿和安置补偿费、勘察设计费、研究试验费、负荷联合试运费、引进技术和进口设备项目的其他费用)。

固定资产投资按建设性质分

建设项目的性质分为:新建、扩建、改建和技术改造、单纯建造生活设施、迁建、恢复、单纯购置。房地产开发企业、农村投资、城镇工矿区私人建房投资不划分建设性质。基本建设按建设项目划分建设性质,更新改造、国有经济中其他固定资产投资及城镇集体投资等按整个企业、事业单位的建设情况确定建设性质。

(1)新建:指从无到有"平地起家"开始建设的项目。现有企业、事业、行政单位投资的项目一般不属于新建。但如有的单位原有基础很小,经过建设后新增的固定资产价值超过该企、事业、行政单位原有固定资产价值(原值)三倍以上的也应作为新建。

(2)扩建:指企业、事业单位在厂内或其他地点,为扩大原有产品的生产能力(或效益)或增加新的产品生产能力,而增建主要的生产车间(或主要工程)独立的生产线、分厂等。行政、事业单位在原单位增建业务用房(如学校增建教学用房、医院增建门诊部、病房等)也作为扩建。

现有企、事业单位为扩大原有主要产品生产能力或增加新的产品生产能力,增建一个或几个主要生产车间(或主要工程)、总厂之下的分厂,如同时进行一些更新改造工程的,则也应作为扩建。

(3)改建和技术改造:指现有企业、事业单位对原有设施进行技术改造或更新(包括相应配套的辅助性生产、生活福利设施)的建设项目。改建项目包括现有企业、事业单位为适应市场变化的需要,而改变企业的主要产品种类(如军工企业转民产品等)的建设项目,原有产品生产作业线由于各工序(车间)之间能力不平衡,为填平补齐充分发挥原有生产能力而增建不增加本企业主要产品设计能力的车间的建设项目。技术改造是指企业、事业单位在现有基础上,用先进的技术代替落后的技术,用先进的工艺和装备代替落后的工艺和装备,以改变企业落后的技术经济面貌,实现以内涵为主的扩大再生产,达到提高产品质量、促进产品更新换代、节约能源、降低消耗、扩大生产规模、全面提高社会经效益的目的。技术改造具体包括以下内容:机器设备和工具的更新改造;生产工艺改革、节约能源和原材料的改造;厂房建筑和公共设施的改造;保护环境进行的“三废”治理改造;劳动条件和生产环境的改造等。

(4)单纯建造生活设施:是指企(事)业及行政单位在不扩建、改建生产性工程和业务用房的情况下,单纯建造职工住宅、托儿所、子弟学校、医务室、浴室、食堂等生活福利设施。

(5)迁建:指为改变生产能力布局或由于城市环境保护和安全生产的需要等原因搬迁到另地建设的企、事业单位。在搬迁另地建设过程中,不论是维持原来规模还是扩大规模都按迁建统计。

(6)恢复:是指因自然灾害、战争等原因,使原有固定资产全部或部分报废,以后又投资恢复建设的单位。不论是按原规模恢复还是在恢复的同时进行扩建的都按恢复项目统计。尚未建成投产的基本建设项目,因自然灾害而损坏重建的,仍按原有建设性质划分。

(7)单纯购置:是指现有企、事业、行政单位单纯购置不需要安装的设备、工具、器具而不进行工程建设的单位。有些单位当年虽然只从事一些购置活动,但其设计中规定有建筑安装活动,应根据设计文件的内容来确定建设性质,不得作为单纯购置统计。

新增固定资产

新增固定资产又称交付使用的固定资产,是指已经完成建造和购置过程,并已交付生产或使用单位的固定资产价值。新增固定资产是以价值形式表示的固定资产投资成果的价值量综合性指标,也是反映建设进度、计算固定资产投资效果的重要数据。

固定资产交付使用率

固定资产交付使用率又称固定资产运用系数,是指一定时期新增固定资产与同期完成投资额的比率。它反映各个时期固定资产动用速度,衡量建设过程中宏观投资效果的综合性指标。

施工项目

施工项目指报告期内进行过建筑或安装施工活动的项目。凡是报告期内施过工的建设项目,不论施工时间长短,均作为施工项目统计。施工项目个数可以反映一定时期固定资产投资的实际规模,与同期建成投产的建设项目个数相比,可以从建设速度的角度反映固定资产投资的效果。根据建设项目施工活动的不同性质,施工项目又分为:本年正式施工项目、本年收尾项目和以前年度全部停缓建项目。

全部建成投产项目

工业项目指设计文件规定形成生产能力的主体工程及其相应配套的辅助设施全部建成,经负荷试运转,证明具备生产设计规定合格产品的条件,并经过验收鉴定合格或达到竣工验收标准,与生产性工程配套的生活福利设施可以满足近期正常生产的需要,正式移交生产的建设项目。非工业项目指设计文件规定的主体工程和相应的配套工程全部建成,能够发挥设计规定的全部效益,经验收鉴定合格或达到竣工验收标准,正式移交使用的建设项目。

建成投产率

指一定时期内全部建成投产项目个数与同期正式施工项目个数的比率。该指标是从建设项目建设速度的角度反映投资效果的指标。

EXPLANATORY NOTES TO MAJOR STATISTICAL INDICATORS

Total Investment in Fixed Assets

Investment in Fixed Assets constitutes an important portion of the national economic reproduction. Fixed assets investment is a general term for both the work volume of production and purchase of fixed assets and relevant expenditure, in the form of currency, during a certain period. It is a comprehensive indicator of scale, structure and development speed of fixed assets investment. As stipulated in the current national statistics regulations, the social fixed assets investment includes the investment for the projects of urban infrastructure, real estate development, and construction projects by non-agricultural farmers in the rural areas.

From 2011 on, the fixed assets items only include those with an investment of 5 million yuan and above.

Investment in Real Estate Development

Investment in Real Estate Development refers to the investment by the real estate development companies of various types of ownership in the construction of house buildings, such as residential buildings, factory buildings, warehouses, hotels, guesthouses, holiday villages, office buildings, and the complementary service facilities and land development projects, such as roads, water supply, water drainage, power supply, heating, telecommunications, land leveling and other projects of infrastructure. It excludes the activities in pure land transactions.

Investment in Fixed Assets by National Economic Sector

Investment in Fixed Assets by National Economic Sector refers to determining the classification of construction projects by the major products or the purpose of the projects when they are put into production or use, and by the nature of their social economic activities. In general, one project or one enterprise or institution can only be classified into one national economic sector.

Investment in Fixed Assets by Composition

Investment in Fixed Assets by Composition is classified by their contents and ways of completion. It is mainly classified into 4 categories, i. e. construction, installation, purchase of equipment, tools and instrument, and other expenses.

(1) Construction projects (work volume of construction) refer to the construction of various houses and buildings. They include construction of various houses; equipment foundations, industrial kilns and stoves, and metal structure work; preparation works for project construction, and clearing up works post project construction; pavement of railways and roads, drilling of mines and putting up of oil pipes; construction of projects of water conservancy; construction of underground air – raid shelters and construction of other special projects; value of equipment for heating, sanitation, ventilation, lighting, gas, painting, etc. that are covered by the budget of housing projects; laying out of various pipelines (for steam, compressed air, petroleum, tap water and sewage) and lines for electric power and for communications; installation of various machinery equipment, testing operation for pre – testing the quality of installation projects, and land and other development work conducted by real estate developers for commercial housing.

(2) Installation projects (work volume of installation) refer to the installation of equipment necessary for the production, motive power, power lifting, transportation, medical services and experiments. They also refer to the trial operation for single equipment and system equipment for the determination of the installation quality. The value of equipment installed is not included in the value of installation projects.

(3) Purchase of equipment, tools and instruments refers to the purchase activities that turn the industrial products into fixed assets, which include the value of equipment, tools, and instruments purchased or self – produced which come up to standards for fixed assets by the construction units for the enterprises and institutions. Equipment, tools and instruments purchased or self – produced for new workshops by newly established or expanded units are categorized as "purchase of equipment, tools and instruments" no matter whether they come up to the standards for fixed assets.

(4) Other expenses refer to expenses other than the above – mentioned investment, which include the expenses that are added into those of the fixed assets, such as purchase expenses for livestock by forest construction units, construction expenses of all kinds of economic forest, purchase of furniture and appliances for office and life, administration expenses for construction units, compensation for land acquisition and young crops and farmer resettlement, other expenses for technology introduction and imported equipment, etc.

Investment in Fixed Assets by Type of Construction

The construction projects can be classified as new construction, expansion, reconstruction and technology transformation, construction of pure living facilities, relocation, restoration, and purchase. Real estate enterprises, rural investment and private investment on building in town industrial zones will not be classified with their types of construction. Capital construction will be classified according to their projects, and other investment on fixed assets in national economy and town collective investment will be classified according to the construction of the whole enterprise and institution.

(1) New construction refers to newly constructed projects from scratch. Generally, projects invested by existing enterprises, institutions and administrative agencies will not be considered as new construction. In case the assets of some units are quite small, and the value of newly added fixed assets exceeds the original value of assets by three times, the expansion will be considered as new construction.

(2) Expansion refers to construction of new major production workshop, branch factory or independent production line within a factory or in other locations of certain enterprises and institutions, for the purpose of increasing the production capacity (or improving efficiency) of the original products. Newly constructed houses for the operation of institutions and administrative organizations (such as the newly constructed buildings for teaching in schools, buildings for clinics or wards in hospitals, etc.) are also considered as expansion.

(3) Reconstruction and technology reforms refer to construction projects by existing enterprises or institutions for technical innovation or transformation of the old facilities (including auxiliary production equipment and welfare facilities). Also considered as reconstruction is the construction of new workshops by the existing enterprises or institutions to change the variety of products to meet the market demand (such as the production of civil products by defense industries), or to bring the designed production capacity into full play through a more balanced production process on production lines. Also included in the expansion are investments by existing enterprises or institutions in building major production lines or branch factories along with some work on innovation, for the purpose of expending the production capacity of original products or producing new products.

(4) Construction of pure living facilities refers to that under the condition of not expanding or reconstructing the productive and operation buildings, enterprises, institutions and administrative agencies construct pure living facilities for welfare such as staff housing, nurseries, schools for staff children, infirmaries, bathrooms and canteens.

(5) Relocation refers to that enterprises and institutions will be relocated for the change of layout of their production throughput or because of environmental protection for the city and for the sake of production safety. During the relocation of another place, maintaining the original scale or expanding the scale will be accounted as relocation.

(6) Restoration refers to that units restore their construction by investment after their original fixed assets have been partially or totally discarded because of natural disasters and war. Restoration ac-

cording to the original scale or expansion while restoring will be accounted as restoration. Capital construction projects that have not been completed and put into use and reconstructed will be classified as their original construction because of natural disasters.

(7) Pure purchase refers to that existing enterprises, institutions and administrative agencies purchase equipment, tools and instrument that are not necessary to be installed or constructed. Although some units purchased some equipment at the current year, there were some activities of construction and installation in their design. The type of construction will be determined according to the contents of design documents and can not be accounted as pure purchase.

Newly Increased Fixed Assets

Newly Increased Fixed Assets, also called fixed assets put into operation, refers to the value of fixed assets that has been put into production or handed over to the production units after the completion of the process of construction and purchase. The newly increased fixed asset is a value indicator of the result of investment. It is also the necessary data for reflecting the construction process and the result of investment in fixed assets.

Rate of Fixed Assets Completed and Put into Operation

Rate of Fixed Assets Completed and Put into Operation, also called the fixed assets-operation ratio, refers to ratio of newly increased fixed assets to total investment completed in the same period, which is a comprehensive indicator, reflecting the development of fixed assets investment and investment efficiency.

Projects under Construction

Projects under Construction refer to projects with construction and installation activities undertaken in the reference period. All projects that have construction activities undertaken during the reference period are reported as projects under construction irrespective of the length of construction work. The number of projects under construction can reflect the actual size of investment in fixed assets during a given period, and when compared with the number of projects completed and put into use during the same period, it demonstrates the results of investment in fixed assets. Depending on the nature of construction activities, projects under construction can also be classified into projects under construction in current year, winding - up projects in current year and stopped or suspended projects in previous years (with preservation work in current year).

Projects Completed and Put into Use

Industrial projects refer to the major projects and accessory facilities completed which result in forming production capacity and have been checked and accepted while the living and welfare facilities have been completed and can ensure normal production and formally put into production. Non-industrial projects refer to the major projects and accessory facilities completed which possess the designed capacity and have been checked, accepted and formally put into production.

Rate of Construction Projects Completed and Put into Use

Rate of Construction Projects Completed and Put into Use refers to the ratio of the number of construction projects completed and put into use in certain period of time to the number of projects under construction in the same period. This reflects the investment efficiency from the perspective of the speed of projects construction.

第四篇

Chapter 4

招商引资

BUSINESS PROMOTION AND FOREIGN-FUND ATTRACTION

表 4－1　历年外商直接投资情况
(1990～2011)

年　份 Year	外商直接投资合同项目(项) Contracted Projects of Foreign Direct Investment(unit)	#中外合资 Joint-venture	中外合作 Sino-foreign Cooperative	外商独资 Solely Foreigner Funded
1990	28	22	2	4
1991	92	79	4	9
1992	567	467	38	56
1993	924	610	38	275
1994	1 035	547	51	432
1995	838	340	41	455
1996	802	285	38	479
1997	615	132	36	447
1998	554	88	30	435
1999	470	71	18	380
2000	693	109	21	563
2001	880	110	10	758
2002	964	119	14	829
2003	1 563	175	15	1 370
2004	1 688	188	9	1 489
2005	1 734	149	8	1 574
2006	1 446	143	7	1 292
2007	1 254	112	3	1 138
2008	803	90	3	710
2009	780	100	4	676
2010	906	140	1	765
2011	995	181	2	809

注：从 2004 年起，外商直接投资实际到位金额中不包含间接吸收外资。
Note：The actual paid amount of foreign direct investment will not include the indirectly-attracted foreign capital after the year of 2004.

Foreign Direct Investment in Main Years

外商直接投资合同金额(亿美元) Contracted Value of Foreign Direct Investment (USD 100 million)				外商直接投资实际到位金额(亿美元) Capital in Place of Foreign Direct Investment (USD 100 million)
	# 中外合资 Joint-venture	中外合作 Sino-foreign Cooperative	外商独资 Solely Foreigner Funded	
0.34	0.29	0.01	0.05	0.13
1.01	0.92	0.03	0.06	0.68
13.53	7.28	0.82	2.77	2.49
17.57	13.08	1.53	2.78	4.29
25.93	14.14	4.10	7.32	6.85
32.56	10.47	2.56	17.43	12.81
18.09	5.04	5.84	7.21	14.25
18.00	13.39	0.82	3.79	10.13
27.90	13.77	0.63	2.90	15.37
10.73	2.95	0.55	6.91	5.92
28.84	2.73	0.47	25.63	8.85
20.02	4.51	1.12	14.16	23.04
26.68	5.72	1.36	17.22	18.47
28.75	6.47	0.12	21.19	18.01
32.24	5.05	0.56	26.08	23.78
56.54	7.84	0.38	42.20	31.11
48.42	7.67	0.32	39.46	32.20
49.49	5.08	0.39	41.30	33.06
49.92	5.87	0.12	43.12	34.35
55.29	4.80	1.22	47.13	39.08
56.25	8.57	0.01	45.35	38.56
65.97	9.31	0.59	55.00	52.97

表4-2 外商直接投资合同项目

Number of Contracted Projects of Foreign Direct Investment

单位:个 (unit)

指 标	Indicators	2000	2005	2010	2011	至2011年末累计 Accumulated by the End of 2011
总 计	**Total**	**693**	**1 734**	**906**	**995**	**19 648**
按投资方式分	**By Way of Investment**					
中外合资	Joint-venture	109	149	140	181	4 308
中外合作	Sino-foreign Cooperative	21	8	1	2	400
外商独资	Solely Foreigner Funded	563	1 574	765	809	14 904
B股企业	B Share		3		3	36
按投资行业分	**By Sector**					
#第二产业	Secondary Industry	168	209	52	42	4 009
#工 业	Industry	167	188	46	38	3 399
第三产业	Tertiary Industry	522	1 524	854	953	15 614
#批发零售业	Wholesale and Retail	2	672	476	551	8 589
交通运输、仓储和邮政业	Transportation, Warehousing, Post and Telecommunications	3	18	20	33	745
房地产业	Real Estate	3	25	3	11	332
租赁和商务服务业	Leasing and Business Service		295	216	241	2 999
按总投资规模分	**By Investment Scale**					
1 000万美元以上	>USD 10 million USD	34	59	51	80	1 185
500~1000万美元	USD 5 ~ 10 million USD	15	51	33	25	552
300~500万美元	USD 3 ~ 5 million USD	14	29	19	22	454
100~300万美元	USD 1 ~ 3 million USD	101	150	128	142	2 484
50~100万美元	USD 0.5 ~1 million USD	150	153	70	100	2 721
30~50万美元	USD 0.3 ~0.5 million USD	70	97	69	75	1 805
30万美元以下	<USD 0.3 million USD	309	1 195	536	551	10 447
按投资国别、地区分	**By Country/Region**					
#中国香港	Hong Kong, China	174	307	301	275	5 557
中国澳门	Macao, China	1	2		1	60
中国台湾	Taiwan, China	40	82	62	39	1 206
日 本	Japan	80	270	101	91	2 639
新加坡	Singapore	41	107	52	58	1 156
韩 国	Republic of Korea	14	80	29	23	565
英 国	United Kingdom	12	35	15	14	357
德 国	Germany	25	52	27	36	524
法 国	France	5	26	10	12	182
荷 兰	the Netherlands	14	24	10	7	228
瑞 士	Switzerland	7	14	8	8	176
美 国	United States of America	104	146	87	79	2 256
加拿大	Canada	6	19	10	10	294
澳大利亚	Australia	12	22	8	14	285
海外中资集团	Overseas Chinese Group Companies	1				72

注：当年增资部分不计算项目个数。

Note: The increase of investment in the current year is not listed as new project.

表4-3 外商直接投资合同金额

Contract Value Capital of Foreign Direct Investment

单位:万美元 (USD 10 000)

指标	Indicators	2000	2005	2010	2011	至2011年末累计 Accumulated by the End of 2011
总　计	**Total**	**288 376**	**565 369**	**562 487**	**659 727**	**6 340 491**
按投资方式分	**By Way of Investment**					
中外合资	Joint-venture	27 318	78 437	85 679	93 081	1 330 276
中外合作	Sino-foreign Cooperative	4 714	3 771	122	5 920	153 650
外商独资	Solely Foreigner Funded	256 295	421 985	453 504	550 004	4 531 628
B股企业	B Share	49	61 176	23 182	10 722	324 937
按投资行业分	**By Sector**					
第二产业	**Secondary Industry**	**235 421**	**172 056**	**98 697**	**43 322**	**1 977 936**
#工　业	Industry		162 312	95 872	40 942	1 502 045
第三产业	**Tertiary Industry**	**52 896**	**393 242**	**463 790**	**616 405**	**4 360 573**
#批发零售业	Wholesale and Retail		61 919	90 922	151 336	
交通运输、仓储和邮政业	Transportation, Warehousing, Post and Telecommunications		114 776	18 896	23 108	350 121
房地产业	Real Estate		49 390	100 310	135 341	
租赁和商务服务业	Leasing and Business Service		114 149	163 058	103 392	
按总投资规模分	**By Investment Scale**					
1000万美元以上	>USD 10 million	240 825	162 738	142 532	265 512	2 869 027
500~1000万美元	USD 5~10 million	7 311	16 141	11 390	25 130	147 361
300~500万美元	USD 3~5 million	4 561	5 620	4 486	12 566	67 712
100~300万美元	USD 1~3 million	14 252	16 233	14 820	33 659	226 501
50~100万美元	USD 0.5~1 million	8 702	6 972	3 316	8 369	93 416
30~50万美元	USD 0.3~0.5 million	2 996	2 464	1 873	3 597	41 256
30万美元以下	<USD 0.3 million	9 729	15 817	6 885	22 892	166 747
当年增资	Capital Increase in Current Year		339 384	401 546	376 467	2 841 297
按投资国别、地区分	**By Country/Region**					
#中国香港	Hong Kong, China	15 543	68 253	200 809	242 094	1 541 874
中国澳门	Macao, China	20	68		155	6 752
中国台湾	Taiwan, China	1 775	2 795	2 936	2 105	60 520
日　本	Japan	15 513	69 789	49 831	41 930	707 890
新加坡	Singapore	8 135	18 363	30 632	70 775	384 859
韩　国	Republic of Korea	1 574	5 438	4 463	11 816	83 433
英　国	United Kingdom	1 554	6 245	10 809	4 023	110 477
德　国	Germany	6 735	54 020	9 016	10 089	198 398
法　国	France	733	2 531	21 750	7 407	113 264
荷　兰	the Netherlands	3 392	8 424	9 744	13 107	186 691
瑞　士	Switzerland	3 788	1 340	1 037	11 142	49 134
美　国	United States of America	16 859	41 169	21 172	20 955	614 121
加拿大	Canada	340	1 101	-92	791	23 901
澳大利亚	Australia	1 400	787	1 024	620	20 443
海外中资集团	Overseas Chinese Group Companies	-35				20 657
当年增资	**Capital Increase in Current Year**		**339 384**	**401 546**	**376 467**	**2 841 297**

注：资金负数是当年项目的投资不抵当年增资(减资)的数值。

Note: The negative figures in the table are the values that the investment of projects in that particular year. is not worth of that of the increase or decrease of investment in that year.

表4-4 当年签约投资2000万美元以上的外商投资企业

FIEs with Current Year Contracted Investment Over USD 20 Million (2011)

单位:万美元 (USD 10 000)

序号 No.	指标 Indicators		国别(地区) Country/Region	总投资 Total Investment	外商合同投资 Contracted Foreign Investment
1	艾美利肯车桥投资管理(上海)有限公司	American Axle Investment Management (Shanghai) Co., Ltd.	卢森堡 Luxembourg	2 500	1 000
2	立邦投资有限公司	Nippon Investment Co., Ltd.	香港 HongKong	3 800	3 800
3	上海永胜半导体设备有限公司	Shanghai Jhcore Semiconductor Equipment Co., Ltd.	香港 HongKong	2 703	676
4	雅瑞资置业(上海)有限公司	Yaruizi Real Estate (Shanghai) Co., Ltd.	新加坡 Singapore	9 296	3 790
5	上海绿洲怡丰投资有限公司	Shanghai Oasis Yifeng Investment Co., Ltd.	香港 HongKong	4 000	4 000
6	丰永(上海)置业有限公司	Toyonaga (Shanghai) Real Estate Co., Ltd.	香港 HongKong	14 114	7 057
7	上海三营融资租赁有限公司	Shanghai San Ying Financial Leasing Co., Ltd.	香港 HongKong	2 030	1 218
8	礼来(中国)研发有限公司	Eli Lilly (China) Research and Development Co., Ltd.	瑞士 Switzerland	9 900	4 000
9	上海荣耀信息技术有限公司	Shanghai Glory Information Technology Co., Ltd.	香港 HongKong	2 000	2 000
10	伊顿上飞(上海)航空管路制造有限公司	Eaton-SAMC (Shanghai) Aviation Pipeline Manufacturing Co., Ltd.	投资性公司投资 Invested by investment companies	5 200	882
11	上海挚信信息技术有限公司	Shanghai Zhixin Information Technology Co., Ltd.	香港 HongKong	4 000	3 000
12	上海仁恒兴唐置业有限公司	Shanghai Renheng Xintang Real Estate Co., Ltd.	新加坡 Singapore	81 092	34 177
13	上海莉源房地产开发有限公司	Shanghai Liyuan Real Estate Development Co., Ltd.	香港 HongKong	86 500	74 500
14	上海超连设备租赁有限公司	Shanghai Chaolian Equipment Leasing Co., Ltd.	香港 HongKong	4 000	4 000
15	勃林格殷格翰(中国)投资有限公司	Boehringer Ingelheim (China) Investment Co., Ltd.	德意志联邦共和国 Germany	3 000	3 000
16	上海崇和船舶融资租赁有限公司	Shanghai Chonghe Ship Leasing Co., Ltd.	香港 HongKong	2 000	500
17	久保田(中国)投资有限公司	Kubota (China) Investment Co., Ltd.	日本 Japan	4 500	4 500
18	上海辉煌定丰贸易有限公司	Shanghai Huihuang Dingfeng Trade Co., Ltd.	香港 HongKong	4 554	4 251
19	三一能源重工有限公司	Sanyi Resources and Heavy Industry Co., Ltd.	香港 HongKong	9 109	2 793
20	龙惠融资租赁有限公司	Longhui Leasing Co., Ltd.	香港 HongKong	4 858	2 943
21	蒂森克虏伯普利斯坦汽车零部件(上海)有限公司	ThyssenKrupp Presta (Shanghai) Co., Ltd.	投资性公司投资 Invested by investment companies	4 648	1 549

单位:万美元　　表 4-4 续表 Continued　　(USD 10 000)

序号 No.	指标	Indicators	国别(地区) Country/Region	总投资 Total Investment	外商合同投资 Contracted Foreign Investment
22	花旗商贸(上海)有限公司	Citigroup Trading (Shanghai) Co., Ltd.	美国 the United States	6 000	2 000
23	久保田环保科技(上海)有限公司	Kubota Environmental Technology (Shanghai) Co., Ltd.	日本 Japan	2 450	980
24	亲和源股份有限公司	Cherish-Yearn Co.,Ltd.	香港 HongKong	3 043	761
25	上海国际医学园区医学产品市场经营管理有限公司	Medical Product Marketing Management Co., Ltd. of Shanghai International Medical Park	香港 HongKong	4 565	2 739
26	乐天融资租赁(中国)有限公司	Lotte Leasing (China) Co., Ltd.	韩国 Korea	3 702	3 702
27	中金再生资源(中国)有限公司	China Metal Renewable Resources (China) Co., Ltd.	投资性公司投资 Invested by investment companies	4 500	1 500
28	建银国际(上海)有限公司	CCB International (Shanghai) Co., Ltd.	香港 HongKong	3 000	3 000
29	上海泽润生物科技有限公司	Shanghai Zerui Biological Technology Co., Ltd.	投资性公司投资 Invested by investment companies	9 980	8 000
30	上海中油能源控股有限公司	Shanghai China Petroleum Engery Holdings Co., Ltd.	香港 HongKong	9 130	7 608
31	上海天行股权投资基金管理有限公司	Shanghai Tianxing Equity Investment Fund Management Co., Ltd.	香港 HongKong	4 565	761
32	庆隆(上海)创业投资有限公司	Qinglong (Shanghai) Investment Co., Ltd.	香港 HongKong	3 333	3 333
33	优艾贝(中国)有限公司	UIB International Holdings	开曼群岛 the Cayman Islands	4 565	1 522
34	上海百迈博制药有限公司	Shanghai Biomabs Pharmaceuticals Co., Ltd.	香港 HongKong	6 848	5 022
35	上海国际集团广场有限公司	Shanghai International Group Plaza Co., Ltd.	新加坡 Singapore	14 271	8 274
36	上海熙可送物流有限公司	Shanghai Xikesong Logistics Co., Ltd.	开曼群岛 the Cayman Islands	3 972	1 200
37	盛旅置业(上海)有限公司	Shengyu Real Estate (Shanghai) Co., Ltd.	英属维尔京群岛 British Virgin Islands	18 218	11 538
38	威茨曼新能源科技(上海)有限公司	Weitzman New Energy Technology (Shanghai) Co., Ltd.	香港 HongKong	3 000	3 000
39	沃尔玛(上海)电子商务有限公司	Walmart (Shanghai) Electronic Business Co., Ltd.	新加坡 Singapore	5 000	1 670
40	寰宇福四通贸易有限公司	Yuanyufu Stone Trading Co., Ltd.	美国 the United States	4 500	1 500
41	住商电子商务(上海)有限公司	Sumitomo Eletronic Business (Shanghai) Co., Ltd.	日本 Japan	2 500	1 000
42	宝洁(中国)营销有限公司	Procter & Gamble (China) Marketing Co., Ltd.	香港 HongKong	2 000	800

表4-5　外商直接投资实际到位金额
Capital in Place of Foreign Direct Investment

单位:万美元　　（USD 10 000）

指　标	Indicators	2005	2010	2011
总　计	**Total**	**311 142**	**385 567**	**529 736**
按投资方式分	**By Way of Investment**			
#中外合资	Joint-venture	105 486	59 492	78 376
中外合作	Sino-foreign Cooperative	14 092	836	8 577
外商独资	Solely Foreigner Funded	191 564	325 239	442 783
按投资行业分	**By Sector**			
#第二产业	Secondary Industry	87 759	50 926	49 931
#工　业	Industry	86 582	48 603	48 889
第三产业	Tertiary Industry	223 383	334 516	479 793
#批发和零售业餐饮业	Wholesale and Retail Catering	28 059	64 727	88 847
房地产业	Real Estate	50 194	64 706	136 141
租赁和商务服务业	Leasing and Business Service	57 667	118 916	92 014
按投资国别、地区分	**By Country/Region**			
#中国香港	Hong Kong, China	23 088	116 495	272 308
日　本	Japan	72 377	37 506	34 687
新加坡	Singapore	8 996	61 672	53 452
英　国	United Kingdom	1 889	4 632	8 784
德　国	Germany	21 414	8 738	10 833
法　国	France	3 095	14 871	16 239
荷　兰	the Netherlands	11 414	27 020	13 218
开曼群岛	Cayman Islands	27 761	12 702	29 552
英属维尔京群岛	British Virgin Islands	93 636	17 901	18 008
美　国	United States of America	28 238	21 956	19 582
萨摩亚	Samoa	695	1 358	1 328

表4-6 内资企业工商注册情况
Registered Domestic Enterprises

指 标	Indicators	单 位 Unit	2010	2011
期末实有注册企业	**Actual Registered Enterprises at End of Term**	**个 unit**	**10 961**	**10 636**
第一产业	Primary Industry	个 unit	170	155
第二产业	Secondary Industry	个 unit	3 070	2 811
#制造业	Manufacturing	个 unit	2 478	2 191
建筑业	Construction	个 unit	521	477
第三产业	Tertiary Industry	个 unit	7 721	7 670
#交通运输、仓储和邮政业	Transportation, Warehousing and Post Service	个 unit	483	463
批发和零售业	Wholesale and Retail	个 unit	2 980	2 860
金融业	Banking	个 unit	76	90
房地产业	Real Estate	个 unit	888	881
期末实际注册资金总额	**Total of Actual Registered Capital at End of Term**	**亿元(100 million yuan)**	**7 229.28**	**7 482.42**
第一产业	Primary Industry	亿元(100 million yuan)	20.24	19.90
第二产业	Secondary Industry	亿元(100 million yuan)	2 092.50	2 163.62
#制造业	Manufacturing	亿元(100 million yuan)	1 349.16	1 352.84
建筑业	Construction	亿元(100 million yuan)	481.80	548.76
第三产业	Tertiary Industry	亿元(100 million yuan)	5 116.54	5 298.90
#交通运输、仓储和邮政业	Transportation, Warehousing and Post Service	亿元(100 million yuan)	456.69	573.81
批发和零售业	Wholesale and Retail	亿元(100 million yuan)	573.42	634.44
金融业	Banking	亿元(100 million yuan)	472.37	377.81
房地产业	Real Estate	亿元(100 million yuan)	892.31	950.96

注：内资注册数和注册资本含市局登记、不含分支机构。

Note: The number of domestic registered enterprises and that of registered capital included those registered in Shanghai municipal bureaus and excluded those registered in branch bureaus.

表4-7 私营企业基本情况
Statistics of Private Enterprises
(2011)

指 标	Indicators	户 数 (户) Number of Enterprises (unit)	投资人数 (人) Number of Investors (person)	雇工人数 (人) Employed Persons (person)	注册资金 (亿元) Registered Capital (100 million yuan)
总 计	**Total**	**96 199**	**182 161**	**685 399**	**3 033.50**
农、林、牧、渔业	Farming, Forestry, Animal Husbandry and Fishery	767	1 269	4 439	6.90
采掘业	Mining and Quarrying	5	9	10	0.79
制造业	Manufacturing	18 022	32 874	244 914	294.37
建筑业	Construction	3 774	6 987	43 158	111.71
交通运输业、仓储和邮政业	Transportation, Warehousing and Post Service	3 441	6 811	26 509	103.01
信息传输、计算机服务	Information Transmission and Computer Service	2 545	5 821	18 955	70.12
批发零售贸易业	Wholesale and Retail	34 629	61 276	168 417	662.29
住宿和餐饮业	Catering	2 453	3 298	18 533	12.82
居民服务和其他服务业	Resident Service and Other Services	3 317	4 865	15 225	38.32
房地产	Real Estate	2 966	4 755	23 992	277.96
其 他	Others	24 280	54 196	121 247	1 455.21

表 4-8 个体工商户基本情况
Self-Employment Business
(2011)

指 标	Indicators	户 数 (户) Number of Enterprises (unit)	从业人数 (人) Employed persons (person)	注册资金 (万元) Registered Capital (10 000 yuan)
总 计	**Total**	**66 727**	**69 974**	**138 411**
农、林、牧、渔	Farming, Forestry, Animal Husbandry and Fishery	344	363	2 028
制造业	Manufacturing	1 833	2 145	4 793
建筑业	Construction	65	72	169
交通运输业、仓储业	Transportation and Warehousing	514	529	2 759
批发零售贸易业、住宿和餐饮业	Wholesale, Retail and Catering Businesses	55 754	57 860	110 425
批发零售贸易业	Wholesale and Retail	52 051	53 202	97 975
住宿和餐饮业	Catering	3 703	4 658	12 450
居民服务和其他服务业	Resident Service and Other Services	7 568	8 328	16 405
其 他	Others	649	677	1 832

主要统计指标解释

外商直接投资

外商直接投资是指外国企业和经济组织或个人(包括华侨、港澳台胞以及我国在境外注册的企业)按我国有关政策、法规,用现汇、实物、技术等在我国境内开办外商独资企业、与我国境内的企业或经济组织共同举办中外合资经营企业、合作经营企业或合作开发资源的投资(包括外商投资收益的再投资)以及企业投资总额内直接投资者对企业的贷款,即外方股东贷款(需在报告期内将相应合同及贷款协议报商务部备案核查)。

合同投资额

是指经有关部门批准的我方与外商正式签订的合同规定的可使用的贷款额、外商投资额和中方对外发行债券、股票总值,以及"补偿贸易"外商提供的设备价款,"国际租赁"境外出租人提供的设备等价款总值。

外商实际投资额

是指按合同(章程)规定,外商以现金、实物及专有技术等工业产权计价的全部实缴资本额,包括经有关部门批准,外商用于扩大再生产、发展企业规模或补充基本建设资金不足而投入的追加资金。外商的实缴资本额一律折成美元计算。

EXPLANATORY NOTES TO MAJOR STATISTICAL INDICATORS

Foreign Direct Investment

Foreign Direct Investment refers to the investments made inside China by foreign enterprises and economic organizations or individuals (including overseas Chinese, compatriots in Hong Kong, Macao and Chinese enterprises registered abroad), in line with the relevant policies and laws of China, for the establishment of wholly foreign-owned enterprises, and joint ventures or development projects launched in China (including re-investment of profits from foreign businesses), and the funds that enterprises borrow from abroad in the total investment of projects which are approved by the relevant departments of the governments and the loans from the direct investors within the total investment of the projects, i. e., foreign shareholders' loans. (The related contracts and loans agreements in the report period should be filed with the Ministry of Commerce)

Agreed (Contracted) Investment

Agreed (Contracted) Investment includes usable loans which are approved by government departments and with contracts signed formally by Chinese units and foreign investors, investment of foreigners, total value of bonds and stocks issued in international market by Chinese units, the value of equipment provided by foreign investors for compensation trade, the value of equipment which are leased from foreign firms, etc.

Actual Investment of Foreign Investors

refers to all foreign investors paid-in capital, in cash, in kind or in special technique, based on contracts, which includes the additional funds used for extensional reproduction, expanding enterprise scale or complements to capital construction. All the foreigners paid-in capital is measured by or converted to US dollars.

第五篇

Chapter 5

农 业

AGRICULTURE

表5-1 主要年份农村户数、人口和劳动力
Rural Households, Population and Workforce in Main Years

指 标	Indicators	单 位 Unit	1990	1993	2000	2005	2010	2011
户 数	Household	万户 10 000 households	15.74	14.67	13.67	12.67	32.90	32.57
人 口	Population	万人 10 000 persons	47.00	42.37	36.82	35.57	82.96	80.94
劳动力使用	Workforce	万人 10 000 persons	27.70	23.70	19.86	19.66	48.70	48.67
#农 业	Agriculture	人 person	68 339	48 325	40 430	16 725	106 229	102 452
工 业	Industry	人 person	141 352	123 940	84 042	107 767	227 127	228 276
建筑业	Construction	人 person	7 723	6 552	5 793	7 499	32 331	31 785
运输、仓储及邮电业	Transportation, Warehousing Post and Telecommunications	人 person	4 363	2 616	3 631	6 276	22 129	27 968
批发零售贸易、餐饮业	Wholesale/Retail/ Catering	人 person	3 633	4 715	7 748	9 542	31 292	23 515
外省市流入劳动力	Migrant Workforce from Other Provinces	人 person	15 262	44 418	91 268	265 223	653 226	663 762
第一产业	Primary Industry	人 person	2 828	4 190	14 743	16 453	40 821	38 868
第二产业	Secondary Industry	人 person	11 846	36 097	52 715	184 437	433 208	404 303
第三产业	Tertiary Industry	人 person	588	4 131	23 810	64 333	179 197	220 591

注：表中涉及的户数、人口和劳动力是指居住在农村地区的本市户籍人口。

Note: The numbers of households, population and labor force involved in this table are referred to those that live in the rural area and are registered in Shanghai.

表5-2 各镇耕地面积

Cultivated Area by Town

单位:公顷 (hectare)

镇 Town		2010年末耕地面积 Cultivated Area (End of 2010)	2011年净减少耕地面积 Net Decrease in Cultivated Area in 2011	2011年末耕地面积 Cultivated Area (End of 2011)	水田 Paddy Field	水浇地 Irrigated land
川沙新镇	Chuansha New Town	2 296.1	47.1	2 249.0	2 141.3	107.7
高桥镇	Gaoqiao Town	258.8		258.8	226.1	32.7
北蔡镇	Beicai Town	373.9		373.9	320.9	53.0
合庆镇	Heqing Town	861.8	24.6	837.2	762.6	74.6
唐镇	Tangzhen Town	271.5		271.5	246.2	25.3
曹路镇	Caolu Town	674.8	73.2	601.6	572.6	29.0
金桥镇	Jinqiao Town	18.8		18.8	14.2	4.6
高行镇	Gaohang Town	324.2		324.2	253.7	70.5
高东镇	Gaodong Town	565.4	17.7	547.7	502.2	45.5
张江镇	Zhangjiang Town	685.7	63.9	621.8	544.6	77.2
三林镇	Sanlin Town	891.6		891.6	818.2	73.4
惠南镇	Huinan Town	1 791.6		1 791.6	1 596.4	195.2
周浦镇	Zhoupu Town	1 638.9		1 638.9	1 483.9	155.0
新场镇	Xinchang Town	2 511.4		2 511.4	2 291.7	219.7
大团镇	Datuan Town	1 910.0		1 910.0	1 456.1	453.9
芦潮港镇	Luchaogang Town	956.9		956.9	873.0	83.9
康桥镇	Kangqiao Town	853.7	10.8	842.9	219.0	623.9
航头镇	Hangtou Town	2 921.1		2 921.1	2 123.4	797.7
六灶镇	Liuzao Town	1 735.7	18.6	1 717.1	990.5	726.6
祝桥镇	Zhuqiao Town	3 557.2		3 557.2	3 414.9	142.3
泥城镇	Nicheng Town	3 169.9		3 169.9	2 899.3	270.6
宣桥镇	Xuanqiao Town	2 024.9	-12.6	2 037.5	1 230.2	807.3
书院镇	Shuyuan Town	3 565.9		3 565.9	3 360.8	205.1
万祥镇	Wanxiang Town	1 462.7		1 462.7	1 334.4	128.3
老港镇	Laogang Town	1 833.8	23.3	1 810.5	1 730.7	79.8
农场	Farm	26.1		26.1	26.1	
棉种场	Cotton Farm	23.5		23.5	23.5	
其他	Others	2 467.1	41.5	2 425.6		2 425.6

注：各镇耕地面积南片为批准数，北片为实际经营数，两者不能加总。

Note: The number in the southern part of cultivated area in each town is what has been authorized, and that in the northern part is what has been operated. These two numbers cannot be accumulated.

表5-3 主要年份耕地面积增减情况
Increase and Decrease of Cultivated Land in Main Years

单位:公顷 (hectare)

指 标	Indicators	2000	2005	2010	2011
年初耕地面积	Cultivated Area(Year Beginning)	12 799	9 483	44 001	43 551
当年减少	Decrease in Current Year	133	634	450	245
年末耕地面积	Cultivated Area (Year-end)	12 666	8 849	43 551	43 319

注：2011 年耕地面积为批准数。
Note：The number of cultivated area in 2011 is what has been authorized.

表5-4 主要年份农业总产值
Gross Output Value of Agriculture in Main Years

单位:万元 (10 000 yuan)

指 标	Indicators	1990	1993	2000	2005	2010	2011
按当年价格计算	**Calculated At Current Year Price**						
总 计	**Total**	**55 318**	**69 277**	**125 732**	**116 248**	**698 552**	**735 789**
种植业	Planting	24 015	31 544	59 584	66 809	396 127	425 407
林 业	Forestry	234	136	1 279	25 424	10 420	17 324
牧 业	Animal Husbandry	29 528	34 608	60 837	19 488	183 084	186 993
渔 业	Fishery	1 541	2 989	4 032	4 527	70 921	67 565
农、林、牧、渔服务业	Agriculture, Forestry, Animal Husbandry and Fishery				38 000	38 500	38 500
构 成(%)	**Composition (%)**						
总 计	**Total**	**100.0**	**100.0**	**100.0**	**100.0**	**100.0**	**100.0**
种植业	Planting	43.4	45.5	47.4	57.5	56.7	57.8
林 业	Forestry	0.4	0.2	1.0	21.9	1.5	2.4
牧 业	Animal Husbandry	53.4	50.0	48.4	16.8	26.2	25.4
渔 业	Fishery	2.8	4.3	3.2	3.8	10.2	9.2
农、林、牧、渔服务业	Agriculture, Forestry, Animal Husbandry and Fishery					5.4	5.2

表5-5 各镇农业总产值
Gross Output Value of Agriculture by Town
(2011)

单位:万元 (10 000 yuan)

指 标 Indicators		农业总产值(按现行价格计算) Gross Output Value of Agriculture (at Current Price)	#种植业 Planting	林 业 Forestry	牧 业 Animal Husbandry	渔 业 Fishery
总 计	**Total**	**735 789**	**425 407**	**17 324**	**186 993**	**67 565**
川沙新镇	Chuansha New Town	40 641	24 612	8 250	3 809	2 060
高桥镇	Gaoqiao Town	1 835	1 655	124		56
北蔡镇	Beicai Town	637	605			32
合庆镇	Heqing Town	9 181	5 388	180	3 152	461
唐 镇	Tangzhen Town	3 862	3 711	114		37
曹路镇	Caolu Town	22 722	8 923	616	12 960	223
金桥镇	Jinqiao Town	267	164	70		33
高行镇	Gaohang Town	372	372			
高东镇	Gaodong Town	2 161	2 111			50
张江镇	Zhangjiang Town	5 841	5 499	112		230
三林镇	Sanlin Town	4 387	1 902	262		127
惠南镇	Huinan Town	34 299	19 745		12 556	1 998
周浦镇	Zhoupu Town	19 646	15 551		3 716	379
新场镇	Xinchang Town	53 346	42 084		9 945	1 317
大团镇	Datuan Town	41 914	30 182		9 443	2 289
芦潮港镇	Luchaogang Town	7 293	6 196		748	349
康桥镇	Kangqiao Town	5 660	3 596	150	1 806	108
航头镇	Hangtou Town	51 606	25 039	2 159	22 990	1 418
六灶镇	Liuzao Town	33 114	21 269		10 047	1 798
祝桥镇	Zhuqiao Town	64 264	36 660	90	24 541	2 973
泥城镇	Nicheng Town	40 990	19 845		16 956	4 189
宣桥镇	Xuanqiao Town	31 639	22 723		7 549	938
书院镇	Shuyuan Town	46 456	32 747	313	6 203	7 193
万祥镇	Wanxiang Town	14 086	8 794		2 858	2 434
老港镇	Laogang Town	42 231	23 367		15 737	3 127
其 他	Others	157 339	62 667	4 884	21 977	33 746

表5-6 各镇粮食和蔬菜作物播种面积和产量

Sown Area and Output of Grain Crops and Vegetables by Town (2011)

指 标	Indicators	粮食播种面积（公顷）Sown Area (hectare)	粮食总产量（吨）Total Output of Grain Crops (ton)	夏粮 Summer Harvested	秋粮 Autumn Harvested	粮食单位面积产量（千克/公顷）Yield Per Unit (kg/hectare)	蔬菜播种面积（公顷）Sown Area of Vegetables (hectare)	蔬菜总产量（吨）Total Output of Vegetables (ton)
总 计	**Total**	**22 081.6**	**148 599**	**29 867**	**118 732**	**6 730**	**25 185.3**	**832 818**
川沙新镇	Chuansha New Town	664.5	4 638	1 418	3 220	6 980	1 844.3	66 520
高桥镇	Gaoqiao Town						237.8	6 571
北蔡镇	Beicai Town						144.9	2 653
合庆镇	Heqing Town	250.1	1 751	561	1 190	7 001	350.1	14 200
唐 镇	Tangzhen Town	114.7	714	179	535	6 225	311.0	5 595
曹路镇	Caolu Town	206.7	1 590	427	1 163	7 692	1 241.7	35 750
金桥镇	Jinqiao Town						56.7	678
高行镇	Gaohang Town						66.7	1 632
高东镇	Gaodong Town						219.2	4 101
张江镇	Zhangjiang Town	152.3	956	250	706	6 277	207.6	6 929
三林镇	Sanlin Town						199.1	7 029
惠南镇	Huinan Town	1 347.2	9 523	2 357	7 166	7 069	1 434.9	37 130
周浦镇	Zhoupu Town	469.0	3 087	783	2 304	6 582	1 822.0	43 246
新场镇	Xinchang Town	1 030.5	7 294	981	6 313	7 078	2 325.9	100 556
大团镇	Datuan Town	1 355.5	10 662	697	9 965	7 866	332.6	41 463
芦潮港镇	Luchaogang Town	1 089.0	4 232	862	3 370	3 886	384.3	6 135
康桥镇	Kangqiao Town	293.0	2 016	508	1 508	6 881	502.1	11 610
航头镇	Hangtou Town	564.0	4 132	604	3 528	7 326	2 395.2	91 048
六灶镇	Liuzao Town	285.3	2 009	242	1 767	7 042	1 900.4	53 850
祝桥镇	Zhuqiao Town	2 689.7	17 253	3 965	13 288	6 414	2 500.2	91 554
泥城镇	Nicheng Town	1 264.7	10 063	1 556	8 507	7 957	1 705.8	46 302
宣桥镇	Xuanqiao Town	696.8	4 028	633	3 395	5 781	2 262.9	70 050
书院镇	Shuyuan Town	4 478.1	33 283	7 819	25 464	7 432	1 119.5	46 295
万祥镇	Wanxiang Town	884.2	6 659	964	5 695	7 531	680.9	12 353
老港镇	Laogang Town	1 979.6	12 051	3 603	8 448	6 088	939.5	29 568
其 他	Others	2 266.7	12 658	1 458	11 200	5 584		

表5-7 主要农产品产量
Output of Main Farm Products

指 标	Indicators	单 位 Unit	2005	2007	2010	2011
粮食作物	Grain Crops	吨 ton	13 671	12 528	148 707	148 599
夏熟作物	Summer Harvested	吨 ton	1 303	1 861	27 147	29 867
#小 麦	Wheat	吨 ton	1 064	1 861	20 291	22 322
秋熟作物	Autumn Harvested	吨 ton	12 368	10 667	121 560	118 732
#单季晚稻	Single-Season Late Harvested Rice	吨 ton	10 580	10 549	116 437	112 968
油菜籽	Rapeseed	吨 ton	89	8	2 315	2 351
蔬 菜	Vegetables	万吨 10 000 tons	30	23	81	83
西甜瓜	Watermelons	万吨 10 000 tons	2	2	23	22
水果产量	Output of Fruits	吨 ton	4 219	4 560	108 714	88 191
#柑 桔	Mandarin Oranges	吨 ton	607	577	56 543	23 741
生 梨	Pears	吨 ton	274	264	7 829	8 889
葡 萄	Grapes	吨 ton	727	895	4 304	7 025
桃 子	Peaches	吨 ton		1 660	39 153	47 813
生猪饲养数	Stock of Hogs	万头 10 000 in number	16.72	13.99	96.61	96.35
生猪出栏数	Hogs on Market	万头 10 000 in number	8.80	8.28	56.36	54.59
猪肉产量	Pork Output	万吨 10 000 tons	0.77	0.72	3.66	4.11
牛奶产量	Milk Output	万吨 10 000 tons	1.27	0.85	4.43	4.43
家禽出栏数	Poultry on Market	万羽 10 000 in number	24.28	23.86	1913.32	1730.18
鲜蛋产量	Output of Fresh Eggs	万吨 10 000 tons	0.17	0.05	2.26	2.06
水产品产量	Output of Aquatic Products	万吨 10 000 tons	0.23	0.26	2.16	1.98
海水产品	Sea Products	万吨 10 000 tons			0.32	0.33
淡水产品	Fresh Water Products	万吨 10 000 tons	0.23	0.26	1.84	1.65

表5-8 农业机械拥有量
Farm Machinery Holding

指标	Indicators	单位 Unit	2005	2010	2011
农业机械总动力	**Total Power of Farm Machinery**	**千瓦 kw**	**18 584**	**112 420**	**117 169**
每公顷耕地拥有动力	Power Per Hectare	千瓦 kw	2	5	5
每万公顷耕地拥有拖拉机	Tractors Per 10 000Hectare	台 set	295	842	876
#耕作机械动力合计	Total Power of Farm Machinery	千瓦 kw	7 591	46 605	47 251
大、中型拖拉机	Large/Medium Tractors	台 set	285	925	965
小型拖拉机	Walking Tractors	台 set	97	938	935
排灌机械动力合计	Total Power of Drainage and Irrigation Machinery	千瓦 kw	5 534	15 603	15 444
种植机械动力合计	Total Power of Cultivation	千瓦 kw	183	2 897	3 274
植物保护机械动力合计	Total Power of Crop Protection Machinery	千瓦 kw	432	6 141	7 445
#机动喷雾器	Motorized Sprayers	台 set	353	2 043	2 238
		千瓦 kw	432	6 052	7 313
收获机械动力合计	Total Power of Harvest Machinery	千瓦 kw	713	14 293	15 338
#联合收割机	Combines	台/千瓦 set/kw	85/688	383/10176	408/11662
农产品加工机械动力合计	Power of Farm Processing Machinery	千瓦 kw	1 060	6 468	5 523
积肥机械动力合计	Power of Manure-Collecting Machinery	千瓦 kw	183	1 629	1 875
畜牧机械动力合计	Power of Animal Husbandry Machinery	千瓦 kw	183	2 831	2 962
渔业机械动力合计	Total Power of Fishery Machinery	千瓦 kw	782	9 673	9 902
园艺机械动力合计	Total Power of Horticultural Machinery	千瓦 kw	624	492	748
其他农业机械动力合计	Total Power of Other Agricultural Machineries	千瓦 kw	1 874	5 788	7 407
#农用载重汽车	Trucks for Agricultural Use	辆 in number	30	75	75
机动运输船	Transport Ships with Mechanical Power	艘 in number	23	43	41

表5-9 农田水利建设情况
Construction of Farmland Water Conservancy

指 标 Indicators		单 位 Unit	2005	2010	2011
有效灌溉面积	Effectively Irrigated Area	公顷 hectare	5 125	18 510	16 168
本年实灌面积	Actually Irrigated Area (Current Year)	公顷 hectare	1 271	11 939	12 411
当年新增改善灌溉面积	Increased and Improved Irrigated Area (Current Year)	公顷 hectare	224	242	833
旱涝保收面积	Ensured Area from Drought and Flood	公顷 hectare	1 271	11 939	12 411
易涝面积	Area Subjected to Flood	公顷 hectare	1 447		282
水 闸	Dams	座 unit	28	11	16
堤 防	Dikes	公里 km	129.14	180.59	180.59
#郊区海塘	Rural/Suburban Sea Wall	公里 km	59.02	115.28	115.28
江 堤	Embankment	公里 km	70.12	65.31	65.31
围垦面积	Enclosed Tideland for Cultivation	公顷 hectare	3 755		
小机口新增	Newly Increased Small Machinery	座/台套/千瓦 unit /set /kw	12/17/123.5	29/29/316.5	27/37/532.5
新增排涝泵站	Newly Built Pump Houses for Draining Water-logging Fields	座/台套/千瓦 unit /set /kw		1/3/10	2/5/37.5
新建排涝涵洞	Newly Built Culvert for Draining Water-logging Fields	座/米 unit /meter	10/717	57/2 681	68/3 627
改造地下渠道	Underground Irrigation Ditch Reformed	公里 km	6.14	101.74	110.33
改造渡槽倒虹吸	Siphon Aqueduct Transformed	条/米 unit/meter	25/426	192/3 851	272/5 369

表 5-10　历年农田水利工程投资
Investment in Farmland Water Conservancy Projects in Main Years (1990～2011)

单位:万元　　(10 000 yuan)

年　份 Year	合　计 Total	国家投资 State-invested	乡村自筹 Funded by Villages	乡村自筹所占比重(%) Percentage of Investment Funded by Villages(%)
1990	1 363.74	668.75	694.99	51.0
1991	906.70	354.80	551.90	60.9
1992	826.30	311.90	514.40	62.3
1993	1 517.22	357.80	1 159.42	76.4
1994	2 673.15	1 253.61	1 419.54	53.1
1995	2 426.99	1 262.82	1 164.17	48.0
1996	3 357.97	1 766.90	1 591.07	47.4
1997	4 203.64	2 154.13	2 049.51	48.8
1998	4 849.08	2 419.01	2 430.07	50.1
1999	4 907.60	2 152.70	2 754.90	56.1
2000	6 321.21	2 333.20	3 988.01	63.1
2001	5 627.80	2 787.75	2 840.05	50.5
2002	7 975.97	3 423.95	4 552.02	57.1
2003	7 259.27	3 281.75	3 977.52	54.8
2004	7 137.29	3 583.26	3 554.03	49.8
2005	10 131.48	4 403.23	5 728.25	56.5
2006	15 053.70	6 661.95	8 391.75	55.7
2007	14 859.89	7 510.40	7 349.49	49.5
2008	43 846.67	21 908.07	21 938.60	50.0
2009	37 513.48	15 601.77	21 911.71	58.4
2010	68 474.03	52 745.21	15 728.82	23.0
2011	59 262.87	41 412.45	17 850.42	30.1

表5-11 孙桥现代农业园区主要经济指标
Major Economic Indicators of Sunqiao Modern Agricultural Park

指　标	Indicators	单　位 Unit	2005	2010	2011
园区面积	**Area of the Park**				
规划面积	Planned Area	公顷 hectare	932	932	932
已开发利用面积	Area Put to Use	公顷 hectare	346	346	346
引进项目情况	**Projects Introduced**				
引进投资项目数	Number of Investment Projects Introduced	项 item	52	76	80
#引进外资项目数	Number of Foreign Investment Projects Introduced	项 item	10	7	7
外省市项目数	Number of Investment Projects Introduced From Other Provinces and Municipalities	项 item	8	22	22
引进投资项目金额	Amount of Investment Projects Introduced	万元 10 000 yuan	60 935	67 936	68 599
#引进外资项目金额	Amount of Foreign Investment Projects Introduced	万美元 10 000 USD	2 714	2 714	2 714
开发总投资	**Total Investment for Development**	**万元 10 000 yuan**	**75 243**	**95 039**	**96 727**
招商引资	Business Promotion and Foreign Funds Attraction	万元 10 000 yuan	60 935	68 563	69 223
政府扶持资金	Government Grants	万元 10 000 yuan	5 192	10 438	11 057
其　它	Others	万元 10 000 yuan	9 116	16 038	16 447
企业和从业人员	**Enterprises and Employed Persons**				
年末实有企业数	Number of Enterprises at Year-end	个 unit	52	64	55
#农产品生产企业	Enterprises Producing Farm Products	个 unit	41	26	21
农产品加工企业	Enterprises Processing Farm Products	个 unit	6	12	10
农产品贸易服务企业	Enterprises Engaged in Trading and Service for Farm Products	个 unit	5	5	6
年末从业人员数	Employed Persons at Year-end	人 person	1 416	2 007	2 138
#各类专业技术人员	All kinds of Technical Professionals	人 person	95	165	168

表 5－11　续表　Continued

指　标　Indicators		单　位　Unit	2005	2010	2011
品牌生产及认证	**Production and Autthentication of Branded Farm Products**				
品牌农产品生产企业	Enterprises Producing Branded Farm Products	个 unit	3	4	4
品牌农产品产值	Output Value of Branded Farm Products	万元 10 000 yuan	2 950	17 151	18 338
认证品牌生产个数	Number of Authenticated Branded Products	个 in number	2	3	3
认证品牌生产面积	Production Area of Authenticated Brands	公顷 hectare	9	142	142
认证品牌生产产值	Output Value of Authenticated Brands	万元 10 000 yuan	2 950	12 793	16 006
生产经营情况	**Operation**				
农业总产值	Output Value of Agriculture	万元 10 000 yuan	96 578	88 543	99 211
农产品出口总额	Total Value of Exported Farm Products	万元 10 000 yuan	8 675	8 590	10 179
农产品加工产值	Output Value of Processed Farm Products	万元 10 000 yuan	8 096	24 778	25 682
农产品服务贸易销售收入	Sales Revenue from Service and Trading of Farm Products	万元 10 000 yuan	1 408	8 037	8 146
利税总额	Total of Profits and Taxes	万元 10 000 yuan	5 579	5 316	1 238
园区产业化生产经营（辐射）能力	**Operating（Influential）Capacity of Park Industrialization**				
带动本市园区外农户户数	Number of Rural Households Outside the Park from Which Have Benefited	户 household	59 882	61 092	66 286
带动外省市农户户数	Number of Rural Households in Other Provinces and Municipalities from Which Have Benefited	户 household	58 148	57 124	61 330
对外省市产品及技术服务输出总额	Total Value of Products and Service Transferred to Other Provinces	万元 10 000 yuan	475	11 170	17 540

表5-12 南汇现代农业园区主要经济指标
Major Economic Indicators of Nanhui Modern Agricultural Park

指 标	Indicators	单 位 Unit	2005	2010	2011
园区面积	**Area of the Park**				
规划面积	Planned Area	公顷 hectare	1 698	1 030	1 030
已开发利用面积	Area Put to Use	公顷 hectare	843	349	349
引进项目情况	**Projects Introduced**				
引进投资项目数	Number of Investment Projects Introduced	项 item	17	22	22
#引进外资项目数	Number of Foreign Investment Projects Introduced	项 item	5	5	5
外省市项目数	Number of Investment Projects Introduced From Other Provinces and Municipalities	项 item	4	8	8
引进投资项目金额	Amount of Investment Projects Introduced	万元 10 000 yuan	66 030	249 831	249 831
#引进外资项目金额	Amount of Foreign Investment Projects Introduced	万美元 10 000 USD	542	2 164	2 164
开发总投资	**Total Investment for Development**	**万元 10 000 yuan**	**25 810**	**42 742**	**43 617**
招商引资	Business Promotion and Foreign Funds Attraction	万元 10 000 yuan	25 810	42 742	43 617
政府扶持资金	Government Grants	万元 10 000 yuan			
其 它	Others	万元 10 000 yuan			
企业和从业人员	**Enterprises and Employed Persons**				
年末实有企业数	Number of Enterprises at Year-end	个 unit	6	7	8
#农产品生产企业	Enterprises Producing Farm Products	个 unit		3	4
农产品加工企业	Enterprises Processing Farm Products	个 unit	5	2	2
农产品贸易服务企业	Enterprises Engaged in Trading and Service for Farm Products	个 unit	1	1	1
年末从业人员数	Employed Persons at Year-end	人 person	600	594	565
#各类专业技术人员	All kinds of Technical Professionals	人 person	59	41	41

表 5－12 续表 Continued

指 标	Indicators	单 位 Unit	2005	2009	2010
品牌生产及认证	**Production and Autthentication of Branded Farm Products**				
品牌农产品生产企业	Enterprises Producing Branded Farm Products	个 unit	5	5	6
品牌农产品产值	Output Value of Branded Farm Products	万元 10 000 yuan	9 709	12 710	15 765
认证品牌生产个数	Number of Authenticated Branded Products	个 in number	3	9	3
认证品牌生产面积	Production Area of Authenticated Brands	公顷 hectare	2 000	362	30
认证品牌生产产值	Output Value of Authenticated Brands	万元 10 000 yuan	2 840	5 946	9 924
生产经营情况	**Operation**				
农业总产值	Output Value of Agriculture	万元 10 000 yuan	10 648	4 898	11 859
农产品出口总额	Total Value of Exported Farm Products	万元 10 000 yuan	9 871	8 112	8 567
农产品加工产值	Output Value of Processed Farm Products	万元 10 000 yuan	9 151	9 412	4 206
农产品服务贸易销售收入	Sales Revenue from Service and Trading of Farm Products	万元 10 000 yuan	9	450	450
利税总额	Total of Profits and Taxes	万元 10 000 yuan		4 857	4 126
园区产业化生产经营（辐射）能力	**Operating (Influential) Capacity of Park Industrialization**				
带动本市园区外农户户数	Number of Rural Households Outside the Park from Which Have Benefited	户 household	3 850	240	70
带动外省市农户户数	Number of Rural Households in Other Provinces and Municipalities from Which Have Benefited	户 household	8 153	12 700	160
对外省市产品及技术服务输出总额	Total Value of Products and Service Transferred to Other Provinces	万元 10 000 yuan	24	244	244

表5-13 浦东临空出口农业园区主要经济指标
Major Economic Indicators of Pudong Linkong Exports-Oriented Agricultural Park

指 标 Indicators		单 位 Unit	2005	2010	2011
园区面积	**Area of the Park**				
规划面积	Planned Area	公顷 hectare	1 038	1 038	1 038
已开发利用面积	Area Put to Use	公顷 hectare	222	222	222
引进项目情况	**Projects Introduced**				
引进投资项目数	Number of Investment Projects Introduced	项 item	35	33	31
#引进外资项目数	Number of Foreign Investment Projects Introduced	项 item	2	2	2
外省市项目数	Number of Investment Projects Introduced From Other Provinces and Municipalities	项 item	16	15	14
引进投资项目金额	Amount of Investment Projects Introduced	万元 10 000 yuan	42 352	46 184	46 682
#引进外资项目金额	Amount of Foreign Investment Projects Introduced	万美元 10 000 USD	121	121	121
开发总投资	**Total Investment for Development**	**万元 10 000 yuan**	**42 352**	**46 184**	**46 682**
招商引资	Business Promotion and Foreign Funds Attraction	万元 10 000 yuan	38 317	39 679	39 979
政府扶持资金	Government Grants	万元 10 000 yuan	4 035	6 505	6 703
其 它	Others	万元 10 000 yuan			
企业和从业人员	**Enterprises and Employed Persons**				
年末实有企业数	Number of Enterprises at Year-end	个 unit	33	33	31
#农产品生产企业	Enterprises Producing Farm Products	个 unit	11	9	9
农产品加工企业	Enterprises Processing Farm Products	个 unit	9	9	8
农产品贸易服务企业	Enterprises Engaged in Trading and Service for Farm Products	个 unit	11	12	11
年末从业人员数	Employed Persons at Year-end	人 person	848	851	831
#各类专业技术人员	All kinds of Technical Professionals	人 person	164	151	149

表5－13 续表 Continued

指 标 Indicators		单 位 Unit	2005	2010	2011
品牌生产及认证	**Production and Autthentication of Branded Farm Products**				
品牌农产品生产企业	Enterprises Producing Branded Farm Products	个 nit	1	1	1
品牌农产品产值	Output Value of Branded Farm Products	万元 10 000 yuan	5 500	7 739	7 200
认证品牌生产个数	Number of Authenticated Branded Products	个 in number	3	3	3
认证品牌生产面积	Production Area of Authenticated Brands	公顷 hectare	700	549	549
认证品牌生产产值	Output Value of Authenticated Brands	万元 10 000 yuan	7 000	7 900	8 150
生产经营情况	**Operation**				
农业总产值	Output Value of Agriculture	万元 10 000 yuan	11 965	11 000	16 035
农产品出口总额	Total Value of Exported Farm Products	万元 10 000 yuan	20 150	34 780	32 380
农产品加工产值	Output Value of Processed Farm Products	万元 10 000 yuan	10 960	17 660	15 886
农产品服务贸易销售收入	Sales Revenue from Service and Trading of Farm Products	万元 10 000 yuan	19 640	29 745	36 015
利税总额	Total of Profits and Taxes	万元 10 000 yuan		1 264	2 864
园区产业化生产经营（辐射）能力	**Operating（Influential）Capacity of Park Industrialization**				
带动本市园区外农户户数	Number of Rural Households Outside the Park from Which Have Benefited	户 household	12 000	8 388	5 188
带动外省市农户户数	Number of Rural Households in Other Provinces and Municipalities from Which Have Benefited	户 household	32 500	32 500	26 500
对外省市产品及技术服务输出总额	Total Value of Products and Service Transferred to Other Provinces	万元 10 000 yuan			

主要统计指标解释

农村从业人员

指乡村人口中16岁以上实际参加生产经营活动并取得实物或货币收入的人员，既包括劳动年龄内实际参加劳动人员，也包括超过劳动年龄但实际参加劳动的人员，但不包括户口在家的在外学生、现役军人和丧失劳动能力的人，也不包括待业人员和家务劳动者。劳动者年龄为16岁以上。

农业总产值

农业总产值是以货币表现的农、林、牧、渔业全部产品的总量和对农林牧渔生产活动进行的各种支持性服务活动的价值。它反映一定时期内农业生产的总规模和总成果。

农、林、牧、渔业的统计范围是：

（1）农业　包括农作物种植业和其他农业。

农作物种植业包括谷物、豆类、薯类、棉、油料、糖料、麻类、烟叶、蔬菜、药材、瓜类和其他农作物的种植，以及茶园、桑园、果园的生产经营。

其他农业包括采集野生植物的果实、纤维、树胶、树脂、油料以及柴草、野生药材、菌类等及农民家庭兼营的商品性工业。

（2）林业　包括林木的栽培（不包括茶园、桑园和果园的栽培、管理和收获等活动）、林产品的采集和村及村以下合作经济组织和农户的竹木采伐。

（3）牧业　包括除渔业养殖以外的一切动物饲养和放牧，以及野生动物的捕猎和饲养。

（4）渔业　包括水生动物和海藻类植物的养殖和捕捞。

（5）农林牧渔服务业　包括农林牧渔业生产活动进行的各种支持性服务活动。但不包括各种科学技术和专业技术服务活动。

从所有制看，包括国有经济的各种专业农（农、林、牧、渔）场以及国家各级机关团体学校、科研机构、部队经营的农业；集体所有制的乡镇村各级办农场；农村各种经济组织经营的农、林、牧、渔业以及工矿企业家属集体经营的农业；农民家庭自营的农林牧渔业及兼营商品性工业等。

农业总产值的计算方法通常是按农林牧渔业产品及其副产品的产量分别乘以各自单位产品价格求得，少数生产周期较长、当年没有产品或产品产量不易统计的，则采用间接方法匡算其产值，然后将四业产品产值和服务业产值相加即为农业总产值。

1957年以前的农业总产值中包括了厩肥和农民自给性手工业（如农民自制衣服、鞋、袜，自己从事粮食初步加工等）。1958年及以后的农业总产值，林业中增加了村及村以下竹木采伐产值；牧业中取消了厩肥产值；副业中取消了农民自给性手工业产值，增加了村及村以下办的工业产值；渔业中增加了海洋捕捞水产品产值。1980年及以后的农业总产值，在副业中增加了农民家庭兼营工业商品部分的产值。从1984年起村及村以下办工业产值划归工业。从1993年起，取消副业。将野生动物的捕猎划入牧业，野生植物采集和农民家庭兼营商品性工业划归农业。从2003年起，农业总产值中包括了农林牧渔服务业产值。

当年价格

当年价格（或现行价格）是指报告期的实际价格，如工业品的出厂价格、农产品的收购价格、商品零售价格等。用当年价格计算的一些以货币表现的物量指标或劳务总量指标，如国内生产总值、工农业总产值、社会商品零售额等，反映当年的实际情况，使国民经济各项指标互相衔接，便于考察当年社会经济效益，便于对生产和流通、生产和分配、生产和消费之间进行经济核算和综合平衡。

按当年价格计算的以货币表现的指标，在不同年份之间进行对比时，因包含各年间价格变动的因素，不能确切地反映实物量的增减变动，必须消除价格变动的因素后，才能真实反映经济发展动态。因此，在计算增长速度时都使用按可比价格计算的数字。

可比价格

可比价格指在对不同时期的价值指标对比时，扣除了价格变动的因素，以确切反映物量的变化。按可比价格计算有两种方法，一种是直接按产品产量乘其某一年的不变价格计算；另一种是用价格指数换算。

不变价格

指以同类产品某年的平均价格作为固定价格，用于计算各年的产品价值。按不变价格计算的产品价值消除了价格变动因素，不同时期对比可以反映生产的发展速度。新中国成立后，随着工农业产品价格水平的变化，国家统计局先后五次制定了全国统一的工业产品不变价格和农业产品不变价格。从1952年到1957年使用1952年工（农）业产品不变价格，从1957年到1970年使用1957年不变价格，从1971年到1980年使用1970年不变价格，从1981年到1990年使用1980年不变价格，从1991年到2000年使用1990年不变价格，从2001年开始使用2000年不变价格。

年末耕地面积

年末耕地面积指能够种植农作物，经常进行耕锄的田地。包括熟地、当年新开荒地、新开垦围垦地、连续撂荒未满三年的耕地和当年休闲地（轮歇地）。以种植农作物为主并附带种植桑树、茶树、果树和其他林木的土地，以及沿海、沿湖地区已围垦利用的“海涂”、“湖田”等也应包括在内，但不包括专业性桑园、茶园、果园、果木苗圃、林地、芦苇地、天然草原等。小于一米宽的渠、路、田埂,包括在耕地中。

农作物播种面积

农作物播种面积指报告期内收获农产品的作物的实际播种或移植有农作物的面积。凡是实际种植农作物的面积,不论种植在耕地上还是种植在非耕地上,均包括在农作物播种面积中。在播种季节基本结束后,因遭灾而重新改种和补种的农作物面积,也包括在内。

粮食产量

指全社会的产量。包括国有经济经营的、集体统一经营的和农民家庭经营的粮食产量,还包括工矿企业办的农场和其他生产单位的产量。粮食除包括稻谷、小麦、玉米、高粱、谷子及其他杂粮外,还包括薯类和豆类。其产量计算方法,豆类按去豆荚后的干豆计算;薯类(包括甘薯和马铃薯,不包括芋头和木薯)1963 年以前按每 4 公斤鲜薯折 1 公斤粮食计算,从 1964 年开始改为按 5 公斤鲜薯折 1 公斤粮食计算。城市郊区作为蔬菜的薯类(如马铃薯等)按鲜品计算,并且不作粮食统计。其他粮食一律按脱粒后的原粮计算。1989 年以前全国粮食产量数据主要靠全面报表取得,1989 年开始使用抽样调查数据。

水产品产量

指人工养殖的水产品和天然生长的水产品的捕捞量。包括海水的鱼类、虾蟹类、贝类和藻类以及内陆水域的鱼类、虾蟹类和贝类,不包括淡水生植物。水产品产量是通过各级水产和统计部门逐级上报取得数据。1995 年及以前,贝类中牡蛎按鲜肉计算;蚶、蛤、蛙按 5 斤鲜品折 1 斤计算。1996 年以后则统一按鲜品计算。

猪、牛、羊肉产量

指当年出栏并已屠宰、除去头蹄下水后带骨肉(即胴体重)的重量。包括全社会范围内的产量。1996 年前为各级逐级上报数据。1996 年第一次农业普查以后,由于畜牧业产品年报数据与普查数据之间存在一定的差距,国家统计局农调总队对畜牧业年报数据与普查数据进行衔接。1999 年以后,国家统计局开展了猪、牛、羊、禽等主要畜禽品种的抽样调查,并用抽样数据作为国家定案数据使用。未开展抽样调查的品种,仍使用各级统计部门逐级上报数据。

农业机械总动力

农业机械总动力指用于农、林、牧、渔业生产的各种动力机械的动力总和。动力机械包括耕作、排灌、种植、植物保护、收获、农产品加工、运输、畜牧、渔业、农田水利等各种机械。不包括专门用于乡办工业、基本建设、非农业运输、科学试验和教学等非农业生产方面用的动力机械与作业机械的数量。

农村经济收益分配主要指标

农村经济收益分配和效益指标,是为了全面观察农村经济收入分配情况,研究农村经济的规模、发展速度、多种经营、商品化程度,国家、集体和个人的分配关系及经济效益。其计算范围包括乡村企业、集体统一经营(含家庭承包)新经济联合体以及农民家庭经营(含家庭承包)四个部分。

(1)总收入:指本单位当年经营的收入中可用以抵偿本年开支并在国家、集体、农民之间进行分配的农、林、牧、渔业、工业、交通运输业、建筑业、商业、饮食业、服务业等各项经营收入和利息、租金等非生产收入,但不包括那些不能用来分配,属于借贷性质或暂收性质的收入,如贷款收入、预购定金、国家投资、农民投资等。

(2)总费用:是指为实现当年各项生产经营收入应由当年负担的各项费用开支,包括生产费用、管理费用和其他费用三项。

(3)净收入总额:是指当年"总收入"减去"总费用"后,当年所得的净收入部分。

(4)农村居民净收入:是指农村居民从当年的净收入中减去国家税金和集体提留以后,归个人支配的部分,包括现金和实物折款。

EXPLANATORY NOTES TO MAJOR STATISTICAL INDICATORS

Personnel Employed in Rural Areas

Personnel Employed in Rural Areas refers to people in rural areas who are older than 16 years and engaged in production and business activities that generate incomes in cash or in practicality. It includes all working laborers, no matter whether they are within the working age or not, whereas students studying outside but with their registered residence at home, active serviceman, people who lost their ability to work, unemployed people, and those engaged in housework are not included. The working age is defined as older than 16 years.

Gross Output Value of Agriculture

Gross Output Value of Agriculture refers to the total volume of products of farming, forestry, animal husbandry and fishery expressed in the monetary terms and output value of all kinds of service activities that support farming, forestry, animal husbandry and fishery production. It reflects the overall scale and achievements of agricultural production during a given period of time.

The scope of statistics on farming, forestry, animal husbandry, and fishery are as follows:

(1) Farming includes cultivation of farm crops and other agri-

cultural activities.

Cultivation of farm crops include cultivation of grain crops, legume crops, tuber-crops, cotton, oil-bearing crops, sugar crops, bastfiber plants, tobacco, vegetables, medicinal herbs, melon crops, and cultivation and management of tea plantations, mulberry fields and orchards.

Other agricultural activities include harvesting wild fruits, fiber, tree gum, resin, oil-bearing plants, firewood, wild medicinal herbs, fungus, and rural-household commodity industries.

(2) Forestry refers to planting trees of various kinds (excluding tea plantations, mulberry fields and orchards), collection of forestry products and cutting and felling of bamboo and trees by villages and other cooperative organizations under village level.

(3) Animal husbandry refers to raising and grazing of all kinds of farm animals except fishing and aquatic cultivating, and hunting and rising of wild animals.

(4) Fishery refers to cultivation and catching of fish and other aquatic products and cultivation and collection of seaweed and other aquatic plants.

(5) Service Industry for Farming, Forestry, Animal Husbandry and Fishery refers to all kinds of service activities that support farming, forestry, animal husbandry and fishery production, whereas activities of science, technology and professional service are not included.

In terms of ownership, China's agriculture includes specialized state farms (for farming, forestry, animal husbandry, fishery), farms managed by various government agencies, organizations, schools, research institutions, and army; farms managed by rural collective organizations at levels of the township, town, and village; farming, forestry, animal husbandry, fishery run by various rural collective organizations and farming run by collective family members' organizations of mining and industrial enterprises; farming, forestry, animal husbandry and fishery and some commodity industries run by individual farmers.

Gross output value of agriculture is obtained by first multiplying the output of products or by-products by their unit price. For a small number of products, annual output of which is not available or difficult to get due to the long production/growing process involved, the output value will be estimated through an indirect approach. The sum of output value of all products of farming, forestry, animal husbandry and fishery and output value of service activities will then and together to form gross output value of agriculture.

Before 1957, China's gross agricultural output value included the value of barnyard manure and handicraft products for self-consumption (clothes, shoes, stockings, and initial grain processing under-taken by peasants). After 1958, the output value of cutting and felling of bamboo and trees by villages and other cooperative organizations under villages have been included in forestry; value of barnyard manure has been excluded from animal husbandry; the value of self-consumed handicrafts has been excluded from sideline occupations, while output value of industries run by villages and cooperative organizations under village level has been included in sideline occupations and output value of fish catches by motor fishing boats has been added to fishery. Since 1980, the output value of handicraft products made for sale by farmer households has been added to sideline occupations, From 1984, industries run by villages and cooperative organizations under village level have been included in the sector of industry. After 1993, the category of sideline occupations has been canceled and hunting of wild animals has been classified into husbandry, and harvesting of wild vegetation and commodity industry run by rural households have been grouped into the category of agriculture. Since 2003, the output value of service industry for farming, forestry, animal husbandry and fishery is included in the gross output value of agriculture.

Current Prices

Current prices refer to the actual prices in the report period, for example, industrial producers prices, procurement prices of agricultural products, retail prices, and so on. Goods and services measured by the current prices, such as gross national product, gross output value of industry and agriculture, total retail sales, reflect the current-year actual activities. The various national economic indicators, such as current-year social economic efficiency, production, exchange, distribution and consumption could be understood and compared directly if they are measured by the current prices.

The indicators measured by the current prices can not exactly reflect the real change over different years, if the price level changes during the period of time. The comparable prices would be used in measuring growth rates, in order to deflate the price change.

Comparable Prices

Comparable Prices are applied when comparing indicators over time to reflect accurately the changes in real term. Two methods are used for calculating comparable prices: 1. output by constant price of certain year; 2. output in current prices divided by relevant price index.

Constant Price

Constant Price refers to the average price of a given product in certain year, which is used for comparison of output value over time. As the output value at constant prices removes the factor of price changes, it reflects the trend of production development over time. Since 1949, with the changes in general price level, National Bureau of Statistics has issued nationally unified constant prices five times: the 1952 constant prices for 1949 - 1957; the 1957 constant prices for 1957 - 1971; the 1970 constant prices for 1971 - 1981; the 1980 constant prices for 1981 - 1990; the 1990 constant prices for 1991 - 2000; and the 2000 constant prices have been used since 2001.

The Actual Area of Plowland at Year End

The Area of Plowland at Year End refers to the area of arable land and frequently-tended farm-fields at the beginning of a year. It includes cultivated land, the newly-reclaimed wasteland and inning land in the year, the farmland which has been laid idle for no more than three consecutive years, and land on fallow that year. It shall also include farmland with mulberry, tea, fruit and other trees but used mainly for growing crops as well as the reclaimed "beach-land" and "lake-land" along the sea coasts and the lake banks. However, it shall not include the land devoted especially for mulberry and the tea gardens, orchards, nurseries, woodlands, reed marches and natural grasslands. Ditches, pathways and ridges of field which are less than one meter wide are included in plowland.

Sown Area of Crops

Sown Area of Crops refers to area of land sown or transplanted with crops that have been harvested during report period, regardless of being in cultivated area or non-cultivated area. Area of land re-sown due to natural disasters is also included.

Grain Output

Grain Output refers to the total output in the whole country including grains produced by state farms, collective units, rural households, as well as by farms affiliated to industrial and mining enterprises and other production units. Grain includes rice, wheat, corn, sorghum, millet and other miscellaneous grains as well as tubers and bean. Output of beans refers to dry beans without pods. The output of tubers (sweet potatoes and potatoes, not including taros and cassava) was converted into that of grain at the ratio 4 : 1, i. e. 4 kilograms of fresh tubers was equivalent to 1 kilogram of grain up to 1963. Since 1964 the ratio for conversion has been 5:1. Tubers supplied as vegetables (such as potatoes) in cities and suburbs are calculated as fresh vegetables and their output is not included in the output of grain. Output of all other grains refers to husked grain. Data on grain production before 1989 were obtained through Comprehensive Statistical Reporting System. Since 1989, data from sample surveys are used.

Output of Aquatic Products

Output of Aquatic Products refers to catches of both artificially cultured and naturally grown aquatic products, including fish, shrimps, crabs and shellfish in sea and inland water as well as seaweed. Freshwater plants are not included. Data on output of aquatic products are reported by aquatic product and statistical agencies level by level. Before 1995, among the shellfish, the oyster was counted as fresh meat; 5 kilograms of ark shell, clams and frogs are equivalent to 1 kilogram of fresh aquatic products; they are all counted as fresh aquatic products since 1996.

Output of Pork, Beef, and Mutton

Output of Pork, Beef, and Mutton refers to the meat of slaughtered hogs, cattle, sheep and goats with head, feet, and offal taken away. Data refers to the production of the whole country. The first agriculture census of China in 1996 revealed some discrepancy between the production of animal products from the annual reports and that from the census. Efforts were made by the Rural Socio-economic Survey Organization of NBS to adjust the output value of animal husbandry to make the figures from the annual reports consistent with the census data. Since 1999, NBS conducted sample survey for the major animal husbandry products, such as hogs, cattle, sheep and goats and fowls, and the data from sample surveys are used as national finalized data. Those products, which are not covered by the sample survey, are still reported by statistical agencies level by level.

Total Power of Farm Machinery

Total Power of Farm Machinery refers to the total mechanical power of machinery used in farming, forestry animal husbandry and fishery, including machines used for ploughing, irrigation and drainage, crop growing, plant protection, harvesting, farm product processing, transport, stock breeding, fishery and water conservancy. Machinery employed for non-agricultural purposes such as township industry, capital construction, non-agricultural transport, scientific experiments and for teaching is excluded.

Major Indicators of Rural Income Distribution

Indicators of rural income distribution and efficiency are used for investigating the overall income distribution in rural area and for studying the rural economy in scale, development, multi-operation, commercialization, income distribution among state, collective units and individuals and economic efficiency. The statistical scope includes village enterprises, collective operations (collectively contracted operation), new economic unions and farmers family operations (family contracted operation).

(1) Gross income refers to current year operating revenue in farming, forestry, animal husbandry, fishery, industry, transportation, construction, commerce, catering, services and interest, rent, which can be used to compensate for current year's expenses and distributed among the state, collective units and farmers, but excludes the credit or actual revenue which can not be distributed, such as loan revenue, advance payments for purchases, state investment and farmers investment.

(2) Total expenses refers to current year expenses which realize current year's productive operating revenue, including production expenses, managerial expenses and other expenses.

(3) Total net income refers to current year's net gross revenue of total expenses.

(4) Net Income of Residents in Rural Area refers to the disposable portion of such residents after deduction of state tax and collective retention from net income, including cash and income in kind in money terms.

第六篇
Chapter 6

工 业
INDUSTRY

2012 / 上海浦东新区统计年鉴

SHANGHAI PUDONG NEW AREA STATISTICAL YEARBOOK

表6-1 主要年份工业总产值及其构成

单位:亿元

指 标	Indicators	1990	1995	1996	1998	1999	2000
总 计	**Total**	**176.85**	**968.03**	**1 130.42**	**1 414.99**	**1 450.81**	**1 625.77**
按隶属关系分	**By Subordination**						
中央工业	Central	42.48	225.99	269.28	331.21	323.62	381.41
市属工业	Municipal	88.44	491.63	562.02	640.62	610.35	599.57
非中央、市属工业	Local	45.93	250.41	299.12	443.16	516.84	644.79
按登记注册类型分	**By Type of Registration**						
国 有	State-owned	110.18	449.57	494.03	396.46	309.87	275.85
集 体	Collective-owned	49.09	122.54	131.93	105.85	90.04	70.91
港澳台及外商投资	Overseas Invested	7.07	231.94	303.77	695.25	851.48	1 012.34
其 他	Others	10.51	163.98	200.69	217.43	199.42	266.67
按轻、重工业分	**By Light/Heavy Industry**						
轻工业	Light Industry	72.08	424.42	509.85	575.55	533.52	514.58
重工业	Heavy Industry	104.77	543.61	620.57	839.44	917.29	1 111.19
按企业规模分	**By Scale of Enterprises**						
大型企业	Large	81.32	632.35	746.06	861.03	988.53	1 138.11
中型企业	Medium	21.40	96.37	106.57	163.34	163.48	187.00
小型企业	Small	74.13	239.31	277.79	390.62	298.80	300.66
构 成(%)	**Composition (%)**						
总 计	**Total**	**100.0**	**100.0**	**100.0**	**100.0**	**100.0**	**100.0**
按隶属关系分	**By Subordination**						
中央工业	Central	24.0	23.3	23.8	23.4	22.3	23.5
市属工业	Municipal	50.0	50.8	49.7	45.3	42.1	36.9
非中央、市属工业	Local	26.0	25.9	26.5	31.3	35.6	39.6
按登记注册类型分	**By Type of Registration**						
国 有	State-owned	62.3	46.4	43.7	28.0	21.4	17.0
集 体	Collective-owned	27.8	12.7	11.7	7.5	6.2	4.3
港澳台及外商投资	Overseas Invested	4.0	24.0	26.9	49.1	58.7	62.3
其 他	Others	5.9	16.9	17.7	15.4	13.7	16.4
按轻、重工业分	**By Light/Heavy Industry**						
轻工业	Light Industry	40.8	43.8	45.1	40.7	36.8	31.7
重工业	Heavy Industry	59.2	56.2	54.9	59.3	63.2	68.3
按企业规模分	**By Scale of Enterprises**						
大型企业	Large	46.0	65.3	66.0	60.9	68.1	70.0
中型企业	Medium	12.1	10.0	9.4	11.5	11.3	11.5
小型企业	Small	41.9	24.7	24.6	27.6	20.6	18.5

注：2011年起，规模以上企业为年主营业务收入2000万元及以上。

Note: Above-scaled enterprises will be refered to those which have an annual main business income of 20 million yuan and above since 2011.

Gross Output Value of Industry and Its Composition in Main Years

(100 million yuan)

2001	2002	2003	2004	2005	2006	2007	2008	2009	2010	2011
1 888.74	**2 193.82**	**2 856.68**	**3 519.71**	**4 242.47**	**4 758.76**	**5 188.12**	**5 649.22**	**7 141.55**	**8 591.50**	**9 553.79**
386.40	431.13	549.05	677.04	1 321.05	1 538.42	1 663.26	1 999.48	1 653.93	2 216.69	2 278.33
779.48	805.98	1 082.55	1 254.17	1 135.29	1 249.74	1 373.81	1 289.49	2 010.76	2 043.34	2 284.38
722.86	956.71	1 225.08	1 588.50	1 786.13	1 970.60	2 151.05	2 360.25	3 476.86	4 331.47	4 991.08
344.02	241.56	290.97	358.04	550.18	573.84	662.21	679.71	729.56	885.71	927.97
57.02	49.57	46.02	49.09	38.67	36.87	34.89	31.60	47.87	34.70	34.67
1 242.91	1 522.31	1 985.30	2 461.66	2 632.70	2 980.46	3 001.98	3 088.54	4 008.58	5 047.75	5 899.02
244.79	380.38	534.39	650.92	1 020.92	1 167.59	1 489.04	1 849.37	2 355.54	2 623.34	2 692.13
535.06	541.28	647.92	764.94	825.40	878.66	952.26	1 070.62	1 402.71	1 535.63	1 677.47
1 353.68	1 652.54	2 208.76	2 754.77	3 417.07	3 880.10	4 235.86	4 578.60	5 738.84	7 055.87	7 876.32
1 294.24	1 564.20	1 229.85	1 426.29	1 989.45	1 976.08	2 309.39	2 731.96	3 318.52	4 097.63	6 154.87
239.26	209.92	862.86	1 083.29	1 173.99	1 725.62	1 841.13	1 822.86	2 022.62	2 593.18	1 477.88
355.24	419.70	763.97	1 010.13	1 079.03	1 057.06	1 037.60	1 094.40	1 800.41	1 900.69	1 921.04
100.0	**100.0**	**100.0**	**100.0**	**100.0**	**100.0**	**100.0**	**100.0**	**100.0**	**100.0**	**100.0**
20.4	19.7	19.2	19.3	31.1	32.3	32.0	35.4	23.2	25.8	23.8
41.3	36.7	37.9	35.6	26.8	26.3	26.5	22.8	28.1	23.8	23.9
38.3	43.6	42.9	45.1	42.1	41.4	41.5	41.8	48.7	50.4	52.3
18.2	11.0	10.2	10.2	13.0	12.1	12.8	12.0	10.2	10.3	9.7
3.0	2.3	1.6	1.4	0.9	0.8	0.7	0.6	0.7	0.4	0.4
65.8	69.4	69.5	69.9	62.0	62.6	57.8	54.7	56.1	58.8	61.7
13.0	17.3	18.7	18.5	24.1	24.5	28.7	32.7	33.0	30.5	28.2
28.3	24.7	22.7	21.7	19.5	18.5	18.4	19.0	19.6	17.9	17.6
71.7	75.3	77.3	78.3	80.5	81.5	81.6	81.0	80.4	82.1	82.4
68.5	71.3	43.1	40.5	46.9	41.5	44.5	48.3	46.5	47.7	64.4
12.7	9.6	30.2	30.8	27.7	36.3	35.5	32.3	28.3	30.2	15.5
18.8	19.1	26.7	28.7	25.4	22.2	20.0	19.4	25.2	22.1	20.1

表6-2　工业总产值、销售产值和出口交货值
(2011)

单位:亿元

指　标	Indicators	工业总产值(按现行价格计算) Gross Output Value of Industry (at Current Price)
总　计	**Total**	**9 553.79**
按隶属关系分	**By Subordination**	
中央工业	Central	2 278.33
市属工业	Municipal	2 284.38
非中央、市属工业	Local	4 991.08
按登记注册类型分	**By Type of Registration**	
内　资	Domestic Funded	3 654.77
国　有	State-owned	927.97
集　体	Collective-owned	34.67
股份合作制	Share-holding	21.86
联　营	Jointly-operated	7.72
有限责任公司	Companies with Limited Liability	832.14
股份有限公司	Companies Limited by Shares	1 005.25
私　营	Private	822.74
其　他	Others	2.43
港澳台商投资	Hong Kong/Macao/Taiwan Invested	1 057.43
#港澳台商独资	Solely Hong Kong/Macao/Taiwan Funded	748.75
外商投资	Foreigner Invested	4 841.59
#外商独资	Solely Foreigner Funded	2 475.63
按轻、重工业分	**By Light/Heavy Industry**	
轻工业	Light Industry	1 677.47
重工业	Heavy Industry	7 876.32
按企业规模分	**By Scale of Enterprises**	
大型企业	Large	6 154.87
中型企业	Medium	1 477.88
小型企业	Small	1 921.04

Gross Output Value, Sales Value and Export Delivery Value

(100 million yuan)

#镇及镇以上 Town and Above	工业销售产值 Sales Value of Industry	#镇及镇以上 Town and Above	出口交货值 Export Delivery Value	#镇及镇以上 Town and Above
4 896.56	**9 443.04**	**4 845.86**	**2 421.13**	**764.67**
2 278.33	2 266.21	2 266.21	458.84	458.84
2 284.38	2 253.66	2 253.66	259.03	259.03
333.85	4 923.17	325.99	1 703.26	46.80
2 572.06	3 624.19	2 556.93	360.31	281.29
921.63	928.03	921.70	18.87	18.19
13.86	36.79	14.12	1.05	1.05
5.24	21.61	4.96	0.54	0.03
3.09	7.59	3.00	0.02	
700.77	822.90	698.95	237.78	228.42
876.41	992.72	865.77	33.97	30.05
50.46	811.99	47.68	66.94	3.56
0.60	2.55	0.75	1.15	
160.34	1 054.82	160.34	407.00	27.82
24.75	754.22	24.94	287.75	11.06
2 164.16	4 764.03	2 128.59	1 653.82	455.56
120.42	2 424.19	122.51	1 125.39	43.09
646.66	1 656.68	638.66	364.94	173.53
4 249.90	7 786.36	4 207.20	2 056.19	591.14
3 930.31	6 069.91	3 889.36	1 837.72	657.58
560.08	1 455.08	553.07	320.43	71.97
406.17	1 918.05	403.43	262.98	35.12

表6-3 主要工业产品生产和销售量
Output and Sales Volume of Major Industrial Products
(2011)

产品名称	Products	单 位 Unit	生产量 Output	销售量 Sales Volume	生产量占全市比重(%) PNA/Shanghai(%)
原油加工量	Volume of Crude Oil Processing	万吨 10 000 tons	1 044.33	1 032.09	49.0
汽　油	Gasoline	万吨 10 000 tons	177.52	162.99	64.7
柴　油	Diesel Oil	万吨 10 000 tons	400.87	400.97	50.2
化学纤维	Chemical Fiber	万吨 10 000 tons	14.37	12.84	28.0
合成纤维聚合物	Synthetic Polymer	万吨 10 000 tons	49.19	47.21	34.5
化学药品原药	Original Chemical Drug	吨 ton	2 469.10	2 484.18	9.5
钢　材	Steel	万吨 10 000 tons	17.30	17.10	0.7
家用洗衣机	Household Washing Machine	万台 10 000 sets	153.57	152.68	70.1
房间空气调节器	Household Air-conditioner	万台 10 000 sets	331.16	331.21	53.4
数字程控交换机	Program-controlled Exchange	万线 10 000 lines	164.00	164.00	100.0
电话单机	Telephone Set	万部 10 000 sets	330.81	304.17	99.9
微型计算机设备	ITS Computer Equipment	万部 10 000 sets	2 814.23	2 823.72	27.7
其中:笔记本计算机	Including Notebooks	万部 10 000 sets	2 388.50	2 379.74	26.7
彩色电视机	Color TV Set	万部 10 000 sets	171.46	172.43	76.3
气体压缩机	Gas Compressor	万台 10 000 sets	1 481.69	1 477.80	78.0
轿　车	Car	万辆 10 000 vehicles	68.67	67.60	39.4
集成电路	Integrated Circuit	亿块 100 million pieces	92.99	93.41	55.9
集成电路圆片	IC Wafer	万片 10 000 pieces	202.26	204.46	75.6
民用钢质船	Civil Steel Ship	万载重吨 10 000 DWT	689.22	689.22	51.6

表6－3 续表 Continued

产品名称	Products	单位 Unit	生产量 Output	销售量 Sales Volume	生产量占全市比重(%) PNA/Shanghai(%)
起重机	Crane	万吨 10 000 tons	42.62	42.60	78.9
微波炉	Microwave Oven	万台 10 000 sets	391.47	391.48	100.0
发电量	Electricity	亿千瓦时 100 mil. kwh	312.35	295.64	33.0
光电子器件	Optoelectronic Device	亿只 100 million units	59.82	59.16	63.6
移动通信基站设备	Base Station Equipment for Mobile Communication	万信道 10 000 information channels	490.40	490.40	100.0
电饭锅	Electric Rice Cooker	万个 10 000 units	33.52	33.40	6.9
原电池(折R20标准只)	Size D Battery(R20 standard)	亿只 100 million units	15.05	15.24	70.4
水　泥	Cement	万吨 10 000 tons	69.93	68.32	8.7
塑料制品	Plastics	万吨 10 000 tons	33.37	33.52	17.3
合成橡胶	Synthetic Rubber	万吨 10 000 tons	25.63	25.04	96.2
初级形态的塑料	Plastics in Primary Form	万吨 10 000 tons	48.22	48.53	14.9
涂　料	Paint	万吨 10 000 tons	41.40	42.98	28.3
化学农药原药	Original Chemicals of Chemical Pesticide	吨 ton	452.89	357.00	3.3
人造板	Man-made Board	万立方米 10 000 cu · m	5.49	5.57	23.9
服　装	Garment	亿件 100 million units	1.03	0.94	20.3
印染布	Printing & Dyeing Cloth	万米 10 000 meters	2 891.33	3 025.80	27.2
布	Cloth	万米 10 000 meters	776.40	760.20	4.5
乳制品	Dairy Products	万吨 10 000 tons	4.10	3.88	9.0
精炼食用植物油	Refined Edible Vegetable Oil	万吨 10 000 tons	62.58	64.60	74.0

表6-4　按行业分的工业总产值、销售产值和出口交货值
Gross Output Value, Sales Value and Export Delivery Value by Sector (2011)

单位:亿元　　(100 million yuan)

指　标	Indicators	工业总产值(按现行价格计算) Gross Output Value of Industry (at Current Price)	工业销售产　值 Sales Value of Industry	出口交货值 Export Delivery Value
总　计	**Total**	**9 553.79**	**9 443.04**	**2 421.13**
#农副食品加工业	Processing of Agricultural Side-line Food	93.73	97.52	0.54
食品制造业	Food Manufacturing	105.33	98.53	1.44
酒、饮料和精制茶制造业	Manufacturing of Liquor, Beverage and Refined Tea	31.11	30.60	2.69
烟草制品业	Tobacco Products	2.95	2.95	0.01
纺织业	Textile Industry	31.04	31.54	10.06
纺织服装、服饰业	Textile, Clothing and Accessories	169.26	169.32	31.39
皮革、毛皮、羽(毛)绒及其制品业	Leather, Fur, Down & Related Products	9.87	10.00	2.94
木材加工及木、竹、藤、棕、草制品业	Timber-processing, Bamboo, Cane, Palm Fiber and Straw Products	5.84	5.85	2.03
家具制造业	Furniture Manufacturing	82.68	82.54	18.62
造纸及纸制品业	Paper-making and Paper Products	54.36	53.23	10.62
印刷业和记录媒介复制业	Printing and Record Pressing	45.48	45.23	4.61
文教、工美、体育和娱乐用品制造业	Manufacturing of Cultural, Educational, Arts, Sports and Leisure Products	40.74	40.20	18.14
石油加工、炼焦及核燃料加工业	Petroleum Processing, Coke Products and Processing of Nuclear Fuel	765.17	756.04	24.40
化学原料及化学制品制造业	Raw Chemical Materials and Chemical Products	533.18	522.80	83.35
医药制造业	Medicine Manufacturing	209.40	198.85	15.44

单位:亿元　　表6-4 续表 Continued　　(100 million yuan)

指标	Indicators	工业总产值(按现行价格计算) Gross Output Value of Industry (at Current Price)	工业销售产值 Sales Value of Industry	出口交货值 Export Delivery Value
化学纤维制造业	Chemical Fiber Manufacturing	0.77	0.77	
橡胶和塑料制品业	Rubber and Plastic Products	125.61	127.37	15.12
非金属矿物制品业	Nonmetal Mineral Products	99.19	96.68	16.33
黑色金属冶炼及压延加工业	Smelting and Pressing of Ferrous Metal	46.22	44.19	1.96
有色金属冶炼及压延加工业	Smelting and Pressing of Nonferrous Metal	82.11	84.86	8.86
金属制品业	Metal Products	155.90	154.22	40.12
通用设备制造业	General Purpose Equipment Manufacturing	672.99	671.49	223.88
专用设备制造业	Special Purpose Equipment Manufacturing	388.55	374.86	64.12
汽车制造业	Automobile Manunfacturing	1 440.98	1 423.84	66.70
铁路、船舶、航空航天和其他运输设备制造业	Manufacturing of Railway, Ships, Aeronautics & Astronautics, and Other Transportation Equipment	332.69	329.98	225.46
电气机械及器材制造业	Electric Equipment and Machinery	460.84	458.04	158.89
计算机、通信和其他电子设备制造业	Manufacturing of Computers, Telecommunications and Other Electronic Equipment	2 327.56	2 295.12	1 312.61
仪器仪表制造业	Manufacturing of Instruments and Apparatuses	84.47	84.47	36.17
其他制造业	Other Manufacturing	31.17	29.20	4.00
废弃资源综合利用业	Comprehensive Reutilization of Discarded Resources	1.27	1.27	
金属制品、机械和设备修理业	Repairing of Metal Products, Machineries and Equipment	20.85	20.88	1.24
电力、热力的生产和供应业	Production and Supply of Electricity and Heating Power	797.75	797.62	
燃气生产和供应业	Production and Supply of Gas	33.47	33.41	
水的生产和供应业	Production and Supply of Tap Water	10.38	8.69	

表6-5　工业重点发展行业主要指标
(2011)

单位:万元

指　标	Indicators	企业单位数(个) Enterprises (unit)	从业人数(人) Employed Persons (person)	工业总产值 Gross Output Value of Industry
总　计	**Total**	**912**	**393 005**	**67 406 829**
按登记注册类型分	**By Type of Registration**			
内　资	Domestic Funded	443	124 983	19 764 396
国　有	State-owned	16	16 664	2 026 078
集　体	Collective-owned	11	1 736	112 482
股份合作制	Share-holding	10	1 487	93 204
联　营	Jointly-operated	5	774	34 871
有限责任公司	Companies with Limited Liability	83	37 932	5 472 137
股份有限公司	Companies Limited by Shares	20	19 960	8 989 937
私　营	Private	296	45 829	3 016 661
其　他	Others	2	601	19 027
港澳台商投资	Hong Kong/Macao/Taiwan Invested	98	43 231	8 472 426
#港澳台商独资	Solely Hong Kong/Macao/Taiwan Funded	67	28 174	6 912 010
外商投资	Foreigner Invested	371	224 791	39 170 007
#外商独资	Solely Foreigner Funded	254	152 365	19 883 333
按轻、重工业分	**By Light/Heavy Industry**			
轻工业	Light Industry	147	46 661	6 081 890
重工业	Heavy Industry	765	346 344	61 324 939
按企业规模分	**By Scale of Enterprises**			
大型企业	Large	65	217 547	49 163 443
中型企业	Medium	170	95 727	9 483 571
小型企业	Small	677	79 731	8 759 815
按行业分	**By Industry**			
电子信息产品制造业	Manufacturing of Electronic and Information Technology Products	259	185 367	25 549 643
汽车制造业	Auto Manufacturing	135	71 111	14 409 800
石油化工及精细化工制造业	Manufacturing of Petrochemical and Fine Chemicals	107	25 737	12 517 668
精品钢材制造业	Manufacturing of High Quality Steel Products	20	2 368	370 390
成套设备制造业	Manufacturing of Complete Plants and Equipment	305	81 180	11 736 368
生物医药制造业	Manufacturing of Biological Medicine	86	27 242	2 822 960

Major Indicators of PNA Pillar Industries

(10 000 yuan)

工业销售产值 Sales Value of Industry	固定资产原价 Original Value of Fixed Assets	资产总计 Total Assets	负债总计 Total Liabilities	实收资本 Paid-in Capital	主营业务收入 Revenue of Primary Operations	税金 Tax	利润总额 Total Profits
66 396 415	**23 843 611**	**63 101 357**	**33 164 476**	**14 883 274**	**76 598 683**	**3 207 147**	**6 584 329**
19 517 620	6 770 678	26 628 075	10 767 359	4 948 084	20 498 800	1 372 117	2 474 820
2 032 062	1 220 374	2 304 551	1 123 675	1 008 654	2 150 278	79 063	134 577
118 720	14 738	75 241	45 189	4 894	121 970	3 275	7 558
91 599	21 619	50 708	22 136	5 626	93 219	2 939	6 964
33 972	9 627	26 880	14 917	5 548	33 833	1 151	2 345
5 404 096	2 296 810	7 853 038	4 718 674	1 439 898	5 448 095	166 131	585 739
8 862 052	2 393 856	13 265 212	3 059 274	1 933 683	9 622 509	1 037 157	1 539 858
2 954 830	803 487	3 032 777	1 779 850	546 681	3 008 608	81 835	196 517
20 288	10 168	19 669	3 645	3 100	20 289	566	1 262
8 427 515	2 327 438	4 568 993	2 568 106	1 407 745	8 588 368	75 646	347 931
6 962 040	1 920 877	3 398 122	1 997 792	1 120 488	7 095 255	47 567	225 884
38 451 280	14 745 494	31 904 290	19 829 011	8 527 446	47 511 515	1 759 384	3 761 578
19 459 342	7 954 172	12 987 393	7 806 167	4 610 942	20 550 560	297 298	777 839
5 898 879	1 722 835	5 618 410	2 673 836	1 658 443	6 134 551	230 561	544 577
60 497 536	22 120 776	57 482 947	30 490 640	13 224 831	70 464 132	2 976 586	6 039 752
48 433 872	17 694 220	45 316 810	23 970 685	10 150 575	57 745 850	2 560 988	4 940 328
9 256 450	3 616 138	9 519 002	4 852 604	2 614 752	9 808 926	394 330	946 796
8 706 093	2 533 253	8 265 545	4 341 187	2 117 947	9 043 907	251 829	697 205
25 329 931	9 746 827	16 624 507	10 002 077	5 976 052	26 157 694	143 889	674 322
14 238 395	4 121 373	21 266 651	8 671 085	2 775 022	23 167 895	1 473 392	4 500 442
12 319 204	3 456 656	5 645 573	2 825 342	2 087 172	12 772 176	1 089 117	239 130
352 734	431 264	473 097	308 730	361 262	380 760	11 171	10 236
11 484 882	5 103 227	15 814 132	9 741 428	2 721 243	11 328 482	330 855	869 111
2 671 269	984 264	3 277 397	1 615 814	962 523	2 791 676	158 723	291 088

表6-6 高技术工业主要指标
(2011)

单位:万元

指 标	Indicators	企业单位数(个) Enterprises (unit)	从业人数(人) Employed Persons (person)	工业总产值 Gross Output Value of Industry
总 计	**Total**	**258**	**198 391**	**27 043 300**
按登记注册类型分	**By Type of Registration**			
内 资	Domestic Funded	85	28 901	1 791 022
国 有	State-owned	2	3 781	294 018
集 体	Collective-owned			
股份合作制	Share-holding			
联 营	Jointly-operated	2	280	14 135
有限责任公司	Companies with Limited Liability	26	10 683	666 858
股份有限公司	Companies Limited by Shares	7	2 919	197 167
私 营	Private	45	10 215	591 245
其 他	Others	3	1 023	27 599
港澳台商投资	Hong Kong/Macao/Taiwan Invested	40	27 710	7 234 882
#港澳台商独资	Solely Hong Kong/Macao/Taiwan Funded	31	20 203	6 230 807
外商投资	Foreigner Invested	133	141 780	18 017 396
#外商独资	Solely Foreigner Funded	98	111 618	13 291 108
按轻、重工业分	**By Light/Heavy Industry**			
轻工业	Light Industry	93	34 294	3 941 888
重工业	Heavy Industry	165	164 097	23 101 412
按企业规模分	**By Scale of Enterprises**			
大型企业	Large	37	142 233	22 594 629
中型企业	Medium	61	36 202	2 794 841
小型企业	Small	160	19 956	1 653 830
按工业行业分	**By Sector**			
信息化学品制造	Manufacturing of Information Chemicals	2	732	106 594
医药制造业	Manufacturing of Medicine	61	22 420	2 094 153
航空航天器制造	Manufacturing of Aviation and Space Vehicles	8	1 013	65 406
电子及通信设备制造业	Manufacturing of Electronics and Telecommunications Equipment	106	103 762	10 887 946
电子计算机及办公设备制造业	Manufacturing of Electronic Computers and Office Equipment	18	55 005	12 542 304
医疗设备及仪器仪表制造业	Manufacturing of Medical Equipment and Instrument	63	15 459	1 346 897

Major Indicators of PNA High-Tech Enterprises

(10 000 yuan)

工业销售产值 Sales Value of Industry	固定资产原价 Original Value of Fixed Assets	资产总计 Total Assets	负债总计 Total Liabilities	实收资本 Paid-in Capital	主营业务收入 Revenue of of Floating Assets	税金 Tax	利润总额 Total Profits
26 660 348	**10 270 556**	**18 734 277**	**10 837 342**	**6 777 556**	**27 526 595**	**283 666**	**949 135**
1 746 499	956 066	2 383 798	1 226 281	696 548	1 791 898	74 601	184 292
296 520	343 077	548 874	323 190	187 477	286 555	7 478	26 619
13 655	2 802	6 895	5 471	1 473	13 655	317	73
658 259	334 436	957 514	508 938	284 469	676 607	37 588	81 589
182 554	81 281	258 747	78 657	74 036	205 461	8 132	34 828
568 147	170 055	574 037	300 093	140 233	582 367	20 557	41 458
27 364	24 416	37 732	9 933	8 860	27 254	529	−276
7 175 832	1 942 629	3 563 539	2 044 839	1 134 428	7 295 246	33 161	273 017
6 256 579	1 727 173	2 836 448	1 728 750	953 909	6 336 415	18 127	189 957
17 738 017	7 371 861	12 786 939	7 566 222	4 946 581	18 439 451	175 904	491 827
13 012 613	6 161 598	7 810 388	4 746 362	3 498 645	13 703 728	100 321	278 035
3 876 663	1 047 172	3 888 871	1 752 920	1 227 234	3 963 138	180 708	370 029
22 783 685	9 223 384	14 845 406	9 084 422	5 550 322	23 563 457	102 958	579 106
22 227 301	8 522 354	13 807 612	8 699 164	5 199 288	22 925 366	133 736	497 611
2 760 479	1 178 482	3 070 005	1 302 112	934 962	2 865 316	86 040	282 410
1 672 568	569 720	1 856 660	836 066	643 306	1 735 913	63 890	169 114
101 756	55 699	132 510	51 382	15 084	129 962	399	12 882
1 988 459	816 866	2 624 085	1 247 096	839 290	2 051 522	140 138	204 491
63 610	75 674	117 544	73 743	85 877	64 167	2 416	−1 209
10 760 782	8 490 564	10 646 989	5 560 388	5 180 389	10 950 273	93 097	486 742
12 414 446	523 027	4 130 411	3 492 182	366 451	12 965 591	12 851	73 744
1 331 294	308 726	1 082 738	412 551	290 465	1 365 080	34 763	172 485

表6-7 独立核算工业企业主要财务指标(规模以上)
(2011)

单位:万元

指 标	Indicators	企业单位数（个） Enterprises (unit)	从业人数（人） Employed Persons (person)	工业总产值 Gross Output Value of Industry
总 计	**Total**	**1 993**	**654 816**	**92 929 060**
按隶属关系分	**By Subordination**			
中央工业	Central	50	60 342	22 777 616
市属工业	Municipal	160	117 519	22 830 509
非中央、市属工业	Local	1 783	476 955	47 320 935
按登记注册类型分	**By Type of Registration**			
内 资	Domestic Funded	1 095	251 660	34 282 161
国 有	State-owned	42	35 832	9 272 542
集 体	Collective-owned	28	3 680	265 044
股份合作制	Share-holding	26	3 190	162 611
联 营	Jointly-operated	13	1 236	60 879
有限责任公司	Companies with Limited Liability	166	50 281	5 185 439
股份有限公司	Companies Limited by Shares	33	25 488	10 043 337
私 营	Private	771	116 437	6 220 793
其 他	Others	16	15 516	3 071 517
港澳台商投资	Hong Kong/Macao/Taiwan Invested	208	74 587	10 490 152
#港澳台商独资	Solely Hong Kong/Macao/Taiwan Funded	118	38 897	7 430 275
外商投资	Foreigner Invested	690	328 569	48 156 747
#外商独资	Solely Foreigner Funded	470	214 080	24 587 705
按轻、重工业分	**By Light/Heavy Industry**			
轻工业	Light Industry	632	188 560	15 655 671
重工业	Heavy Industry	1 361	466 256	77 273 389
按企业规模分	**By Scale of Entrerprises**			
大型企业	Large	92	294 590	61 548 690
中型企业	Medium	324	181 462	14 778 804
小型企业	Small	1 577	178 764	16 601 566

Major Indicators of Industrial Enterprises with Independent Accounting Systems (Above-Certain-Scaled Enterprises)

(10 000 yuan)

工业销售产值 Sales Value of Industry	实收资本 Paid-in Capital	资产总计 Total Assets	流动资产合计 Total Circulating Assets	固定资产合计 Total Fixed Assets	固定资产原价 Original Value of Fixed Assets
91 821 604	**20 504 827**	**93 933 253**	**51 525 923**	**27 824 121**	**52 848 851**
22 656 470	4 645 755	28 762 080	10 360 385	15 105 898	26 909 284
22 523 311	7 351 105	30 686 391	16 767 776	5 549 741	12 035 316
46 641 823	8 507 967	34 484 782	24 397 762	7 168 482	13 904 251
33 976 362	7 736 132	47 472 392	19 564 778	18 057 013	31 085 089
9 273 175	1 947 722	15 799 097	2 120 618	11 939 604	21 055 992
286 308	12 445	183 663	144 380	31 519	66 793
160 106	13 806	118 689	87 501	27 811	49 157
59 595	10 730	58 981	45 979	10 804	30 597
5 095 652	1 871 526	6 230 783	3 094 964	2 509 184	4 194 477
9 918 057	2 104 983	14 515 790	6 797 213	1 351 922	2 528 325
6 113 245	931 213	5 497 672	3 743 086	1 210 094	1 687 598
3 070 223	843 707	5 067 716	3 531 037	976 075	1 472 150
10 464 116	1 999 938	6 599 220	4 468 718	1 447 994	3 328 831
7 485 064	1 346 548	4 007 577	2 899 630	922 656	2 332 124
47 381 126	10 768 757	39 861 641	27 492 428	8 319 114	18 434 931
24 073 233	5 649 693	16 855 830	11 625 875	3 963 987	9 628 786
15 447 796	3 751 640	14 119 232	9 466 954	3 167 646	5 570 459
76 373 808	16 753 187	79 814 021	42 058 969	24 656 475	47 278 392
60 699 148	11 902 265	62 660 043	31 077 044	19 834 653	39 132 192
14 550 767	4 035 277	14 736 921	9 777 716	3 455 253	6 418 444
16 571 689	4 567 285	16 536 289	10 671 163	4 534 215	7 298 215

单位:万元

表 6－7　续表　Continued

指　标	Indicators	本年折旧 Depreciation of the Current Year	负债合计 Total Liabilities	所有者权益 Owner's Equity
总　计	**Total**	**3 217 332**	**45 647 829**	**48 285 425**
按隶属关系分	**By Subordination**			
中央工业	Central	1 631 610	12 393 782	16 368 297
市属工业	Municipal	679 990	13 672 108	17 014 283
非中央、市属工业	Local	905 732	19 581 939	14 902 845
按登记注册类型分	**By Type of Registration**			
内　资	Domestic Funded	1 860 590	17 949 741	29 522 651
国　有	State-owned	1 358 915	4 251 843	11 547 255
集　体	Collective-owned	5 495	119 367	64 296
股份合作制	Share-holding	4 287	56 145	62 545
联　营	Jointly-operated	1 074	35 527	23 455
有限责任公司	Companies with Limited Liability	196 993	3 101 545	3 129 238
股份有限公司	Companies Limited by Shares	140 434	3 676 091	10 839 699
私　营	Private	106 420	3 219 378	2 278 294
其　他	Others	46 974	3 489 846	1 577 870
港澳台商投资	Hong Kong/Macao/Taiwan Invested	187 413	3 729 684	2 869 535
#港澳台商独资	Solely Hong Kong/Macao/Taiwan Funded	112 609	2 308 062	1 699 515
外商投资	Foreigner Invested	1 169 328	23 968 403	15 893 239
#外商独资	Solely Foreigner Funded	606 253	9 797 044	7 058 787
按轻、重工业分	**By Light/Heavy Industry**			
轻工业	Light Industry	299 394	7 244 665	6 874 566
重工业	Heavy Industry	2 917 938	38 403 164	41 410 859
按企业规模分	**By Scale of Entrerprises**			
大型企业	Large	2 451 302	29 150 107	33 509 937
中型企业	Medium	341 057	7 552 626	7 184 295
小型企业	Small	424 973	8 945 096	7 591 193

(10 000 yuan)

主营业务收入 Revenue of Primary Operations	税　金 Tax	#本年应交增值税 Current Year Value-Added Tax Payable	营业利润 Operation Profits	利润总额 Total Profits	应付职工薪酬 Wage/Fringe Benefits
103 178 319	**4 093 996**	**2 498 760**	**7 592 586**	**7 940 422**	**4 706 476**
22 609 084	1 428 323	618 410	224 080	316 742	1 034 522
32 004 106	1 715 381	1 044 552	4 942 755	5 040 508	1 147 710
48 565 129	950 292	835 798	2 425 751	2 583 172	2 524 244
35 341 871	1 928 473	1 023 462	2 836 577	2 996 317	1 866 691
9 493 797	403 191	338 090	159 816	172 820	570 139
298 585	6 717	5 767	6 226	12 505	16 001
161 786	4 936	4 505	13 917	16 322	9 523
59 152	1 749	1 620	2 310	2 607	3 802
5 207 803	223 159	197 393	441 563	479 382	369 315
10 893 295	1 096 996	309 637	1 708 086	1 733 230	271 391
6 158 888	169 318	150 666	319 885	357 028	413 607
3 068 566	22 409	15 784	184 774	222 423	212 913
10 619 269	142 610	116 323	505 710	522 701	412 561
7 620 792	56 990	46 887	246 110	255 572	214 501
57 217 179	2 022 913	1 358 975	4 250 300	4 421 404	2 427 225
25 570 861	468 482	409 901	1 110 051	1 196 710	1 347 303
16 259 029	589 088	526 479	1 229 285	1 300 096	1 046 362
86 919 290	3 504 908	1 972 281	6 363 301	6 640 326	3 660 114
70 465 663	3 090 176	1 612 649	5 320 885	5 520 329	2 584 256
15 478 469	552 559	491 880	1 196 710	1 261 417	1 113 804
17 234 187	451 261	394 231	1 074 991	1 158 676	1 008 416

表6-8 独立核算工业企业经济效益指标(规模以上)
(2011)

指 标	Indicators	工业经济效益综合指数 Composite Index of Industry Economic Results	总资产贡献率(%) Total Assets Contribution Ratio(%)
总 计	**Total**	**290.1**	**14.5**
按隶属关系分	**By Subordination**		
中央工业	Central	540.2	6.7
市属工业	Municipal	510.8	24.5
非中央、市属工业	Local	198.5	12.1
按登记注册类型分	**By Registration Categories**		
内 资	Domestic Funded	274.5	11.4
国 有	State-owned	499.7	3.8
集 体	Collective-owned	179.1	12.7
股份合作制	Share-holding	191.1	19.9
联 营	Jointly-operated	150.0	8.6
有限责任公司	Companies with Limited Liability	268.8	10.0
股份有限公司	Companies Limited by Shares	464.8	20.7
私 营	Private	165.2	11.3
其 他	Others	178.8	11.0
港澳台商投资	Hong Kong/Macao/Taiwan Invested	210.1	11.3
#港澳台商独资	Solely Hong Kong/Macao/Taiwan Funded	206.5	8.9
外商投资	Foreigner Invested	321.8	18.7
#外商独资	Solely Foreigner Funded	211.0	11.5
按轻、重工业分	**By Light/Heavy Industry**		
轻工业	Light Industry	229.8	15.5
重工业	Heavy Industry	314.5	14.3
按企业规模分	**By Scale of Enterprises**		
大型企业	Large	368.0	15.2
中型企业	Medium	229.5	14.5
小型企业	Small	214.5	11.8

Economic Results Indicators of Industrial Enterprise with Independent Accounting Systems(Above-Certain-Scaled Enterprises)

资本保值增值率(%) Ratio of Capital Holding and Adding(%)	资产负债率(%) Ratio of Capital to Liabilities(%)	流动资产周转率(次) Turnover Period of Circulating Assets(time)	成本费用利润率(%) After-tax Profit/Cost(%)	工业全员劳动生产率(元/人) Overall Industrial Labor Productivity (yuan/person)	工业产品销售率(%) Sales Rate of Industrial Products(%)
114.5	**48.6**	**2.0**	**8.2**	**283 068**	**98.8**
106.7	43.1	2.2	1.5	760 461	99.5
123.5	44.6	1.9	17.5	558 131	98.7
114.2	56.8	2.0	5.6	156 088	98.6
117.1	37.8	1.8	8.9	265 383	99.1
105.6	26.9	4.5	1.8	663 238	100.0
113.2	65.0	2.1	4.3	127 359	108.0
124.3	47.3	1.8	10.4	90 206	98.5
109.0	60.2	1.3	4.6	105 706	97.9
115.2	58.4	1.2	9.4	266 619	98.9
131.3	25.3	1.6	16.7	501 993	98.8
126.5	58.6	1.6	6.1	103 119	98.3
106.4	18.5	1.8	6.6	123 812	106.6
115.5	56.5	2.4	5.1	173 695	99.8
112.9	57.6	2.6	3.4	181 790	100.7
109.8	60.1	2.1	8.4	321 233	98.4
114.2	58.1	2.2	4.9	179 670	97.9
111.6	51.3	1.7	8.5	183 808	98.7
115.0	48.1	2.1	8.2	323 087	98.8
115.5	46.5	2.3	8.4	403 936	98.6
114.0	51.2	1.6	8.8	186 857	98.5
110.6	54.1	1.6	7.1	180 594	99.8

表6-9 独立核算大中型工业企业主要指标
(2011)

单位:万元

指 标	Indicators	企业单位数(个) Enterprises (unit)	从业人数(人) Average Number of Employed Persons (person)	工业总产值 Gross Output Value of Industry
总 计	**Total**	**416**	**476 052**	**76 327 494**
按隶属关系分	**By Subordination**			
中央工业	Central	27	57 240	22 508 129
市属工业	Municipal	76	106 200	20 580 860
非中央、市属工业	Local	313	312 612	33 238 505
按登记注册类型分	**Type of Registration**			
内 资	Domstic Funded	160	150 829	26 607 006
国 有	State-owned	16	32 383	8 950 269
集 体	Collective-owned	2	774	39 382
股份合作制	Share-holding	2	656	12 567
联 营	Jointly-operated			
有限责任公司	Companies with Limited Liability	53	48 432	5 935 410
股份有限公司	Companies Limited by Shares	15	23 147	9 734 945
私 营	Private	71	44 921	1 921 412
其他内资	Other Domestic Investment	1	516	13 022
港澳台商投资	Hong Kong/Macao/Taiwan Invested	60	54 894	8 887 940
#港澳台商独资	Solely Hong Kong/Macao/Taiwan Funded	30	26 256	6 348 843
外商投资	Foreigner Invested	196	270 329	40 832 547
#外商独资	Solely Foreigner Funded	122	174 067	19 522 568
按轻、重工业分	**By Light/Heavy Industry**			
轻工业	Light Industry	155	132 099	11 418 181
重工业	Heavy Industry	261	343 953	64 909 313
按从业人数分	**By Number of Employees**			
5 000 人及以上	≥5 000 persons	3	58 139	14 872 557
3 000 ~ 4 999 人	3 000 ~ 4 999 persons	12	46 218	11 294 708
1 000 ~ 2 999 人	1 000 ~ 2 999 persons	97	220 238	36 532 051
999 及以下	≤ 999 persons	304	151 457	13 628 178
按工业总产值分	**By Gross Output Value of Industry**			
5 亿元及以上	≥500 million yuan	175	343 739	71 508 200
10000 ~ 49999 万元	100 ~ 499.99 million yuan	179	109 531	4 405 382
5 000 ~ 9 999 万元	50 ~ 99.99 million yuan	46	17 367	350 635
5 000 万元以下	<50 million yuan	16	5 415	63 277
按固定资产原价分	**By Original Value of Fixed Assets**			
5 亿元及以上	≥500 million yuan	71	219 506	53 184 107
10000 ~ 49999 万元	100 ~ 499.99 million yuan	150	146 532	14 546 434
5 000 ~ 9 999 万元	50 ~ 99.99 million yuan	80	48 683	5 975 549
1 000 ~ 4 999 万元	10 ~ 49.99 milion yuan	86	43 866	2 283 438
1 000 万元以下	<10 million yuan	29	17 465	337 966
按利税总额分	**By Profits and Taxes**			
1 亿元及以上	≥100 million yuan	92	188 939	45 942 564
5 000 ~ 9 999 万元	50 ~ 99.99 milion yuan	36	36 291	3 258 520
1 000 ~ 4 999 万元	10 ~ 49.99 milion yuan	108	88 324	7 511 358
1 000 万元以下	<10 million yuan	180	162 498	19 615 052

Major Indicators of Large and Medium Industrial Enterprises with Independent Accounting Systems

(10 000 yuan)

工业销售产值 Sales Value of Industry	固定资产原价 Original Value of Fixed Assets	资产总计 Total Assets	固定资产合计 Total Fixed Assets	流动资产合计 Total Floating Assets	主营业务收入 Revenue of of Floating Assets	利润总额 Total Profits
75 249 915	**45 550 636**	**77 396 964**	**23 289 906**	**40 854 760**	**85 944 132**	**6 781 746**
22 383 966	26 749 260	28 477 769	15 038 055	10 166 830	22 337 048	305 130
20 266 735	9 476 172	27 478 679	3 845 804	15 544 894	29 669 914	4 845 449
32 599 214	9 325 204	21 440 516	4 406 047	15 143 036	33 937 170	1 631 167
26 340 038	27 075 602	39 624 280	15 332 514	15 108 460	27 499 614	2 550 767
8 959 142	20 880 518	15 447 726	11 850 089	1 891 562	9 177 809	164 446
41 826	6 359	15 710	3 465	11 994	46 717	876
11 593	6 694	12 147	3 481	8 237	11 593	568
5 822 202	3 192 519	8 308 521	1 758 590	5 502 575	5 920 459	525 603
9 619 422	2 419 939	14 112 365	1 285 551	6 568 224	10 452 677	1 713 314
1 873 071	561 697	1 714 442	425 676	1 118 162	1 877 577	145 210
12 783	7 875	13 369	5 662	7 706	12 783	752
8 866 748	2 540 241	4 942 967	986 243	3 414 265	8 992 786	444 171
6 411 633	1 838 540	2 884 507	585 928	2 205 798	6 512 019	208 942
40 043 129	15 934 793	32 829 718	6 971 149	22 332 035	49 451 732	3 786 808
19 016 104	7 952 860	12 318 422	3 012 421	8 238 355	20 141 519	784 968
11 223 086	3 950 300	9 958 438	2 235 958	6 586 373	11 830 924	1 031 047
64 026 829	41 600 336	67 438 526	21 053 948	34 268 387	74 113 208	5 750 699
14 664 075	20 047 486	17 114 118	11 252 372	4 507 823	14 770 125	38 740
11 192 695	3 643 005	6 333 150	1 900 277	3 591 693	11 263 312	326 216
35 914 466	15 989 322	40 387 408	7 002 889	23 713 487	45 582 214	5 259 353
13 478 679	5 870 823	13 562 288	3 134 368	9 041 757	14 328 481	1 157 437
70 517 948	43 050 661	71 681 136	21 843 968	37 545 406	81 028 635	6 461 476
4 318 804	2 230 703	5 224 387	1 315 242	2 970 564	4 474 275	307 750
351 783	234 852	428 605	110 253	300 874	379 770	15 494
61 380	34 420	62 836	20 443	37 916	61 452	-2 974
52 340 157	41 119 299	60 967 839	20 789 989	28 528 135	61 969 484	5 237 231
14 364 211	3 558 176	11 367 257	1 995 612	8 157 103	15 258 046	1 181 024
6 011 232	593 471	3 287 380	342 555	2 728 632	6 085 430	230 154
2 201 722	265 878	1 583 917	150 113	1 284 970	2 296 831	112 165
332 593	13 812	190 571	11 637	155 920	334 341	21 172
45 618 582	31 077 154	54 064 422	16 024 056	27 347 336	55 504 235	6 605 663
3 111 024	956 793	2 664 108	621 350	1 831 287	3 338 772	258 070
7 218 071	4 223 625	9 640 021	2 715 515	5 728 581	7 490 326	277 757
19 302 238	9 293 064	11 028 413	3 928 985	5 947 556	19 610 799	-359 744

表6-10 港澳台及外商投资工业企业主要指标

(2011)

单位:万元

指 标	Indicators	企业单位数(个) Enterprises (unit)	从业人数(人) Employed Persons (person)	工业总产值 Gross Output Value of Industry
总 计	**Total**	**898**	**403 156**	**58 646 899**
按登记注册类型分	**By Type of Registration**			
与港澳台商合资经营企业	China-Hong Kong/Macao/Taiwan Joint Venture	76	26 053	1 962 472
与港澳台商合作经营企业	China-Hong Kong/Macao/Taiwan Cooperative	9	3 297	122 677
港澳台商独资企业	Solely Hong Kong/Macao/Taiwan Funded	118	38 897	7 430 275
港澳台商投资股份有限公司	Hong Kong/Macao/Taiwan Investment Companies Limited by Shares	4	6 172	971 487
其他港澳台商投资	Other HongKong/Macao/Taiwan Investment	1	168	3 242
中外合资经营企业	Sino-Foreign Jointly-operated	197	91 364	19 142 263
中外合作经营企业	Sino-Foreign Cooperative	16	7 753	568 021
外商独资企业	Solely Foreigner Funded	470	214 080	24 587 705
外商投资股份有限公司	Foreign Investment Company Limited by Shares	6	15 344	3 852 506
其他外商投资	Other Foreign Investment	1	28	6 251
按行业分	**By Sector**			
农副食品加工业	Processing of Agricultural Side-line Food	11	2 042	745 821
食品制造业	Food Manufacturing	12	4 710	948 203
酒、饮料和精制茶制造业	Manufacturing of Liquor, Beverage and Refined Tea	5	4 620	298 382
烟草制品业	Tobacco Products	1	500	29 463
纺织业	Textile Industry	11	1 871	124 761
纺织服装、服饰业	Textile, Clothing and Accessories	47	24 108	449 616
皮革、毛皮、羽毛及其制品和制鞋业	Leather, Fur, Feather and their Products and Shoe-making	5	894	27 036
木材加工及木、竹、藤、棕、草制品业	Timber-Processing, Bamboo, Cane, Palm Fiber and Straw Products	4	842	29 466
家具制造业	Furniture Manufacturing	6	8 651	782 597
造纸及纸制品业	Paper-making and Paper Products	16	4 382	376 814

Major Indicators of HK/Macao/Taiwan & Overseas Invested Industrial Enterprises

(10 000 yuan)

工业销售产值 Sales Value of Industry	固定资产原价 Original Value of Fixed Assets	资产总计 Total Assets	负债总计 Total Liabilities	实收资本 Paid-in Capital	主营业务收入 Revenue of of Floating Assets	税金 Tax	利润总额 Total Profits
57 845 242	**21 763 762**	**46 460 861**	**27 698 088**	**14 725 744**	**67 836 448**	**2 165 523**	**4 944 106**
1 944 068	764 867	1 908 849	1 035 076	476 351	1 930 962	77 847	213 665
124 233	82 307	130 857	109 439	43 933	121 574	3 720	848
7 485 064	2 332 124	4 007 577	2 308 062	1 346 548	7 620 792	56 990	255 572
907 509	146 875	548 822	274 936	132 815	942 699	4 000	52 194
3 242	2 658	3 116	2 171	291	3 242	53	422
18 884 615	5 793 523	15 037 264	9 268 254	3 619 616	27 220 342	1 468 612	3 118 262
545 553	264 259	530 983	290 871	2 174 498	656 722	22 850	39 771
24 073 233	9 628 786	16 855 830	9 797 043	5 649 693	25 570 861	468 482	1 196 710
3 871 474	2 748 310	7 433 027	4 608 998	1 281 903	3 762 782	62 585	65 068
6 251	53	4 536	3 238	96	6 472	384	1 594
783 813	93 506	629 407	354 941	71 929	891 424	13 109	34 167
878 655	199 941	639 490	479 483	149 795	895 273	73 385	123 253
292 834	240 494	228 793	155 036	141 820	371 815	12 247	- 8 196
29 463	46 503	52 542	10 561	28 974	29 843	4 827	9 033
127 812	43 622	106 924	66 014	36 645	124 572	1 255	5 833
444 936	106 684	327 997	211 927	76 519	461 159	13 885	6 342
26 559	6 994	16 300	14 248	5 885	26 559	124	3 416
29 901	21 828	44 330	36 832	21 834	31 070	589	766
783 296	129 981	562 610	350 117	51 159	780 807	33 287	123 528
369 983	371 295	462 574	255 110	193 295	371 626	7 698	9 561

单位:万元　　　　表6－10　续表　Continued

指　标	Indicators	企业单位数(个) Enterprises (unit)	从业人数(人) Employed Persons (person)	工业总产值 Gross Output Value of Industry
印刷业、记录媒介的复制	Printing and Record Medium Reproduction	10	2 297	132 289
文教、工美、体育和娱乐用品制造业	Manufacturing of Cultural, Educational, Arts, Sports and Leisure Products	17	4 600	171 679
石油加工、炼焦及核燃料加工业	Petroleum Processing, Coke Products and Processing of Nuclear Fuel	8	1 106	266 775
化学原料及化学制品制造业	Raw Chemical Materials and Chemical Products	65	15 136	3 934 054
医药制造业	Medicine Manufacturing	28	12 725	1 265 572
橡胶和塑料制品业	Rubber and Plastic Products	62	13 201	542 728
非金属矿物制品业	Nonmetal Mineral Products	36	6 356	513 479
黑色金属冶炼及压延加工业	Smelting and Pressing of Ferrous Metal	6	1 731	273 964
有色金属冶炼及压延加工业	Smelting and Pressing of Nonferrous Metal	7	1 258	418 115
金属制品业	Metal Products	43	10 038	848 404
通用设备制造业	General Purpose Equipment Manufacturing	124	32 480	5 303 045
专用设备制造业	Specialized Equipment Manufacturing	78	20 266	2 725 600
汽车制造业	Automobile Manufacturing	61	37 424	11 289 595
铁路、船舶、航空航天和其他运输设备制造业	Manufacturing of Railway, Ships, Aeronautics &Astronautics, and Other Transportation Equipment	22	4 045	404 811
电气机械及器材制造业	Electric Equipment and Machinery	80	31 205	3 101 532
计算机、通信和其他电子设备制造业	Manufacturing of Computers, Telecommunication and other Electronic Equipment	89	140 798	22 444 749
仪器仪表制造业	Manufacturing of Instrument and Apparatus	28	8 699	772 292
工艺品及其他制造业	Handicrafts and Other Production	8	4 731	283 015
金属制品、机械和设备修理业	Repairing of Metal Products, Machine and Equipment	5	862	50 577
电力、热力生产和供应业	Production and Supply of Electricity and Heating Power	2	232	24 599
水的生产和供应业	Production and Supply of Tap Water	1	1 346	67 870

(10 000 yuan)

工业销售产值 Sales Value of Industry	固定资产原价 Original Value of Fixed Assets	资产总计 Total Assets	负债总计 Total Liabilities	实收资本 Paid-in Capital	主营业务收入 Revenue of of Floating Assets	税金 Tax	利润总额 Total Profits
131 139	96 676	130 124	69 812	35 311	131 123	6 848	14 729
171 215	34 742	127 119	77 787	20 882	166 469	869	3 792
275 233	38 941	129 856	58 419	35 128	276 240	9 156	21 501
3 832 595	1 429 139	3 094 893	1 613 204	909 393	4 140 260	121 912	266 447
1 179 141	420 677	1 455 175	732 455	412 952	1 219 580	87 804	102 558
562 598	314 158	488 037	190 791	188 441	575 731	17 207	23 642
499 856	535 294	872 377	382 407	394 478	564 287	14 736	37 059
252 036	402 106	373 706	240 857	344 893	283 243	9 602	13 656
424 516	123 204	380 420	285 521	85 197	437 487	3 986	6 653
849 084	277 732	702 421	365 456	202 474	884 213	20 259	80 401
5 325 174	3 049 679	7 446 550	4 425 382	1 204 964	5 587 428	154 843	286 436
2 646 319	603 528	2 135 625	1 180 840	423 190	2 683 096	117 585	267 727
11 102 582	2 745 797	8 586 514	5 863 454	1 362 063	19 222 797	1 284 596	2 684 978
384 773	86 776	351 445	177 061	87 241	410 824	5 590	25 126
3 135 277	731 403	2 007 766	1 088 535	489 760	3 217 881	44 226	195 016
22 140 948	8 480 374	13 468 420	8 289 478	5 294 859	22 848 045	83 644	470 162
771 012	170 934	585 912	245 650	148 082	791 084	10 673	83 036
263 383	273 359	385 114	102 731	90 932	271 430	2 537	44 371
50 577	74 562	101 930	67 366	78 701	50 574	1 874	
23 274	98 067	101 907	7 054	29 800	33 198	1 153	12 932
57 260	515 771	464 586	299 560	152 000	57 314	6 018	26

表6-11 私营工业企业主要指标
(2011)

单位:万元

指 标	Indicators	企业单位数(个) Enterprises (unit)	从业人数(人) Average Number of Employed Persons (person)	工业总产值 Gross Output Value of Industry
总 计	**Total**	**771**	**116 437**	**6 220 793**
按轻、重工业分	**By Light/Heavy Industry**			
轻工业	Light Industry	255	42 825	1 932 628
重工业	Heavy Industry	516	73 612	4 288 165
按主要工业行业分	**By Main Sector**			
#农副食品加工业	Processing of Agricultural Side-line Food	6	5 317	183 311
食品制造业	Food Producing	6	699	27 019
纺织业	Textile Industry	21	2 223	115 078
纺织服装、鞋、帽制造业	Manufacturing of Textile Clothing, Shoes and Hats	63	10 257	307 114
皮革、毛皮、羽毛及其制品和制鞋业	Leather, Fur, Feather and their Products and Shoe-making	12	2 793	63 082
木材加工及木、竹、藤、棕、草制品业	Timber-processing, Bamboo, Cane, Palm Fiber and Straw Products	4	384	28 894
家具制造业	Furniture Making	11	1 803	44 160
造纸及纸制品业	Paper-making and Paper Products	16	2 218	103 887
印刷业和记录媒介的复制	Printing and Record Medium Reproduction	22	4 478	160 373
文教、工美、体育和娱乐用品制造业	Manufacturing of Cultural, Educational, Arts, Sports and Leisure Products	10	1 579	186 316
石油加工、炼焦及核燃料加工业	Petroleum Processing, Coke Products and Processing of Nuclear Fuel	4	186	30 117
化学原料及化学制品制造业	Raw Chemical Material and Chemical Products	34	2 923	236 022
医药制造业	Medicine Manufacturing	15	2 882	295 066
化学纤维制造业	Chemical Fiber Manufacturing	1	50	7 724
橡胶和塑料制品业	Rubber and Plastic Products	80	9 005	460 345
非金属矿物制品业	Nonmetal Mineral Products	32	2 894	153 532
黑色金属冶炼及压延加工业	Smelting and Pressing of Ferrous Metal	21	1 988	148 647
有色金属冶炼及压延加工业	Smelting and Pressing of Nonferrous Metal	19	911	181 236
金属制品业	Metal Products	78	9 738	438 987
通用设备制造业	Manufacturing of General Purpose Equipment	84	11 667	715 733
专用设备制造业	Specialized Equipment Manufacturing	36	5 107	314 100
汽车制造业	Automobile Manufacturing	48	10 774	455 272
铁路、船舶、航空航天和其他运输设备造业	Manufacturing of Railway, Ship, Aviation and Aerospace, and other Transportation Equipment	25	4 611	150 766
电气机械及器材制造业	Manufacturing of Electrical Machinery and Equipment	92	12 265	1 089 759
计算机、通信和其他电子设备制造业	Manufacturing of Telecommunications Equipment, Computers and Other Electronic Equipment	16	5 847	226 996
仪器仪表制造业	Manufacturing of Instrument, Meter and Office Machineries	8	939	40 417
其他制造业	Handicrafts and Other Production	3	543	28 640
金属制品、机械和设备修理业	Recycling of Abandoned Resources and Wastes	4	2 356	28 200

Major Indicators of PNA Private Industrial Enterprises

(10 000 yuan)

工业销售产值 Sales Value of Industry	固定资产原价 Original Value of Fixed Assets	资产总计 Total Assets	负债总计 Total Liabilities	实收资本 Paid-in Capital	主营业务收入 Revenue of of Floating Assets	税金 Tax	利润总额 Total Profits
6 113 245	**1 687 598**	**5 497 672**	**3 219 378**	**931 214**	**6 158 888**	**169 318**	**357 028**
1 899 739	582 662	1 507 877	831 274	270 798	1 901 276	56 035	93 248
4 213 506	1 104 936	3 989 795	2 388 104	660 416	4 257 612	113 283	263 780
183 247	39 623	68 055	39 049	12 161	183 783	2 817	4 932
28 117	11 818	25 383	12 994	3 935	27 002	1 356	1 280
116 417	33 160	104 048	70 884	11 513	116 801	2 132	1 415
299 172	83 132	196 372	141 594	26 827	301 215	7 503	2 249
64 842	10 591	38 613	26 540	6 693	63 887	2 159	2 321
28 623	4 077	13 447	8 142	3 132	27 952	562	544
42 109	7 582	40 698	21 025	5 923	40 754	1 033	1 120
100 698	46 767	94 704	57 573	7 376	103 075	3 079	2 900
159 392	77 506	146 792	84 261	22 853	160 404	6 127	13 662
186 226	18 748	77 369	39 818	18 310	182 293	4 212	12 285
28 451	3 565	27 369	16 185	8 958	65 845	247	396
234 900	54 108	227 538	73 361	38 223	241 192	8 566	24 354
273 052	102 495	326 566	154 438	106 945	283 281	11 314	23 702
7 724	432	659	351	50	7 724	61	47
460 289	139 460	411 523	216 682	57 600	461 696	13 777	28 911
149 838	60 891	156 870	104 530	31 603	155 945	6 386	6 378
148 922	51 091	124 447	81 042	20 617	147 226	2 306	1 663
183 816	16 794	114 870	90 521	9 517	183 553	1 488	800
423 993	140 101	388 929	231 850	49 888	420 287	12 498	19 334
695 759	189 848	644 885	342 510	112 446	693 083	19 967	63 310
300 226	73 717	331 474	187 209	47 217	293 269	8 174	27 839
443 642	210 370	603 173	406 265	122 103	438 110	16 116	37 076
146 583	54 175	173 752	118 757	31 626	145 155	5 327	6 050
1 083 506	189 910	906 163	537 919	145 480	1 085 318	21 051	57 794
225 127	50 237	177 731	107 704	21 588	230 553	5 529	11 255
41 736	9 271	48 187	27 929	5 550	41 155	2 383	4 270
28 640	5 778	11 129	7 173	2 580	28 615	501	161
28 200	2 352	16 926	13 072	500	29 715	2 647	980

表6-12　工业企业单位数和从业人员平均人数的各种分组
Classification of Industrial Enterprises and Average Number of Persons Employed

指　标 Indicators		企业单位数(个) Enterprises (unit)		从业人员平均人数(人) Average Number of Persons Employed (person)	
		2010	2011	2010	2011
总　计	**Total**	**8 872**	**6 469**	**767 898**	**794 901**
按隶属关系分	**By Subordination**				
中央工业	Central	58	55	67 713	60 265
市属工业	Municipal	177	174	97 279	119 672
非中央、市属工业	Local	8 637	6 240	602 906	614 964
按登记注册类型分	**By Type of Registration**				
内　资	Domestic Funded	7 481	5 223	412 538	367 428
国　有	State-owned	57	50	37 482	36 321
集　体	Collective-owned	272	177	10 990	9 048
股份合作	Share-holding	138	108	8 448	6 665
联　营	Jointly Operated	36	30	2 483	1 803
有限责任公司	Companies with Limited Liabilities	345	304	75 184	70 958
股份有限公司	Companies Limited by Shares	51	52	28 315	26 381
私　营	Private	6 565	4 489	248 584	215 443
其　他	Others	17	13	1 052	809
港澳台商投资	HK/Macao/Taiwan Invested	340	298	75 035	79 672
#港澳台商独资	Solely HK/Macao/Taiwan Funded	198	176	38 733	41 780
外商投资	Foreigner Invested	1 051	948	280 325	347 801
#外商独资	Solely Foreigner Funded	704	647	182 616	227 246
按轻、重工业分	**By Light/Heavy Industry**				
轻工业	Light Industry	3 638	2 679	265 918	261 073
重工业	Heavy Industry	5 234	3 790	501 980	533 828
按企业规模分	**By Scale of Enterprises**				
大型企业	Large	31	92	155 961	298 999
中型企业	Medium	369	324	244 972	183 134
小型企业	Small	8 472	6 053	366 965	312 768

注：表中没有注明的即为全社会统计口径，后续各表相同。
Note: The fields that have not been specified in this table have been counted with the total statistical approuch. The tables followed are the same.

表6-13　规模以上工业企业分行业能源消费情况

Energy Consumption of Above-scaled Industrial Enterprises by Sector (2011)

指　标	Indicators	企业单位数（个）Enterprises (in Number)	综合能源消费量（吨标准煤）Comprehensive Energy Consumption (tons of standard coal)	产值能耗（吨标准煤/万元）Energy Consumption of Production Value (tons of standard coal/10 000 yuan
总　计	**Total**	**1 985**	**8 941 263**	**0.097**
农副食品加工业	Processing of Agricultural Side-line Food	19	61 320	0.067
食品制造业	Food Manufacturing	25	36 782	0.038
饮料制造业	Beverage Manufacturing	6	33 481	0.109
烟草制品业	Tobacco Products	1	3 644	0.124
纺织业	Textile Industry	81	72 327	0.133
纺织服装、鞋、帽制造业	Textile Products, Clothes, Shoes and Hats	90	42 816	0.029
皮革、毛皮、羽毛(绒)及其制品业	Leather, Fur, Down & Related Products	17	3 487	0.045
木材加工及木、竹、藤、棕、草制品业	Timber-processing, Bamboo, Cane, Palm Fiber and Straw Products	10	5 004	0.040
家具制造业	Furniture Manufacturing	18	20 061	0.027
造纸及纸制品业	Paper-making and Paper Products	39	176 565	0.328
印刷业和记录媒介的复制	Printing and Record Pressing	48	39 817	0.087
文教体育用品制造业	Stationery, Educational and Sports Goods	24	10 274	0.049
石油加工、炼焦及核燃料加工业	Petroleum Processing, Coke Products and Processing of Nuclear Fuel	17	2 403 546	0.314
化学原料及化学制品制造业	Raw Chemical Materials and Chemical Products	124	650 964	0.122
医药制造业	Medicine Manufacturing	57	125 531	0.060
化学纤维制造业	Chemical Fiber Manufacturing	4	814	0.050
橡胶制品业	Rubber Products	21	34 205	0.247
塑料制品业	Plastic Products	138	157 175	0.149
非金属矿物制品业	Nonmetal Mineral Products	89	220 447	0.203
黑色金属冶炼及压延加工业	Smelting and Pressing of Ferrous Metal	16	71 891	0.223
有色金属冶炼及压延加工业	Smelting and Pressing of Nonferrous Metal	36	69 732	0.082
金属制品业	Metal Products	142	92 953	0.062
通用设备制造业	General Purpose Equipment Manufacturing	251	290 709	0.044
专用设备制造业	Special Purpose Equipment Manufacturing	132	73 322	0.020
交通运输设备制造业	Transportation Equipment Manufacturing	202	655 625	0.036
电气机械及器材制造业	Electric Equipment and Machinery	184	138 960	0.030
通信设备、计算机及其他电子设备制造业	Manufacturing of Electronic and Telecommunications Equipment, Computersand Other Electronic Equipment	117	650 731	0.029
仪器仪表及文化、办公用机械制造业	Instruments, Meters, Cultural and Office Equipment	40	16 565	0.018
工艺品及其他制造业	Handicrafts and other Productions	21	35 378	0.072
废弃资源和废旧材料回收加工业	Recycling of Abandoned Recources and Wastes	2	186	0.013
电力、热力的生产和供应业	Production and Supply of Electricity and Heating Power	9	2 536 397	0.318
燃气生产和供应业	Production and Supply of Gas	2	167 320	0.500
水的生产和供应业	Production and Supply of Tap Water	3	43 234	0.430

表6-14 规模以上工业企业分行业主要能源品种消费情况

(2011)

指标	Indicators	原 煤(吨) Raw Coal (tons)	洗精煤(吨) Cleaned Coal (tons)	其他洗煤(吨) Other Washed Coals(tons)
总 计	**Total**	**12 673 752**	**766 002**	**43 349**
农副食品加工业	Processing of Agricultural Side-line Food	32 856	991	
食品制造业	Food Manufacturing	4 677	5 723	
饮料制造业	Beverage Manufacturing			
烟草制品业	Tobacco Products			
纺织业	Textile Industry	33 007	7 094	51
纺织服装、鞋、帽制造业	Textile Products, Clothes, Shoes and Hats	18 746	20	8
皮革、毛皮、羽毛(绒)及其制品业	Leather, Fur, Down & Related Products	53	78	35
木材加工及木、竹、藤、棕、草制品业	Timber-Processing, Bamboo, Cane, Palm Fiber and Straw Products	5	32	
家具制造业	Furniture Manufacturing	536		
造纸及纸制品业	Paper-making and Paper Products	150 727	11 854	4 388
印刷业和记录媒介的复制	Printing and Record Medium Reproduction			734
文教体育用品制造业	Stationery, Educational and Sports Goods			
石油加工、炼焦及核燃料加工业	Petroleum Processing, Coke Products and Processing of Nuclear Fuel			
化学原料及化学制品制造业	Raw Chemical Materials and Chemical Products	1 051 608		4 900
医药制造业	Medicine Manufacturing	65 454		
化学纤维制造业	Chemical Fiber Manufacturing			
橡胶制品业	Rubber Products	17 542	1 914	1 940
塑料制品业	Plastic Products		7 300	29 271
非金属矿物制品业	Nonmetal Mineral Products	15 110		720
黑色金属冶炼及压延加工业	Smelting and Pressing of Ferrous Metal	4 743	593	804
有色金属冶炼及压延加工业	Smelting and Pressing of Nonferrous Metal	26 362		
金属制品业	Metal Products	3 524		78
通用设备制造业	General Purpose Equipment Manufacturing	1 191	4 931	420
专用设备制造业	Specialized Equipment Manufacturing			
交通运输设备制造业	Transportation Equipment Manufacturing	9 124	21	
电气机械及器材制造业	Electrical Machinery and Equipment	5 388		
通信设备、计算机及其他电子设备制造业	Manufacturing of Telecommunications Equipment, Computers and Other Electronic Equipment			
仪器仪表及文化、办公用机械制造业	Instrument, Meter, and Office Machines	18		
工艺品及其他制造业	Handicrafts and other Productions	2 420		
废弃资源和废旧材料回收加工业	Recycling of Abandoned Resources and Wastes			
电力、热力的生产和供应业	Production and Supply of Electricity and Heating Power	11 230 661		
燃气生产和供应业	Production and Supply of Gas		725 451	
水的生产和供应业	Production and Supply of Tap Water			

Consumption of Main Kinds of Engery in Above-scaled Industrial Enterprises by Sector

煤制品(吨) Coal Products (tons)	焦炭(吨) Coke (tons)	焦炉煤气(万立方米) Coke Oven Gas (10 000 cu·m)	发生炉煤气(万立方米) Generator Gas (10 000 cu·m)	天然气(气态)(万立方米) Natural Gas (gas state) (10 000 cu·m)	液化天然气(液态)(吨) LNG(liquid state) (tons)	原油(吨) Crude Oil (tons)
18 469	**82 977**	**22 545**	**21 610**	**44 376**	**2 596**	**10 468 999**
				166		
				128		
				6		
				3		
				167		
				36	10	
				5		
				93		
	78			124		
				163		
				40		
				646		10 468 999
16 449				1 064		
			29	258		
				12		
290				3 408		
1 730	327			2 361		
	1 540		2 936	26		
	56			631		
	2 832			558	1 393	
				346	1	
			5 675	4 451	1 192	
				242		
			50	2 261		
				6		
				313		
			148	14 653		
	78 144	22 545	12 772	12 209		

表6－14 续表1 Continued

指标	Indicators	汽油(吨) Gasoline (tons)	煤油(吨) Kerosene (tons)	柴油(吨) Diesel Oil (tons)	燃料油(吨) Fuel Oil (tons)
总 计	**Total**	**50 249**	**24 350**	**126 929**	**164 822**
农副食品加工业	Processing of Agricultural Side-line Food	319		2 859	823
食品制造业	Food Manufacturing	292		845	161
饮料制造业	Beverage Manufacturing	111		1 489	1 923
烟草制品业	Tobacco Products				
纺织业	Textile Industry	1 452		1 253	145
纺织服装、鞋、帽制造业	Textile Products, Clothes, Shoes and Hats	1 769		1 463	17
皮革、毛皮、羽毛(绒)及其制品业	Leather, Fur, Down & Related Products	516		35	
木材加工及木、竹、藤、棕、草制品业	Timber-Processing, Bamboo, Cane, Palm Fiber and Straw Products	104		154	
家具制造业	Furniture Manufacturing	249	1	297	
造纸及纸制品业	Paper-making and Paper Products	716	11	2 141	971
印刷业和记录媒介的复制	Printing and Record Medium Reproduction	1 660	2	1 796	1 034
文教体育用品制造业	Stationery, Educational and Sports Goods	740		237	
石油加工、炼焦及核燃料加工业	Petroleum Processing, Coke Products and Processing of Nuclear Fuel	706	20 731	37 131	50 751
化学原料及化学制品制造业	Raw Chemical Materials and Chemical Products	4 155	2 990	6 594	25 872
医药制造业	Medicine Manufacturing	830	1	1 674	
化学纤维制造业	Chemical Fiber Manufacturing	34		4	
橡胶制品业	Rubber Products	516		124	
塑料制品业	Plastic Products	2 392		2 568	203
非金属矿物制品业	Nonmetal Mineral Products	1 260	5	9 914	1 668
黑色金属冶炼及压延加工业	Smelting and Pressing of Ferrous Metal	158	6	277	205
有色金属冶炼及压延加工业	Smelting and Pressing of Nonferrous Metal	387	354	3 443	2 752
金属制品业	Metal Products	2 450	56	3 494	1 292
通用设备制造业	General Purpose Equipment Manufacturing	4 939	83	19 122	1 509
专用设备制造业	Specialized Equipment Manufacturing	2 398	39	727	230
交通运输设备制造业	Transportation Equipment Manufacturing	10 890	71	20 387	16 274
电气机械及器材制造业	Electrical Machinery and Equipment	2 854		2 222	65
通信设备、计算机及其他电子设备制造业	Manufacturing of Telecommunications Equipment, Computers and Other Electronic Equipment	1 655		428	
仪器仪表及文化、办公用机械制造业	Instrument, Meter, and Office Machines	311		120	
工艺品及其他制造业	Handicrafts and other Productions	298		2 900	
废弃资源和废旧材料回收加工业	Recycling of Abandoned Resources and Wastes	4			
电力、热力的生产和供应业	Production and Supply of Electricity and Heating Power	5 420		2 390	58 927
燃气生产和供应业	Production and Supply of Gas	426		819	
水的生产和供应业	Production and Supply of Tap Water	238		22	

液化石油气（吨）LPG（tons）	炼厂干气（吨）Dry Gas from Refineries（tons）	其他石油制品（吨）Other Petrolium Products（tons）	热　力（百万千焦）Heating Power（1 million KJ）	电　力（万千瓦时）Electric Power（10 000 KWH）	其他燃料（吨标准煤）Other Fuels（tons/standard coal）
47 400	**241 431**	**1 101 155**	**16 400 799**	**1 832 963**	**66 961**
2			114 874	8 286	
32			151 364	6 506	
337			100 671	8 104	
			30 513	855	
20		1	125 426	10 564	
4			4 550	7 857	
8				825	
				1 127	
73		1	1 301	5 672	
47			51 548	13 284	
256			59 209	9 976	
8			28 823	2 614	
17 401	224 613	1 064 995	9 619 714	102 543	
27 140	16 818	28 789	2 653 305	117 499	
13		48	621 534	22 326	
			16 768	63	
5		113		5 181	
591		5	99 724	41 281	
60		7	86 488	47 700	
1				11 571	
9				15 967	
8		110	23 805	23 344	422
93		420	90 974	77 123	
5		102	23 483	21 003	
240		6 522	1 351 484	151 418	
748		9	41 058	40 573	
294		3	628 367	198 692	
		28	7 185	5 187	
1		2		8 303	
				60	
			26 529	845 311	66 539
			442 102	7 866	
4				14 282	

表6-15 规模以上工业企业能源消费分组情况
Energy Consumption of Above-scaled Industrial Enterprises by Group (2011)

指标	Indicators	综合能源消费量（吨标准煤）Comprehensive Energy Consumption (tons of standard coal)	单位产值能耗（吨标准煤/万元）Energy Consumption of Production Value (tons of standard coal/10 000 yuan)
按轻、重工业分	**By Light/Heavy Industry**		
轻工业	Light Industry	937 219	0.061
重工业	Heavy Industry	8 004 044	0.105
按企业规模分	**By Scale of Enterprises**		
大型企业	Large	5 324 512	0.116
中型企业	Medium	1 968 644	0.070
小型企业	Small	1 648 107	0.094
按高载能行业分	**By High Engery Bearing**		
石油加工、炼焦及核燃料加工业	Raw Chemical Materials and Chemical Products	2 403 546	0.314
非金属矿物制品业	Nonmetal Mineral Products	650 964	0.122
化学原料及化学制品制造业	Raw Chemical Materials and Chemical Products	655 625	0.036
黑色金属冶炼及压延加工业	Smelting and Pressing of Ferrous Metal	650 731	0.029
电力、热力的生产和供应业	Production and Supply of Electricity and Heating Power	2 536 397	0.318
按重点行业分	**By Key Industry**		
电子信息产品制造业	Manufacturing of Electronic and Information Products	763 274	0.031
汽车制造业	Automobile Industry	453 475	0.031
石油化工及精细化工制造业	Petrochemical and Refining Industry	2 967 034	0.234
精品钢材制造业	Manufacturing of Refined Steel Products	71 272	0.223
成套设备制造业	Manufacturing of Complete Equipment	408 702	0.036
生物医药制造业	Manufacturing of Biological Medicine	144 870	0.051
按高技术行业分	**By High-tech Industry**		
信息化学品制造	Manufacturing of Information Chemicals	248	0.040
医药制造业	Manufacturing of Medicines	125 531	0.060
航空航天器制造	Manufacturing of Aviation and Space Vehicles	2 861	0.066
电子及通信设备制造业	Manufacuring of Electronic and Communication Equipment	602 599	0.058
电子计算机及办公设备制造业	Manufacturing of Electronic Computer and Office Equipment	48 578	0.004
医疗设备及仪器仪表制造业	Manufacturing of Medical Equipment, Instrument and Meters	20 659	0.019

主要统计指标解释

工　业

指从事自然资源的开采，对采掘品和农产品进行加工和再加工的物质生产部门。具体包括：(1)对自然资源的开采，如采矿、晒盐等(但不包括禽兽捕猎和水产捕捞)；(2)对农副产品的加工、再加工，如粮油加工、食品加工、缫丝、纺织、制革等；(3)对采掘品的加工、再加工，如炼铁、炼钢、化工生产、石油加工、机器制造、木材加工等，以及电力、自来水、煤气的生产和供应等；(4)对工业品的修理、翻新，如机器设备的修理、交通运输工具(包括小卧车)的修理等。

1984年以前农村的村及村以下办工业归属农业，1984年以后划归工业。

工业统计调查单位为独立核算法人工业企业。

独立核算法人工业企业指从事工业生产经营活动的单位。独立核算法人工业企业应同时具备以下条件：①依法成立，有自己的名称、组织机构和场所，能够承担民事责任；②独立拥有和使用资产，承担负债，有权与其他单位签订合同；③独立核算盈亏，并能够编制资产负债表。

轻工业

指主要提供生活消费品和制作手工工具的工业。按其所使用的原料不同，可分为两大类：(1)以农产品为原料的轻工业，是指直接或间接以农产品为基本原料的轻工业。主要包括食品制造、饮料制造、烟草加工、纺织、缝纫、皮革和毛皮制作、造纸以及印刷等工业；(2)以非农产品为原料的轻工业，是指以工业品为原料的轻工业。主要包括文教体育用品、化学药品制造、合成纤维制造、日用化学制品、日用玻璃制品、日用金属制品、手工工具制造、医疗器械制造、文化和办公用机械制造等工业。

重工业

指为国民经济各部门提供物质技术基础的主要生产资料的工业。按其生产性质和产品用途，可以分为下列三类：(1)采掘(伐)工业，是指对自然资源的开采，包括石油开采、煤炭开采、金属矿开采、非金属矿开采等工业；(2)原材料工业，指向国民经济各部门提供基本材料、动力和燃料的工业。包括金属冶炼及加工、炼焦及焦炭、化学、化工原料、水泥、人造板以及电力、石油和煤炭加工等工业；(3)加工工业，是指对工业原材料进行再加工制造的工业。包括装备国民经济各部门的机械设备制造工业、金属结构、水泥制品等工业，以及为农业提供的生产资料如化肥、农药等工业。

根据上述划分原则，修理业中以重工业产品为修理作业对象的划为重工业，反之划为轻工业。

工业总产值

(1)定义：工业总产值是以货币形式表现的，工业企业在一定时期内生产的工业最终产品或提供工业性劳务活动的总价值量。它反映一定时间内工业生产的总规模和总水平。

(2)计算原则：工业生产的原则，即凡是企业在报告期生产的经检验合格的产品，不管是否在报告期销售，均包括在内。

最终产品的原则，即凡是计入工业总产值的产品，必须是本企业生产的经检验合格的，不需要再进行任何加工的最终产品。如果企业有中间产品(半成品)对外销售，则对外销售的中间产品应视为企业的最终产品。

工厂法原则，即工业总产值是以工业企业作为基本计算(核算)单位，即按企业的最终产品计算工业总产值。按这种方法计算的工业总产值，不允许同一产品价值在企业内部重复计算，不能把企业内部各个车间(分厂)生产的成果相加，但允许企业间的重复计算。

(3)内容及计算方法：1995年全国工业普查对工业总产值(原规定)的内容及计算原则和方法做了某些修订，修订后的工业总产值(新规定)包括三项内容：即本期生产成品价值、对外加工费收入、在制品半成品期末期初差额价值三部分。

本期生产成品价值：指企业本期生产，并在报告期内不再进行加工，经检验、包装入库的全部工业成品(半产品)价值合计，包括企业生产的自制设备及提供给本企业在建工程、其他非工业部门和福利部门等单位使用的成品价值。本期生产成品价值为按自备原材料生产的产品的数量乘以本期不含增值税(销项税额)的产品实际销售平均单价计算；会计核算中按成本价格转帐的自制设备和自产自用的成品，按成本价格计算生产成品价值。生产成品价值中不包括用定货者来料加工的成品(半产品)价值。

对外加工费收入：指企业在报告期内完成的对外承接的工业品加工(包括用定货者来料加工产品)的加工费收入和对外工业修理作业所取得的加工费收入。对外加工费收入按不含增值税(销项税额)的价格计算，可根据会计"产品销售收入"科目的有关资料取得。

对于本企业对内非工业部门提供的加工修理、设备安装的劳务收入，如果企业会计核算基础较好，能取得这部分资料，而且这部分价值所占比重较大，应包括在对外加工费收入中。

自制半成品在制品期末期初差额价值：指企业报告期在制品期末减期初的差额价值，本指标一般可以从会计核算资料中取得。如果会计产品成本核算中不计算半成品、在制品的成本，则总产值中也不包括这部分价值，反之则包括。

(4)工业总产值统计范围变化和计算方法修订情况：1984年以前工业总产值不包括村办工业，村办工业总产值划归农业。1984年以后工业总产值包括村办工业。

1995年工业普查对工业总产值计算方法做了修订，即从1995年始按新修订(新规定)方法计算工业总产值。新规定与原规定的区别如下：

全价与加工费的计算原则不同:新规定为凡自备原材料,不论其生产繁简程度如何,一律按全价计算工业总产值;凡来料加工,允许按加工费计算工业总产值。原规定则视生产加工的繁简程度不同,规定哪些行业按全价,哪些行业按加工费计算工业总产值。

自制半成品、在产品期末期初差额价值的计算原则不同:新规定要求,凡会计产品成本核算时计算了成本的差额价值,总产值中就应包括,否则可不包括;原规定则按生产周期六个月的界限区分,凡生产周期六个月以上的企业,总产值计算中应包括这部分差额价值,否则可不包括。

计算价格不同:新规定按不含增值税(销项税额)的价格计算;原规定则按含增值税(销项税额)的价格计算。

工业销售产值

是以货币表现的工业企业在一定时期内销售的、本企业生产的工业产品总量。包括已销售的成品、半成品价值,对外提供的工业性作业价值和对本单位基本建设部门、生活福利部门等提供的产品和工业性作业及自制设备的价值。工业销售产值依循的是以产品所有权转移为计算原则,因此,已销售的成品、半成品不论是本期生产的、还是上期生产的,只要是本期销售出去的均包括在内。对外提供的工业性作业是指企业按合同对外提供的工业性劳务。

工业销售产值的计算范围、计算价格和计算方法与工业总产值一致,但两者计算的基础不同,工业销售产值计算的基础是产品销售总量,工业总产值计算的基础是工业产品生产总量。

出口交货值

是指工业企业交给外贸部门或自营(委托)出口(包括销往香港、澳门地区、台湾省)的产品价值;批量销于国内或在过境批量出口等但用外汇价格结算的产品价值;外商来样、来料加工,来件装配和补偿贸易等生产,分别参照计算总产值的规定要求按全价或加工费计算的价值。

大、中、小型企业

根据工业和信息化部、国家统计局、国家发展改革委、财政部《关于印发中小企业划型标准规定的通知》(工信部联企业【2011】300 号),依据从业人员、营业收入、资产总额等指标或替代指标,将我国的企业划分为大型、中型、小型、微型等四种类型,原划分办法废止。工业企业划型标准见下表:

指标名称	计量单位	大　型	中　型	小　型	微　型
从业人员(X)	人	X≥1000	300≤X<1000	20≤X<300	X<20
主营业务收入(Y)	万元	Y≥40000	2000≤Y<40000	300≤Y<2000	Y<300

说明:大型、中型和小型企业必须同时满足所列指标下限,否则下划一档;微型企业只须满足所列指标中的一项即可。

独立核算工业企业、非独立核算工业生产单位

工业企业按其行政和财务是否独立,分为独立核算工业企业和非独立核算工业生产单位。

独立核算工业企业应同时具备下列三个条件:(1)行政上有独立的组织形式;(2)经济上独立核算,自负盈亏,编制独立的资金平衡表(或资产负债表);(3)有权与其他单位签订合同,并在银行设有独立帐户。独立核算工业企业不论是单一性生产或联合性生产的企业,均以整个企业作为一个基层单位进行统计,而不按分厂、车间统计。

非独立核算工业生产单位是指不同时具备独立核算工业企业三个条件,附设于其他企业、事业、机关、团体、学校、科研机构、部队等单位的工业生产单位。非独立核算工业生产单位必须同时具备下列三个条件,才可列入工业统计范围,即:(1)有固定的生产场所和生产设备;(2)有固定的生产工人和学徒在 10 人以上;(3)一般单位常年生产,季节性生产的单位全年开工时间在三个月以上。

资产总计

资产是指企业拥有或者控制的能以货币计量的经济资源,包括各种财产、债权和其他权利。资产按其流动性(即资产的变现能力和支付能力)划分为:流动资产、长期投资、固定资产、无形资产、递延资产和其他资产。该指标根据企业会计"资产负债表"中"资产总计"项目的期末数增列。

流动资产合计

指可以在一年或者超过一年的一个营业周期内变现或者耗用的资产,包括现金及各种存款、短期投资、应收及预付货款、存款等。

流动资产平均余额

指企业在报告期内全部流动资产的平均余额。

固定资产净值年平均余额

指固定资产净值在报告期内余额的平均数。计算公式为:

固定资产净值年平均余额 = 1 至 12 月各月月初、月末固定资产净值之和/24

该指标根据"资产负债表"中"固定资产原价"、"累计折旧"指标的期初、期末数计算填列。

固定资产净值指固定资产原价减去历年已提折旧额后的净额。计算公式为:

固定资产净值 = 固定资产原价 - 累计折旧

负债合计

负债合计是指企业所承担的能以货币计量,将以资产或劳务偿付的债务总计。负债一般按偿还期长短分为流动负债和长期负债。流动负债合计是指企业在一年内或超过一年的一个营业周期内偿还的债务;长期负债合计是指偿还期在一年以上或者超过一年的一个营业周期内偿还债

务。

所有者权益

指企业投资人对企业净资产的所有权。企业净资产等于企业全部资产减去全部负债后的余额,包括企业投资人对企业的最初投入的实际到位的资产及资本公积金、盈余公积金和未分配利润。所有者权益合计数小于零,表示企业资不抵债。

利润总额

指企业生产经营活动的最终成果,是企业在一定时期内实现的盈亏相抵后的利润总额(亏损以"-"号表示),它等于营业利润加上补贴收入加上投资收益加上营业外净收入再加上以前年度损益调整。

总资产贡献率

反映企业全部资产的获利能力,是企业经营业绩和管理水平的集中体现,是评价和考核企业盈利能力的核心指标。计算公式为:

总资产贡献率(%)=利润总额+税金总额+利息支出/平均资金总额×100%

公式中:税金总额为产品销售税金及附加与应缴增值税之和;平均资产总额为期初期末资产之和的算术平均值。

资产负债率

该指标既反映企业经营风险的大小,也反映企业利用债权人提供的资金从事经营活动的能力。计算公式为:

资产负债率(%)=负债总额/资产总额×100%

资产与负债均为报告期期末数。

流动资产周转次数

指一定时期内流动资产完成的周转次数,反映投入工业企业流动资金的周转速度。计算公式为:

流动资产周转次数=产品销售收入/全部流动资产平均余额

公式中:全部流动资产平均余额为期初和期末的流动资产之和的算术平均值。

产品销售率

该指标反映工业产品已实现销售的程度,是分析工业产销衔接情况、研究工业产品满足社会需求的指标。计算公式为:

产品销售率(%)=工业销售产值/工业总产值(现价)×100%

资本保值增值率

该指标反映企业净资产的变动状况,是企业发展能力的集中体现。计算公式为:

资本保值增值率=报告期期末所有者权益/上年同期期末所有者权益

所有者权益等于资产总计减负债总计。

成本费用利润率

反映企业投入的生产成本及费用的经济效益,同时也反映企业降低成本所取得的经济效益。计算公式为:

成本费用利润(%)=利润总额/成本费用总额×100%

公式中:成本费用总额为产品销售成本、销售费用、管理费用、财务费用之和。

全员劳动生产率

该指标反映企业的生产效率和劳动投入的经济效益。计算公式为:

$$全员劳动生产率(元/人)=\frac{工业增加值}{全部从业人员平均人数}$$

EXPLANATORY NOTES TO MAJOR STATISTICAL INDICATORS

Industry

Industry refers to the material production sector which is engaged in extraction of natural resources and processing and reprocessing of minerals and agricultural products, including (1) extraction of natural resources, such as mining, salt production (but not including hunting and fishing); (2) processing and reprocessing of farm and sideline produces, such as rice husking, flour milling, wine making, oil pressing, silk reeling, spinning and weaving, and leather making; (3) manufacture of industrial products, such as steel making, iron smelting, chemicals manufacturing, petroleum processing, machine building, timber processing; water and gas production and electricity generation and supply; (4) repairing of industrial products such as the repairing of machinery and means of transport (including cars).

Prior to 1984, the rural industry run by villages and cooperative organizations under village was classified into agriculture. Since 1984, it has been grouped into industry.

Units of industrial statistics survey corporate industrial enterprises with independent accounting system.

Corporate industrial enterprises with independent accounting system refer to enterprises engaging in industrial production activities, which meet the following requirements: ①They are established legally, having their own names, organizations, location, able to take civil liability; ②They possess and use their assets independently, assume liabilities, and are entitled to sign contracts with other units; ③They are financially independent and compile their own balance sheets.

Light Industry

refers to the industry that produces consumer goods and hand tools. It consists of two categories, depending on the materials used:

(1) Industries using farm products as raw materials. These are branches of light industry which directly or indirectly use farm products as basic raw materials, including the manufacture of food and beverages, tobacco processing, textile, clothing, fur and leather manufacturing, paper making, printing, etc.

(2) Industries using non farm products as raw materials. These are branches of light industry which use manufactured goods as raw materials, including the manufacture of cultural, educational articles and sports goods, chemicals, synthetic fiber, chemical products for daily use, glass products for daily use, metal products for daily use, hand tools, medical apparatus and instruments, and the manufacture of cultural and clerical machinery.

Heavy Industry

refers to the industry which produces capital goods, and provides various sectors of the national economy with necessary material and technical basis. It consists of the following three branches according to the purpose of production or the use of products:

(1) Mining, quarrying and logging industry refers to the industry that extracts natural resources, including extraction of petroleum, coal, metal and non-metal ores.

(2) Raw materials industry refers to the industry that provides various sectors of the national economy with raw materials, fuels and power. It includes smelting and processing of metals, coking and coke chemistry, chemical materials and building materials such as cement, plywood, and power, petroleum refining and coal dressing.

(3) Manufacturing industry refers to the industry that processes raw materials. It includes machine building industry which equips sectors of the national economy, industries of metal structure and cement products, industries producing means of agricultural production, such as chemical fertilizers and pesticides. According to the above principle of classification, the repairing trades which are engaged primarily in repairing products of heavy industry are classified into heavy industry while these engaged in repairing products of light industry are classified into light industry.

Gross Output Value of Industry

(1) Definition: Gross industrial output value is the total volume of final industrial products produced and industrial services provided during a given period. It reflects the total achievements and overall scale of industrial production during a given period.

(2) Principles for calculation: Statistics on industrial production follow the principle that all products produced by the enterprises and accepted during the reference period are to be included no matter whether they are sold or not during the reference period.

Determination of final products follow the principle that all products that are included in the calculation of grow industrial output value are the final products of the enterprise which have been accepted through quality check and require no further processing. If an enterprise has intermediate (semi-finished) products to sell, these intermediate products are considered as the final products of the enterprise.

Gross industrial output value is calculated following the principle of factory approach, i. e. industrial enterprise is used as the basic accounting unit in calculating the gross industrial output value. By this approach, value of the same product is not to be double counted, and the output value of different workshops (branch factories) should not be added. However, this approach does not exclude the possibility of double counting between enterprises.

(3) Content and calculation method: The old definition of gross industrial output value was modified duringthe national industrial census in 1995. The revised (new) definition of gross industrial output value consists of 3 components: value of the finished products during the reference period, income from external processing, and value of change in semi-finished products at the end and at the beginning of the reference period.

Value of the finished products during the reference period: refers to the value of all finished (semi-finished) industrial products that are produced during the reference period without the need for further processing, checked for acceptance, packed and put into the warehouse of the enterprise, including the value of own-produced equipment and the value of products provided to the projects under construction of the enterprise, and to other non-industrial or welfare units. Value of finished products during the reference period is calculated by the quantity of products produced using own materials multiplied by the average unit prices at which products are sold (excluding value-added tax). Own-produced equipment and products produced for own use are value at cost prices as in the case of enterprise accounting. Value of finished products does not include the value of finished products (semi-finished products) that are produced using the materials from the clients who make the orders.

Income from external processing: refers to income from contracted external processing of industrial products (including processing of industrial products using materials from the clients), and the income from industrial repairing work provided to other units. Income from external processing is calculated using information from the item "products sales income" in the enterprise accounting at the prices excluding value-added tax.

For income from services such as processing, repairing and installation of equipment provided to non-industrial units within the enterprise, if the accounting work of the enterprise is good enough to separate it from other records, and the share of such services is significant, it should also be included in the income from external processing.

Value of change in semi-finished products at the end and at the beginning of the reference period: refers to the value of change in semi-finished products at the end and at the beginning of the reference period, which generally can be obtained from accounting records of enterprises. If the enterprise accounting excludes the cost of semi-finished products, then it should not be included in the gross industrial output value, and vice versa.

(4) Changes in the coverage and method of calculation of gross industrial output value: Prior to 1984, the value of rural industry run by villages was classified into agriculture instead of industry. Since 1984, it has been included in the gross industrial output value.

Method of calculation for the gross industrial output value was modified in the industrial census in 1995. The difference in the new method as compared with the old one is outlined below:

Principle in using full value vs. processing fee: The new method stipulates that all products produced using own materials are to be calculated with full value in reporting the gross industrial output value irrespective of sophistication of production, and for external processing, it allows calculation using processing fee. In the old method, however, the use of full value or processing fee was determined by the degree of sophistication of production in different branches of industries.

Principle in determining the value of change in semi-finished products: The new method requires that value of the change in semi-finished products should be included in the gross industrial output value if it is included in the accounting record of the enterprise, otherwise it should not be included. By the old method, it is determined by the type of enterprises in terms of production cycle. If the production cycle is over 6 months, the value of change in semi-finished products is included in the gross industrial output value, otherwise it is excluded.

Difference in prices: The new method uses prices excluding value-added tax in the calculation of gross industrial output value, while the old method used prices including value-added tax.

Sales Output Value of Industry

refers to total sales value of products produced by industrial enterprises during a given period, including sales of finished goods, value of semi-products, value of industrial services provided to other units, value of products provided for capital construction sector, welfare sector and value of industrial services provided and self produced equipment within enterprises. Sales of finished goods and-semi-products in current period are taken into account regardless of their production period.

The coverage, pricing, and calculation method for sales output value of industry are the same as for gross output value of industry except that the former is based on sales of products and the latter is based on the output of products.

Export Delivery Value of Industry

refers to the product value which industrial enterprises deliver to Foreign Trade Department, or value of products which are exported directly from producers (including the sales to Hong Kong, Macao and Taiwan); the product value, (at foreign exchange rate,) of domestic batch sale or transit batch export; full price or processing fee of the production with design, materials, assembling parts supplied by foreign businessmen and compensation trade.

Large, Medium and Small Enterprises

According to the Notice of the Ministry of Industry and Information Technology, National Bureau of Statistics, National Development and Reform Commission and the Ministry of Finance on printing and distributing the classification standard for middle and small enterprises (<2011> No. 300), we will divide our national enterprises into four kinds that are large, middle, small and mini in accordance with the indicators or substitute indicators such as employed persons, operation income and total assets. The former method for classification will be discarded. The classification standard for industrial enterprises are shown as followed.

Indicators	Unit	Large	Middle	Small	Mini
Employed Persons(X)	Persons	X≥1000	300≤X<1000	20≤X<300	X<20
Main Operation Income(Y)	10 000 yuan	Y≥40000	2000≤Y<40000	300≤Y<2000	Y<300

Note: Large, middle and small enterprises must meet all of the lowest limit of the listed indicators, or they will be classified into the lower kind, respectively. Mini enterprises can meet only one of the listed indicators.

Industrial Enterprises with Independent Accounting

Systems and Industrial Production Units with Non-Independent Accounting Systems.

Depending on whether they have independent administration and accounting, industrial enterprises can be divided into industrial enterprises with independent accounting system and industrial production units with non-independent accounting system. An industrial enterprise with independent accounting system shall operate simultaneously under the following three conditions: (1) having an independent organization in terms of administration; (2) economically having independent accounting, taking care of its own profits and losses, and filing independent balance sheets; and (3) enjoying the right to sign contracts with other units and to open independent bank accounts. An industrial enterprise with independent accounting system, no matter under a unitary management or cooperative operation, shall be counted as single grassroots unit in statistics and its branch factories and workshops shall not be calculated separately.

An industrial production unit with non-independent accounting system is an industrial production unit which does not operate simultaneously under the above mentioned three conditions of industrial enterprises with independent accounting systems and is attached to an enterprise, institution, government department, organization, school, scientific research institution, or army unit. An industrial production with non-independent accounting system unit can be included into the industrial statistics only when it operates simultaneously under the following three conditions: (1) having fixed production sites and production equipment; (2) having more than 10 permanent workers and apprentices; and (3) operating all year round if it's a normal production unit or operating more than three months a year if it's a seasonal production unit.

Aggregate Assets

Total Assets refer to all economic resources, in monetary terms, that is owned or controlled by enterprises, including properties, creditors equity and other economic rights of all forms. Classified by the degree of equitability, total assets include circulating assets, long-term investment, fixed assets, intangible assets and deferred assets, and other assets. Data on this indicator can be obtained by the year-end figures of total assets in the Assets and Liability Table of accounting records of enterprises.

Total of Working Capitals

Total of Working Capitals refer to capitals which can be cashed in or spent or consumed in an operating cycle of one year or over one year, including cash, all kinds of deposits, short term investment, receivable and payable payment for goods or deposits.

Average Value of Working Capitals

Average Value of Working Capitals refers to the average value of all working capitals of the enterprise during the reference period.

Annual Average of Net Value of Fixed Assets

refer to average of the net value of fixed assets during the reference period, calculated with the following formula:

Annual Average of Net Value of Fixed Assets = sum of net value of fixed assets at the beginning and at the end of each month from January to December / 24.

Information on this indicator can be obtained from the beginning and ending figures of the original value of fixed assets and cumulative depreciation from the Assets and Liability Table of enterprises.

Net value of fixed assets refers to the original value of fixed assets minus depreciation over the years, i. e. :

Net value of fixed assets = original value of fixed assets-cumulative depreciation

Aggregate Liabilities

Aggregate liabilities refer to the total debts of an enterprise which can be calculated in monetary term and will be repaid in the forms of assets or service. Usually, the debts are divided into liquid liability and long-term debt according to the length of the payback period. The liquid liability is the debt that an enterprise will pay back during an operation cycle which is either shorter or longer than a year. The long-term debt refers to a debt whose payback period is longer than a year or which will be repaid during an operation cycle that is longer than a year.

Creditors' Equity

Creditors'Equity refers to investors ownership of net assets of the enterprise, which is equal to the total assets of the enterprise minus its total liabilities, including the primary input actually received at the enterprise from investors, capital accumulation fund, surplus accumulation fund and undistributed profit. When the total of creditors' equity is less than zero, that indicates the liability of the enterprise is larger that its assets.

Total Profits

Total Profits refer to the final achievements of production and operation of the enterprises, represented by the total profits after deducting losses (loss is expressed by the negative figure). It is the sum of profits from operation, income from subsidies, investment earnings, net income from activities other than operation, and adjustment of profits and losses of previous years.

Ratio of Profits, Taxes and Interests to Average Assets

Ratio of Profits, Taxes and Interests to Average Assets reflects the profit-making capability of all assets of the enterprise and is a key indicator manifesting the performance and management and evaluating the profit-making potential of the enterprise. It is calculated as follows:

Ratio of Profits, Taxes and Interests to Average Assets (%) = [(total profits + total taxes + interest payment) / average assets] ×100%

In the above formula, total taxes is the sum of tax and extra charges on the sales of products and value-added tax payable; and average assets is the arithmetic mean of the sum of beginning assets and ending assets.

Ratio of Debts to Asset

Ratio of Debts to Assets reflect both the operation risk and the capability of the enterprise in making use of the capital from the creditors. It is calculated as follows:

Ratio of Debts to Assets (%) = (total debts / total assets) × 100%

Both assets and debts are figures at the end of the reference period.

Turnover of Working Capital

Turnover of Working Capital refers to the number of times of turnover of working capital in a given period of time, which reflects the speed of the turnover of working capital of industrial enterprises, and is calculated as follows:

Turnover of Working Capital = (sales revenue of products) / (average balance of total working capital)

In the above formula, average balance of total working capital refers to the arithmetic mean of the sum of working capital at the beginning and at the end of the reference period.

Ratio of Sales to Gross Output Value

Ratio of Sales to Gross Output Value reflects the degree at which industrial products are sold. It helps to analyze the linkage between production and sales and the extent of the needs of the society that has been met by the supply of industrial products. It is calculated as follows:

Ratio of Sales to Gross Output Value = (Industrial sales / Gross industrial output value at current prices) ×100%

Capital Maintenance and Appreciation Rate

Capital Maintenance and Appreciation Rate reflects the changes of an enterprise's net assets. It epitomizes the growth capability of an enterprise. Its calculating formula is:

Capital maintenance and appreciation rate = Ownership equity at the end of the reporting period/Ownership equity at the same period of the previous year. Ownership equity is the result of total assets minus total liabilities.

Ratio of Profits to Total Industrial Costs

Ratio of Profits to Total Industrial Costs refers to the ratio of profits realized in a given period to the total costs in the same period, which reflects the economic efficiency of input cost and is calculated as follows:

Ratio of Profits to Total Industrial Cost(%) = (total profits/ total costs) ×100%

Total costs in the above formula is the sum of cost of products sold, marketing cost, management cost and financial cost.

Overall Labour Productivity

Overall Labour Productivity is an indicator reflecting the production efficiency of an enterprise and the economic efficiency of its labour input, calculated by the formula:

Overall Labour Productivity (yuan/person) = industrial value-added/average of all persons engaged.

第七篇

Chapter 7

建筑业

CONSTRUCTION

表7-1　主要年份建筑业企业主要指标

指　标　Indicators		单　位　Unit	1995	2000
施工企业单位数	Number of Construction Enterprises	个 unit	243	367
年末从业人员数	Employed Persons (Year End)	人 person	125 627	93 753
全年从业人员平均数	Annual Average Employed Persons	人 person	140 994	116 722
建筑业总产值	Gross Output Value of Construction	万元 10 000 yuan	1 045 601	935 731
#建筑工程	Construction Projects	万元 10 000 yuan	905 848	886 356
安装工程	Installation Projects	万元 10 000 yuan	110 763	115 164
竣工产值	Output Value of Construction Projects Completed	万元 10 000 yuan	446 202	786 808
房屋建筑面积	Floor Space of Buildings			
施工面积	Floor Space Under Construction	万平方米 10 000 sq・m	1 042.05	1 149.25
#本年新开工	New Start in Current Year	万平方米 10 000 sq・m	285.02	426.18
竣工面积	Floor Space Completed	万平方米 10 000 sq・m	290.25	520.61
#住　宅	Housing	万平方米 10 000 sq・m	150.63	350.65
全员劳动生产率	Overall Labor Productivity	元/人 yuan/person	74 159	80 167
房屋建筑面积竣工率	Ratio of Floor Space Completed	%	27.9	45.3
平均每个职工竣工房屋面积	Floor Space Completed Per Staff Member	平方米/人 sq・m/person	20.59	44.60

注：建筑业总产值为建筑业企业自行完成的施工产值。
Note: Gross output value of construction refers to output value of construction completed by construction enterprises themselves.

Major Indicators of Construction Industry in Main Years

2005	2006	2007	2008	2009	2010	2011
398	489	469	522	680	699	720
159 099	176 109	123 957	181 687	293 496	253 822	259 056
208 807	237 537	273 887	203 498	408 349	361 140	424 530
3 353 790	4 168 060	5 416 041	6 607 274	8 938 091	9 801 257	11 353 474
2 599 981	3 555 436	4 655 203	5 421 540	7 323 235	8 001 415	9 746 424
643 346	487 822	611 949	1 020 528	760 443	1 526 037	1 440 514
2 322 347	2 716 496	3 319 285	3 507 229	5 335 389	6 858 981	5 650 019
3 009.91	3 542.14	3 798.19	4 324.58	6 237.41	6 886.55	8 451.28
1 291.18	1 284.94	1 430.47	1 569.64	2 153.29	2 501.17	2 675.90
903.45	1 042.95	1 066.82	877.13	1 611.78	1 641.86	1 520.70
523.94	543.25	469.87	477.70	724.81	695.52	677.63
160 617	175 470	197 747	324 685	218 884	271 398	267 436
30.0	29.4	28.1	20.3	25.8	23.8	18.0
43.27	43.91	38.95	43.10	39.47	45.46	35.82

表7-2 建筑业企业主要指标
(2011)

指 标	Indicators	企业单位数(个) Number of Enterprises (unit)	年末从业人员数(人) Employed Persons at Year-end (person)	年从业人员平均数(人) Annual Average Employed Persons (person)	建筑业总产值(万元) Gross Output Value of Construction (10 000 yuan)	竣工产值(万元) Output Value of Completed Construction Projects (10 000 yuan)
合 计	**Total**	**720**	**259 056**	**424 530**	**11 353 474**	**5 650 019**
#外省市	Non-Shanghai	78	14 912	14 725	342 800	197 256
按注册登记类型分	**By Type of Registration**					
内 资	Domestic Investment	681	243 933	401 684	10 381 886	5 136 318
国 有	State-owned	45	14 472	37 203	1 079 866	708 906
集 体	Collective-owned	15	1 423	1 627	39 726	39 166
股份合作	Share-holding	6	304	366	7 364	721
联 营	Jointly Operated	4	516	515	11 911	3 235
国有独资公司	Wholly state-owned company	8	11 152	22 218	593 237	361 968
责任有限公司	Companies with Limited Liabilities	103	102 111	123 299	4 925 512	1 756 624
股份有限公司	Companies Limited by Shares	16	8 980	31 302	820 916	834 795
私 营	Private	484	104 975	185 154	2 903 354	1 430 903
港澳台商投资	HK/Macao/Taiwan Invested	17	2 958	5 615	491 127	149 002
外商投资	Foreigner Invested	22	12 165	17 231	480 461	364 699
按行业分	**By Sector**					
房屋和土木工程建筑业	Housing and Civil Engineering Construction	373	215 400	300 352	9 124 874	4 499 542
建筑安装业	Installation	168	20 788	89 802	1 105 189	589 684
建筑装饰业	Decoration	148	21 362	32 880	1 059 773	526 062
其他建筑业	Other Constructions	31	1 506	1 496	63 638	34 731
按建筑业资质等级分	**By Qualification of Construction Industry**					
#特 级	Special Grade	13	81 340	100 563	4 156 528	1 961 649
一 级	Grade I	131	81 148	142 605	4 199 299	1 867 314
二 级	Grade II	198	59 475	69 661	2 009 306	1 168 118
三 级	Grade III	378	37 093	111 701	988 341	652 938

注：建筑业总产值为建筑业企业自行完成的施工产值；建筑业资质等级为新标准资质。

Note: Gross Output Value of Construction refers to Output Value of Construction Completed by Construction Enterprises themselves. Qualification of Construction Industry refers to qualification under new standards.

Major Indicators of Construction Enterprises

房屋建筑施工面积（万平方米）Floor Space Under Construction (10 000 sq·m)	#本年新开工 New Start in Current Year	房屋竣工面积（万平方米）Floor Space Completed (10 000 sq·m)	#住宅 Residential Housing	全员劳动生产率（元/人）Overall Labor Productivity (yuan/person)	平均每个职工竣工房屋面积（平方米/人）Floor Space Completed Per Staff Member (sq·m/person)	房屋建筑面积竣工率（%）Ratio of Floor Space Completed (%)
8 451.28	**2 675.90**	**1 520.70**	**677.63**	**267 436**	**35.82**	**18.0**
222.76	46.90	48.65	24.97	232 801	33.04	21.8
8 283.32	2 559.21	1 454.38	677.63	258 459	36.21	17.6
211.86	75.02	90.57	60.93	290 263	24.34	42.7
17.97	13.60	2.65	2.65	244 167	16.29	14.7
				201 202		
1.87	1.87			231 282		
296.78	102.24	95.52	63.08	267 007	42.99	32.2
5 501.30	1 666.26	635.34	376.02	399 477	51.53	11.5
926.99	270.45	217.14	21.03	262 257	69.37	23.4
1 326.55	429.77	413.16	154.02	156 808	22.31	31.1
				874 670		
167.96	116.69	66.32		278 835	38.49	39.5
8 424.55	2 674.00	1 512.07	677.63	303 806	50.34	17.9
22.95	1.90	8.11		123 070	0.90	35.3
3.78		0.52		322 315	0.16	13.8
				425 388		
6 050.16	1 824.79	702.62	305.52	413 326	69.87	11.6
1 237.30	484.72	442.38	203.03	294 471	31.02	35.8
915.99	264.13	262.91	123.76	288 441	37.74	28.7
247.83	102.26	112.79	45.32	88 481	10.10	45.5

表 7-3　建筑业财务报表
(2011)

单位:万元

指　标	Indicators	合　计 Total	内　资 Domestic Investment	国　有 State-owned
企业单位数(个)	**Number of Enterprises (unit)**	**642**	**604**	**21**
年末资产负债	**Balance Sheet at Year-end**			
资产总计	Total Assets	14 595 665	13 235 385	2 518 674
#流动资产	Floating Assets	11 427 594	10 192 919	1 525 685
固定资产	Fixed Assets	1 045 704	941 417	69 612
固定资产原价	Initial Value of Fixed Assets	1 630 746	1 527 224	118 457
累计折旧	Accumulated Depreciation	682 654	645 534	56 755
#本年折旧	Depreciation This Year	112 985	105 214	14 869
无形资产及递延资产	Intangible Assets and Deferred Assets	57 303	53 372	21 509
负债总计	Total Liabilities	11 055 205	9 971 458	1 957 322
流动负债	Floating Liabilities	10 480 846	9 465 074	1 735 621
长期负债	Long-term Liabilities	574 359	506 384	221 701
所有者权益总计	Total Rights and Interests of Owners	3 540 460	3 263 927	561 352
损益及分配	**Profit and Loss and Their Distribution**			
工程结算收入	Project Settlement Income	13 322 989	11 948 767	1 598 250
工程结算成本	Project Settlement Costs	11 999 802	10 856 480	1 474 698
工程结算税金及附加	Project Settlement Taxes and Additional Taxes	366 978	342 742	37 862
工程结算利润	Project Settlement Profits	956 209	749 545	85 690
管理费用	Administrative Expenses	451 492	378 624	45 373
#税　金	Taxes	7 988	7 474	813
财务费用	Financial Expenses	78 414	65 961	19 636
营业利润	Operation Profits	447 367	332 768	36 310
利润总额	Total Profits	471 907	356 916	40 237

注：以上财务数据不包含外省市进沪建筑业企业。
Note: The above-mentioned financial data exclude construction enterprises from other provinces and cities that enter the construction market in Shanghai.

Financial Statements of Construction Industry

(10 000yuan)

集　体 Collective-owned	股份合作 Share-holding	联　营 Jointly-operated	国有独资公司 Wholly state-owned company	责任有限公司 Companies with Limited Liability	股份有限公司 Companies Limited by Shares	私　营 Private	港澳台商投资 Hong kong/ Macao/ Taiwan Investment	外商投资 FIE
12	**4**	**4**	**6**	**82**	**6**	**469**	**17**	**21**
59 001	23 535	21 016	714 365	5 401 900	1 287 040	3 209 854	534 364	825 916
55 818	20 218	13 719	344 603	4 453 348	969 624	2 809 904	459 817	774 858
2 195	3 277	1 173	319 672	268 907	39 443	237 138	62 438	41 849
6 285	4 406	2 181	498 851	424 462	86 858	385 724	38 756	64 766
4 126	1 130	1 206	181 149	193 423	48 784	158 961	14 203	22 917
386	65	103	21 844	36 580	3 112	28 255	2 116	5 655
97	41	3	3 996	16 966	3 397	7 363	1 837	2 094
36 466	15 972	8 964	406 933	4 598 429	969 119	1 978 253	384 224	699 523
36 310	15 972	8 636	362 971	4 536 128	890 519	1 878 917	349 134	666 638
156		328	43 962	62 301	78 600	99 336	35 090	32 885
22 535	7 563	12 052	307 432	803 471	317 921	1 231 601	150 140	126 393
42 912	4 390	18 501	606 678	5 636 436	1 100 332	2 941 268	731 724	642 498
35 822	3 850	16 930	535 330	5 161 742	1 040 855	2 587 253	583 562	559 760
1 205	101	517	12 347	172 841	33 191	84 678	13 980	10 256
5 885	439	1 054	59 001	301 853	26 286	269 337	134 182	72 482
3 458	622	1 205	11 082	157 770	20 747	138 367	34 320	38 548
149	1	137	248	1 668	692	3 766	202	312
-51	88	-15	1 822	29 498	1 808	13 175	11 307	1 146
3 096	-271	10	51 812	114 022	8 029	119 760	87 541	27 058
3 115	-269	96	53 724	119 849	11 387	128 777	87 686	27 305

主要统计指标解释

建筑业总产值

建筑业总产值是以货币形式表现的建筑业企业在一定时期内生产的建筑业产品和提供的服务的总和。建筑业总产值包括：

（1）建筑工程产值：指列入建筑工程预算内的各种工程价值。

（2）安装工程产值：指设备安装工程价值，不包括被安装设备本身价值。

（3）其他产值：建筑业总产值中除建筑工程、安装工程以外的产值。包括房屋构筑物修理产值、非标准设备制造产值、总包企业向分包企业收取的管理费以及不能明确划分的施工活动所完成的产值。

a. 房屋构筑物修理产值：指房屋和构筑物修理所完成的产值，但不包括被修理房屋、构筑物本身价值和生产设备的修理产值。

b. 非标准设备制造产值：指加工制造没有定型的非标准生产设备的加工费和原材料价值（如化工厂、炼油厂用的各种罐、槽，矿井生产统一使用的各种漏斗、三角槽、阀门等）以及附属加工厂为本企业承建工程制作的非标准设备的价值。

房屋建筑施工面积

房屋建筑施工面积指在报告期内施过工的全部房屋建筑面积，包括本期新开工的房屋面积、上期施工跨入本期继续施工的房屋面积、上期停缓建在本期恢复施工的房屋面积、本期竣工的房屋面积及本期施工后又停缓建的房屋面积。

房屋建筑竣工面积

房屋建筑竣工面积 指在报告期内房屋建筑按照设计要求全部完工，达到了使用条件，经验收鉴定合格的房屋建筑面积。

房屋建筑面积竣工率

指一定时期内房屋竣工面积占同期房屋施工面积的比率。该指标从房屋建筑施工速度的角度反映投资效果的指标。

EXPLANATORY NOTES TO MAJOR STATISTICAL INDICATORS

Gross Output Value of Construction

Gross Output Value of Construction refers to total of construction products and services, expressed in money terms, produced or rendered by (completed by) construction enterprises during a given period of time. It includes:

(1) Output value of construction projects, that is the value of projects covered by the project budgets;

(2) Output value of installation projects, that is the value of the installation of equipment, (excluding the value of the equipment to be installed);

(3) Output value of other projects refers to other output value of gross output value of construction industry besides construction and installation projects. It includes the output value of building repairing, nonstandard equipment manufacturing, the management fees going from subcontractor to original contractor and other construction output value which can not be measure off definitely.

a. Output value of repair of buildings and structures, that is the value created through the repairs of buildings or structures, but does not include the value of buildings or structures being repaired and the value of the repair of production equipment;

b. Output value of manufactured non – standard equipment that is the value of non – standard production equipment (including raw materials and manufacturing cost) made for the construction project, irrespective of whether the equipment is manufactured on the construction site or by subsidiary workshops.

Floor Space of Buildings under Construction

Floor Space of Buildings under Construction refers to floor space of buildings under construction during the reference period, including newly started buildings, buildings started earlier and continued during the reference period, and buildings suspended earlier but restarted during the reference period, buildings completed during the reference period, and buildings under construction and then suspended during the reference period.

Floor Space of Buildings Completed

Floor Space of Buildings Completed refers to the floor space of buildings that are completed in the reference period in accordance with the requirements of the design, up to the standard for putting them into use, and have been checked and accepted by concerned departments as qualified ones.

Completion Rate of Floor Space of Buildings

Completion Rate of Floor Space of Buildings refers to the ratio of the floor space of buildings completed in certain period of time to the floor space of buildings under construction in the same period. This indicator reflects the investment result from the perspective of the speed of construction.

第八篇

Chapter 8

金融业及要素市场

FINANCE AND BANKING, AND FACTOR MARKETS

SHANGHAI PUDONG NEW AREA STATISTICAL YEARBOOK

表8-1　各类金融机构数
Statistics of all Kinds of Financial Institutions

单位:个 (unit)

指　标	Indicators	2005	2010	2011
总　计	**Total**	**369**	**649**	**692**
银行类机构合计	**Subtotal of Banks**	**141**	**211**	**221**
中资银行	Chinese Banks	19	29	32
外资银行法人行	Foreign Banks and Corporate Banks		18	18
外资银行分行	Branches of Foreign Banks	53	57	61
外资银行代表处	Representative Offices of Foreign Banks	44	60	63
银行营运中心	Bank Operation Centers	14	23	24
非银行金融机构	Non-banking Financial Institutions	11	24	23
证券类机构合计	**Subtotal of Securities Institutions**	**117**	**261**	**276**
中资证券(包括中介机构)	Chinese Securities Institutions (including intermediary organs)	50	68	75
外资证券(包括代表处)	Foreign Securities Institutions (including representative offices)	36	53	55
基金公司	Fund Companies	25	46	49
期货公司	Futures Companies		81	83
非证券金融机构	Non-securities Financial Institutions	6	13	14
保险机构合计	**Subtotal of Insurance Companies**	**111**	**177**	**195**
中资保险(集团)	Chinese Insurance Companies (Groups)	30	46	49
外资保险	Foreign Insurance Companies	20	27	29
外资保险代表处	Representative Offices of Foreign Insurance Companies	20	23	27
保险中介	Agencies of Insurance Companies	39	76	84
保险营运中心	Insurance Operation Centers	2	5	6

表8-2 主要年份中资银行人民币存贷款年末余额
Chinese Banks' Year-end RMB Balance of Deposits and Loans in Main Years

单位:亿元 (100 million yuan)

指标	Indicators	1990	1995	2000	2005	2010	2011
存款余额合计	**Total Deposit Balance**	**36.48**	**503.69**	**1 046.81**	**2 915.41**	**8 848.87**	**10 243.30**
#企业存款	Enterprise Deposits	9.67	286.20	644.79	1 530.99	5 239.12	5 923.46
居民储蓄存款	Resident Savings Deposits	20.62	180.94	360.99	1 105.96	2 943.49	3 375.71
其他存款	Others	1.66	13.73	10.61	166.38	427.38	667.37
贷款余额合计	**Total Loan Balance**	**28.19**	**417.05**	**891.59**	**2 674.76**	**6 434.95**	**7 238.06**
#企业贷款	Enterprise Loans				2 014.23	5 343.68	5 929.33
#短期贷款	Short Term Loans				716.01	1 504.28	1 615.62
中长期贷款	Medium and Long Term Loans				1 298.22	3 839.40	4 313.71
票据融资	Securities Financing				193.73	82.59	157.07
个人贷款	Individual Loans				464.40	1 007.62	1 150.64
#住房按揭贷款	Housing Mortgage Loans				431.28	888.58	935.71
汽车消费贷款	Car Loans				4.08	14.76	25.60

表8-3 外资银行主要指标
(2011)

指 标 Indicators		单位数(个) Enterprises (unit)	从业人数(人) Employed Persons (person)	普通贷款(万美元) Ordinary Loans (USD 10 000)
总 计	**Total**	**77**	**13 207**	**2 068 061**
按各大洲分	**By Continent**			
亚洲地区	Asia	40	9 535	1 358 495
欧洲地区	Europe	26	1 728	459 734
美洲地区	America	8	1 882	209 124
大洋洲地区	Oceania Region	2	48	40 491
非洲地区	Africa	1	14	217
按进驻各大厦分	**By Mansion Where Enterprises Handle Their Businesses**			
环球金融中心大厦	Shanghai World Financial Center	12	1 833	374 692
汇亚大厦	Azia Center	10	1 999	379 764
金茂大厦	Jinmao Building	7	403	211 314
中银大厦	Bank of China Tower	4	118	55 094
恒生银行大厦	Hangseng Bank Tower	5	444	163 459
证券大厦	Shanghai Stock Exchange Building	2	635	183
花旗大厦	Citigroup Mansion	4	1 400	116 730
星展银行大厦	DBS Tower	3	422	106 850
船舶大厦	Marine Tower	3	107	35 295
东亚银行大厦	Global Financial Tower	3	1 156	55 793
国金中心	Shanghai International Financial Center	4	2 504	196 991
其他大厦	Other Buildings	20	2 186	371 896
按普通贷款分	**By Regular Loans**			
7亿美元以上	> USD 700 million	10	4 578	1 280 196
5～7亿美元	USD 500～700 million	2	438	109 866
3～5亿美元	USD 300～500 million	6	1 700	230 729
1～3亿美元	USD 100～300 million	19	1 116	347 673
1亿美元以下	< USD 100 million	40	5 375	99 597
按普通存款分	**By Regular Deposit**			
10亿美元以上	> USD 10 000 million	7	4 041	943 394
3～10亿美元	USD 300～10 000 million	4	1 116	242 473
1～3亿美元	USD 100～300 million	9	1 746	282 281
1千万～1亿美元	USD 10～100 million	16	1 652	220 799
1千万美元以下	< USD 10 million	41	4 652	379 114
按资产总额分	**By Total Assets**			
10亿美元以上	> USD 1 000 million	22	9 738	1 471 105
5～10亿美元	USD 500～1 000 million	11	1 707	262 466
3～5亿美元	USD 300～500 million	11	555	156 476
1～3亿美元	USD 100～300 million	21	1 013	149 388
1亿美元以下	< USD 100 million	12	194	28 626
按税金分	**By Tax**			
2000万元以上	≥20 million yuan	23	9 451	1 499 584
500～2000万元	5～20 million yuan	23	2 536	369 191
100～500万元	1～5 million yuan	17	393	166 807
100万元以下	< 1 million yuan	14	827	32 479

Major Indicators of Foreign Banks

普通存款（万美元） Ordinary Deposits (USD 10 000)	人民币贷款（万元） RMB Loans (10 000 yuan)	人民币存款（万元） RMB Deposits (10 000 yuan)	资产总额（万美元） Total Assets (USD 10 000)	利润总额（万元） Operation Profit (10 000 yuan)	拆入同业（万元） Borrowing from Correspondence Banks (10 000 yuan)	拆放同业（万元） Banker Call Loans (10 000 yuan)
1 716 303	**20 109 886**	**37 145 372**	**7 948 016**	**694 045**	**1 388 229**	**4 431 860**
1 229 471	12 174 119	23 431 401	4 984 374	463 888	1 069 375	3 133 312
295 874	6 000 312	8 872 130	2 116 761	119 885	318 854	986 829
190 574	1 935 455	4 841 841	743 086	103 759		311 719
113			97 442	5 912		
271			6 353	601		
315 610	3 014 213	5 377 057	1 563 199	210 772	150 431	264 005
401 761	2 401 626	5 247 935	1 191 328	168 174	159 710	723 608
17 437	827 218	656 572	430 054	40 734	171 815	136 000
3 651	125 665	236 304	83 317	13 092	20 000	
73 220	1 698 216	1 969 568	373 441	57 602	75 273	
8 509		23 000	270 736	-29 618	147 000	65 000
167 936	1 557 116	3 801 381	531 553	88 756	15 000	294 500
59 341	1 011 943	26 261 310	242 727	41 034	205 000	1 062 562
1 489	342 468	69 138	74 428	18 186	16 000	6 000
27 276	1 179 403	1 620 536	341 017	8 442	100	30 000
284 406	2 021 533	5 345 638	1 388 818	185 002	83 000	807 948
355 667	5 930 485	10 172 103	1 457 398	-108 131	344 900	1 042 237
1 322 884	11 451 772	24 983 355	3 220 763	504 487	699 274	2 609 606
40 794	1 520 645	2 071 862	193 922	44 176	273	
192 791	2 825 160	5 656 304	854 464	264 920	150 432	586 341
110 818	2 695 013	2 922 158	962 586	156 942	115 540	199 228
49 016	1 617 296	1 511 693	2 716 281	-27 648	422 710	1 036 685
1 314 886	10 422 213	22 267 588	2 676 341	462 457	372 000	1 479 554
189 158	2 247 381	5 555 726	525 569	186 899	220 000	1 352 973
146 185	3 518 347	6 218 067	910 000	153 478	83 813	440 297
62 050	2 848 914	2 571 240	1 001 782	163 900	267 432	83 100
4 024	1 037 031	532 751	2 834 324	-272 689	444 984	1 075 936
1 412 406	13 289 411	29 057 232	6 298 908	568 691	1 132 979	4 251 886
214 011	3 791 620	5 209 937	776 358	-23 422	84 540	96 979
39 750	1 282 895	1 145 849	425 234	66 956	95 000	21 000
40 559	1 681 129	1 676 140	370798	79 627	75 710	61 995
9 577	64 831	56 214	76 718	2 193		
1 634 217	16 865 804	35 002 833	5 561 095	825 564	761 344	3 761 924
69 708	2 940 954	1 981 376	1 592 556	-126 686	594 985	588 063
10 304	288 653	160 658	526 568	65 003	16 900	58 878
2 074	14 475	505	267 797	-69 836	15 000	22 995

表8-4　外资银行存贷款年末余额
Foreign Banks' Year-end Balance of Deposits and Loans

指　标 Indicators		单　位 Unit	2005	2009	2010	2011
外汇存贷款	**Deposits and Loans of Foreign Exchange**	**亿美元 USD 100 million**	**197.19**	**273.91**	**327.45**	**378.44**
客户存款	Deposits of Customers	亿美元 USD 100 million	59.43	109.96	132.06	171.63
#短　期	Short Term	亿美元 USD 100 million	22.35	36.40	52.96	82.26
同业存款	Inter-bank Deposits	亿美元 USD 100 million	4.13	8.22	33.73	22.23
拆入同业	Deposits From Other Banks	亿美元 USD 100 million	29.30	96.96	128.33	102.37
普通贷款	Ordinary Loans	亿美元 USD 100 million	137.76	163.95	195.39	206.81
#短　期	Short Term	亿美元 USD 100 million	67.05	77.21	93.98	97.63
投　资	Investment	亿美元 USD 100 million	8.21	15.21	9.51	2.58
拆放同业	Deposits to Other Banks	亿美元 USD 100 million	15.64	105.02	101.07	77.52
人民币存贷款	**RMB Deposits and Loans**	**亿元 100 million yuan**	**1 203.72**	**3 915.83**	**4 910.27**	**5 725.50**
客户存款	Deposits of Customers	亿元 100 million yuan	615.44	2 233.65	3 000.91	3 714.54
拆入同业	Deposits From Other Banks	亿元 100 million yuan	53.76	203.83	157.13	138.82
普通贷款	Ordinary Loans	亿元 100 million yuan	588.28	1 682.18	1 909.36	2 010.99
投　资	Investment	亿元 100 million yuan	115.83	1 500.46	1 657.37	2 370.55
拆放同业	Deposits to Other Banks	亿元 100 million yuan	5.63	191.82	449.44	443.19

表8-5 历年中资保险机构原保险保费收入和赔款支出

Former Premium Income and Indemnity Expenditure of Chinese Insurance Business in Main Years (1992~2011)

单位:亿元 (100 million yuan)

年 份 Year	原保险保费收入 Former Premium Income	财产险 Property Insurance	人身险 Life Insurance	原保险赔款支出 Former Indemnity Expenditure	财产险 Property Insurance	人身险 Life Insurance	赔款率(%) Rate of Indemnity(%)	财产险 Property Insurance	人身险 Life Insurance
1992	1.13	0.75	0.38	0.69	0.20	0.49	61.1	26.7	128.9
1993	2.51	1.42	1.09	0.30	0.06	0.24	12.0	4.2	25.9
1994	5.37	3.30	2.07	1.77	1.63	0.14	33.0	49.4	6.8
1995	13.63	10.42	3.21	3.12	2.97	0.15	22.9	28.5	4.7
1996	22.02	7.70	14.32	3.83	3.41	0.42	17.4	44.3	2.9
1997	38.34	9.19	29.15	4.91	4.71	0.20	12.8	51.3	0.7
1998	44.09	9.93	34.16	6.28	4.48	1.80	14.2	45.1	5.3
1999	51.42	10.84	40.58	7.76	5.71	2.05	15.1	52.7	5.1
2000	63.31	13.40	49.91	7.06	3.87	3.19	11.2	28.9	6.4
2001	99.36	13.73	85.63	9.08	4.92	4.16	9.1	35.8	4.9
2002	118.31	16.55	101.76	10.12	7.17	2.95	8.6	43.3	2.9
2003	129.83	21.88	107.95	20.73	9.04	11.69	16.0	41.3	10.8
2004	118.09	29.52	88.57	19.59	11.62	7.97	16.6	39.4	9.0
2005	140.63	40.03	100.60	23.16	20.09	3.07	16.5	50.2	3.1
2006	171.47	45.51	125.96	26.17	22.16	4.01	15.3	48.7	3.2
2007	182.33	52.47	129.86	29.29	24.54	4.75	16.1	46.8	3.7
2008	230.84	55.25	175.59	37.01	30.99	6.02	16.0	56.1	3.4
2009	221.20	68.75	152.45	43.54	36.26	7.28	19.7	52.7	4.8
2010	329.82	100.41	229.41	45.65	39.93	5.72	13.8	39.8	2.5
2011	374.73	134.18	240.55	70.33	62.35	7.98	18.8	46.5	3.3

表8-6 中资保险机构主要险种的原保险保费收入和赔款支出

Former Premium Income and Indemnity Expenditure of Major Types of Chinese Funded Insurance Business

(2011)

单位:亿元 (100 million yuan)

指 标	Indicators	原保险保费收入 Former Premium Income	原保险赔款支出 Former Indemnity Expenditure	赔款率(%) Rate of Indemnity(%)
总 计	**Total**	**295.18**	**61.71**	**20.9**
财产险小计	Subtotal of Property Insurance	120.53	56.19	46.6
企业财产险	Enterprise Property Insurance	12.23	4.02	32.9
机动车辆险	Motor Vehicle Insurance	86.63	44.52	51.4
其 他	Others	21.67	7.65	35.3
人身险小计	Subtotal of Life Insurance	174.65	5.52	3.2
个 险	Individual Insurance	152.72	1.18	0.8
团 险	Team Insurance	21.93	4.34	19.8

表8-7 外资保险机构主要险种的原保险保费收入和赔款支出

Former Premium Income and Indemnity Expenditure of Major Types of Foreign Funded Insurance Business

(2011)

单位:亿元 (100 million yuan)

指 标	Indicators	原保险保费收入 Former Premium Income	原保险赔款支出 Former Indemnity Expenditure	赔款率(%) Rate of Indemnity(%)
总 计	**Total**	**77.64**	**6.73**	**8.7**
财产保险小计	Subtotal of Property Insurance	13.50	3.95	29.3
#企业财产险	Enterprise Property Insurance	3.74	0.91	24.3
货运险	Cargo Transportation Insurance	4.89	2.17	44.4
家财险	Household Property Insurance	0.04	0.01	25.0
责任保险	Liability Insurance	3.86	0.77	19.9
人身险	Life Insurance	64.14	2.78	4.3

表8-8 上海证券交易所市场交易主要指标
Statistics of Shanghai Stock Exchange

指标	Indicators	单位 Unit	2000	2005	2010	2011
交易天数	**Trading Days**	**天 day**	**239**	**242**	**242**	**244**
上市证券数	**Number of Securities Traded**	**个 unit**	**657**	**1 073**	**1 500**	**1 691**
股　票	Stocks	个 unit	614	878	938	975
A　股	A Share	个 unit	559	824	884	921
B　股	B Share	个 unit	55	54	54	54
债　券	Bonds	个 unit	25	165	536	680
政府债	Government Bonds	个 unit	7.00	43.00	199	213
公司债	Corporate Bonds	个 unit	10	65	284	417
回　购	Repurchase	个 unit	8	57	53	50
证券投资基金	Funds of Securities Investment	个 unit	18	25	13	13
ETF	Exchange Traded Funds	个 unit		1	12	23
权　证	Warrant	个 unit		4	1	0
股票市价总值	**Total Value of Stock Price**	**亿元 100 million yuan**	**27 294.80**	**38 067.81**	**179 007.24**	**148 376.22**
成交金额	**Turnover Value**	**亿元 100 million yuan**	**49 901.47**	**49 775.61**	**398 395.73**	**454 651.56**
股　票	Stocks	亿元 100 million yuan	31 373.86	19 240.21	304 312.01	237 560.45
A　股	A Share	亿元 100 million yuan	31 029.69	19 061.49	303 215.93	236 814.27
B　股	B Share	亿元 100 million yuan	344.17	178.72	1 096.08	746.18
债　券	Bonds	亿元 100 million yuan	16 895.82	28 138.41	74 914.42	210 714.87
政府债	Government Bonds	亿元 100 million yuan	3 657.06	2 772.79	1 590.04	1 243.11
公司债	Corporate Bonds	亿元 100 million yuan	91.55	446.56	3 306.79	4 850.47
回　购	Repurchase	亿元 100 million yuan	13 147.21	24 919.06	70 017.59	204 621.29
基　金	Funds	亿元 100 million yuan	1 334.18	576.78	4 771.71	2 901.41
权　证	Warrant	亿元 100 million yuan		1 763.07	14 397.58	3 474.82
其　他	Others	亿元 100 million yuan	297.61	57.14		
成交数量	**Volume Turnover**					
股　票	Stocks	亿手 100 million contracts		3 986.59	25 964.43	21 193.87
A　股	A Share	亿手 100 million contracts	2 310.87	3 926.89	25 812.40	21 079.68
B　股	B Share	亿手 100 million contracts	126.78	59.70	152.03	114.19
债　券	Bonds	亿手 100 million contracts	16.53	28.15	74.81	210.69
政府债	Government Bonds	亿手 100 million contracts	3.31	2.81	1.57	1.25
公司债	Corporate Bonds	亿手 100 million contracts	0.07	0.42	3.22	4.82
回　购	Repurchase	亿手 100 million contracts	13.15	24.92	70.02	204.62
基　金	Funds	亿手 100 million contracts	995.32	778.73	3 580.37	2 370.84
权　证	Warrant	亿手 100 million contracts		1 274.79	10 735.99	1 395.94
其　他	Others	亿手 100 million contracts	31.65	0.12		

注：2010 年起，上交所统计口径有调整，原表中“国债现货”和“地方政府债”数据，现合并为“政府债”；原表中“公司债”和“可转债”数据，现合并统称为“公司债”。

Note: Shanghai Stock Exchange has changed its statistical approach for its data since 2010. The data in the fields of “National Debts on Spots” and “Local Government Bonds” in the former table have been merged as those of “Government Bonds” and the fields of “Corporate Debts” and “Convertible Bonds” have been merged as “Corporate Bonds”.

表8-9　上海证券交易所市盈率和换手率
P/E Ratio & Turnover Rate of Shanghai Stock Exchange

指　标	Indicators	2000	2005	2010	2011
市盈率(%)	**P/E Rate**	**58.2**	**16.3**	**21.61**	**13.4**
A　股	A　Share	59.1	16.4	21.6	13.4
B　股	B　Share	25.2	12.4	23.9	12.3
换手率(%)	**Turnover Rate**	**449.1**	**274.4**	**198.5**	**124.8**
A　股	A　Share	504.1	290.7	199.3	125.1
B　股	B　Share	151.2	58.5	119.0	86.8

表8-10　上海证券交易所市场筹集资金
Capital Raising of Shanghai Stock Exchang

单位:亿元　　(100 million yuan)

指　标	Indicators	2000	2005	2010	2011
A股小计	**Subtotal of A Shares**	**882.41**	**308.75**	**5 532.14**	**3 199.69**
A股首次发行	IPO of A Shares	568.67	28.55	1 891.51	1 014.01
A股再次发行	Second Issuing of A Shares	313.74	280.20	3 640.62	2 185.68
#A股增发	Additional Issuing of A Shares	62.86	278.78	2 102.90	1 774.07
A股配股	Rights Issuing of A Shares	250.88	1.42	1 415.73	378.37
A股行权	Rights Claiming of A Shares			84.28	29.49

表8-11　浦东新区上市公司分行业汇总情况
Listed Companies in PNA by Sector
(2011)

指　标	Indicators	单　位　Unit	地产类 Real Estate	工业类 Industry	公用事业类 Public Utilities	商业类 Commerce	综合类 Comprehens-ive
发行股数	Number of Stocks Issued	亿股 100 million in number	76.05	216.21	382.47	31.47	720.55
流通股数	Number of Stocks Circulated	亿股 100 million in number	71.88	184.51	294.28	30.65	668.51
成交额	Volume	亿元 100 million yuan	944.94	4 998.02	1 829.19	703.78	5 489.92
成交股数	Number of Stock Transacted	亿股 100 million in number	109.83	417.21	221.52	64.57	586.83
市盈率	P/E Ratio	%	12.6	21.4	11.4	24.2	9.2
换手率	Turnover Rate	%	160.5	240.1	75.4	174.6	94.6
市价总值	Total Market Value	亿元 100 million yuan	485.60	1 590.09	1 497.58	268.04	4 244.80
流通市值	Circulating Market Value	亿元 100 million yuan	446.76	1 371.21	1 118.19	262.24	3 788.93

注：1. 浦东新区上市公司指公司注册地含"浦东"的公司。
2. 数据包含A股和B股。
3. "成交额"、"成交股数"、"换手率"为2011年整年数据。
4. "发行股数"、"流通股数"、"市盈率"、"市值总值"、"流通市值"为2011年12月31日数据。

Note: 1. Newly listed companies in PNA refer to those companies that registered in Pudong.
2. The data include both A shares and B shares.
3. The items of Business Volume, Number of Transacted Stocks and Turnover Rate are data in the whole year of 2011.
4. The items of Number of Issued Stocks, Number of Circulated Stocks, P/E Ratio, Total Market Value and Circulating Market Value are data of December 31, 2011.

表8-12 上海联合产权交易所基本情况
Shanghai United Assets and Equity Exchange

指 标	Indicators	单 位 Unit	2000	2005	2010	2011
成交企业数	**Number of Enterprises Acquired /Merged**	**户 unit**	**2 794**	**3 395**	**1 981**	**1 749**
按企业产权出让分	By Property Rights Transferring Out					
# 国有企业	State-owned Enterprises	户 unit	748	1 457	1 099	1 039
集体企业	Collective-owned Enterprises	户 unit	719	488	136	123
有限责任	Limited Liability	户 unit		659	211	191
按企业产权受让分	By Property Rights Transferring In					
# 国有企业	State-owned Enterprises	户 unit	255	777	766	557
集体企业	Collective-owned Enterprises	户 unit	222	76	38	75
有限责任	Limited Liability	户 unit		567	233	178
外商独资	Solely Foreigner Funded	户 unit	29	231	62	63
私营企业	Private Enterprises	户 unit	38	385	270	307
自然人	Natural Person	户 unit		1 329	563	520
交易额合计	**Total Volume of Trade**	**亿元 100 million yuan**	**480.31**	**4 002.80**	**2 325.35**	**1 016.91**
按企业产权出让分	By Property Rights Transferring Out					
# 国有企业	State-owned Enterprises	亿元 100 million yuan	68.73	1 489.64	1 807.25	788.43
集体企业	Collective-owned Enterprises	亿元 100 million yuan	38.82	46.78	7.69	13.89
有限责任	Limited Liability	亿元 100 million yuan		225.29	47.01	93.61
按企业产权受让分	By Property Rights Transferring In					
# 国有企业	State-owned Enterprises	亿元 100 million yuan	42.58	690.52	1 702.79	569.88
集体企业	Collective-owned Enterprises	亿元 100 million yuan	13.85	11.95	32.67	9.48
有限责任	Limited Liability	亿元 100 million yuan		835.91	99.21	169.90
外商独资	Solely Foreigner Funded	亿元 100 million yuan	9.56	116.72	31.68	62.11
私营企业	Private Enterprises	亿元 100 million yuan	0.52	96.07	87.72	130.05
自然人	Natural Person	亿元 100 million yuan		4.86	12.19	19.66

注：交易额，原指“产权交易标的对应总资产金额”，2010年调整为“产权交易合同价款金额”。
Note: Total Volume of Trade“formerly referred to” Total Capital Corresponding to Transacted Object of Property Rights “and it was readjusted as” Contracted Value of Transacted Property Rights“in 2010”.

表8-13　上海期货交易所市场交易主要指标
Major Indicators of Shanghai Futures Exchange

指　标	Indicators	单　位　Unit	2000	2005	2010	2011
会员单位	**Membership**	**户 unit**	**216**	**215**	**209**	**208**
经纪单位	Broking	户 unit	162	175	164	163
非经纪单位	Non-Broking	户 unit	54	40	45	45
交易天数	Business Days in the Year	天 day	241	242	242	244
上市交易品种	Business Lines	个 unit	3	4	8	9
成交量	**Total Volume of Business**	**万手 10 000 contracts**	**825.27**	**6 757.95**	**124 379.64**	**61 647.84**
铜	Copper	万手 10 000 contracts	534.72	2 470.41	10 157.71	9 792.23
铝	Aluminum	万手 10 000 contracts	91.00	425.00	3 452.40	1 990.78
锌	Zinc	万手 10 000 contracts			29 317.87	10 732.7
铅	Lead	万手 10 000 contracts				58.66
黄　金	Gold	万手 10 000 contracts			679.41	1 444.35
天然橡胶	Natural Rubber	万手 10 000 contracts	199.53	1 900.63	33 482.98	20 857.28
燃料油	Fuel Oil	万手 10 000 contracts		1 961.91	2 136.44	394.23
螺纹钢	Rebar	万手 10 000 contracts			45 122.48	16 376.96
线　材	Wire Rod	万手 10 000 contracts			30.35	0.65
成交金额	**Total Value of Business**	**亿元 100 million yuan**	**6 663.42**	**65 402.03**	**1234 794.76**	**869 068.72**
铜	Copper	亿元 100 million yuan	5 037.73	40 463.23	296 437.54	299 334.19
铝	Aluminum	亿元 100 million yuan	731.79	3 714.46	28 342.48	17 070.34
锌	Zinc	亿元 100 million yuan			255 725.62	92 365.50
铅	Lead	亿元 101 million yuan				2 561.59
黄　金	Gold	亿元 100 million yuan			18 291.92	50 976.08
天然橡胶	Natural Rubber	亿元 100 million yuan	893.90	15 601.79	426 464.81	330 474.23
燃料油	Fuel Oil	亿元 100 million yuan		5 622.55	9 886.37	1 928.77
螺纹钢	Rebar	亿元 100 million yuan			199 517.15	74 355.03
线　材	Wire Rod	亿元 100 million yuan			128.87	2.99
年末持仓量	**Year End Contracts**	**万手 10 000 contracts**	**14.85**	**30.95**	**206.46**	**214.00**
铜	Copper	万手 10 000 contracts	11.10	10.58	37.31	42.96
铝	Aluminum	万手 10 000 contracts	2.04	7.89	23.73	24.99
锌	Zinc	万手 10 000 contracts			40.24	37.37
铅	Lead	万手 10 000 contracts				0.26
黄　金	Gold	万手 10 000 contracts			7.88	10.23
天然橡胶	Natural Rubber	万手 10 000 contracts	1.71	5.70	21.46	29.93

表 8－13 续表 Continued

指 标 Indicators		单 位 Unit	2000	2005	2010	2011
燃料油	Fuel Oil	万手 10 000 contracts		6.78	10.44	0.09
螺纹钢	Rebar	万手 10 000 contracts			65.40	68.17
线 材	Wire Rod	万手 10 000 contracts			0.01	0.01
交割量	**Volume of Transaction**	**万手 10 000 contracts**	**7.20**	**8.73**	**37.69**	**27.75**
铜	Copper	万手 10 000 contracts	5.23	3.07	3.84	3.17
铝	Aluminum	万手 10 000 contracts	1.49	2.18	11.52	12.16
锌	Zinc	万手 10 000 contracts			6.15	6.71
铅	Lead	万手 10 000 contracts				0.13
黄 金	Gold	万手 10 000 contracts			0.05	0.07
天然橡胶	Natural Rubber	万手 10 000 contracts	0.48	1.52	2.57	1.01
燃料油	Fuel Oil	万手 10 000 contracts		1.96	6.90	4.18
螺纹钢	Rebar	万手 10 000 contracts			6.00	0.32
线 材	Wire Rod	万手 10 000 contracts			0.66	
交割金额	**Value of Transaction**	**亿元 100 million yuan**	**61.93**	**88.29**	**349.06**	**312.44**
铜	Copper	亿元 100 million yuan	47.69	54.54	113.40	106.24
铝	Aluminum	亿元 100 million yuan	12.09	18.07	90.41	102.86
锌	Zinc	亿元 100 million yuan			53.77	57.57
铅	Lead	亿元 101 million yuan				4.89
黄 金	Gold	亿元 100 million yuan			1.46	2.30
天然橡胶	Natural Rubber	亿元 100 million yuan	2.15	10.79	32.21	17.12
燃料油	Fuel Oil	亿元 100 million yuan		4.89	30.28	19.92
螺纹钢	Rebar	亿元 100 million yuan			24.89	1.54
线 材	Wire Rod	亿元 100 million yuan			2.64	
交割率	**Rate of Transaction**					
铜	Copper	%	1.8	0.2	0.1	0.1
铝	Aluminum	%	4.1	1.0	0.7	1.0
锌	Zinc	%			0.1	0.1
铅	Lead	%				0.5
黄 金	Gold	%			…	
天然橡胶	Natural Rubber	%	0.8	0.3	…	
燃料油	Fuel Oil	%		0.2	0.5	0.7
螺纹钢	Rebar	%			…	
线 材	Wire Rod	%			2.0	

表8-14 上海钻石交易所市场交易主要指标
Major Indicators of Shanghai Diamond Exchange

指标	Indicators	单位 Unit	2009	2010	2011
会员单位	**Membership**	**户 unit**	**243**	**283**	**326**
外资会员	Foreign Member	户 unit	165	193	215
中资会员	Chinese Member	户 unit	78	90	111
成交量	**Total Volume of Business**	**万克拉 10 000 carat**	**9 978.77**	**19 762.53**	**14 821.08**
钻石进境量	Volume of Diamond Coming in Border	万克拉 10 000 carat	55.60	92.60	78.62
钻石出境量	Volume of Diamond Leaving our Country	万克拉 10 000 carat	12.81	24.03	20.54
钻石进口量	Volume of Imports	万克拉 10 000 carat	76.11	118.53	140.35
钻石出口量	Volume of Exports	万克拉 10 000 carat	9 820.91	19 518.03	14 573.90
钻石保税交易量	Volume of Bonded Transactions	万克拉 10 000 carat	12.06	7.54	6.06
钻石加工贸易量	Volume of Processing Trade	万克拉 10 000 carat	1.28	1.80	1.61
成交金额	**Total Value of Transactions**	**万美元 10 000 USD**	**150 400.40**	**288 568.49**	**470 669.41**
钻石进境额	Amount of Diamond Coming in Border	万美元 10 000 USD	52 738.89	104 620.22	171 616.92
钻石出境额	Amount of Diamond Leaving our Country	万美元 10 000 USD	14 539.04	38 044.48	78 816.94
钻石进口额	Amount of Imports	万美元 10 000 USD	69 621.25	131 092.79	204 010.28
钻石出口额	Amount of Exports	万美元 10 000 USD	783.67	1 281.58	1 809.73
钻石保税交易额	Amount of Bonded Transactions	万美元 10 000 USD	12 244.57	13 042.58	13 334.89
钻石加工贸易额	Amount of Processing Trade	万美元 10 000 USD	472.98	486.84	1 080.65

表8-15 新区属人才交流市场基本情况
Basic Statistics of PNA Professional Resources Market(PPRM)

指 标	Indicators	单位 Unit	2000	2005	2010	2011
全年举办交流活动	Number of Exchange Activites in the Year	场 in number	54	133	193	214
参与人才招聘单位	Number of Participating Organizations	个 unit	1 890	3 859	7 462	7 220
接待咨询服务人次	Job-seeking Visitors Received	万人次 10 000 person-times	8.27	19.67	37.00	35.00
办理择业登记人数	Job-seeking Visitors Registered	人次 person-time	26 670	90 452	211 000	205 000
达成意向人数	Number of Job-seekers Who Have Signed Letters of Intent	人 person	68 963	37 302	39 949	34 433
获得上海市居住证人数	Number of Persons Who Have Obtained Shanghai Residence Permits	人 person		7 158	30 985	43 606
后续服务	**Follow-up Services**					
档案保管	File-keeping	件 file	2 727	5 691	13 489	13 561
户籍挂靠(迁入)	Domiciling(immigration)	户 unit		1 605	1 175	2 278

主要统计指标解释

存　款

是企业、机关、团体或居民等根据资金必须收回的原则，把货币资金存入银行或其他信用机构保管并取得一定利息的一种信用活动形式。根据存款对象的不同可划分为企业存款、财政存款、机关团体存款、储蓄存款等科目。它是银行信贷资金的主要来源。

贷　款

是银行或其他信用机构根据资金必须归还的原则，按一定利率，为企业、个人等提供资金的一种信用活动形式。我国银行贷款分为短期贷款、中期流动资金贷款、中长期贷款、信托贷款以及工业贷款、商业贷款等科目。

居民储蓄存款年末余额

居民和农民个人在银行、信用社等金融机构储蓄存款年末余额。不包括居民的手存现金和企事业单位、部队、机关团体等的集体存款。

保险金额

指保险人承担赔偿或者给付保险金责任的最高限额。

保险费

保险费是指投保人根据保险合同的有关规定，为保险受益人取得因保险事故发生所造成的经济损失予以补偿(或给付)权利，付给保险人的代价。包括财产险和人身险储金类支出。

保险赔款及给付

保险赔款及给付指保险事故发生后，经查证确属保险责任范围以内的保险标的损失，保险人根据保险合同的规定履行赔偿义务，给予被保险人(或投保人指定的受益人)的款项。

市价总值

市价总值即全部股份乘上市场价格。

流通市值

流通市值指在某特定时间内当时可交易的流通股股数乘以当时股价得出的流通股票总价值。

市盈率

市盈率是某种股票每股市价与每股盈利的比率。

市盈率 = 普通股每股市场价格 ÷ 普通股每年每股盈利

换手率

换手率是指在一定时间内市场中股票转手买卖的频率。

金融债券

金融债券，是指银行和非银行金融机构为筹集资金而发行的债券。其债务人为发行债券的金融机构。

企业债券

企业债券通常又称为公司债券，是企业依照法定程序发行，约定在一定期限内还本付息的债券。企业债券代表着发债企业和投资者之间的一种债权债务关系。债券持有人是企业的债权人，不是所有者，无权参与或干涉企业经营管理，但债券持有人有权按期收回本息。企业债券与股票一样，同属有价证券，可以自由转让。

可转换债券

可转换债券，又译可换股债券，是债券的一种，它可以转换为债券发行公司的股票，其转换比率一般会在发行时确定。可转换债券通常具有较低的票面利率，因为可以转换成股票的权利是对债券持有人的一种补偿。另外，将可转换债券转换为普通股时，所换得的股票价值一般远大于原债券价值。可转换债券是在发行公司债券的基础上，附加了一份期权，并允许购买人在规定的时间范围内将其购买的债券转换成指定公司的股票。

持仓量

持仓量指的是在交易所市场上未平仓的期权合约的数量，也指某一种类或系列中未平仓的期权合约的数量。

成交量

成交量指当天成交的股票数量。

交　割

交割概念来源于期货，分为：实物交割和现金交割。

实物交割，是指期货合约的买卖双方于合约到期时，根据交易所制订的规则和程序，通过期货合约标的物的所有权转移，将到期未平仓合约进行了结的行为。商品期货交易一般采用实物交割的方式。

现金交割，是指到期未平仓期货合约进行交割时，用结算价格来计算未平仓合约的盈亏，以现金支付的方式最终了结期货合约的交割方式。这种交割方式主要用于金融期货等期货标的物无法进行实物交割的期货合约。

EXPLANATORY NOTES TO MAJOR STATISTICAL INDICATORS

Deposits

Deposits are a form of credit by which enterprises, institutions, organizations or residents put money into banks and other credit institutions for safekeeping and earn interests under the principle of free withdrawal. According to different depositors, deposits are divided into enterprise deposits, treasury deposits, deposits of institutions and organizations, urban savings deposits and other deposits. Deposits constitute a major source of bank credit funds.

Loans

Loans are a form of credit by which banks and other credit institutions provide funds with a specified interest to enterprises and individuals under the principle of free repayment. Loans from Chinese banks include short term loans, medium term circulating capital loans, long term loans, trust loans, industrial loans and commercial loans.

Savings Deposit Balance of Urban and Rural Residents

refers to year-end savings deposit balance of urban residents and farmers at banks, credit unions and other financial institutions, excluding cash held by residents and collective savings of enterprises, institutions, military units and government agencies.

Amount Insured

Amount Insured refers to the maximum that the insurant will get for the claim of the case insured .

Premium

Premium is the fee paid by the insurant to the insurer to obtain the obligation of compensation from the insurance within the agreed terms. It includes saving payment for property and life insurance.

Insurance Indemnity

Insurance Indemnity is the compensation paid by the insurer to the insurant or the beneficiary, when an accident has happened to the insured property or life and the loss has been investigated and verified to be within the insurance obligation.

Total Market Value

Total Market Value means all of the stock shares multiplied by their relevant market price.

Circulation Value on the Market

Circulation Value on the Market means the tradable circulation shares multiplied by their relevant share prices during a certain period of time.

P/E Ratio

P/E Ratio refers to the ratio between the price of a certain share and its earnings per year. The P/E ratio is the price of a traded common share divided by its annual earnings.

Exchange Rate

Exchange Rate means the trading frequency of certain stock shares on the market during a certain period of time.

Financial Bonds

Financial Bonds refer to those that banks and non-banking financial institutions issue to raise funds. Their debtors are the financial institutions that issue the bonds.

Corporate Bonds

Corporate Bonds usually refer to business bonds, which will be issued in accordance with the statutory procedures of the business and repay the original investment plus agreed interest within a certain period of time. Corporate bonds represent a kind of debtor-creditor relationship between the issuing enterprises and the investors. Bondholders are creditors of the certain enterprise, not the owners, and they do not have the right to participate or interfere with the business management. However, the bondholders have the right to claim the principal and interest on time. Like the stock shares, corporate bonds belong to marketable securities and can be freely transferable.

Convertible Bonds

Convertible Bonds, also translated into convertible exchangeable bonds, can be converted into the stock shares of the enterprise that issue the bonds. The conversion rate will usually be determined at the time of distribution. Convertible bonds generally have lower nominal interest rates, because the right of being converted into stock shares is a kind of compensation to the bondholders. In addition, when the bonds are converted into ordinary shares, the prices of these shares usually are far higher than the original value of the bonds. In essence, the convertible bonds have an additional option on the basis of the business bonds, and these bondholders are allowed to convert the convertible bonds they have purchased into the stock shares of specific companies during the specific period.

Open Interest

Open Interest refers to the number of open option contracts in the exchange market, also refers to the number of one or series of open option contracts.

Turnover

Turnover refers to the transaction volume of stock shares traded on that certain day.

Delivery

Delivery, its concept comes from futures, can be divided into physical delivery and cash delivery.

Physical delivery refers to the behavior that the vendor and the purchaser finish the open contracts at the end of the term by means of the ownership transfer of the object of futures contracts in accordance with rules and procedures of the stock exchange when the contract expires. The transaction of commodity futures usually adopts the physical delivery.

Cash delivery refers to the way that the two sides finally close their futures contracts by means of cash, with the settlement price used to calculate earnings or loss of the open contracts when the open futures contracts are delivered at the end of term. This kind of delivery is mainly used for futures contracts that their objects can not be dealt with physical delivery such as the financial futures.

第九篇

Chapter 9

房地产

REAL ESTATE

SHANGHAI PUDONG NEW AREA STATISTICAL YEARBOOK

表9-1　房地产开发投资
(2011)

单位:亿元

指　标 Indicators		企业个数(个) Enterprises (unit)	本年完成投资 Current Year Investment Completed	
				建筑工程 Construction Project
总　计	**Total**	**729**	**589.45**	**347.57**
按登记注册类型分	**By Type of Registration**			
内　资	Domestic Investment	610	479.49	294.21
国　有	State-owned	64	60.01	44.92
集　体	Collective-owned	12	11.80	10.27
股份合作	Share-holding	1	0.42	
联　营	Jointly-operated	9	23.68	17.08
有限责任公司	Companies with Limited Liability	230	230.20	123.51
股份有限公司	Companies Limited by Shares	49	12.14	11.00
私　营	Private	240	134.50	85.47
其　他	Others	5	6.73	1.96
港澳台商投资	Hong Kong/Macao/Taiwan Investment	73	56.04	32.52
#港澳台商独资	Solely Hong Kong/Macao/Taiwan Funded	31	35.00	16.22
外商投资	FIE	46	53.92	20.84
#外商独资	Solely Foreign Funded	26	18.78	13.34
按隶属关系分	**By Subordination**			
中央属	Central Government	22	33.61	23.52
市(局)属	Municipality/Bureau	89	76.83	45.67
区　属	PNA	157	100.43	72.42
外省市属	Non-Shanghai	6	5.91	4.95
其他属	Others	455	372.66	201.01
按企业资质等级分	**By Qualifications of Enterprises**			
一　级	Grade 1	42	15.44	11.87
二　级	Grade 2	156	85.46	64.22
三　级	Grade 3	117	36.50	29.10
无　级	No Grade	414	452.04	242.38

Investment in Real Estate Development

(100 million yuan)

完成投资按构成分 By Composition of Completed Investment			完成投资按工程用途分 By Project Use of Completed Investment			
安装工程 Installation	设备工器具购置 Equipment Purchasing	其他费用 Other Cost	住　宅 Residential Housing	办公楼 Office Buildings	商业营业用房 Commerce/ Operation	其　他 Others
34.69	**3.47**	**203.72**	**404.60**	**52.42**	**62.30**	**70.13**
29.92	3.47	151.88	338.85	33.27	45.08	62.30
3.11	0.27	11.72	45.13	4.02	2.11	8.75
0.47		1.06	10.73		0.22	0.86
		0.42				0.42
0.10		6.50	19.64		0.37	3.67
19.52	2.79	84.38	171.59	12.27	21.00	25.34
		1.15	3.46	4.73	2.15	1.80
6.69	0.41	41.93	84.95	12.26	15.83	21.46
0.04		4.73	3.34		3.39	
2.20		21.32	33.16	13.78	6.67	2.43
0.64		18.14	24.91	4.16	5.51	0.42
2.56		30.52	32.60	5.38	10.55	5.40
1.66		3.78	8.41	5.08	2.72	2.56
1.12		8.98	23.89	3.99	3.04	2.68
5.96	0.15	25.05	51.88	4.68	9.62	10.66
4.68	0.56	22.77	61.69	12.49	8.88	17.36
		0.96	1.92	3.02	0.48	0.49
22.93	2.76	145.96	265.21	28.24	40.28	38.94
2.07	0.11	1.41	13.70	0.08	0.63	1.04
4.95	0.24	16.05	61.66	6.92	5.57	11.31
2.29		5.12	26.29	1.86	4.16	4.20
25.39	3.12	181.15	302.95	43.57	51.94	53.59

表9-2　房地产开发企业投资资金来源
(2011)

单位:亿元

指　标	Indicators	本年资金来源合计 Total Sources of Funds	上年末结余资本 Remnant Capital of Previous Year	本年资金来源小计 Subtotal of Current Year
总　计	**Total**	**1 087.50**	**358.90**	**728.60**
按登记注册类型分	**By Type of Registration**			
内　资	Domestic Investment	868.98	256.78	612.21
国　有	State-owned	78.28	10.09	68.19
集　体	Collective-owned	14.62	1.86	12.76
股份合作	Share-holding	0.67	0.67	
联　营	Jointly-operated	25.54	3.22	22.32
有限责任公司	Companies with Limited Liability	444.29	166.10	278.19
股份有限公司	Companies Limited by Shares	14.96		14.96
私　营	Private	282.65	74.52	208.14
其　他	Others	7.97	0.32	7.66
港澳台商投资	Hong Kong/Macao/Taiwan Investment	114.40	56.89	57.50
#港澳台商独资	Solely Hong Kong/Macao/Taiwan Funded	32.10	8.51	23.59
外商投资	FIE	104.12	45.23	58.89
#外商独资	Solely Foreign Funded	54.41	23.77	30.64
按隶属关系分	**By Subordination**			
中央属	Central Government	46.25	3.21	43.04
市(局)属	Municipality/Bureau	92.10	19.45	72.64
区　属	PNA	156.56	16.43	140.13
外省市属	Non-Shanghai	12.27	1.54	10.73
其他属	Others	780.32	318.27	462.06
按企业资质等级分	**By Qualifications of Enterprises**			
一　级	Grade 1	13.00	1.47	11.54
二　级	Grade 2	142.48	36.42	106.06
三　级	Grade 3	77.48	20.95	56.53
无　级	No Grade	854.54	300.06	554.47

Sources of Funds of Investment in Real Estate Development

(100 million yuan)

国内贷款 Domestic Loans	利用外资 Foreign Funds	自筹资金 Self-raised Funds	# 自有资金 Self-owned	其他资金来源 Other Funds	本年各项应付款合计 Current Year Total Amount Payable	# 工程款 Project Funds
183.42	**3.26**	**294.85**	**131.94**	**247.07**	**122.05**	**48.41**
136.73	0.12	271.78	115.77	203.58	96.95	41.77
33.12		23.05	7.40	12.02	13.84	10.53
3.60		4.15		5.01	0.19	0.13
7.15		13.74	10.93	1.44	2.13	0.89
44.31		153.12	54.90	80.76	24.32	19.74
2.76		12.20	11.53			
45.40	0.12	61.68	27.88	100.94	56.47	10.48
0.40		3.85	3.13	3.41		
17.93	1.16	12.18	6.17	26.23	19.07	2.23
12.87	1.16	2.00	2.00	7.56	18.67	1.83
28.75	1.99	10.89	10.00	17.26	6.03	4.40
17.85	1.99			10.80	2.91	2.57
0.68		36.94	13.17	5.42	2.49	1.90
16.90		47.29	27.32	8.45	8.10	7.78
37.25		49.94	26.43	52.94	23.54	17.76
2.31		1.72		6.70		
126.27	3.26	158.97	65.02	173.55	87.93	20.97
3.90		4.59	4.59	3.05	9.35	5.75
31.09		38.45	18.33	36.52	8.85	7.31
19.61		16.53	5.12	20.39	12.92	3.59
128.82	3.26	235.29	103.90	187.11	90.94	31.76

表9-3　房地产开发企业房屋施工面积、竣工面积和销售面积 (2011)

单位:万平方米

指　标	Indicators	施工面积 Floor Area Under Construction	#新开工面积 Floor Area of New Starts	竣工面积 Floor Area Completed
总　计	**Total**	**3 511.82**	**884.07**	**487.81**
按登记注册类型分	**By Type of Registration**			
内　资	Domestic Investment	3 064.74	812.70	423.72
国　有	State-owned	440.59	97.68	5.39
集　体	Collective-owned	110.35	47.12	
股份合作	Share-holding			
联　营	Jointly-operated	142.04	16.25	6.57
有限责任公司	Companies with Limited Liability	1 360.66	354.67	223.03
股份有限公司	Companies Limited by Shares	170.21	41.81	20.42
私　营	Private	806.69	232.62	162.71
其　他	Others	34.20	22.55	5.60
港澳台商投资	Hong Kong/Macao/Taiwan Invested	269.90	38.73	14.88
#港澳台商独资	Solely Hong Kong/Macao/Taiwan Funded	116.06	11.21	9.13
外商投资	FIE	177.18	32.64	49.21
#外商独资	Solely Foreign Funded	118.32	10.96	40.50
按隶属关系分	**By Subordination**			
中央属	Central Government	256.06	126.87	5.60
市(局)属	Municipality/Bureau	458.73	95.38	101.67
区　属	PNA	892.74	208.06	84.28
外省市属	Non-Shanghai	29.14		
其他属	Others	1 875.14	453.75	296.26
按企业资质等级分	**By Qualifications of Enterprises**			
一　级	Grade 1	108.61	22.18	5.19
二　级	Grade 2	731.83	170.62	64.96
三　级	Grade 3	297.90	54.70	64.10
无　级	No Grade	2 373.48	636.57	353.56

Floor Space Under Construction, Completed and Sold in Real Estate Development in Real Estate Development

(10 000 sq · m)

			竣工价值(亿元) Completion Value (100 million yuan)	现房销售面积 Sold Floor Space for Completed Housing	期房销售面积 Area of Forward Sale of Future Marketable Housing
#住 宅 Housing	办公楼 Office Building	商业营业用房 Commerce/ Operation			
286.14	**56.76**	**73.01**	**253.25**	**107.04**	**287.65**
274.68	44.44	44.48	201.28	92.83	266.58
	4.69		1.35	9.98	19.06
				0.22	1.57
4.80		1.76	2.97	2.29	13.53
160.63	27.64	11.04	99.16	40.62	141.24
		7.93	15.39	2.02	
109.24	12.10	18.14	80.36	37.30	91.18
		5.60	2.06	0.39	
8.46	3.57	1.05	16.61	3.61	9.34
2.71	3.57	1.05	9.79	0.67	2.79
3.01	8.75	27.49	35.36	10.60	11.73
3.01	8.75	27.49	33.29	9.88	4.04
		5.60	2.06	2.12	15.52
46.16	8.80	26.77	48.85	7.66	15.43
39.27	21.89	8.39	37.64	17.44	62.85
				0.06	4.84
200.71	26.07	32.26	164.70	79.76	189.01
	2.39	2.80	1.87	1.77	
38.00	4.69	4.30	33.69	11.86	48.28
57.79		0.95	36.46	44.55	26.22
190.36	49.68	64.96	181.23	48.85	213.16

表9-4 历年全社会房屋施工面积、竣工面积

Total Floor Space Under Construction and Completed in Main Years (1992～2011)

年 份 Year	施工面积（万平方米）Floor Space Under Construction (10 000 sq·m)	#住 宅 Residential Housing	竣工面积（万平方米）Floor Space Completed (10 000 sq·m)	#住 宅 Residential Housing	房屋建筑面积竣工率（%）Construction Completion Rate(%)	#住 宅 Residential Housing
1992	312.15	123.00	104.70	69.27	33.5	56.3
1993	764.36	285.34	169.44	76.68	22.2	26.9
1994	1 158.24	450.03	458.33	113.92	39.6	25.3
1995	1 577.21	583.96	404.58	199.84	25.7	34.2
1996	2 226.58	904.18	674.49	355.31	30.3	39.3
1997	1 954.70	768.15	581.03	271.64	29.7	35.4
1998	2 014.17	911.68	578.31	301.41	28.7	33.1
1999	1 766.88	856.25	573.20	268.27	32.4	31.3
2000	1 549.57	711.80	544.22	255.21	35.1	35.9
2001	1 526.45	879.01	469.53	249.96	30.8	28.4
2002	2 328.47	1 737.98	611.48	512.11	26.3	29.5
2003	2 242.65	1 607.68	671.70	498.85	29.9	31.0
2004	2 250.62	1 569.76	632.76	453.83	28.1	28.9
2005	2 390.79	1 695.24	684.96	512.42	28.6	30.2
2006	2 204.65	1 589.11	779.65	597.52	35.4	37.6
2007	1 983.86	1 255.32	516.59	419.29	26.0	33.4
2008	1 964.30	1 058.98	477.85	255.77	24.3	24.2
2009	2 977.23	1 792.12	742.28	505.70	24.9	28.2
2010	3 211.12	2 085.07	424.90	296.70	13.2	14.2
2011	3 511.82	2 296.52	487.81	286.14	13.9	12.5

表9-5 主要年份房地产开发企业房屋建筑面积和造价

Floor Space and Cost of Constructions Developed by Real Estate Companies in Main years

指 标	Indicators	1998	1999	2000	2005	2010	2011
房屋施工面积（万平方米）	**Floor Space Under Construction (10 000 sq·m)**	**1 458.94**	**1 097.51**	**1 119.67**	**2 390.79**	**3 211.12**	**3 511.82**
住 宅	Residential Housing	789.35	661.96	712.17	1 695.24	2 085.07	2 296.52
#别墅、高档公寓	Villas and Flats	77.46	54.65	72.64	490.51	394.58	389.13
办公楼	Office Buildings	404.07	250.74	199.39	196.68	300.14	355.28
商业营业用房	Commercial Buildings	155.58	110.28	106.63	222.13	389.62	374.73
其 他	Others	109.94	74.53	101.48	276.74	436.30	485.29
房屋竣工面积（万平方米）	**Floor Space Completed (10 000 sq·m)**	**360.36**	**313.70**	**384.03**	**684.96**	**424.90**	**487.81**
住 宅	Residential Housing	231.94	235.73	264.91	512.42	296.70	286.14
#别墅、高档公寓	Villas and Flats	26.10	15.92	23.59	168.59	85.58	82.00
办公楼	Office Buildings	71.15	27.30	54.62	54.08	31.61	56.76
商业营业用房	Commercial Buildings	41.16	24.55	28.10	32.85	35.85	73.01
其 他	Others	16.11	26.12	36.40	85.61	60.74	71.90
房屋竣工价值（亿元）	**Value of Buildings Completed (100 million yuan)**	**141.19**	**104.99**	**110.16**	**204.11**	**173.20**	**253.25**
住 宅	Residential Housing	61.74	44.56	55.36	147.55	127.76	137.29
#别墅、高档公寓	Villas and Flats	16.91	5.13	9.86	61.51	71.53	61.26
办公楼	Office Buildings	53.89	25.33	35.25	26.18	13.98	36.45
商业营业用房	Commercial Buildings	20.61	20.86	11.02	10.09	12.98	53.16
其 他	Others	4.95	14.24	8.53	20.29	18.47	26.35
竣工房屋平均造价（元/平方米）	**Average Construction Cost (yuan/sq. m)**	**3 918**	**3 347**	**2 869**	**2 980**	**4 076**	**5 192**
住 宅	Residential Housing	2 662	1 890	2 090	2 879	4 306	4 798
#别墅、高档公寓	Villas and Flats	6 481	3 221	4 179	3 648	8 358	7 471
办公楼	Office Buildings	7 575	9 276	6 454	4 841	4 423	6 421
商业营业用房	Commercial Buildings	5 007	8 498	3 921	3 075	3 622	7 281
其 他	Others	3 078	5 452	2 345	2 371	3 042	3 666

表9-6 浦东房地产交易中心交易情况
Transactions in Pudong Real Estate Trading Center

指 标 Indicators		单 位 Unit	2009	2010	2011
商品房交易登记	**Registered Transaction of Commodity Housing**				
#商品房出售套数	Number of Commodity Housing Sold	套 set	62 513	73 892	50 670
商品房出售面积	Floor Space of Commodity Housing Sold	平方米 sq・m	6 353 507	7 197 092	5 096 893
商品房出售金额	Value of Commodity Housing Sold	万元 10 000 yuan	5 587 208	6 799 748	6 015 128
商品房预售套数	Number of Forward Sale of Commodity Housing	套 set	37 345	14 905	10 726
商品房预售面积	Floor Space of Forward Sale of Commodity Housing	平方米 sq・m	4 153 784	1 629 081	1 238 582
商品房预售金额	Value of Forward Sale of Commodity Housing	万元 10 000 yuan	6 990 759	3 283 668	2 810 003
存量房交易登记	**Registered Transaction of Housing at Stock**				
存量房交易过户套数	Trading Number of Housing at Stock	套 set	66 107	43 162	30 890
存量房交易过户面积	Trading Floor Space of Housing at Stock	平方米 sq・m	6 437 403	4 537 343	2 893 805
存量房交易过户金额	Trading Value of Housing at Stock	万元 10 000 yuan	7 820 027	6 277 733	4 765 762

主要统计指标解释

房地产开发投资

指各种登记注册类型的房地产开发公司、商品房建设公司及其他房地产开发法人单位和附属于其他法人单位实际从事房地产开发或经营活动的单位统一开发的包括统代建、拆迁还建的住宅、厂房、仓库、饭店、宾馆、度假村、写字楼、办公楼等房屋建筑物和配套的服务设施，土地开发工程（如道路、给水、排水、供电、供热、通讯、平整场地等基础设施工程）的投资；不包括单纯的土地交易活动。

施工面积

指报告期内施工的全部房屋建筑面积。包括本期新开工的面积和上期开工跨入本期继续施工的房屋面积，以及上期已停建在本期恢复施工的房屋面积。本期竣工和本期施工后又停缓建的房屋，其建筑面积仍计入本期房屋施工面积中。

竣工面积

指在报告期内房屋建筑按照设计要求已经全部完工，达到住人和使用条件，经验收鉴定合格（或达到竣工验收标准），正式移交使用单位的各栋房屋建筑面积的总和。

房屋建筑面积竣工率

指一定时期内房屋竣工面积占同期房屋施工面积的比率。该指标从房屋建筑施工速度的角度反映投资效果的指标。

别墅、高档公寓

指建筑造价和销售价格明显高于一般商品住宅的商品住宅。别墅一般指地处郊区，独立成栋的商品住宅；高档公寓一般指地处市内高尚社区，高层或多层的商品住宅。别墅、高档公寓的确定标准：一是经有房地产投资计划审批权的主管部门审批建设的别墅、高档公寓开发项目；二是销售价格高于当地同等地段商品住宅平均销售价格一倍以上的别墅、公寓开发项目。该指标可以分析房地产投资结构，反映高收入家庭商品住宅的供求平衡情况。

EXPLANATORY NOTES TO MAJOR STATISTICAL INDICATORS

Investment in Real Estate Development

It includes the investment by the real estate development companies, commercial buildings construction companies and other real estate development units of various types of ownership in the construction of house buildings, such as residential buildings, factory buildings, warehouses, hotels, guesthouses, holiday villages, office buildings, and the complementary service facilities and land development projects, such as roads, water supply, water drainage, power supply, heating, telecommunications, land leveling and other projects of infrastructure. It excludes the activities in simple land transactions.

Floor Space under Construction

Floor Space under Construction refers to total floor space of all buildings under construction during the reference period, including floor space of newly started buildings during the reference period, floor space of construction extended from the previous period to the current period, and floor space of construction suspended during the previous period and resumed in the current period. Floor space of construction completed in the current period, and floor space of construction started and then suspended in the current period are also included in the floor space under construction of the current year.

Floor Space of Buildings Completed

Floor Space of Buildings Completed refers to the floor space of all buildings completed in the reference period, which have been appraised and accepted (or come up to the designed standards) and have been transferred to the owners for use.

Completion Rate of Floor Space of Buildings

Completion Rate of Floor Space of Buildings refers to the ratio of the floor space of buildings completed in certain period of time to the floor space of buildings under construction in the same period. This indicator reflects the investment result from the perspective of the speed of construction.

Villas, High-Grade Apartments

Villas, High-Grade Apartments refers to commercial houses whose construction costs and marketing prices are significantly higher than ordinary housing. Villas are independent structures generally located in the suburbs; high-grade apartments are multi-story buildings located in elegant urban neighborhoods. Criteria for villas and high-grade apartments include: 1) projects for the construction of villas or high-grade apartments have to be approved by competent departments in charge of real estate development and investment plans, and 2) prices for projects on villas or high-grade apartments are higher by over 100% compared with the average prices of ordinary commercial housing projects in similar location. This indicator helps to analyze the investment structure of the real estate industry and the demand and supply of housing for high-income households.

第十篇

Chapter 10

国内外贸易

DOMESTIC AND FOREIGN TRADES

表10-1　历年商品销售总额

Total Sales of Commercial Goods in Main Years (1994～2011)

单位:亿元　　(100 million yuan)

年　份 Year	商品购进总额 Total Value of Goods Purchased	商品销售总额 Total Value of Goods Sold	期末库存 Inventory at Year-End
1994	150.11	171.46	10.40
1995	186.38	200.05	17.03
1996	202.48	242.39	15.90
1997	278.41	274.26	37.23
1998	260.70	306.12	26.75
1999	517.13	593.37	57.62
2000	686.44	752.94	62.63
2001	891.30	1 004.89	64.55
2002	1 152.32	1 787.51	51.08
2003	2 366.49	2 422.87	187.75
2004	2 788.95	2 932.10	258.35
2005	2 499.25	2 807.47	224.16
2006	2 638.45	2 944.96	220.71
2007	3 337.31	3 613.46	245.43
2008	4 174.85	4 646.70	376.29
2009	4 913.26	5 905.20	495.57
2010	8 386.78	8 263.56	1 509.06
2011	12 866.04	10 502.98	1 169.80

表10-2 历年社会消费品零售总额
Total Retail Sales of Social Consumer Goods in Main Years (1993~2011)

单位:亿元 (100 million yuan)

年份 Year	消费品零售总额 Total Retail Sales of Consumer Goods	#餐饮 Catering	按商品用途分 By Use 食品 Food	衣着 Clothing	用品 Articles	燃料 Fuel	商品销售总额 Total Sales of Retail Goods
1993	41.92		14.04	4.74	22.80	0.34	
1994	82.74	3.18	39.58	6.47	36.08	0.61	171.46
1995	110.00	4.07	49.50	8.36	51.59	0.55	200.05
1996	140.21	4.03	53.13	12.17	74.01	0.90	242.39
1997	162.23	5.41	62.89	12.54	84.72	2.08	274.26
1998	178.97	4.78	65.06	16.61	96.27	1.03	306.12
1999	198.31	19.02	74.17	15.26	104.17	4.71	593.37
2000	215.17	25.80	81.55	13.65	117.94	2.03	752.94
2001	233.02	28.50	81.27	13.99	135.28	2.48	1 004.89
2002	284.24	25.19	75.12	14.08	190.61	4.43	1 787.51
2003	313.24	24.50	72.53	14.49	220.21	6.01	2 422.87
2004	358.21	31.49	83.73	17.84	251.42	5.22	2 932.10
2005	353.69	43.80	111.00	27.53	213.52	1.64	2 807.47
2006	400.02	51.55	125.88	32.24	240.83	1.07	2 944.96
2007	456.04	60.52	128.66	35.63	283.45	8.30	3 613.46
2008	526.89	68.16	167.23	45.39	306.53	7.74	4 646.70
2009	859.63	102.74	256.11	77.78	498.41	27.33	5 905.20
2010	1 036.88	138.03	268.69	92.32	604.08	71.79	8 263.56
2011	1 204.04	152.43	309.09	114.46	650.35	130.14	10 502.98

表10-3 连锁商业零售额
Retail Sales of Commercial Chains

单位:万元 (10 000 yuan)

指 标	Indicators	2009	2010	2011
连锁商业零售总额	**Total Retail Sales of Commercial Chains**	**2 030 051**	**2 259 603**	**2 439 773**
超市及大型超市	Supermarkets and Shopping Malls	873 207	934 491	917 676
便利店	Convenience Stores	146 910	136 299	167 699
家居建材商店	Stores of Building Materials for House Decorations	45 966	35 972	35 233
家电连锁店	House Appliance Chain Stores	418 867	438 901	439 006
连锁餐饮	Catering Chains	102 460	127 810	114 881
医药连锁	Pharmcy Chains	19 852	13 377	14 101
成品油连锁	Refined Oil Chains	376 796	518 197	694 528
其他连锁	Other Chains	45 993	54 556	56 649

表10-4 社会商业商品购、销、存总额
Total Values of Social Products on Purchase, Sales and Inventory

单位:亿元 (100 million yuan)

指 标	Indicators	2009	2010	2011
商品购进总额	**Total Goods Purchased**	**4 913.26**	**8 386.78**	**12 866.04**
#进 口	Imports	1 036.39	1 632.04	2 568.25
商品销售总额	**Total Goods Sold**	**5 905.20**	**8 263.56**	**10 502.98**
商品零售总额	Total Sales of Retail Goods	859.63	1 036.88	1 204.04
商品批发销售总额	Total Sales of Wholesale Goods	5 045.57	7 226.68	9 298.94
#出 口	Exports	463.09	663.82	941.75
年末库存总额	**Total Inventory at Year-end**	**495.57**	**1 509.06**	**2 303.33**

表10-5 社会消费品零售总额
Total Retail Sales of Consumer Goods

单位:万元 (10 000 yuan)

指 标	Indicators	2005	2010	2011
社会消费品零售总额	**Total Retail Sales of Consumer Goods**	**3 536 860**	**10 368 802**	**12 040 411**
按登记注册类型分	**By Type of Registration**			
内 资	Domestic Funded	2 665 074	6 947 927	8 086 101
国 有	State-owned	205 063	697 711	838 801
集 体	Collective-owned	140 382	552 532	321 702
股份有限公司	Companies with Limited Liability	225 844	1 151 463	1 248 803
私 营	Private	816 919	2 157 908	2 980 805
其 他	Others	1 276 866	2 388 313	2 695 990
港澳台商投资	Hong Kong/Macao/Taiwan Invested	280 623	1 243 829	1 573 804
外商投资	Foreigner Invested	591 163	2 177 046	2 380 506
按行业分	**By Sector**			
商业零售额	Commerce	3 097 392	8 988 464	10 516 109
餐饮业零售额	Catering	439 420	1 380 338	1 524 302
其 他	Others	48		
按商品用途分	**By Use**			
食品类	Food	1 110 039	2 686 915	3 090 903
衣着类	Clothing	275 260	923 241	1 144 602
用品类	Articles	2 135 181	6 040 820	6 503 501
燃料类	Fuel	16 380	717 826	1 301 405
构 成(%)	**Composition (%)**			
总 计	**Total**	**100.0**	**100.0**	**100.0**
按登记注册类型分	**By Type of Registration**			
内 资	Domestic Funded	75.4	67.0	67.2
国 有	State-owned	5.8	6.7	7.0
集 体	Collective-owned	4.0	5.3	2.7
股份有限公司	Company with Limited Liability	6.4	11.1	10.4
私 营	Private	23.1	20.8	24.7
其 他	Others	36.1	23.1	22.4
港澳台商投资	Hong Kong/Macao/Taiwan Invested	7.9	12.0	13.0
外商投资	Foreigner Invested	16.7	21.0	19.8
按行业分	**By Sector**			
商业零售额	Commerce	87.6	86.7	87.3
餐饮业零售额	Catering	12.4	13.3	12.7
其 他	Others	…	…	…
按商品用途分	**By Use**			
食品类	Food	31.4	25.9	25.7
衣着类	Clothing	7.8	8.9	9.5
用品类	Articles	60.3	58.3	54.0
燃料类	Fuel	0.5	6.9	10.8

表10-6　主要商品销售量
Sales Amount of Main Goods

指　标	Indicators	单　位　Unit	2009	2010	2011
粮　食	Grain	吨 ton	600 348	643 354	630 082
食用植物油	Vegetable Oil	吨 ton	529 556	726 381	717 760
猪　肉	Pork	吨 ton		16 402	19 922
牛　肉	Beef	吨 ton		4 804	4 952
羊　肉	Mutton	吨 ton		457	456
禽　肉	Fowl	吨 ton		56 871	67 477
鲜　蛋	Fresh Eggs	吨 ton		682	809
彩色电视机	Color TV Set	台 set	108 771	110 971	111 136
电　脑(微型计算机)	Computer (PC)	台 set	1 794 760	2 013 445	2 868 448
电冰箱(家用电冰箱)	Refrigerator	台 set	35 713	38 799	39 174
家用空调器(房间空调器)	Household Air Conditioners (Room)	台 set	80 377	85 861	87 192
煤　炭	Coal	吨 ton	17 822 885	26 460 753	31 427 825
汽　油	Gasoline	吨 ton	898 034	1 732 210	2 043 081
柴　油	Diesel Oil	吨 ton	939 148	1 385 488	1 654 806
化学肥料	Fertilizer	吨 ton	31 067	175 383	147 470
化学农药	Chemical Pesticide	吨 ton	14 675	44 194	41 237
钢　材	Steel Products	吨 ton	3 616 411	21 924 603	24 479 566
铜	Copper	吨 ton	5 568 335	7 612 231	7 930 189
铝	Aluminium	吨 ton	904 325	2 597 057	2 595 391
水　泥	Cement	吨 ton	531 241	1 886 303	1 155 264
汽　车	Motor Vehicles	辆 unit	126 790	234 266	239 909
#轿　车	Cars	辆 unit	96 493	144 215	148 703

表 10-7 限额以上商业企业主要财务指标
Major Financial Indicators of Above-Quota Commercial Enterprises

单位:万元 (10 000 yuan)

指标	Indicators	2005	2010	2011
企业单位数(个)	**Number of Enterprises (unit)**	**569**	**1 524**	**1 746**
年末资产负债	**Assets and Liabilities at Year-end**			
资产总计	Total Assets	8 981 028	35 132 544	50 081 988
#流动资产合计	Circulating Assets	7 334 193	28 436 799	41 362 051
#存　货	Goods in Stock	2 000 913	6 637 479	10 044 123
固定资产合计	Total Fixed Assets	586 373	1 936 378	2 445 981
固定资产原价	Original Value of Fixed Assets	774 941	2 713 858	3 462 058
累计折旧	Accumulated Depreciation	229 104	962 398	1 272 434
#本年提取折旧	Current Year Depreciation	49 695	177 580	181 675
负债总计	Total Liabilities	6 153 100	24 413 996	35 211 001
所有者权益总计	Owner's Equity	2 827 928	10 718 548	14 870 987
#实收资本	Paid-up Capital	1 302 017	4 116 682	5 507 911
#国家资本	State-owned Capital Assets	77 825	1 470 542	1 023 164
港澳台商资本	Hong Kong/Macao/Taiwan Capital Assets	26 705	414 141	777 974
外商资本	Foreign Capital Assets	302 926	811 726	1 139 568
法人资本	Legal Person Capital Assets	642 054	726 655	1 590 981
损益及分配(限批发零售贸易业填)	**Profit, Loss and Distribution (Only for Wholesale and Retails)**			
营业收入	Operating Revenue	22 736 239	833 143 406	128 133 473
#主营业务收入	Main Operation Revenue	22 672 300	828 879 416	127 666 389
主营业务成本	Main Operation Cost	19 722 827	770 844 602	117 854 883
营业费用	Operating Expense	790 284	23 609 805	4 253 014
业务税金及附加	Operation Tax & Surtax	12 575	1 115 249	157 597
主营业务利润	Profit From Main Business	1 498 530	56 919 565	9 653 909
其他业务利润	Other Earnings	107 241	3 319 656	502 260

表 10-8 商品交易市场基本情况
Commodity Market Transactions
(2011)

指 标	Indicators	市场数（个）Number of Markets(unit)	营业面积（平方米）Business Space(sq·m)	成交额（万元）Transaction Value (10 000 yuan)
合 计	**Total**	**184**	**1 043 812**	**18 847 787**
综合市场	**Integrated Markets**	**54**	**160 402**	**1 106 440**
生产资料综合市场	Integrated Market for Productive Materials	2	19 000	6 535
农产品综合市场	Integrated Market for Agricultural Products	33	79 462	1 023 685
其他综合市场	Other Integrated Markets	19	61 940	76 220
专业市场	**Professional Markets**	**130**	**883 410**	**17 741 347**
生产资料市场	Market for Productive Materials	17	363 844	13 416 500
农产品市场	Market for Agricultural Products	69	231 699	577 539
食品饮料烟酒市场	Market of Food, Beverage, Tobacco and Liquor	6	17 756	12 199
纺织品服装鞋帽市场	Market of Textiles, Clothes, Shoes and Hats	8	30 220	21 795
日用品及文化用品市场	Market of Commodities and Stationers Goods	3	9 226	3 056 831
家俱、五金装饰材料市场	Market of Furniture, Hardware and Decorative Materials	14	158 427	37 993
汽车及零配件市场	Market of Automobiles and Spare and Accessory Parts	3	34 767	311 880
电器、通讯器材市场	Market of Electric Appliances and Communication Equipment	2	8 534	83 610
花、鸟、鱼、虫市场	Market of Flowers, Birds, Fishes and Insects	2	16 700	10 200
其他专业市场	Other Professional Markets	6	12 237	212 800

表 10-9 商品交易市场摊位数量及成交额
Number of Stalls and Transaction Value in Commodity Market (2011)

指标 Indicators		数 量（个）Stalls (unit)	成交额（万元）Transaction Value (10000 yuan)
已出租摊位总计	**Total Stalls Leased**	**25 835**	**18 847 787**
食品、饮料、烟酒类	Food, Beverage, Tobacco and Liquor	15 676	1 612 753
服装、鞋帽、针、纺织品类	Garments, Shoes, Hats and Knitwear	3 015	32 317
化妆品类	Cosmetics	18	97
金银珠宝类	Gold, Silver and Jewelry	12	415
日用品类	Articles for Daily Use	374	3 075 179
五金电料类	Hardware Materials	161	1 496
书报杂志类	Books and Newspapers	5	67
电子出版物及音像制品	Electronic Publications and Audio-Video Products	4	39
家用电器和音像器材类	Household Appliances and Audio-Video Equipment	18	370
中西药品	Western and Traditional Chinese Medicine	3	167
文化办公用品类	Culture and Office Articles	485	93 018
通讯器材类	Telecommunications Equipment	17	262
家具类	Furniture	700	29 608
木材及制品类	Timber and Its Products	58	2 570
石油及制品类	Petroleum and its products	506	12 600 000
金属材料及制品类	Metal Materials and Products	530	502 100
建筑及装潢材料类	Building and Decoration Materials	2 494	315 373
汽车类	Automobiles	104	311 880
种子饲料类	Seeds and Feeding Stuff	2	12
其他类	Others	1 653	270 064

表10-10 电子商务交易情况
Transactions of E-businesses

单位:亿元 (100 million yuan)

指标	Indicators	2010年	2011年
商品类电子商务交易额	**E-business Trading Volume for Commodities**	**2 324.95**	**3 106.63**
提供交易平台发生的电子商务交易额	E-business Trading Volume by Providing Platforms	2 065.27	2 745.25
B2B	B to B	2 059.59	2 724.51
B2C	B to C	3.82	16.25
C2C	C to C	1.85	4.48
企业自营发生的电子商务销售额	E-business Trading Volume by Enterprises	59.72	104.64
B2B	B to B	41.32	69.37
B2C	B to C	18.40	35.27
企业自营发生的电子商务采购额	E-business Purchasing Volume by Enterprises	199.97	256.74
服务类电子商务交易额	**E-business Trading Volume for Services**	**5 223.24**	**1 4907.87**
#第三方支付	Paid by Third Party	4 871	13 625

表 10-11 历年进出口货物总值
Total Value of Imports and Exports in Main Years
(1993～2011)

单位:亿美元 (USD 100 million)

年份 Year	进出口总值 Total Value of Imports and Exports	出口总值 Total Export Value	#一般贸易 Ordinary Trade	加工贸易 Processing Trade	海关特殊监管区域物流货物 Goods for Logistics within Special Supervision of the Customs	进口总值 Total Import Value	#一般贸易 Ordinary Trade	加工贸易 Processing Trade	海关特殊监管区域物流货物 Goods for Logistics within Special Supervision of the Customs
1993	25.92	12.02	6.67			13.90	5.26		
1994	47.35	23.21	13.73			24.14	5.60		
1995	71.96	39.63	24.40			32.34	11.72		
1996	80.78	38.75	21.31			42.03	14.12		
1997	99.01	45.86	23.06			53.15	17.00		
1998	119.82	52.80	25.14			67.02	21.74		
1999	153.65	66.67	28.58			86.98	35.90		
2000	254.86	95.80	44.21			159.06	71.91		
2001	297.83	110.22	49.56			187.61	87.74		
2002	368.98	136.02	62.96			232.96	98.94		
2003	581.33	211.92	102.80			369.41	156.60		
2004	808.07	323.78	145.55			484.29	185.68		
2005	894.75	372.12	175.38			522.63	186.52		
2006	1 073.10	444.71	212.50			628.39	198.72		
2007	1 280.52	528.10	257.50			752.42	248.66		
2008	1 449.59	604.23	300.42			845.36	286.70		
2009	1 389.89	576.50	241.40			813.39	332.19		
2010	1 865.62	738.79	306.50	286.05	127.51	1 126.83	430.70	123.24	506.01
2011	2 260.00	888.98	356.82	339.00	167.03	1 371.02	537.42	152.78	600.65

表10-12 重要商品的出口货物总值
Total Value of Important Exported Goods

单位:万美元 (USD 10 000)

指 标	Indicators	2010	2011
总 计	**Total**	**7 387 919**	**8 889 777**
#机电产品	Mechanic and Electric Products	4 908 703	5 819 110
高新技术产品	Hi-tech Products	2 706 210	3 416 114
自动数据处理设备及其部件	Automatic Data Processing Equipment and its Parts	758 895	934 617
服装及衣着附件	Clothing and its Accessories	694 477	801 968
集成电路	Integrated Circuits	617 975	650 302
船 舶	Ships	559 185	565 330
电话机	Telephone Sets	109 818	491 137
纺织纱线、织物及制品	Textile Yarns, Fabrics and their Products	283 143	342 867
液晶显示板	LCDs	223 104	279 722
自动数据处理设备的零件	Parts of Automatic Data Processing Equipment	192 436	167 403
汽车零件	Automobile Parts	120 276	146 386
成品油	Refined Oils	121 714	143 432
医药品	Medicines	92 357	128 447
通断保护电路装置及零件	Protection Circuit Devices and their Parts	111 210	121 695
未锻造的铜及铜材	Unwrought Copper and its Bar	28 486	107 407
箱包及类似容器	Boxes and Similar Containers	74 984	94 040
家具及其零件	Furniture and its Parts	84 306	89 646
珍珠、钻石、宝石及半宝石	Pearls, Diamonds, Precious Stones and Half-precious Stones	41 440	82 604
二极管及类似半导体器件	Diodes and Similar Semiconductor Devices	120 321	78 752
农产品	Farm Products	72 138	77 188
钢 材	Steel	63 506	74 582
塑料制品	Plastic Products	59 063	67 703
电视、收音机及无线电讯设备的零附件	Partsand Accessories of TV Sets, Radios and Telecommunication Equipment	47 813	62 743
未锻造的铝及铝材	Unwrought Aluminium and its Bar	28 993	56 913

表 10-13 重要商品的进口货物总值
Total Value of Important Imported Goods

单位:万美元 (USD 10 000)

指 标	Indicators	2010	2011
总 计	**Total**	**11 268 269**	**13 710 166**
#机电产品	Mechanic and Electric Products	6 645 326	8 010 976
高新技术产品	Hi-tech Products	4 355 345	4 924 091
集成电路	Integrated Circuits	1 769 679	2 111 820
未锻造的铜及铜材	Unwrought Copper and its Bar	677 566	816 420
汽车(包括整套散件)	Cars (including complete parts)	259 256	688 467
自动数据处理设备及其部件	Automatic Data Processing Equipment and its Parts	625 398	614 323
初级形状的塑料	Primarily-formed Plastic	528 622	584 947
农产品	Farm Products	497 393	568 825
计量检测分析自控仪器及器具	Automatically-controlled Equipment and Devices for Measuring and Checking Analysis	301 112	363 290
医药品	Medicines	251 626	352 572
成品油	Refined Oils	229 461	321 223
通断保护电路装置及零件	Protection Circuit Devices and their Parts	263 799	298 636
钻 石	Diamonds	167 854	251 453
自动数据处理设备的零件	Parts of Automatic Data Processing Equipment	279 864	204 880
医疗仪器及器械	Medical Instrument and Appliances	116 852	157 661
手 表	Wrist Watches	84 491	150 648
印刷、装订机械及零件	Printing and Binding Machineries and their Parts	127 342	142 529
汽车零件	Automobile Parts	121 100	140 933
飞 机	Aeroplanes	198 081	136 762
变压、整流、电感器及零件	Tranformers, Rectifiers, Inductors and their Parts	109 231	127 450
纺织纱线、织物及制品	Textile Yarns, Fabrics and their Products	107 716	122 377
酒 类	Alcohols	68 587	112 936
建筑及采矿用机械及零件	Machineries and their Parts for Construction and Mining	81 063	110 588
铁矿砂及其精矿	Iron Ore and its Concentrate	126 282	108 534

表10-14　主要年份按国别(地区)分的出口货物总值
Total Value of Exports by Country/Region in Main Years

单位:万美元　　(USD 10 000)

国别(地区)	Country/Region	2000	2005	2010	2011
总　计	**Total**	**958 044**	**3 721 174**	**7 387 919**	**8 889 777**
#亚　洲	**Asia**	**450 329**	**1 697 530**	**3 340 974**	**4 008 927**
#中国香港	Hong Kong, China	94 198	468 087	717 639	894 808
中国澳门	Macao, China	1 377	1 789	5 557	2 538
中国台湾	Taiwan, China	14 717	130 197	271 421	252 646
印　度	India	4 126	35 233	133 175	172 209
孟加拉国	Bangladesh	4 194	13 023	24 808	23 996
印度尼西亚	Indonesia	7 730	26 669	71 303	106 161
日　本	Japan	190 858	451 176	774 154	941 837
马来西亚	Malaysia	12 120	66 363	244 468	239 705
巴基斯坦	Pakistan	1 857	10 116	15 838	19 206
菲律宾	Philippines	3 855	64 628	71 219	52 081
沙特阿拉伯	Saudi Arabia	3 463	14 897	31 085	39 014
新加坡	Singapore	42 076	109 379	305 192	358 309
韩　国	Republic of Korea	30 633	136 003	260 049	345 273
斯里兰卡	Sri Lanka	1 316	4 348	5 962	19 966
泰　国	Thailand	9 777	33 224	96 554	121 400
阿拉伯联合酋长国	United Arab Emirates	8 124	46 529	100 559	128 450
欧　洲	**Europe**	**210 148**	**843 460**	**1 893 937**	**2 078 237**
#欧　盟	European Union	186 765	785 409	1 701 505	1 876 080
#比利时	Belgium	17 404	61 105	101 144	108 887
英　国	United Kingdom	27 804	114 380	178 263	205 468
德　国	Germany	42 909	187 924	380 488	402 674
法　国	France	23 646	63 802	166 625	195 189
爱尔兰	Ireland	883	15 151	16 467	16 139
意大利	Italy	20 043	51 163	184 868	128 924
荷　兰	Netherlands	35 022	108 070	225 709	286 581
西班牙	Spain	8 945	42 824	78 986	91 665
波　兰	Poland	1 882	12 284	44 788	46 238
瑞　典	Sweden	3 264	22 954	39 060	37 447
瑞　士	Switzerland	2 757	11 441	26 010	31 282
俄罗斯	Russia	1 531	25 442	126 041	135 989
拉丁美洲	**Latin America**	**34 315**	**144 120**	**384 886**	**481 649**
#阿根廷	Argentina	1 551	5 739	24 892	30 188
巴　西	Brazil	5 542	34 310	120 169	131 689
智　利	Chile	3 200	11 408	23 641	34 166
墨西哥	Mexico	12 266	28 773	99 863	131 568
巴拿马	Panama	3 137	19 659	17 688	35 555
北美洲	**North America**	**213 309**	**863 433**	**1 279 355**	**1 691 715**
#加拿大	Canada	13 468	92 621	97 013	114 692
美　国	United States of America	198 503	770 807	1 182 329	1 576 981

表 10-15　主要年份按国别(地区)分的进口货物总值
Total Value of Imports by Country/Region in Main Years

单位:万美元　　(USD 10 000)

国别(地区)	Country/Region	2000	2005	2010	2011
总　计	**Total**	**1 590 555**	**5 226 325**	**11 268 269**	**13 710 166**
#亚　洲	**Asia**	**822 675**	**3 046 147**	**6 234 946**	**7 380 567**
#中国香港	Hong Kong, China	97 992	46 910	38 575	37 730
中国台湾	Taiwan, China	65 545	379 850	762 696	739 051
印　度	India	8 089	58 457	184 487	228 127
印度尼西亚	Indonesia	31 850	76 588	84 572	142 256
日　本	Japan	325 970	919 062	1 738 090	1 873 155
马来西亚	Malaysia	43 211	220 785	736 065	1 085 857
新加坡	Singapore	68 694	199 594	251 998	311 494
韩　国	Repubic of Korea	105 468	511 641	949 805	1 194 667
泰　国	Thailand	24 166	148 120	330 108	361 610
非　洲	**Africa**	**12 083**	**39 824**	**214 711**	**205 600**
欧　洲	**Europe**	**377 161**	**1 122 993**	**2 515 255**	**3 599 233**
#欧　盟	European Union	331 542	998 473	2 092 754	3 001 599
#比利时	Belgium	19 322	52 002	200 446	309 580
英　国	United Kingdom	22 873	72 078	113 428	290 432
德　国	Germany	140 814	385 695	797 961	1 074 889
法　国	France	59 653	159 106	293 253	395 971
意大利	Italy	30 726	102 266	192 625	250 713
荷　兰	Netherlands	12 997	44 876	77 545	120 438
西班牙	Spain	4 792	19 596	50 883	67 389
波　兰	Poland	378	4 920	18 727	33 896
瑞　典	Sweden	35 893	34 688	114 719	136 830
瑞　士	Switzerland	13 788	68 211	214 630	318 329
俄罗斯	Russia	10 962	31 450	144 899	197 925
拉丁美洲	**Latin America**	**53 163**	**127 155**	**645 571**	**748 629**
#巴　西	Brazil	15 523	26 441	107 078	125 129
智　利	Chile	25 086	35 236	299 182	340 495
墨西哥	Mexico	1 755	26 439	103 963	148 394
北美洲	**North America**	**296 704**	**820 607**	**1 420 899**	**1 513 938**
#加拿大	Canada	53 818	61 936	129 762	155 054
美　国	United States of America	242 869	758 389	1 291 123	1 358 874
大洋洲	**Oceania**	**28 769**	**69 599**	**235 546**	**259 117**
#澳大利亚	Australia	21 627	56 073	173 509	202 708
新西兰	New Zealand	6 058	9 197	52 040	51 641

主要统计指标解释

社会消费品零售总额

指批发和零售业、餐饮业、新闻出版业、邮政业和其他服务业等，售予城乡居民用于生活消费的商品和社会集团用于公共消费的商品之总量。社会消费品零售总额包括：

（1）批发和零售业企业（单位）：

①售予城乡居民的各种生活消费品；

②售予入境旅游的外国人、华侨、港澳台同胞的各类商品；

③售予行政事业单位、社会团体、军队和武警等机构的商品，以及以零售方式售予各类企业的商品。具体包括：用于非生产和社会交往的办公用品，如通讯设备、计算器具和设备、电讯网络设备、文印设备、音像视听器材和设备、纸张、本册、文具及装订文印材料、家具、日用电器、针纺织品、清洁卫生用品、文体用品、奖品、纪念品、礼品等；供内部人员乘坐的交通工具和燃料；用于办公设施修缮的各类配件、材料、工具等；用于取暖和防暑降温的设备、燃料、材料及食品等；专用于教学的用品和设备；非营利医疗机构的中、西药品、中药材和医疗设备器材；非专用的劳动保护用品；不对外营业的内部食堂用的餐具、炊具、设备、清洁卫生工具和食品、燃料等；军队、武警用于其人员生活的衣着品和个人用品；其他各类非生产性设备和用品。

（2）餐饮业出售的主食、菜肴、烟酒饮料和其他商品。

（3）新闻出版业、邮政业售予城乡居民、企事业单位、军队和武警等机构的书报杂志、音像制品、邮品等。

（4）其他服务业出售的食品、烟酒饮料、服装鞋帽、日常生活用品、医药保健用品、艺术品、工艺美术品、玩具、殡葬用品以及其他消费品。

批发零售贸易业商品购、销、存总额

指各种登记注册类型的批发、零售贸易企业（单位）以本企业（单位）为总体的，从上海、上海以外市场购进的商品总量、销售和出口的商品总量、库存商品总量等情况。该指标对促进工农业生产发展、活跃市场、平抑物价、保障供给、满足需求具有举足轻重的作用。该指标可以反映商品流转过程中商品的购进、销售、库存之间的比例关系和存在的问题。

商品购进总额

指从本企业（单位）以外的单位和个人购进（包括从境外直接进口）作为转卖或加工后转卖的商品总额。它反映批发零售贸易业从国内、国外市场上购进商品的总量。商品购进总额包括：①从工农业生产者购进的商品；②从出版社、报社的出版发行部门购进的图书、杂志和报纸；③从各种登记注册类型的批发零售贸易企业（单位）购进的商品；④从其他单位购进的商品，如从机关、团体、企业等单位购进的剩余物资，从餐饮业、服务业购进的商品，从海关、市场管理部门购进的缉私和没收的商品，从居民手中收购的废旧商品等；⑤从国（境）外直接进口的商品。不包括企业（单位）为自身经营用和未通过买卖行为而收入的商品以及销售退回、商品升溢等。

商品销售总额

商品销售总额指对本企业以外的单位和个人出售（包括对国（境）外直接出口）的商品。这个指标反映批发零售贸易业在上海市场以及上海以外市场上销售商品的总量。商品销售总额包括：①售给城乡居民和社会集团消费用的商品；②售给工业、农业、建筑业、运输邮电业、批发零售贸易业、餐饮业、服务业等作为生产、经营使用的商品；③售给批发零售贸易业作为转卖或加工后转卖的商品；④对国（境）外直接出口的商品。不包括：出售本企业自用的废旧包装用品，未通过买卖行为付出的商品，经本单位介绍，由买卖双方直接结算，本单位只收取手续费的业务，购货退出的商品以及商品损耗和损失等。

批发零售贸易业年末库存

是指年末各种经济类型的批发零售贸易企业（单位）已取得所有权的商品，它反映各地区、各批发零售贸易企业的商品库存情况和对市场商品供应的保证程度。期末库存包括：①存放在批发零售贸易业经营单位（如门市部、批发站、经营处）仓库、货场、货柜和货架中的商品；②挑选、整理、包装中的商品；③已记入购进而尚未运到本单位的商品，即发货单或银行承兑凭证已到而货未到部份；④寄放他处的商品，如因购货方拒绝承付而暂存放在购货方的商品和已办完加工成品收回手续而未提回的商品；⑤委托其他单位代销（未作销售或调出）尚未售出的商品；⑥代其他单位购进尚未交付的商品。不包括所有权不属于本单位的商品、拨付除批发零售贸易业以外的其他行业所属独立核算加工厂等加工生产尚未收回成品的商品，代国家物资储备部门保管的商品等。期末库存总额计算方法是：农副产品采购单位按购进价计算；批发单位按进货价计算；零售单位按什么价格核算就按什么价格计算。

主营业务收入

指企业在销售商品、提供劳务等日常活动中所产生的收入总额。

主营业务成本

指企业已销商品应负担的进货原价和商品进价成本。

营业费用

指批发零售贸易企业在购、销、存过程中发生的各项经营费用。包括运输费、装卸费、包装费、保险费、展览费、差旅费、广告费、商品损耗、进出口商品累计佣金、经营人员的工资及福利费等。

外贸进出口总额

外贸进出口总额是指海关统计中按经营单位即进出口企业在海关注册地的行政区域口径统计的数据，它反映的是上海浦东新区行政辖区内各类具有进出口经营权企业（外贸企业）的进出口。它不包含外省市外贸企业途经上海浦东新区口岸由上海海关结关放行及统计的进出口商品，但包含上海浦东新区外贸企业经由非上海口岸进出口结关放行及统计的商品。

商品类电子商务交易额

指借助网络订单且实际交割的商品总额，借助网络订单指通过网络发送订单。付款可以是网上，也可以是网下进行。

提供交易平台发生的电子商务交易额

指为电子商务交易双方提供的平台中实现的商品类电子商务交易额。

企业自营发生的电子商务销售额

指企业在自己的电子商务平台上借助网络订单实际销售的商品总额。

企业自营发生的电子商务采购额

指企业在自己的电子商务平台上借助网络订单实际采购的商品总额。

服务类电子商务交易额

指服务类电子商务产生的交易额，非实物商品交易。包含金融服务、住宿旅游服务、交通仓储服务以及通信服务等等。

B2B

指企业对企业的电子商务交易。

B2C

指企业对个人的电子商务交易。

C2C

指个人对个人的电子商务交易。

第三方支付

是指非金融机构作为第三方在收付款人之间作为中介机构通过网络提供货币资金转移服务。

EXPLANATORY NOTES TO MAJOR STATISTICAL INDICATORS

Total Retail Sales of Consumer Goods

Total Retail Sales of Consumer Goods refer to the sum of retail sales of commodities sold by wholesale, retail, catering, publishing, post and telecommunications and other service industries to urban and rural households for private consumption and to social institutions for public consumption. Retail sales of consumer goods include:

(1) Sales by wholesale and retail units:

①of consumer goods sold to urban and rural households

②of commodities sold to foreigners, overseas Chinese and Chinese compatriots from Hong Kong, Macau and Taiwan visiting in China

③of commodities sold to government agencies, institutions, social organizations, military and armed police units, and commodities sold to enterprises in the form of retail sales. More specifically, they include: office facilities and articles for non-production purposes such as communications equipment, computing equipment and instruments, TV and network equipment, printing and copying equipment, audio-visual equipment and instruments, paper, notebooks, stationeries, furniture, electric appliances, knitwear, sanitation and cleaning articles, cultural and sport articles, articles for prizes, souvenirs, etc. ; transport vehicles and fuels for employees; materials, spare parts and tools for the maintenance of office facilities; equipment, fuels, materials and food for winter heating or summer cooling purposes; articles and equipment for teaching purpose; Chinese and western medicines and medical equipment and facilities purchased by non profit-making medical institutes; non – specialized work safety articles; cooking utensils, tableware, equipment, cleaning articles, food and fuels purchased by internal cafeterias; clothes and personal articles purchased by military or armed police units for their officials and soldiers; and other equipment and articles for non-production purposes.

(2) Sales of stable food, cooked dishes, beverages, tobaccos and other articles by catering units.

(3) Sales of books, newspapers, magazines, audio-visual products and post products by publishing, post and telecommunications departments to urban and rural households and to enterprises, institutions, military and armed police units.

(4) Sales of food, beverages, tobaccos, clothing, hats, footwear, articles for daily use, medicines, medical and health articles, work of art, handicrafts, toys, funeral articles and other articles by other service industries.

Purchase, Sales and Stock of Commodities by Wholesale and Retail Trades

Purchase, Sales and Stock of Commodities by Wholesale and Retail Trades refer to the total volume of commodities purchased, total volume of sales and exports, and the stock of commodities by wholesale and retail enterprises (establishments) of different status of registration from Shanghai and out-of-Shanghai markets. This indicator plays an important role in promoting industrial and agricultural production, thriving market, stabilizing prices, ensuring market supply and meeting the needs of consumers. It also reflects the relationship among purchase, sales and stock of commodities in the circulation of goods and reveals the existing problems.

Total Purchase of Commodities

Total purchase of commodities refers to purchase of commodities from other establishments or individuals (including direct import abroad) for the purpose of reselling, either with or without further processing of the commodities purchased. This indicator shows the total value of purchases of commodities by wholesale and retail establishments from domestic and overseas markets, they include: ① agricultural and industrial products purchased from producers; ② books, magazines and newspapers purchased from distribution departments of the publishers; ③ commodities purchased from wholesale and retail establishments; ④ commodities purchased from other units, such as surplus materials purchased from government agencies, enterprises or institutions, commodities purchased from catering and service establishments, confiscated goods purchased from customs authorities or market management agencies, second hand goods and reusable stuff purchased from residents; ⑤ commodities directly imported abroad. Excluded are commodities purchased by establishments for their own business operation, commodities obtained without buying or selling procedures, rejected commodities, etc.

Total Sales of Commodities

Total Sales of Commodities refer to the selling of commodities to other establishments and individuals (including direct export). Reflecting the total value of sales of commodities at Shanghai markets and out – of – Shanghai markets, this indicator includes: ① commodities sold to urban and rural households and institutions for their consumption; ② commodities sold to establishments in industry, agriculture, construction, transportation, post and telecommunications, wholesale and retail trade, catering and service trade and public utility for their production and operation; ③ commodities sold to wholesale and retail establishments for re-selling, with or without further processing; and ④ commodities for direct export to other countries. Excluded are selling of waste packaging materials used by enterprises themselves commodities transferred without buying or selling procedures, commission income from brokerage in transactions whose settlement is directly handled by buyers and sellers, rejected commodities in the purchase, loss in commodities, etc.

Commodities Stock of Wholesale and Retail Enterprises at Year-end

refers to total commodities possessed by wholesale and retail enterprises (units of various ownership, which reflects the commodity stock level of various wholesale and retail enterprises and the potential for market supply. This indicator includes; ① commodities located in storage, rooms, garages, counters, and shelves of operating units (such as sales stores, wholesale stations, and operating offices) of wholesale and retail enterprises; ② commodities in the process of selecting, sorting, and packing; ③ commodities not arrived but recorded as purchase in the account, i. e. commodities have not arrived but payment receipts for the commodities from the sellers or the banks have arrived; ④ commodities deposited in other places rather than places mentioned above, for instance; commodities in the hold of purchasers temporarily due to the refusal of payment and commodities not taken back after going through processing procedures; ⑤ commodities entrusted to other units to sell but not sold out yet; ⑥ commodities purchased for other units but not delivered yet. Commodities not included as stock are those not owned by enterprises, those allocated to financially independent factories rather than wholesale and retail enterprises for processing but not taken back yet, and finally those put in stock by wholesale and retail enterprises on behalf of the state material reserves units. The value of commodities stock at the end of period, the value is calculated at purchasing price of agricultural goods purchasing units and wholesale units and retail units at accounting prices.

Prime Operating Revenue

Prime Operating Revenue refers to the earnings a corporation receives in daily activity such as selling goods and offering labor service.

Operating Cost

Operating Cost refers to the cost a corporation paid to buy and deliver the commodities.

Operating Expenses

Operating Expenses refer to the spendings that a wholesaler or retailer pays in buying, selling or stocking goods. It includes fees incurred in transport, loading and unloading, packaging, insurance, exhibition, business trip, advertisement, commodity wastage, commissions in import and export, salaries and bonus paid to workers involved.

The Volume of Foreign Trade

The Volume of Foreign Trade is offered by Customs authorities, covering the operation units, or the enterprises involved in import and export, that have registered in the administrative regions where the Customs operate. It reflects the import and export of all the enterprises with import and export rights (foreign trade enterprises) under the administration of Shanghai Pudong New Area Municipality. It excludes those commodities of foreign trade enterprises from out of town that underwent customs clearance at Shanghai Pudong New Area ports but includes commodities of foreign trade enterprises of Shanghai Pudong New Area that underwent customs clearance in non – Shanghai ports.

E-business Trading Volume for Commodities

refers to the total volume of commodities that have been ordered and actually transacted through the network, and the term of "through the network" means sending orders via the internet. Payment can be made both online and offline.

Paid by Third Party

refers to the services of monetary transfers provided by non-financial institutions as a third party agency between the payee and the payer through the network.

E-business Trading Volume by Enterprises

refers to the total volume that enterprises make actual sales by means of orders through the network under their own E-business platforms.

E-business Purchasing Volume by Enterprises

refers to the total volume that enterprises make actual purchases by means of orders through the network under their own E-business platforms.

E-business Trading Volume for Services

refers to the trading volume provided by Service E-business, which is not commodity E-business. It includes services such as finance, accommodations, tourism, transportation, warehousing and communications.

B2B

refers to E-business transactions between business to business.

B2C

refers to E-business transactions between business to consumer.

C2C

refers to E-business transactions between consumer to consumer.

E-business Trading Volume by Providing Platforms

refers to the E-business trading volume for commodities that certain platforms are provided for the two parties for E-businesses.

第十一篇

Chapter 11

服务、旅游和住宿业

SERVICES, TOURISM AND HOTELS

表 11－1　社会服务业经济总量(营业收入)
Total Economics of Social Services (Operating Revenue)
(2009 ~ 2011)

单位:亿元　　　　(100 million yuan)

指　标	Indicators	2009	2010	2011
总　计	**Total**	**1 883.60**	**2 515.23**	**2 762.27**
装卸搬运和其他运输服务业、仓储业	Handling, Other Transportation Services and Warehousing	229.72	322.92	329.29
信息传输、计算机服务和软件业	Information Transmission, Computer Services and Software	720.28	881.51	1 004.49
#软件业	Software	281.03	321.01	344.27
租赁和商务服务业	Leasing and Business Services	605.55	931.83	964.56
#商务服务业	Commercial Services	572.61	886.33	892.44
#企业管理服务	Business Management Services	302.85	480.49	524.07
咨询与调查	Consulting and Surveys	100.59	111.09	161.88
广告业	Advertising	55.17	66.28	69.54
科学研究、技术服务和地质勘查业	Scientific Researches, Technology Services and Geologic Prospecting	237.50	266.04	341.26
水利、环境和公共设施管理业	Water Conservancy, Environment and Public Facilities Management	29.32	35.32	27.72
居民服务和其他服务业	Resident Services and Other Services	32.79	40.54	45.77
教　育	Education	10.27	12.43	15.71
卫生、社会保障和社会福利业	Public Health, Social Guarantee and Social Welfare	5.07	6.16	8.13
文化、体育和娱乐业	Culture, Sports and Entertainment	13.10	18.49	25.34

表 11-2 社会服务业经济总量
Total Economics of Social Services
(2011)

单位:亿元 (100 million yuan)

指 标	Indicators	营业收入 Operating Revenue	增 幅(%) Increased by	比 重(%) Percentage
总 计	**Total**	**2 762.27**	**9.8**	**100.0**
装卸搬运和其他运输服务业、仓储业	Handling, Other Transportation Services and Warehousing	329.29	2.0	11.9
信息传输、计算机服务和软件业	Information Transmission, Computer Services and Software	1 004.49	13.9	36.4
#软件业	Software	344.27	7.2	12.5
租赁和商务服务业	Leasing and Business Services	964.56	3.5	34.9
#商务服务业	Commercial Services	892.44	0.7	32.3
#企业管理服务	Business Management Services	524.07	9.1	19.0
咨询与调查	Consulting and Surveys	161.88	45.7	5.9
广告业	Advertising	69.54	4.9	2.5
科学研究、技术服务和地质勘查业	Scientific Researches, Technology Services and Geologic Prospecting	341.26	28.3	12.3
水利、环境和公共设施管理业	Water Conservancy, Environment and Public Facilities Management	27.72	-21.5	1.0
居民服务和其他服务业	Resident Services and Other Services	45.77	12.9	1.7
教 育	Education	15.71	26.4	0.6
卫生、社会保障和社会福利业	Public Health, Social Guarantee and Social Welfare	8.13	32.0	0.3
文化、体育和娱乐业	Culture, Sports and Entertainment	25.34	37.1	0.9

表11-3 社会服务业从业人员数
Number of Employees of Social Services
(2009～2011)

单位:万人 (10 000 persons)

指 标	Indicators	2009	2010	2011
总 计	**Total**	**36.07**	**38.35**	**39.88**
装卸搬运和其他运输服务业、仓储业	Handling, Other Transportation Services and Warehousing	3.37	3.41	3.53
信息传输、计算机服务和软件业	Information Transmission, Computer Services and Software	9.25	9.83	10.78
#软件业	Software	5.28	5.47	6.05
租赁和商务服务业	Leasing and Business Services	13.06	14.77	14.42
#商务服务业	Commercial Services	12.59	14.37	14.05
#企业管理服务	Business Management Services	4.01	4.67	4.45
咨询与调查	Consulting and Surveys	2.41	2.69	2.76
广告业	Advertising	0.53	0.47	0.50
科学研究、技术服务和地质勘查业	Scientific Researches, Technology Services and Geologic Prospecting	5.31	5.20	5.89
水利、环境和公共设施管理业	Water Conservancy, Environment and Public Facilities Management	1.01	0.98	0.89
居民服务和其他服务业	Resident Services and Other Services	2.91	2.91	2.99
教 育	Education	0.35	0.44	0.55
卫生、社会保障和社会福利业	Public Health, Social Guarantee and Social Welfare	0.31	0.31	0.32
文化、体育和娱乐业	Culture, Sports and Entertainment	0.50	0.49	0.51

表11-4 社会服务业从业人员数
Number of Employees of Social Services
(2011)

单位:万人 (10 000 persons)

指标	Indicators	从业人员数 Number of Employees	增幅(%) Increased by	比重(%) Percentage
总计	**Total**	**39.88**	**4.0**	**100.0**
装卸搬运和其他运输服务业、仓储业	Handling, Other Transportation Services and Warehousing	3.53	3.4	8.9
信息传输、计算机服务和软件业	Information Transmission, Computer Services and Software	10.78	9.2	27.0
#软件业	Software	6.05	10.5	15.2
租赁和商务服务业	Leasing and Business Services	14.42	-2.4	36.1
#商务服务业	Commercial Services	14.05	-2.2	35.2
#企业管理服务	Business Management Services	4.45	-4.6	11.2
咨询与调查	Consulting and Surveys	2.76	2.5	6.9
广告业	Advertising	0.50	7.2	1.3
科学研究、技术服务和地质勘查业	Scientific Researches, Technology Services and Geologic Prospecting	5.89	13.3	14.8
水利、环境和公共设施管理业	Water Conservancy, Environment and Public Facilities Management	0.89	-8.7	2.2
居民服务和其他服务业	Resident Services and Other Services	2.99	3.1	7.5
教育	Education	0.55	24.0	1.4
卫生、社会保障和社会福利业	Public Health, Social Guarantee and Social Welfare	0.32	2.4	0.8
文化、体育和娱乐业	Culture, Sports and Entertainment	0.51	3.2	1.3

表 11-5 主要年份接待国内外游客情况
Foreign and Domestic Tourists Received in Main Years

单位:万人次 (10 000 persons)

指标	Indicators	2000	2005	2010	2011
接待游客总数	**Total Tourists Received**	**1 133**	**1 660**	**3 215**	**3 133**
国内游客数	Domestic	1 092	1 566	3 085	3 033
国外游客数	Foreign	41	94	130	100
按接待单位分	By Receiving Agency				
#宾馆接待游客	Hotels	153	164	278	255
旅行社接待游客	Tourist Agencies	30	111	185	180
景点接待游客	Tourist Attractions	950	1 385	2 752	2 698
平均每天接待旅游人数(人次/天)	Average Number of Tourists Received Everyday (person-time/day)	31 041	45 474	88 094	85 836

表 11-6 旅馆、旅行社经营情况
Operation of Hotels and Travel Agencies

指标	Indicators	单位 Unit	2000	2005	2010	2011
旅馆业	**Hotel Industry**					
接待能力状况	**Receiving Capacity**					
客房数	Rooms	间 room	8 766	12 692	15 780	17 755
客房床位数	Beds	张 bed	15 635	20 245	22 652	26 129
实际住宿人次数	Actual Staying Guests	万人次 10 000 person-times	152.50	163.84	278.33	254.82
#境外来沪住宿人次数	Overseas Guests	万人次 10 000 person-times	24.10	73.03	99.21	99.66
实际住宿人天数	Actual Staying Days	万人天 10 000 person · days	235.60	371.18	491.33	429.30
#境外来沪住宿人天数	Staying Days of Overseas Guests	万人天 10 000 person · days	55.10	195.58	187.84	180.16
财务经营状况	**Financial Operation**					
固定资产原值	Original Value of Fixed Assets	亿元 100 million yuan	40.21	82.35	119.19	137.17
营业收入	Operation Earning	亿元 100 million yuan	15.52	37.09	55.85	51.56
#客房收入	Hotel Room Earning	亿元 100 million yuan	7.51	21.77	31.87	26.82
餐饮收入	Catering Earning	亿元 100 million yuan	6.53	15.32	19.22	21.84
旅行社	**Travel Agency**					
旅行社接待人次数	Persons Received by PNA Travel Agencies	万人次 10 000 person-times	29.81	110.69	185.25	180.27
国内旅行社	Domestic Travel Agencies	万人次 10 000 person-times	26.03	89.86	154.52	152.61
国际旅行社	International Travel Agencies	万人次 10 000 person-times	3.78	20.83	30.73	27.66
旅行社营业收入	Operation Earnings of PNA Travel Agencies	亿元 100 million yuan	3.85	14.68	30.00	33.50
国内旅行社	Domestic Travel Agencies	亿元 100 million yuan	2.67	8.44	16.08	23.00
国际旅行社	International Travel Agencies	亿元 100 million yuan	1.18	6.24	13.92	10.50

表 11－7 旅游景点经营情况
Operation of Tourist Attractions

指 标 Indicators		单 位 Unit	2000	2005	2010	2011
主要景点营业情况	**Business in Major Tourist Attractions**					
主要景点个数	Main Tourist Attractions	个 in number	14	23	25	27
接待参观人次	Visitors Received	万人次 10 000 person-times	1 385	1 908	2 752	2 698
营业收入	Operation Earnings	万元 10 000 yuan	63 036	87 500	144 781	121 532

表 11－8 会议、展览情况
Conferences and Fairs

指 标 Indicators		单 位 Unit	2005	2009	2010	2011
举办展览（博览）	**Number of Exhibitions Hosted**	**次 time**	**114**	**112**	**120**	**156**
#国际性	International	次 time	91	87	100	135
#三万平方米及以上	≥30 000 sq. m	次 time	29	42	38	54
#五万平方米及以上	≥50 000 sq. m	次 time	15	29	28	37
展览面积	Display Area	万平方米 10 000 sq·m	238	373	400	551.36
参展客商	Exhibition-Attending Investors	个 unit	48 412	61 750	69 713	90 670
接待（参观）人数	Visitors Received	万人次 10 000 person-times	266.90	283.82	309.70	444.70
召开会议	Conferences Hosted	次 time	1 583	1 340	1 504	13 486
#跨省市	Trans-provincial	次 time	61	66	112	
国际性	International	次 time	199	17	26	1 949
参加会议人员	Number of Participants	万人次 10 000 person-times	16.69	15.90	17.03	132.34
#海外与会人员	Overseas Participants	万人次 10 000 person-times	3.00	1.22	1.34	16.31

注：2011 年会议统计的范围为浦东四星级以上宾馆。
Note: The statistical scope for the conferences in 2011 refers to the hotels with four stars or more in Pudong.

主要统计指标解释

接待国外游客人数

指来上海浦东新区参观、访问、旅行、探亲、访友、休养、考察、参加会议和从事经济、科技、文化、教育、体育、宗教等活动的外国人、华侨、港澳和台湾同胞的人数。不包括来上海浦东新区常住1年以上的外国专家、留学生等。上海浦东新区入境的境外旅游人数包括从上海浦东新区口岸入境的境外旅游人数和从我国其他口岸入境的境外旅游人数。

EXPLANATORY NOTES TO MAJOR STATISTICAL INDICATORS

Number of Overseas Tourists Through Shanghai Customs

Number of Overseas Tourists through Shanghai Pudong New Area Customs refers to the number of foreigners, overseas Chinese, and compatriots from Hong Kong, Macao and Taiwan coming to Shanghai Pudong New Area for sightseeing, visits, tours, family reunions, meeting friends, vacations, study tours, attending meetings and other activities of an economic, scientific and technological, cultural, physical culture and religious nature. This does not include foreign experts and students residing in Shanghai Pudong New Area for over 1 year. The number of overseas tourists to Shanghai Pudong New Area includes those overseas tourists entering China through Shanghai Pudong New Area customs and through customs other than Shanghai.

第十二篇

Chapter 12

科学技术

SCIENCE AND TECHNOLOGY

SHANGHAI
PUDONG
NEW AREA
STATISTICAL
YEARBOOK

表12-1 历年科技成果

Achievements in Scientific & Technological Research in Main Years (1995～2011)

单位:项 (item)

年 份 Year	获上海市高新技术成果转化百佳项目 Top 100 Projects Which Have Successfully Commercialized Achievements in Scientific & Technological Research	获上海市以上科技进步奖 Shanghai and Above Level Achievement Awards in Science and Technology	按奖项分 Award Grade				
			一等奖 First Prize	#国家级 National Grade	二等奖 Second Prize	#国家级 National Grade	三等奖 Third Prize
1995		2			1		1
1996							
1997		2			1		1
1998		14			3		11
1999		12	2		3		7
2000		11			5		6
2001		16			5		11
2002		37	8		13		16
2003	11	34	8		10		16
2004	11	45	10		16		19
2005	25	35	5	1	10	3	20
2006	17	48	11	1	23	5	14
2007		73	11	2	31	11	31
2008		66	10		27	6	29
2009		50	5		23	5	22
2010		63	8		29	10	26
2011		92	15		43	12	34

注：上海市高新技术成果转化百佳项目从2001年起评比。
Note：We started to appraise the above-mentioned Top 100 Projects since 2001.

表 12-2 历年各类技术合同项目
All Kinds of Technical Contracts in Main Years
(1994~2011)

单位:项 (item)

年份 Year	各类合同项目 Item of Contracts	技术开发 Technical Development	技术转让 Technology Tranfer	技术咨询 Technical Consultation	技术服务 Technical Service
1994	595	25	43	98	429
1995	924	42	33	147	702
1996	1 525	12	16	215	1 282
1997	1 742	23	56	291	1 372
1998	1 659	57	49	282	1 271
1999	1 998	85	21	406	1 486
2000	1 940	79	24	458	1 379
2001	2 253	260	86	405	1 502
2002	2 281	372	116	465	1 328
2003	2 406	500	284	422	1 200
2004	2 362	580	148	406	1 228
2005	3 034	1 155	225	353	1 301
2006	2 636	1 448	100	204	884
2007	2 545	1 326	118	86	1 015
2008	2 294	1 448	94	262	490
2009	2 518	1 757	112	194	455
2010	2 550	1 774	139	100	537
2011	2 932	2 269	137	181	345

表12-3　历年各类技术合同成交金额

Business Volume of All Kinds of Technical Contracts in Main Years (1994~2011)

单位:万元　　　　(10 000 yuan)

年　份 Year	成交金额 Business Volume	技术开发 Technical Development	技术转让 Technology Tranfer	技术咨询 Technical Consultation	技术服务 Technical Service
1994	6 225	284	404	492	5 045
1995	12 514	3 863	2 105	936	5 610
1996	21 255	599	573	1 772	18 311
1997	15 644	749	1 286	2 386	11 223
1998	21 286	3 924	2 106	2 098	13 158
1999	24 788	7 194	1 509	2 929	13 156
2000	39 707	7 969	15 893	2 524	13 321
2001	62 892	30 778	8 709	3 317	20 088
2002	86 786	51 233	12 303	4 585	18 665
2003	112 355	79 274	12 978	5 217	14 886
2004	221 295	185 897	13 881	4 030	17 487
2005	386 406	335 848	33 096	3 087	14 375
2006	641 015	525 942	96 628	2 952	15 493
2007	839 052	694 197	125 175	2 586	17 094
2008	957 346	870 937	69 244	3 512	13 653
2009	1 299 693	1 145 384	137 907	2 111	14 291
2010	1 210 256	1 023 716	96 063	16 254	74 224
2011	1 269 191	1 125 001	66 825	2 508	74 857

表 12-4 历年专利申请情况
Statistics of Patent Claiming in Main Years (1999～2011)

单位:项 (item)

年 份 Year	专利申请总量 Total Patent Claimings	发 明 Inventions	实用新型 Utility Models	外观设计 Design in Appearance
1999	386	67	216	103
2000	718	209	241	268
2001	1 103	222	453	428
2002	2 397	467	591	1 339
2003	2 580	1 064	852	664
2004	2 871	1 676	719	476
2005	3 141	1 794	863	484
2006	6 767	2 557	1 224	2 986
2007	8 435	3 054	1 386	3 995
2008	8 980	3 065	1 893	4 022
2009	14 645	5 372	3 936	5 337
2010	17 587	6 576	4 902	6 109
2011	18 819	9 218	6 973	2 628

表 12-5 历年专利授权情况
Statistics of Patents Authorized in Main Years (2001～2011)

单位:项 (item)

年 份 Year	专利授权总量 Total Patents Authorized	发 明 Inventions	实用新型 Utility Models	外观设计 Design in Appearance
2001	519			
2002	668			
2003	1 542			
2004	1 066	95	528	443
2005	1 204	329	576	299
2006	1 432	375	655	402
2007	4 086	409	1 152	2 525
2008	3 677	841	1 442	1 394
2009	8 046	1 557	2 266	4 223
2010	12 764	1 503	3 950	7 311
2011	12 685	2 149	5 423	5 113

表12-6　区属企业、事业单位各类专业技术人员(2011年末)

Professional Personnel Working in Enterprises and Institutions in PNA (Total by the End of 2011)

单位:人 (person)

指　标	Indicators	合　计 Total	#女　性 Female	按学历分 By Education Level 研究生 Post Graduate	大　学 本　科 University	高　等 专　科 Junior University	中等专科 Specialized Secondary School	高中及以下 Senior High School and Below
总　计	**Total**	**43 602**	**30 372**	**1 715**	**27 647**	**10 587**	**2 864**	**789**
工程技术人员	Engineering	2 622	639	264	1 351	560	199	248
农业技术人员	Agricultural	518	137	36	216	136	102	28
科学研究人员	Research	39	16	15	21	3		
卫生技术人员	Healthcare	10 641	7 591	609	4 659	3 394	1 784	195
教学人员	Teaching	25 786	19 775	516	19 689	5 152	402	27
经济人员	Economic	1 328	488	167	518	432	81	130
会计人员	Financial/Accounting	1 419	1 022	52	584	536	189	58
统计人员	Statistical	179	120	2	89	61	20	7
翻译人员	Interpreter/Translator	10	6	2	6	2		
图书档案文博人员	Librarian/Archivist/Museum Staff	599	411	23	289	205	43	39
新闻、出版人员	News-Reporting/Publishing	65	31	7	51	5		2
律师、公证人员	Lawyer/Notary	44	21	7	37			
播音人员	Radio Crew Member	15	9		13	2		
工艺美术人员	Artisan	6		1	1	3	1	
体育人员	PE	64	23		45	17		2
艺术人员	Actor/Actress	42	20	1	13	11	1	16
政工人员	Political	225	63	13	65	68	42	37

表 12-7 区属企业、事业单位各年龄组专业技术职务及专业技术人员(2011 年末)

Technical Professions and Technicians Grouped by Ages in PNA Enterprises and Institutions (Total by the End of 2011)

单位:人 (person)

指 标 Indicators		合 计 Total	按年龄分 By Age					
			35 岁及以下 35 Years Old and Below	36 至 40 岁 36 ~ 40 Years Old	41 至 45 岁 41 ~ 45 Yeas Old	46 至 50 岁 46 ~ 50 Years Old	51 至 54 岁 51 ~ 54 Years Old	55 岁以上 55 Years Old and Above
总 计	**Total**	**43 602**	**17 281**	**8 836**	**7 897**	**5 125**	**2 526**	**1 937**
按专业技术职务分	**By Professional Position**							
高级职务	Senior	3 814	55	610	1 193	1 168	388	400
中级职务	Intermediate	19 207	3 684	5 582	5 042	2 803	1 189	907
初级职务	Junior	19 123	12 300	2 580	1 609	1 106	918	610
未聘职务	Laid-off	1 458	1 242	64	53	48	31	20
按专业技术类别分	**By Profession**							
工程技术人员	Engineering	2 622	972	432	405	374	250	189
农业技术人员	Agricultural	518	112	60	109	88	58	91
科学研究人员	Scientific	39	17	9	2	5	3	3
卫生技术人员	Healthcare	10 641	4 435	2 140	1 557	1 069	847	593
教学人员	Teaching	25 786	10 607	5 481	5 199	2 935	877	687
经济人员	Economic	1 328	349	218	178	229	181	173
会计人员	Financial/Accounting	1 419	453	285	238	219	150	74
统计人员	Statistical	179	70	43	28	24	10	4
图书档案文博人员	Librarian/Archivist/Museum Staff	599	158	112	101	104	78	46
政工人员	Political	225	30	11	38	44	47	55
其他专业技术人员	Others	246	78	45	42	34	25	22

表 12-8　大中型工业企业科技活动人员情况

Scientific and Technical Personnel of Large and Medium Industrial Enterprises (2011)

指　标	Indicators	有科技活动企业数(个) Number of Enterprises with Scientific Technical Activities (unit)	从事科技活动人员(人) Total Number of Personnel Undertaking Scientific Technical Activities (person)	#高中级技术职称人员(人) People with Senior and Intermediate Technical Titles (person)
总　计	**Total**	**166**	**52 105**	**15 248**
按注册登记大类分组	**Grouped by Type of Registration**			
国　有	State-owned	12	5 332	2 848
集　体	Collective-owned			
股份制及其他有限公司	Share-holding	43	10 878	2 968
私　营	Private	25	3 296	410
外商及港澳台投资	Overseas Invested Enterprises	86	32 599	9 022
其　他	Others			
按隶属关系分组	**Grouped by Subordination**			
中央工业	Central	21	13 995	5 846
地方工业	Local	145	38 110	9 402
按企业规模分组	**Grouped by Enterprise Scale**			
大型企业	Large	62	40 625	13 071
中型企业	Medium	104	11 480	2 177
按工业行业大类分组	**Grouped by Sector**			
农副食品加工业	Processing of Agricultural Side-line Food	1	245	10
饮食制造业	Food Manufacturing			
烟草制品业	Tobacco Manufacturing	1	25	9
纺织业	Textile Industry	2	121	10
家具制造业	Furniture Manufacturing	1	812	45
造纸及纸制品业	Paper-making and Paper Products Manufacturing	2	188	10
印刷业和记录媒介的复制	Printing and Record Duplicating	6	468	162
石油加工、炼焦及核燃料加工业	Petroleum Processing, Coke Making and Nuclear Fuel Processing	1	47	47
化学原料及化学制品制造业	Raw Chemical Materials and Chemicals	1	73	57
医药制造业	Medicine Manufacturing	7	852	207
橡胶制品业	Rubber Products	16	2 934	1 093
塑料制品业	Plastic Products	2	175	68
非金属矿物制品业	Nonmetal Mineral Products	5	475	144
有色金属冶炼及压延加工业	Smelting and Pressing of Nonferrous Metal	1	124	50
金属制品业	Metal Products	3	181	17
通用设备制造业	Manufacturing of General Equipment	16	3 754	1 193
专用设备制造业	Manufacturing of Special Purpose Equipment	15	3 258	554
交通运输设备制造业	Manufacturing of Transportation Equipment	27	11 772	2 664
电气机械及器材制造业	Manufacturing of Electric Machinery and Equipment	22	3 720	600
通信设备、计算机及其他电子设备制造业	Manufacturing of Communications Equipment, Computer and Other Electronic Equipment	27	18 859	5 906
仪器仪表及文化、办公用机械制造业	Manufacturing of Instruments, Meters, Culture and Office Equipment	5	624	186
电力、热力的生产和供应业	Production and Supply of Electricity and Thermal Power	2	3 349	2 179
燃气生产和供应业	Production and Supply of Gas	2	23	12
水的生产和供应业	Production and Supply of Tap Water	1	26	25

表 12-9 大中型工业企业技术开发项目和人员情况
Technical Development Projects and Personnel of Large and Medium Industrial Enterprises (2011)

指标	Indicators	项目数（项）Number of Projects (item)	从事技术开发人数（人）Number of Technical Development Personnel (person)	科技项目经费内部支出（千元）Internal Expenditure for Projects of Science and Technology (1 000 yuan)
总　计	**Total**	**4 344**	**44 018**	**14 593 661**
按注册登记大类分组	**Grouped by Type of Registration**			
国　有	State-owned	358	4 909	875 769
集　体	Collective-owned			
股份制及其他有限公司	Share-holding	711	8 936	2 842 380
私　营	Private	233	2 590	383 611
外商及港澳台投资	Overseas Invested Enterprises	3 042	27 583	10 491 901
其　他	Others			
按隶属关系分组	**Grouped by Subordination**			
中央工业	Central	866	12 552	3 891 225
地方工业	Local	3 478	31 466	10 702 436
按企业规模分组	**Grouped by Enterprise Scale**			
大型企业	Large	2 943	34 912	12 176 472
中型企业	Medium	1 401	9 106	2 417 189
按工业行业大类分组	**Grouped by Sector**			
农副食品加工业	Processing of Agricultural Side-line Food	6	200	19 390
饮食制造业	Food Manufacturing			
烟草制品业	Tobacco Manufacturing	5	21	3 150
纺织业	Textile Industry	10	79	14 491
家具制造业	Furniture Manufacturing	237	677	120 990
造纸及纸制品业	Paper-making and Paper Products Manufacturing	11	158	33 904
印刷业和记录媒介的复制	Printing and Record Duplicating	32	405	71 508
石油加工、炼焦及核燃料加工业	Petroleum Processing, Coke Making and Nuclear Fuel Processing	3	45	930
化学原料及化学制品制造业	Raw Chemical Materials and Chemicals	53	71	8 536
医药制造业	Medicine Manufacturing	167	695	307 094
橡胶制品业	Rubber Products	298	2 518	675 268
塑料制品业	Plastic Products	9	137	20 979
非金属矿物制品业	Nonmetal Mineral Products	33	357	88 235
有色金属冶炼及压延加工业	Smelting and Pressing of Nonferrous Metal	11	124	10 317
金属制品业	Metal Products	18	147	18 292
通用设备制造业	Manufacturing of General Equipment	305	2 723	1 323 333
专用设备制造业	Manufacturing of Special Purpose Equipment	200	2 664	748 380
交通运输设备制造业	Manufacturing of Transportation Equipment	909	9 916	4 520 213
电气机械及器材制造业	Manufacturing of Electric Machinery and Equipment	167	2 888	629 320
通信设备、计算机及其他电子设备制造业	Manufacturing of Communications Equipment, Computer and Other Electronic Equipment	1 593	16 321	5 433 828
仪器仪表及文化、办公用机械制造业	Manufacturing of Instruments, Meters, Culture and Office Equipment	39	584	167 109
电力、热力的生产和供应业	Production and Supply of Electricity and Thermal Power	232	3 243	376 884
燃气生产和供应业	Production and Supply of Gas	5	22	510
水的生产和供应业	Production and Supply of Tap Water	1	23	1 000

表12-10 大中型工业科技活动经费支出情况
(2011)

单位:千元

指 标	Indicators	企业内部科技活动支出合计 Total Expenditures of Scientific and Technological Activities Within Enterprises
总 计	**Total**	**17 238 552**
按注册登记大类分组	**Grouped by Type of Registration**	
国 有	State-owned	912 153
集 体	Collective-owned	
股份制及其他有限公司	Share-holding	4 259 104
私 营	Private	471 927
外商及港澳台投资	Overseas Invested Enterprises	11 595 368
其 他	Others	
按隶属关系分组	**Grouped by Subordination**	
中央工业	Central	4 666 184
地方工业	Local	12 572 368
按企业规模分组	**Grouped by Enterprise Scale**	
大型企业	Large	14 269 507
中型企业	Medium	2 969 045
按工业行业大类分组	**Grouped by Sector**	
农副食品加工业	Processing of Agricultural Side-line Food	27 310
饮食制造业	Food Manufacturing	
烟草制品业	Tobacco Manufacturing	7 834
纺织业	Textile Industry	14 907
家具制造业	Furniture Manufacturing	202 422
造纸及纸制品业	Paper-making and Paper Products Manufacturing	40 022
印刷业和记录媒介的复制	Printing and Record Duplicating	75 084
文教体育用品制造业	Manufacturing of Cultural, Educational and Sports Goods	930
石油加工、炼焦及核燃料加工业	Petroleum Processing, Coke Making and Nuclear Fuel Processing	10 744
化学原料及化学制品制造业	Raw Chemical Materials and Chemicals	326 185
医药制造业	Medicine Manufacturing	1 039 342
塑料制品业	Plastic Products	23 908
非金属矿物制品业	Nonmetal Mineral Products	88 828
有色金属冶炼及压延加工业	Smelting and Pressing of Nonferrous Metal	10 317
金属制品业	Metal Products	24 032
通用设备制造业	Manufacturing of General Equipment	1 486 153
专用设备制造业	Manufacturing of Special Purpose Equipment	939 376
交通运输设备制造业	Manufacturing of Transportation Equipment	5 738 317
电气机械及器材制造业	Manufacturing of Electric Machinery and Equipment	764 950
通信设备、计算机及其他电子设备制造业	Manufacturing of Communications Equipment, Computer and Other Electronic Equipment	5 864 826
仪器仪表及文化、办公用机械制造业	Manufacturing of Instruments, Meters, Culture and Office Equipment	174 221
电力、热力的生产和供应业	Production and Supply of Electricity and Thermal Power	376 884
燃气生产和供应业	Production and Supply of Gas	510
水的生产和供应业	Production and Supply of Tap Water	1 450

Expenditures of Large and Medium-sized Industrial Science and Technology Activities

(1 000 yuan)

委托外单位科技活动支出合计 Total Expenditures of Scientific and Technological Activities Organized by Other Enterprises	其他技术活动费用支出 Expenses of Other Technological Activities			
	技术改造经费支出 Expenditures on Technical Transformation	技术引进经费支出 Expenditures on Technical Introdnction	消化吸收经费支出 Expenditures on Technical Digestion and Absorption	购买国内技术经费支出 Expenditure in Buying Domestic Technology
1 393 674	3 875 494	3 205 765	1 267 096	149 780
123 700	1 730 911	8 231		
652 976	1 173 228	594 137	73 006	111 529
572	49 531	28 000	4 200	
616 426	921 824	2 575 397	1 189 890	38 251
234 932	2 424 473	462 049	52 505	47 627
1 158 742	1 451 021	2 743 716	1 214 591	102 153
1 277 910	3 447 783	2 886 801	1 239 546	84 727
115 764	427 711	318 964	27 550	65 053
	10 000			
500	1 400			
8 020				
	5 343			
3 874	270 260			
5 908	115 460	23 166	6 550	585
24 501	56 171	41 758	29 409	39 100
	7 000			
200	3 950			
	1 000			
16 528	328 053	332 718	8 124	
31 017	65 767	6 292	38 568	871
771 069	910 026	2 205 409	1 070 973	47 627
166 421	63 152	236 322	95 339	58
247 091	331 016	360 100	18 133	61 539
3 134	15 026			
114 345	1 655 623			
1 066	19 900			
	16 347			

表 12-11 大中型工业企业技术开发机构情况

Technical Development Institutions of Large and Medium Industrial Enterprises (2011)

指 标	Indicators	企业办技术开发机构数（个）Technical Development Institutions in Enterprises (unit)	技术开发机构科技活动人数（人）Technical Development Personnel (person)	技术开发机构科技经费内部支出（千元）Expenditure of Technical Development (1 000 yuan)
总 计	**Total**	**151**	**28 055**	**12 279 914**
按注册登记大类分组	**Grouped by Type of Registration**			
国 有	State-owned	8	930	236 495
股份制及其他有限公司	Share-holding	34	6 892	2 609 297
私 营	Private	22	1 587	229 598
外商及港澳台投资	Overseas Invested Enterprises	87	18 646	9 204 524
按隶属关系分组	**Grouped by Subordination**			
中央工业	Central	12	7 849	3 110 588
地方工业	Local	139	20 206	9 169 326
按企业规模分组	**Grouped by Enterprise Scale**			
大型企业	Large	63	22 564	11 116 446
中型企业	Medium	88	5 491	1 163 468
按工业行业大类分组	**Grouped by Sector**			
农副食品加工业	Processing of Agricultural Side-line Food	1	98	680
饮食制造业	Food Manufacturing			
烟草制品业	Tobacco Manufacturing			
纺织业	Textile Industry	2	66	14 607
家具制造业	Furniture Manufacturing	1	427	202 422
造纸及纸制品业	Paper-making and Paper Products Manufacturing	1	8	1 150
印刷业和记录媒介的复制	Printing and Record Duplicating	3	134	52 367
文教体育用品制造业	Manufacturing of Cultural, Educational and Sports Goods			
石油加工、炼焦及核燃料加工业	Petroleum Processing, Coke Making and Nuclear Fuel Processing			
化学原料及化学制品制造业	Raw Chemical Materials and Chemicals	15	575	194 920
医药制造业	Medicine Manufacturing	18	1 847	552 470
塑料制品业	Plastic Products	1	60	86
非金属矿物制品业	Nonmetal Mineral Products	4	209	30 161
有色金属冶炼及压延加工业	Smelting and Pressing of Nonferrous Metal	1	26	10 317
金属制品业	Metal Products	3	72	3 220
通用设备制造业	Manufacturing of General Equipment	11	2 056	991 851
专用设备制造业	Manufacturing of Special Purpose Equipment	14	2 153	360 478
交通运输设备制造业	Manufacturing of Transportation Equipment	21	8 987	4 626 325
电气机械及器材制造业	Manufacturing of Electric Machinery and Equipment	24	1 334	283 675
通信设备、计算机及其他电子设备制造业	Manufacturing of Communications Equipment, Computer and Other Electronic Equipment	28	9 255	4 769 012
仪器仪表及文化、办公用机械制造业	Manufacturing of Instruments, Meters, Culture and Office Equipment	2	419	130 443
电力、热力的生产和供应业	Production and Supply of Electricity and Thermal Power	1	329	55 730
燃气生产和供应业	Production and Supply of Gas			
水的生产和供应业	Production and Supply of Tap Water			

表 12-12 大中型工业企业专利情况
Patents Utilized by Large and Medium-sized Industrial Enterprises (2011)

单位:件 (item)

指标	Indicators	专利申请数 Patent Applications	#发明专利数 Patents of Creations and Inventions	有效发明专利数 Number of Effective Patents	#境外授权 Authorized Overseas
总计	**Total**	**4 498**	**2 753**	**2 230**	**125**
按注册登记大类分组	**Grouped by Type of Registration**				
国有	State-owned	437	168	86	5
集体	Collective-owned				
股份制及其他有限公司	Share-holding	960	437	415	5
私营	Private	241	67	129	2
外商及港澳台投资	Overseas Invested Enterprises	2 860	2 081	1 600	113
其他	Others				
按隶属关系分组	**Grouped by Subordination**				
中央工业	Central	714	439	522	17
地方工业	Local	3 784	2 314	1 708	108
按企业规模分组	**Grouped by Enterprise Scale**				
大型企业	Large	3 668	2 358	1 590	93
中型企业	Medium	830	395	640	32
按工业行业大类分组	**Grouped by Sector**				
农副食品加工业	Processing of Agricultural Side-line Food	32			
饮食制造业	Food Manufacturing				
烟草制品业	Tobacco Manufacturing	3	1		
纺织业	Textile Industry	76	1	2	
家具制造业	Furniture Manufacturing	25	9	3	
造纸及纸制品业	Paper-making and Paper Products Manufacturing			1	
印刷业和记录媒介的复制	Printing and Record Duplicating	25	9	15	
石油加工、炼焦及核燃料加工业	Petroleum Processing, Coke Making and Nuclear Fuel Processing			1	
化学原料及化学制品制造业	Raw Chemical Materials and Chemicals	28	24	99	2
医药制造业	Medicine Manufacturing	73	53	155	14
塑料制品业	Plastic Products	16	2	13	
非金属矿物制品业	Nonmetal Mineral Products	26	19	36	
有色金属冶炼及压延加工业	Smelting and Pressing of Nonferrous Metal	6	6		
金属制品业	Metal Products	14	1	22	
通用设备制造业	Manufacturing of General Equipment	285	92	144	14
专用设备制造业	Manufacturing of Special Purpose Equipment	325	178	79	15
交通运输设备制造业	Manufacturing of Transportation Equipment	904	235	200	2
电气机械及器材制造业	Manufacturing of Electric Machinery and Equipment	186	40	62	1
通信设备、计算机及其他电子设备制造业	Manufacturing of Communications Equipment, Computer and Other Electronic Equipment	2 255	1 998	1 372	74
仪器仪表及文化、办公用机械制造业	Manufacturing of Instruments, Meters, Culture and Office Equipment	9	2	12	3
电力、热力的生产和供应业	Production and Supply of Electricity and Thermal Power	209	83	12	
燃气生产和供应业	Production and Supply of Gas	1			
水的生产和供应业	Production and Supply of Tap Water			2	

表 12-13　大中型工业企业新产品产出情况

Output of New Products of Large and Medium Industrial Enterprises
(2011)

单位:千元　　　　(1 000 yuan)

指　标	Indicators	新产品产　值 Output of New Products	新产品销售收入 Sales Revenue	#出　口 Export
总　计	**Total**	**234 617 872**	**303 659 216**	**50 593 629**
按注册登记大类分组	**Grouped by Type of Registration**			
国　有	State-owned	11 389 410	11 940 863	31 921
集　体	Collective-owned			
股份制及其他有限公司	Share-holding	44 449 251	42 569 789	19 008 736
私　营	Private	5 615 927	5 451 264	1 034 450
外商及港澳台投资	Overseas Invested Enterprises	173 163 284	243 697 300	30 518 522
其　他	Others			
按隶属关系分组	**Grouped by Subordination**			
中央工业	Central	57 953 668	55 539 883	32 603 674
地方工业	Local	176 664 204	248 119 333	17 989 955
按企业规模分组	**Grouped by Enterprise Scale**			
大型企业	Large	209 666 546	278 068 408	48 038 354
中型企业	Medium	24 951 326	25 590 808	2 555 275
按工业行业大类分组	**Grouped by Sector**			
农副食品加工业	Processing of Agricultural Side-line Food	289 040	289 040	
纺织业	Textile Industry	215 323	339 513	
家具制造业	Furniture Manufacturing	3 233 430	3 233 430	
造纸及纸制品业	Paper-making and Paper Products Manufacturing	817 894	799 839	618 017
印刷业和记录媒介的复制	Printing and Record Duplicating	627 719	1 000 820	1 000
石油加工、炼焦及核燃料加工业	Petroleum Processing, Coke Making and Nuclear Fuel Processing	79 760	79 760	
化学原料及化学制品制造业	Raw Chemical Materials and Chemicals	5 123 989	5 076 501	694 954
医药制造业	Medicine Manufacturing	6 560 995	5 997 643	42 834
塑料制品业	Plastic Products	96 610	141 822	16 345
非金属矿物制品业	Nonmetal Mineral Products	197 022	303 253	100 816
有色金属冶炼及压延加工业	Smelting and Pressing of Nonferrous Metal	235 763	235 410	46 832
金属制品业	Metal Products	51 478	48 012	32 788
通用设备制造业	Manufacturing of General Equipment	23 612 392	22 768 877	9 559 642
专用设备制造业	Manufacturing of Special Purpose Equipment	5 421 590	6 151 405	14 700
交通运输设备制造业	Manufacturing of Transportation Equipment	132 803 808	202 464 908	19 610 763
电气机械及器材制造业	Manufacturing of Electric Machinery and Equipment	15 302 165	14 986 540	4 250 469
通信设备、计算机及其他电子设备制造业	Manufacturing of Communications Equipment, Computer and Other Electronic Equipment	38 899 672	38 693 221	15 514 866
仪器仪表及文化、办公用机械制造业	Manufacturing of Instruments, Meters, Culture and Office Equipment	1 049 222	1 049 222	89 603

表 12-14 主要年份科技企业主要经济指标
Major Economic Indicators of Technical Research Enterprises Run by Entrepreneurs in Main Years

指 标	Indicators	单 位 Unit	1998	2000	2005	2009	2010	2011
企业单位数	Number of Enterprises	个 unit	592	828	700	2 551	2 525	3 768
企业专利总数	Number of Enterprise Patents	项 item				981	4 918	3 829
职工人数	Employees	万人 10 000 persons	2.43	3.04	5.76	13.98	9.47	34.21
从事科技活动人员	Persons Employed in Science and Technology	万人 10 000 persons				2.97	1.59	9.01
资产总额	Total Assets	亿元 100 million yuan	69.10	122.40	575.47	3 337.84	766.56	4 896.10
技工贸销售总额	Total Sales	亿元 100 million yuan	38.99	82.01	521.45	3 126.08	858.06	3 707.86
产品销售收入	Income for Selling Products	亿元 100 million yuan				2 429.38	770.89	3 530.08
利润总额	Total Profits	亿元 100 million yuan	0.43	4.64	35.58	120.41	64.99	482.79
上交税收	Tax Payable	亿元 100 million yuan	1.37	2.70	18.22	122.14	44.66	195.93
创汇总额	Total Foreign Exchange	亿美元 USD 100 million	0.43	0.95	12.65	287.84	25.67	108.63
投入科研开发费	Investment in Research and Development	亿元 100 million yuan	2.35	4.18	34.72	46.03	26.56	223.77

注：2011 年数据含 2000 万以上科技企业。
Note: Data in 2011 include technology enterprises that have the output value of more than 20 million yuan.

主要统计指标解释

专　利

是专利权的简称，是对发明人的发明创造经审查合格后，由专利局依据专利法授予发明人和设计人对该项发明创造享有的专有权。包括发明、实用新型和外观设计。反映拥有自主知识产权的科技和设计成果情况。

发　明

指对产品、方法或者其改进所提出的新的技术方案。是国际通行的反映拥有自主知识产权技术的核心指标。

实用新型

指对产品的形状、构造或者其结合所提出的适于实用的新的技术方案。反映具有一定技术含量的技术成果情况。

外观设计

指对产品的形状、图案、色彩或者其结合所作出的富有美感并适于工业上应用的新设计。反映拥有自主知识产权的外观设计成果情况。

专业技术人员

专业技术人员指事业、企业单位中已被聘任专业技术职务的从事专业技术工作和专业技术管理的人员，以及虽未被聘任专业技术职务，但现在专业技术岗位上工作的人员。

国有企业

指企业全部资产归国家所有，并按《中华人民共和国企业法人登记管理条例》规定登记注册的非公司制的经济组织。不包括有限责任公司中的国有独资公司。

集体企业

集体企业指企业资产归集体所有，并按《中华人民共和国企业法人登记管理条例》规定登记注册的经济组织。

科技活动

指在自然科学、农业科学、医药科学、工程与技术科学、人文与社会科学领域（简称科学技术领域）中，与科技知识的产生、发展、传播和应用密切相关的有组织的活动。可分为研究与试验发展（R&D）、研究与试验发展成果应用及相关的科技服务三类活动。该定义是联合国教科文组织考虑成员国特别是发展中国家开展科技统计工作的需要，而对科技活动所作的统计界定。

科技活动人员

指直接从事科技活动、以及专门从事科技活动管理和为科技活动提供直接服务，累计从事科技活动的时间占全年制度工作时间10%及以上的人员。（1）直接从事科技活动的人员，包括：在独立核算的科学研究与技术开发机构、高等学校、各类企业及其他事业单位内设的研究室、实验室、技术开发中心及中试车间（基地）等机构中从事科技活动的研究人员、工程技术人员、技术工人及其它人员；虽不在上述机构工作，但编入科技活动项目（课题）组的人员；科技信息与文献机构中的专业技术人员；从事论文设计的研究生等。（2）专门从事科技活动管理和为科技活动提供直接服务的人员包括：独立核算的科学研究与技术开发机构、科技信息与文献机构、高等学校、各类企业及其他事业单位主管科技工作的负责人，专门从事科技活动的计划、行政、人事、财务、物资供应、设备维护、图书资料管理等工作的各类人员，但不包括保卫、医疗保健人员、司机、食堂人员、茶炉工、水暖工、清洁工等为科技活动提供间接服务的人员。该指标用来反映投入科技活动人力的规模。

科学家和工程师

科学家与工程师指科技活动人员中具有高、中级技术职称（职务）的人员和不具有高、中级技术职称（职务）的大学本科及以上学历人员。

科技活动经费筹集

指从各种渠道筹集到的计划用于科技活动的经费，包括政府资金、事业资金、企业资金、银行贷款和其他收入等。反映各社会经济主体对促进科技进步所作的努力。

政府资金

指从各级政府部门获得的计划用于科技活动的经费，包括科学事业费、科技三项费、科研基建费、科学基金、教育等部门事业费中计划用于科技活动的经费以及政府部门预算外资金中计划用于科技活动的经费等。

新产品

指采用新技术原理、新设计构思研制、生产的全新产品，或在结构、材质、工艺等某一方面比原有产品有明显改进，从而显著提高了产品性能或扩大了使用功能的产品。既包括政府有关部门认定并在有效期内的新产品，也包括企业自行研制开发、在统计规定的新产品跟踪期限内的产品。跟踪期限规定如下：装备类跟踪五年，消费品类跟踪二年，其他类跟踪三年。用来反映科技产出及对经济增长的直接贡献。

R&D

是"科学研究与试验发展"(Research and Development)的英文缩写。其含义是指在科学技术领域,为增加知识总量,以及运用这些知识去创造新的应用进行的系统的创造性的活动。R&D 包括基础研究、应用研究、试验发展三类活动。

EXPLANATORY NOTES TO MAJOR STATISTICAL INDICATORS

Patent

Patent is an abbreviation for the patent right and refers to the exclusive right of ownership by the inventors or designers for the creation or inventions, given from the patent offices after due process of assessment and approval in accordance with the Patent Law. Patents are granted for inventions, utility models and designs. This indicator reflects the achievements of S&T and design with independent intellectual property.

Invention

Inventions refer to the new technical proposals to the products or methods or their modifications. This is universal core indicator reflecting the technologies with independent intellectual property.

Utility Models

Utility Models refer to the practical and new technical proposals on the shape and structure of the product or the combination of both. This indicator reflects the condition of technological results with certain technical content.

Exterior Design

Designs refer to the aesthetics and industrially applicable new designs for the shape, pattern and color of the product, or their combinations. This indicator reflects the appearance design achievements with independent intellectual property.

Professional and Technical Personnel

Professional and Technical Personnel refer to professional, technical and managerial staff members in institutions or enterprises who not only have professional and technical titles but also hold professional and technical posts. They also include those who work on professional and technical posts but do not have professional and technical titles.

State-owned Enterprises

State-owned Enterprises refer to non-corporation economic units where the entire assets are owned by the state and which have registered in accordance with the Regulation of the People's Republic of China on the Management of Registration of Corporate Enterprises. Excluded from this category are sole state-funded corporations in the limited liability corporations.

Collective-owned Enterprises

Collective-owned Enterprises refer to economic units where the assets are owned collectively and which have registered in accordance with the Regulation of the People's Republic of China on the Management of Registration of Corporate Enterprises.

Scientific and Technological Activities (S&T Activities)

Scientific and Technological Activities (S&T Activities) refer to organized activities which are closely related with the creation, development, dissemination and application of the scientific and technical knowledge in the fields of natural sciences, agricultural sciences, medical sciences, engineering and technological sciences, humanities and social sciences (referred to as scientific and technological fields). S&T activities can be classified into 3 categories: research and development (R&D) activities, application of R&D results, and related S&T services. This statistical definition is made by UNICHIEF for scientific and technological activities to meet the need of carrying out statistical work in this field for its member countries in particular those developing countries.

Personnel Engaged in S&T Activities

Personnel Engaged in S&T Activities refer to personnel directly engaged in S&T activities, in the management of S&T activities, and in providing direct service to S&T activities, who spend over 10% of the total working hours in a year in S&T activities. (1) Personnel directly engaged in S&T activities include researchers, engineers, technicians and other related personnel engaged in S&T activities in independent-accounting R&D institutions, institutions of higher learning, and in research institutes, laboratories, technology development centers and central experiment workshops under enterprises and institutions. Also included are people working in S&T information archiving institutes, and graduate students working on the design of their thesis. (2) Personnel engaged in the management of S&T activities and in providing direct service to S&T activities include senior management people responsible for S&T activities in independent-accounting R&D institutions, S&T information archiving institutes, institutions of higher learning, and in enterprises and institutions where S&T activities are undertaken. Also included are people responsible for the planning, administration, personnel management, financial management, logistics supply, equipment maintenance, information and library management that are related with S&T activities. People providing indirect services are excluded, such as security, medical service, drivers, plumbers, cleaners and those providing catering and related service. This indicator reflects the size of personnel engaged in S&T activities.

Scientists and Engineers

Scientists and Engineers refer to persons engaged in S&T activities who have obtained titles of senior and middle level professional positions, and those without such position but have completed university or higher education.

Funding for S&T Activities

Funding for S&T Activities refers to funds obtained from various sources for S&T activities, including government funds, self-raised funds by institutions, self-raised funds by enterprises, loans from banks and other funds. This indicator reflects the efforts made by various social economic entities in promoting the development of S&T.

Government Funds

Government Funds refer to funds obtained from government agencies at all levels to be used for S&T activities, including fund for scientific undertakings, 3 kinds of fund for S&T activities, fund for capital construction for scientific researches, science fund, funds from education expenditures by education departments for S&T activities, and extra-budget fund from government agencies for S&T activities.

New Products

New Products refer to new products produced with new technology and new design, or products that represent noticeable improvement in terms of structure, material, or production process so as to improve significantly the character or function of the older versions. They include new products certified by relevant government agencies within the period of certification, as well as new products designed and produced by enterprises within the new product track time limit prescribed by the statistical regulations. The new product track time limit is prescribed as following: equipment products 5 years, consumption products 2 years, other products 3 years. This indictor reflects the direct contribution of S&T output to economic growth.

R&D

R&D is an abbreviation which stands for 'Science Research and Experimental Development', which means systematic and creative endeavors aimed at expanding the overall volume of knowledge and applying the knowledge in systematic creation. R&D includes basic studies, application research and experimental development.

第十三篇

Chapter 13

人民生活

PEOPLE'S LIVELIHOOD

表13-1 从业人员报酬
Wages of Employed Persons
(2011)

单位:亿元 (100 million yuan)

指 标	Indicators	合 计 Total	国有单位 State-owned Enterprises	集体单位 Collective-owned Enterprises	港澳台及外商投资单位 Overseas Invested Enterprises	其 他 单 位 Others
总 计	**Total**	**1 355.74**	**240.40**	**7.23**	**595.21**	**512.91**
农、林、牧、渔业	Farming, Forestry, Animal Husbandry and Fishery	0.77	0.40	0.09	0.03	0.25
采矿业	Mining	0.37				0.37
制造业	Manufacturing	364.66	29.70	1.09	270.71	63.16
电力、燃气及水的生产和供应业	Production and Supply of Electricity, Gas and Tap Water	14.46	10.69	0.02	1.38	2.37
建筑业	Construction	92.38	8.23	0.62	14.30	69.23
交通运输、仓储和邮政业	Transportation, Warehousing and Post Service	77.04	22.73	0.25	8.98	45.08
信息传输、计算机服务和软件业	Information Transmission, Computer Service and Computer Software	57.89	26.49		30.15	1.25
#信息传输	Information Transmission	24.10	21.55		1.89	0.66
批发和零售业	Wholesale and Retail	186.05	4.73	0.94	146.23	34.15
住宿和餐饮业	Hotel and Catering	10.48	1.74	0.04	5.99	2.71
金融业	Banking	356.10	33.29	0.01	53.93	268.87
房地产业	Real Estate	26.43	5.09	0.18	10.09	11.07
租赁和商务服务业	Leasing and Business Service	46.86	7.74	0.28	32.49	6.35
科学研究、技术服务和地质勘查业	Scientific Research, Technical Service and Geological Prospecting	32.09	9.89	0.03	18.89	3.28
水利、环境和公共设施管理业	Water Conservancy, Environment and Public Facilities Administration	4.88	2.75	0.02	0.71	1.40
#公共设施管理业	Public Facilities Administration	1.47	0.37			1.10
居民服务和其他服务业	Resident Service and Other Services	1.24	0.65		0.25	0.34
教 育	Education	35.82	32.47	0.46	0.68	2.22
卫生、社会保障和社会福利业	Healthcare, Social Security and Social Welfare	23.70	20.89	2.81		
卫 生	Healthcare	23.07	20.41	2.66		
社会保障	Social Security	0.25	0.13	0.12		
社会福利业	Social Welfare	0.38	0.35	0.03		
文化、体育和娱乐业	Culture, Sports and Entertainment	3.48	2.19	0.08	0.40	0.81
文 化	Culture	1.89	0.91	0.08	0.10	0.81
体 育	Sports	1.03	1.03			
娱乐业	Entertainment	0.56	0.25		0.31	
公共管理和社会组织	Public Administration and Social Organizations	21.04	20.73	0.31		

表13-2 从业人员平均报酬
Average Wages of Employed Persons
(2011)

单位:元 (yuan)

指 标	Indicators	合 计 Total	国有单位 State-owned Enterprises	集体单位 Collective-owned Enterprises	港澳台及外商投资单位 Overseas Invested Enterprises	其 他 单 位 Others
总平均	**Annual Average Wages**	**91 995**	**89 722**	**55 646**	**91 440**	**94 656**
农、林、牧、渔业	Farming, Forestry, Animal Husbandry and Fishery	54 616	53 640	62 020	31 958	58 805
采矿业	Mining	207 477				207 477
制造业	Manufacturing	69 455	73 139	46 673	68 037	75 008
电力、燃气及水的生产和供应业	Production and Supploy of Electric Power, Gas and Tap Water	109 543	108 991	40 438	82 177	142 382
建筑业	Construction	59 952	78 545	51 474	79 931	55 599
交通运输、仓储和邮政业	Transportation, Warehousing and Post Service	69 627	66 239	43 091	83 823	69 307
信息传输、计算机服务和软件业	Information Transmission, Computer Service and Computer Software	132 659	140 546		132 678	60 676
#信息传输	Information Transmission	131 878	137 977		158 838	45 067
批发和零售业	Wholesale and Retail	116 085	99 127	39 990	136 990	73 586
住宿和餐饮业	Hotel and Catering	40 482	49 820	25 053	32 651	69 685
金融业	Banking	165 686	181 636	116 917	299 978	150 535
房地产业	Real Estate	62 467	69 861	45 219	56 978	65 437
租赁和商务服务业	Leasing and Business Service	100 951	56 522	38 239	139 063	73 659
科学研究、技术服务和地质勘查业	Scientific Research, Technical Service and Geological Prospecting	131 716	88 747	64 690	179 790	122 942
水利、环境和公共设施管理业	Water Conservancy, Environment and Public Facilities Administration	48 882	57 328	76 724	19 162	95 482
#公共设施管理业	Public Facilities Administration	108 412	80 980			122 327
居民服务和其他服务业	Resident Service and Other Services	79 771	91 127		63 833	75 712
教 育	Education	78 525	79 291	84 721	227 296	57 808
卫生、社会保障和社会福利业	Healthcare, Social Security and Social Welfare	93 782	98 194	70 316		
卫 生	Healthcare	95 716	99 963	72 188		
社会保障	Social Security	62 093	62 029	62 161		
社会福利业	Social Welfare	49 871	54 327	24 828		
文化、体育和娱乐业	Culture, Sports and Entertainment	66 830	66 673	73 139	43 926	90 487
文 化	Culture	80 557	73 365	73 139	85 211	91 196
体 育	Sports	62 494	62 494			
娱乐业	Entertainment	46 166	62 990		38 080	21 778
公共管理和社会组织	Public Administration and Social Organizations	88 693	88 576	97 417		

表13-3 历年职工工资总额

Total Wages of Staff and Workers in Main Years (1990～2011)

单位:亿元 (100 million yuan)

年 份 Year	总 计 Total	国有单位 State-owned Enterprises	集体单位 Collective-owned Enterprises	其他单位 Others	#港澳台及外商投资单位 Overseas Invested Enterprises
1990	11.52	9.05	2.24	0.23	
1991	13.69	10.55	2.77	0.37	
1992	23.17	19.01	3.52	0.64	
1993	47.26	35.49	4.24	7.53	
1994	60.75	44.77	5.02	10.96	
1995	80.29	58.22	5.88	16.19	
1996	83.37	55.98	6.35	21.04	
1997	84.18	52.32	6.23	25.63	
1998	89.70	47.13	4.63	37.94	
1999	106.67	53.08	4.95	48.64	
2000	120.59	54.98	4.25	61.36	
2001	140.36	53.14	3.47	83.75	
2002	160.37	54.79	3.29	102.29	
2003	170.99	56.99	2.83	111.17	49.99
2004	184.02	66.16	2.85	115.01	48.92
2005	235.03	66.55	2.70	165.78	64.67
2006	278.91	63.83	2.81	212.27	97.78
2007	354.32	94.30	3.28	256.74	124.93
2008	480.32	88.50	3.43	388.39	174.64
2009	627.92	129.68	5.07	493.17	265.16
2010	765.95	139.43	5.13	621.39	277.86
2011	1 243.20	234.78	6.84	1 001.58	532.74

表13-4 职工工资总额
Total Wages of Staff and Workers
(2011)

单位:亿元 (100 million yuan)

指 标	Indicators	合 计 Total	国有单位 State-owned Enterprises	集体单位 Collective-owned Enterprises	港澳台及外商投资单位 Overseas Invested Enterprises	其他单位 Others
总 计	**Total**	**1 243.20**	**234.78**	**6.84**	**532.74**	**468.84**
农、林、牧、渔业	Farming, Forestry, Animal Husbandry and Fishery	0.75	0.38	0.09	0.03	0.25
采矿业	Mining	0.36				0.36
制造业	Manufacturing	347.81	29.67	1.00	255.59	61.55
电力、燃气及水的生产和供应业	Production and Supply of Electricity, Gas and Tap Water	14.42	10.65	0.02	1.38	2.37
建筑业	Construction	48.43	5.72	0.58	9.76	32.37
交通运输、仓储和邮政业	Transportation, Warehousing and Post Service	75.81	22.48	0.25	8.55	44.53
信息传输、计算机服务和软件业	Information Transmission, Computer Service and Software	56.09	26.49		28.36	1.24
#信息传输	Information Transmission	24.10	21.59		1.86	0.65
批发和零售业	Wholesale and Retail	163.55	4.66	0.92	124.58	33.39
住宿和餐饮业	Hotel and Catering	8.25	1.61	0.03	4.74	1.87
金融业	Banking	344.52	34.13		43.23	267.14
房地产业	Real Estate	23.67	4.59	0.16	9.13	9.79
租赁和商务服务业	Leasing and Business Service	43.23	7.22	0.29	29.17	6.55
科学研究、技术服务和地质勘查业	Scientific Research, Technical Services and Geological Prospecting	29.66	9.68	0.03	16.76	3.19
水利、环境和公共设施管理业	Water Conservancy, Environment and Public Facilities Administration	4.65	2.56	0.02	0.71	1.36
#公共设施管理业	Public Facilities Administration	1.43	0.36			1.07
居民服务和其他服务业	Resident Service and Other Services	1.19	0.63		0.23	0.33
教 育	Education	34.00	31.67	0.45	0.11	1.77
卫生、社会保障和社会福利业	Healthcare, Social Security and Social Welfare	22.75	20.11	2.64		
卫 生	Healthcare	22.20	19.69	2.51		
社会保障	Social Security	0.25	0.13	0.12		
社会福利业	Social Welfare	0.30	0.29	0.01		
文化、体育和娱乐业	Culture, Sports and Entertainment	3.27	2.02	0.08	0.39	0.78
文 化	Culture	1.84	0.88	0.08	0.10	0.78
体 育	Sports	0.90	0.90			
娱 乐	Entertainment	0.54	0.24		0.29	
公共管理和社会组织	Public Administration and Social Organizations	20.79	20.51	0.28		

表13-5 历年职工平均工资
Average Wages of Staff and Workers in Main Years (1990~2011)

单位:元 (yuan)

年份 Year	年平均工资 Annual Average Wages	国有单位 State-owned Enterprises	集体单位 Collective-owned Enterprises	其他单位 Others	#港澳台及外商投资单位 Overseas Invested Enterprises
1990	2 939	3 069	2 466	3 665	
1991	3 363	3 479	2 906	4 305	
1992	4 350	4 532	3 468	5 506	
1993	5 999	5 927	4 984	7 241	
1994	7 906	7 616	6 584	10 514	
1995	9 995	10 087	6 749	11 651	
1996	11 351	11 623	7 445	12 559	
1997	12 425	12 463	7 863	14 359	
1998	13 417	12 977	7 421	15 615	
1999	15 563	14 561	8 659	18 443	22 911
2000	17 607	15 721	9 243	21 216	24 656
2001	20 349	17 503	9 092	24 066	29 710
2002	22 740	19 410	9 863	26 255	32 342
2003	25 620	22 655	10 748	28 543	38 753
2004	29 512	26 863	11 727	32 585	41 812
2005	33 186	27 707	12 390	37 153	50 779
2006	41 725	36 065	16 953	44 698	68 658
2007	56 878	49 004	20 656	59 710	68 674
2008	69 872	49 891	24 017	78 338	71 199
2009	76 026	63 747	23 419	82 074	74 376
2010	89 424	66 802	27 984	98 719	83 679
2011	90 721	85 168	48 915	92 679	85 597

表13-6 职工平均工资

Average Wages of Staff and Workers

(2011)

单位:元 (yuan)

指标	Indicators	合计 Total	国有单位 State-owned Enterprises	集体单位 Collective-owned Enterprises	港澳台及外商投资单位 Overseas Invested Enterprises	其他单位 Others
总平均工资	**Annual Average Wages**	**90 721**	**85 168**	**48 915**	**85 597**	**102 296**
农、林、牧、渔业	Farming, Forestry, Animal Husbandry and Fishery	53 465	51 911	60 824	32 549	57 979
采矿业	Mining	212 807				212 807
制造业	Manufacturing	66 330	64 040	39 216	65 425	72 568
电力、燃气及水的生产和供应业	Production and Supply of Electricity, Gas and Tap Water	109 940	109 495	46 882	81 621	142 546
建筑业	Construction	77 766	75 589	61 482	97 553	73 970
交通运输、仓储和邮政业	Transportation, Warehousing and Post service	69 052	64 248	42 394	80 664	70 003
信息传输、计算机服务和软件业	Information Transmission, Computer Service and Computer Software	126 222	140 315		120 597	60 640
#信息传输	Information Transmission	131 705	137 680		158 227	45 191
批发和零售业	Wholesale and Retail	104 107	84 623	26 885	121 175	73 625
住宿和餐饮业	Hotel and Catering	46 890	50 241	22 902	43 353	56 154
金融业	Banking	162 023	171 947	60 167	255 354	151 916
房地产业	Real Estate	62 489	68 695	50 280	53 584	70 741
租赁和商务服务业	Leasing and Business Service	70 280	33 204	20 882	127 346	42 284
科学研究、技术服务和地质勘查业	Scientific Research, Technical Service and Geological Prospecting	126 138	89 056	64 690	165 699	128 360
水利、环境和公共设施管理业	Water Conservancy, Environment and Public Facilities Administration	49 600	60 108	70 375	19 162	97 634
#公共设施管理业	Public Facilities Administration	111 183	83 582			125 242
居民服务和其他服务业	Resident Service and Other Services	56 249	46 875		64 791	79 225
教育	Education	82 209	83 698	85 826	69 515	62 404
卫生、社会保障和社会福利业	Healthcare, Social Security and Social Welfare	95 802	99 196	75 985		
卫生	Healthcare	96 984	100 269	77 137		
社会保障	Social Security	61 293	61 204	61 389		
社会福利业	Social Welfare	67 184	68 694	40 250		
文化、体育和娱乐业	Culture, Sports and Entertainment	66 227	64 939	64 101	44 838	93 652
文化	Culture	80 264	71 920	64 101	85 211	94 436
体育	Sports	59 746	59 746			
娱乐	Entertainment	46 823	63 171		38 742	21 778
公共管理和社会组织	Public Administration and Social Organizations	90 264	90 084	105 528		

表 13-7 城镇居民家庭基本情况
Background of Urban Families

指标	Indicators	单位 Unit	2005	2010	2011
调查户数	Households Surveyed	户 household	500	600	600
调查户总人口	Total Population of Households Surveyed	人 person	1 460	1 704	1 692
调查户就业人口	Employed Persons in Households Surveyed	人 person	710	918	906
#国有单位就业人口	Employed by State-owned Enterprises	人 person	370	402	402
城镇集体单位就业人口	Employed by Collective-owned Enterprises	人 person	55	48	42
其他各类单位就业人口	Employed by Other Enterprises	人 person	145	222	222
平均每户常住人口	Average Number of Permanent Residents Per Household	人 person	2.92	2.84	2.82
平均每户就业人口	Average Number of Employed Persons Per Household	人 person	1.42	1.53	1.51
平均每户就业面	Average Employment Rate Per Household	%	48.6	53.9	53.5
平均每一就业者赡养人口	Number of Persons Supported by Each Employed Person	人 person	2.06	1.86	1.87
恩格尔系数	Engel's Coefficient	%	36.2	34.8	34.5
平均消费倾向	Average Propensity to Consumption	%	69.8	67.7	68.6
平均每人年实际收入	Annual Actual Income Per Capita	元 yuan	20 990	36 399	41 257
平均每人年可支配收入	Annual Disposable Income Per Capita	元 yuan	19 089	32 330	36 815
平均每人年消费性支出	Annual Consumption Spending Per Capita	元 yuan	13 328	21 897	25 239
平均每人住房建筑面积	Average Floor Space Per Capita	平方米 sq·m	22.44	39.26	36.30

注：本表至表 13－18 为住户调查资料，人均住房面积由建交委提供。
Note: The contents in from this table to Table 13－18 are the survey data of households in Pudong. The data of housing space per capita are provided by Pudong Construction and Transport Committee.

表 13-8 历年城乡居民收支情况
Income and Expenditure of Urban and Suburban Residents in Main Years (2005～2011)

单位:元 (yuan)

指 标	Indicators	2005	2006	2007	2008	2009	2010	2011
城镇居民收支状况	**Income and Expenditure of Urban Residents**							
人均总收入	Gross Income Per Capita	20 990	23 625	26 856	30 900	33 983	36 399	41 257
#可支配收入	Disposable Income	19 089	21 452	24 273	27 797	30 390	32 330	36 815
工薪收入	Wage Income	14 149	16 320	18 690	21 728	23 789	21 706	24 554
经营净收入	Operational Income	775	590	494	400	549	869	1 018
财产性收入	Property Income	397	391	544	597	648	715	891
转移性收入	Transferable Income	5 669	6 324	7 128	8 175	8 997	9 040	10 352
人均总支出	Total Expenses Per Capita	18 923	21 443	26 862	29 055	33 290	30 102	36 408
#消费支出	Consumption Expenses	13 328	14 349	17 802	19 579	22 379	21 897	25 239
#食 品	Foodstuff	4 826	5 299	6 272	6 921	7 757	7 631	8 696
医疗与保健	Medical Care	895	804	831	1 064	1 331	1 143	1 044
教育文化娱乐服务	Education, Culture and Amusement Services	2 119	2 362	2 861	3 027	3 326	3 324	3 528
社会保障支出	Social Security Expenses	1 506	1 758	2 018	2 248	2 679	2 941	3 329
农村居民收入状况	**Income and Expenditure of Suburban Residents**							
人均总收入	Gross Income Per Capita	10 443	11 715	13 157	14 869	16 080	14 759	17 191
#可支配收入	Disposable Income	9 779	10 911	12 246	13 778	14 963	13 898	15 861
工薪收入	Wage Income	7 458	8 223	9 117	10 179	10 751	10 223	11 362
经营净收入	Operational Income	460	320	298	249	260	743	823
财产性收入	Property Income	1 078	1 522	1 914	2 303	2 604	1 314	1 439
转移性收入	Transferable Income	1 447	1 650	1 828	2 138	2 465	1 618	2 237

注：1. 2010 年起居民各项结构性收入改为可支配收入口径。
2. 城镇居民人均年可支配收入和农村居民人均年可支配收入数据，为住户调查数据。剔除 2010 年调查范围变化影响，按可比口径计算，分别增长 11% 和 12.1%。

Note: 1. All kinds of structural income of suburban residents in 2010 were changed to the item of disposable income.
2. Data of annual disposable incomes per capita for both urban and rural citizens are those for household interviews. Deducted from the influence of the change in the survey scope in 2010, they were increased by 11% and 12.1% respectively according to the comparable approach.

表13-9　城镇居民家庭人均收入与支出状况(按收入水平分)
Average Income and Expenses of Urban Families(by income level)
(2011)

单位:元　　(yuan)

指　标	Indicators	总平均 Overall Average	低收入户 Low-income Household	较低收入户 Lower-income Household	中等收入户 Medium-income Household	较高收入户 Medium Higher-income Household	高收入户 High-income Household
人均总收入	**Gross Income Per Capita**	**41 257**	**17 085**	**26 634**	**34 827**	**45 042**	**84 870**
#人均可支配收入	Disposable Income Per Capita	36 815	15 452	24 066	31 268	40 657	74 546
工资性收入	Wage Income	24 554	10 193	14 105	19 487	27 003	53 398
经营净收入	Operational Income	1 018	221	406	524	386	3 636
财产性收入	Property Income	891	65	306	279	1 120	2 777
转移性收入	Transferable Income	10 352	4 974	9 249	10 979	12 148	14 735
人均总支出	**Total Expenses Per Capita**	**36 408**	**15 647**	**25 110**	**31 109**	**38 913**	**73 055**
消费性支出	Consumption Expenses	25 239	12 760	20 624	22 426	25 326	46 017
食　品	Foodstuff	8 696	5 933	8 012	8 495	9 335	11 889
衣　着	Clothing	2 035	1 017	1 590	1 762	2 072	3 818
家庭设备用品及服务	Family Appliances and Services	1 898	673	1 267	1 697	1 942	4 011
医疗保健	Medical Care	1 044	703	1 024	937	1 034	1 544
交通和通信	Traffic and Communications	4 537	1 537	3 513	3 338	4 309	10 228
教育文化娱乐服务	Education, Culture and Amusement Services	3 528	1 638	2 199	3 052	3 907	7 021
居　住	Habitation	2 162	931	2 240	2 021	1 528	4 151
其他商品及服务	Miscellaneous Commodities and Services	1 339	328	778	1 124	1 198	3 354
财产性支出	Property Expenses	377	111	121	438	366	876
转移性支出	Transferable Expenses	4 427	1 377	2 218	3 409	5 283	10 145
社会保障支出	Social Security Expenses	3 329	1 362	2 147	2 943	3 535	6 830
购、建房支出	Expenses for Purchasing/Building Houses	3 036	37		1 894	4 403	9 186

注：收入水平根据居民家庭人均可支配收入由低到高排序，分别按家庭数量的20%分为5组。

Note: Income levels are sorted from the low to the high according to the disposable income per capita of urban families. They are divided into five groups from 20% of the total number of families respectively.

表 13-10 每百户城镇居民家庭年末耐用消费品拥有量
Possession of Durable Consumer Goods Per 100 Urban Households at Year-End

指 标	Indicators	单 位 Unit	2005	2010	2011
摩托车	Mototrcycle	辆 in number	5	9	9
助力车	Scooter	辆 in number	15	22	25
家用汽车	Household Car	辆 in number	4	18	22
洗衣机	Washing Machine	台 set	97	100	100
电冰箱	Household Refrigerator	台 set	102	102	103
彩色电视机	Color TV Set	台 set	178	198	198
家用电脑	Computer	台 set	76	116	125
组合音响	Stereo System	套 set	38	47	45
摄像机	Video Camera	架 set	8	15	17
照相机	Camera	架 set	62	72	75
钢 琴	Piano	架 set	4	5	5
微波炉	Microwave Oven	台 set	93	95	97
空调器	Air Conditioner	台 set	155	206	202
淋浴热水器	Water Heater	台 set	93	104	102
健身器材	Sports Goods	套 set	8	9	9
普通电话	Fixed Telephone	部 set	105	96	94
移动电话	Mobile Phone	部 set	174	216	221

表13－11　城镇居民家庭生活质量
Living Conditions of Urban Families

指　标	Indicators	单　位　Unit	2005	2010	2011
生活用水	**Tap Water for Residential Use**				
独用自来水	Private Tap Water	%	97.8	100.0	100.0
公用自来水	Shared Tap Water	%	2.2		
居室卫生设备	**Sanitary Equipment**				
无卫生设备	Without any Sanitary Equipment	%	1.8		
有厕所浴室	With Lavatory	%	94.4	98.2	97.5
有厕所无浴室	With Lavatory but no Bathroom	%	2.4	1.4	1.9
公　用	Shared Sanitary Equipment	%	1.4	0.4	0.6
居室取暖设备	**Heating Equipment**				
无取暖设备	Without any Heating	%	14.4	2.3	1.7
冷暖空调	Air Conditioner	%	76.0	97.1	98.1
暖　气	Heating	%			
其　他	Others	%	9.6	0.6	0.2
炊用燃气	**Gas for Cooking**				
天然气	Natural Gas	%	93.8	92.1	87.8
液化石油气	Liquefied Petroleum Gas	%	4.6	6.9	11.6
煤	Coal	%	0.2	0.6	0.3
其　他	Others	%	1.4	0.4	0.3
通信设备	**Telecommunications Equipment**				
无电话	Without Telephone	%	1.0		
固定电话	Fixed Telephone	部/百户 set / hundred households	104.6	95.7	94.0
移动电话	Mobile Telephone	部/百户 set / hundred households	173.6	216.2	221.4

表 13-12 城镇居民家庭人均可支配收入
Annual Disposable Income Per Capita for Urban Families

按人均年可支配收入分组	Grouped by Annual Disposable Income Per Capita	比重 Proportion	2005	2010	2011
总计	**Total**	%	**100.0**	**100.0**	**100.0**
6 000 元以下	Below 6 000 yuan	%	3.6		2.0
6 000 ~ 12 000 元	6 000 ~ 12 000 yuan	%	28.3	4.7	6.0
12 000 ~ 18 000 元	12 000 ~ 18 000 yuan	%	30.0	12.8	9.4
18 000 ~ 24 000 元	18 000 ~ 24 000 yuan	%	14.8	20.5	14.4
24 000 ~ 30 000 元	24 000 ~ 30 000 yuan	%	10.0	19.0	16.7
30 000 ~ 36 000 元	30 000 ~ 36 000 yuan	%	3.5	11.2	14.8
36 000 ~ 42 000 元	36 000 ~ 42 000 yuan	%	3.5	10.5	10.2
42 000 ~ 48 000 元	42 000 ~ 48 000 yuan	%	2.4	5.8	6.5
48 000 元以上	Above 48 000 yuan	%	3.9	15.5	20.0

表 13-13 城镇居民家庭人均消费性支出
Annual Consumer Spending Per Capita for Urban Families

按人均年消费性支出分组	Grouped by Annual Nonproductive Expenditure Per Capita	比重 Proportion	2005	2010	2011
总计	**Total**	%	**100.0**	**100.0**	**100.0**
6 000 元以下	Below 6 000 yuan	%	9.0	1.7	5.6
6 000 ~ 12 000 元	6 000 ~ 12 000 yuan	%	48.1	19.3	14.3
12 000 ~ 18 000 元	12 000 ~ 18 000 yuan	%	25.7	28.6	25.9
18 000 ~ 24 000 元	18 000 ~ 24 000 yuan	%	8.7	21.7	20.6
24 000 ~ 30 000 元	24 000 ~ 30 000 yuan	%	3.5	11.7	13.5
30 000 ~ 36 000 元	30 000 ~ 36 000 yuan	%	1.8	4.3	5.2
36 000 ~ 42 000 元	36 000 ~ 42 000 yuan	%	1.1	3.0	3.3
42 000 ~ 48 000 元	42 000 ~ 48 000 yuan	%	0.6	3.0	3.5
48 000 元以上	Above 48 000 yuan	%	1.5	6.7	8.1

表 13-14　城镇居民家庭人均年消费支出状况
Annual Nonproductive Expenditure Per Capita for Urban Families

单位:元 (yuan)

指　标	Indicators	2005	2010	2011
总　计	**Total**	**13 328**	**21 897**	**25 239**
食　品	**Food**	**4 826**	**7 631**	**8 696**
#粮油类	Cereals & Oils	447	772	892
肉禽蛋水产品	Meat Poultry Eggs and Aquatic Products	1 376	2 018	2 401
蔬菜类	Vegetables	404	640	694
糖烟酒饮料类	Sugar Tobacco Alcoholic Drinks and Other Beverages	568	923	1 036
干鲜瓜果类	Dry and Fresh Fruits	346	654	785
糕点、奶及奶制品	Cakes Milk and Dairy Products	359	599	693
衣　着	**Clothing**	**945**	**1 831**	**2 035**
#服　装	Clothes	698	1 350	1 492
鞋　类	Shoes	191	389	434
家庭设备用品及服务	**Household Appliances and Service**	**807**	**1 695**	**1 898**
#耐用消费品	Durable Consumer Goods	404	685	847
室内装饰品	Household Ornaments	29	55	33
家具材料	Furniture and Materials	1	4	3
家庭服务	Household Service	78	176	172
医疗保健	**Health Care**	**895**	**1 143**	**1 044**
#药品费	Medicines	259	424	394
滋补保健品	Nutritious Health Products	232	313	336
医疗费	Medical Treatment	350	330	252
交通和通信	**Transportation and Communications**	**1 950**	**3 456**	**4 537**
交　通	Transportation	1 157	2 310	3 300
通　信	Communications	793	1 146	1 237
教育文化娱乐服务	**Education Culture Entertainment Services**	**2 119**	**3 324**	**3 528**
文化娱乐用品	Cultural and Entertainment Products	545	968	926
文化娱乐服务	Cultural and Entertainment Services	500	1 429	1 550
教　育	Education	1 074	927	1 051
居　住	**Housing**	**1 294**	**1 649**	**2 162**
住　房	Accommodation	643	742	1 222
水电燃料及其他	Water Electricity Fuel and Others	533	727	749
居住服务费	Accommodation Services	118	180	190
杂项商品及服务	**Miscellancous Utensils and Services**	**492**	**1 167**	**1 339**

表13-15 农村居民家庭基本情况
Basic Information of Rural Families

指 标	Indicators	单 位 Unit	2005	2010	2011
调查户数	Households Surveyed	户 household	1 200	500	500
调查户总人口	Total Population of Households Surveyed	人 person	3 932	1 453	1 412
调查户总劳动力	Total Number of Laborers in the Household Surveyed	人 person	2 548	1 002	961
调查户就业人口	Employed Persons in Households Surveyed	人 person	2 367	897	883
#纯务农	Totally Engaged in Agriculture	人 person	70	48	92
本镇内企业	Employed by Enterprises in the Town	人 person	1 006	515	511
本镇外企业	Employed by Enterprises in Other Towns	人 person	810	277	224
平均每户人口	Average Number of Residents Per Household	人 person	3.28	2.91	2.82
平均每户劳动力	Average Number of Laborers Per Household	人 person	2.12	2.00	1.92
平均每户就业人口	Average Employed Persons Per Household	人 person	1.97	1.79	1.77
平均每户就业面	Average Employed Persons Per Household	%	60.1	61.7	62.5
平均每一就业者赡养人口	Number of Persons Supported by Each Employed Person	人 person	1.66	1.63	1.59

表 13－16　农村居民收入情况
Incomes of Suburban Citizens

单位:元　　(yuan)

指　标 Indicators		2005	2010	2011
人均总收入	Total Income Per Capita	10 443	14 759	17 191
# 可支配收入	Disposable Income	9 779	13 898	15 861
工资性收入	Wage Income	7 458	10 223	11 362
# 非企业组织中劳动所得	Income from Other Sources	957	894	1 121
本镇企业中劳动所得	Income from Working in Enterprises in the Town	3 372	6 955	7 301
常住人口外出从业所得	Income from Working in Enterprises in Other Places	2 719	2 364	2 940
财产性收入	Unearned Income	1 078	1 314	1 439
# 股　息	Stock Dividend	5		
租　金	Rent	762	1 014	972
红　利	Dividend	16	34	77
转移性收入	Transferable Income	1 447	1 618	2 237
# 农村以外亲友赠送	Gifts from Relatives and Friends in Urban Area	13	23	24
救济金、保险年金	Relief and Life Annuity	19	13	18
退休金、抚恤金	Pension and Compensation	1 293	1 902	2 359
家庭经营所得	Income from Family-Run Operations	460	743	823
财产性支出	Property Expenditure	29	4	
转移性支出	Transfer Expenditure	577	1 060	1 341
# 赠送农村以外亲友	Gifts to Relatives and Friends in Urban Area	85	82	117
缴纳保险金	Insurance Premium Payment	394	186	239

主要统计指标解释

从业人员报酬

从业人员报酬指各单位在一定时期内直接支付给本单位全部从业人员的劳动报酬总额。包括在岗职工工资总额和本单位其他从业人员劳动报酬两部分。

职工工资总额

工资总额指各单位在一定时期内直接支付给本单位全部职工的劳动报酬总额。工资总额的计算原则应以直接支付给职工的全部劳动报酬为根据。各单位支付给职工的劳动报酬以及其他根据有关规定支付的工资,不论是计入成本的还是不计入成本的,不论是按国家规定列入计征奖金税项目的,还是未列入计征奖金税项目的,不论是以货币形式支付的还是以实物形式支付的,均包括在工资总额内。

职工平均工资

平均工资指企业、事业、机关单位的职工在一定时期内平均每人所得的货币工资额。它表明一定时期职工工资收入的高低程度,是反映职工工资水平的主要指标。计算公式为:

平均工资 = 报告期实际支付的全部职工工资总额/报告期全部职工平均人数

城镇居民可支配收入

城镇居民可支配收入指居民可用于最终消费支出和其他非义务性支出以及储蓄的总和,即居民家庭可以用来自由支配的收入。它是家庭总收入扣除交纳的所得税、个人交纳的社会保障费以及调查户的记账补贴后的收入。不包括出售财物和借贷收入。

城镇居民家庭消费支出

指城镇居民家庭用于日常生活的全部支出,包括食品、衣着、家庭设备用品及服务、医疗保健、交通和通信、教育文化娱乐服务、居住、杂项商品和服务等八大类。

城镇居民家庭人均服务性消费支出

指调查户用于本家庭支付社会提供的各种文化和生活方面的非商品性服务费用。服务性消费的特点在于其劳动过程和消费过程在时间与空间上的统一。在居民家庭八大类消费中,服务消费支出包括:(1)食品类中加工服务费和部分在外饮食费用;(2)衣着类中衣着加工服务费;(3)家庭设备用品及服务类中家庭服务(如家政服务费用);(4)医疗保健类中医疗费(如诊疗费、上门出诊费、护工费用);(5)交通和通信类中交通工具服务费(如汽车使用、维修费用)、交通费中使用飞机、轮船、火车等交通工具费用、通信服务费(如电信费、邮费);(6)教育文化娱乐服务类中文化娱乐服务费(如参观、游览费用、健身活动费、团体旅游、其他文娱活动费)、文娱用品修理服务费、教育费(如义务、非义务教育支出)、成人教育支出、家教费、培训班费用、择校费;(7)居住类中租赁费用、部分房屋装潢费用(人工费用)、居住服务费(如物业管理、维修费用);(8)杂项商品和服务(如美容、洗澡、理发费用,旅馆住宿等费用)。

农村居民可支配收入

指一定时期内农村居民总收入中,扣除家庭经营费用支出、生产性固定资产折旧、交纳税金和上交承包金、公益性及转移支付后的(包括养老、失业、合作医疗、保险基金及罚款等支付),可用于生活消费、生产投资和储蓄的收入。它与纯收入的主要区别是扣除了转移性支付,加上实际得到的公益性及转移性收入后的余额。农村居民可支配收入包括:工资性收入、家庭经营净收入、财产性收入、转移性净收入。

农村居民家庭生活消费支出

指农村住户用于物质生活和精神生活方面的支出。包括食品,衣着,居住,家庭设备用品及服务,医疗保健,交通和通信,文化教育娱乐用品及服务,其他商品和服务等消费支出。

财产性收入

指金融资产或有形非生产性资产的所有者向其他机构单位提供资金或将有形非生产性资产供其支配,作为回报而从中获得的收入。

转移性收入

指农村住户和住户成员无须付出任何对应物而获得的货物、服务、资金或资产所有权等,不包括无偿提供的用于固定资本形成的资金。一般情况下,是指农村住户在二次分配中的所有收入。

基本养老保险

(1)参加保险人数:指报告期末按照国家法律、法规和有关政策规定参加基本养老保险的职工人数。包括不能正常缴费、已中断缴费但未终止保险关系的职工人数。

(2)社会统筹基金收入:指根据国家规定,由纳入基本养老保险范围的单位,按照国家规定的缴费基数和缴费比例缴纳的社会统筹基金,以及通过其他方式取得的形成基金来源的收入,包括:单位缴纳的社会统筹基金收入、财政补贴收入、利息收入、其他收入。

(3)社会统筹基金支出:指按照国家政策规定的开支范围和开支标准从社会统筹基金中支付给参加基本养老保险的离休、退休、退职人员个人的养老金、丧葬抚恤补助,以及由于保险关系转移、上下级之间调剂资金等原因而发生的支出。包括:基础性养老金、过渡性养老金、离休金、退休金、退职金、补贴、丧葬抚恤补助、其他支出。

(4)社会统筹基金结余:指截止报告期末基本养老保险的社会统筹基金结余金额。包括银行存款、财政专户、债券投资和其他。

城镇登记失业人员

城镇登记失业人员指有非农业户口,在一定的劳动年龄内(16 岁以上及男 50 岁以下、女 45 岁以下),有劳动能力,无业而要求就业,并在当地就业服务机构进行求职登记的人员。

EXPLANATORY NOTES TO MAJOR STATISTICAL INDICATORS

Labor Compensation

Labor Compensation refers to total payment by various units to their employees during a certain period of time, including wages to permanent staff and workers and payment to other employees.

Total Wages Bill

Total Wages Bill refers to the total remuneration payment to staff and workers in various units during a certain period of time. The calculation of total wages is based on the total remuneration payment to the staff and workers. Therefore, all the wages and salaries and other payments to staff and workers are included in the total wages regardless of their sources, category, and forms (in kind or cash). (Total wages of staff and workers in this yearbook include only total wages of fully employed staff and workers, excluding the living allowances distributed to those who have left their working units while keeping their labor contract/employment relation unchanged).

Average Wage

Average Wage refers to the average wage in money terms per person during a certain period of time for staff and workers in enterprises, institutions, and government agencies, which reflects the general level of wage income during a certain period of time and is calculated as follows: Average Wage = Total Wages of Staff and Workers at Reference Time / Average Number of Staff and Workers at Reference Time.

Disposable Income of Urban Households

Disposable Income of Urban Households refers to the actual income at the disposal of members of the households which can be used for final consumption, other non-compulsory expenditure and savings, which is part of the urban households' income that can be disposed by the urban households themselves. It is the income after deducting personal income tax, social insurance paid by individuals and investigation allowance from the total income of the households. The income from selling properties and borrowing are not included.

Consumption Expenditures of Urban Households

Consumption Expenditures of Urban Households refer to all the expenditures paid by urban households for consumption in daily life, including 8 categories as follows: food; clothing; household facilities, articles and services; medical care; traffic and telecommunication; education, culture and recreation services; housing; miscellaneous commodities and services.

Urbanities'per-capita Spending on Services

Urbanities'per-capita spending on services refers to urbanites pay for services rather than commodities. Services are offered and consumed at the same time and place. The service spending for an urban family falls into the following eight types: (1)Money paid for food processing and money spent while eating out; (2)Money paid for clothing processing; (3)Domestic services and services for home amenities; (4) Medical cost (including medical diagnosis and treatment, in-home medical services and nursing cost); (5)Transport tool service fees (such as for the use of a car and maintenance fee thereby arising), transport tools (plane, ship, train) fees, post and telecommunications fees; (6)Fees for culture and entertainment services (such as tour and fitness building), fees for repair of sports and entertainment items, education cost (spending on obligatory and non-obligatory education), adult education cost, tutor fees, training courses fees and extra money paid as sponsorship fee to a school a student outside his or her education community; (7)Housing rents, some interior decoration cost (for labor), residence service fees (such as for property management and repairs); (8)Fees for other services (such as at a beauty salon, bathhouse, hairdresser's and hotels).

Disposable Income of Rural Households

Disposable Income of Rural Households refers to the part of the rural households' income in a certain period after deducting family business expenditure, depreciation of productive fixed assets, taxes, contract expenditure, welfare funds and transferred expenditure, (including pensions, unemployment relief, cooperative medical funds, premiums and fines), which can be used for personal consumption, production investment and deposit. It differs from the net income in that it is the balance of the actual welfare and transferred income after deducting transferred expenditure. The disposable income includes: wages and salaries, net income from household business, property income, net transferred income.

Living Expenditures for Consumption of Rural Households

Living Expenditures for Consumption of Rural Households refer to expenditures of material and culture life of rural household, including expenses on food, clothing, housing, household appliances and service, medical and health care, traffic and communication items, cultural, education and recreation items and service and other commodities and service.

Income from Properties

Income from Properties refers to the income received as returns by owners of financial assets or tangible non-productive assets by providing capitals or tangible non-productive assets to other institutional units.

Income from Transfers

Income from Transfers refers to the receipt by rural households and their members of goods, services, capitals or rights of assets without giving or repaying accordingly, excluding capitals provided to them for the formation of fixed assets. In general, it refers to all income received by rural households through redistribution.

Basic Endowment Insurance

(1) Number of people participating in the insurance program: by the end of reference period, number of staff and workers participating in the insurance program in line with national laws, regulations and related policies, including those who can not make regular payment or interrupt payment but not terminate the insurance program.

(2) Revenue of social comprehensive funds: according to national provision, payments made by units covered in basic endowment insurance program, and income from other resources, including: income of social comprehensive funds paid by unites, financial subsidies, interest income and others.

(3) Expenditure of social comprehensive funds: refer to payment made to those retired and resigned people covered in endowment insurance program in terms of pension or compensation within the expenditure scope and standards according to related national policies, and the expenditure occurred due to shift of the insurance relationship or adjustment funds among agencies, including: basic pension, transitional pension, pension for resigned people, pension for retired people, pension for people quitting jobs, subsidies, funeral subsidies and other expenditure.

(4) Balance of social comprehensive funds: refer to the balance of basic endowment insurance of social comprehensive funds at the end of the reference period, including: bank savings, special fiscal account, investment in bonds and others.

Registered Urban Unemployment

Registered Urban Unemployment refers to those non-agricultural population within working age (16 – 50 years for male and 16 – 45 years for females) who are able and willing to work but unemployed and have registered for job in local employment service agencies.

第十四篇

Chapter 14

就业与社会保障

EMPLOYMENT AND SOCIAL SECURITY

SHANGHAI PUDONG NEW AREA STATISTICAL YEARBOOK

表 14-1　历年从业人员数
Number of Employed Persons in Main Years
(1993～2011)

单位:人　　　　(person)

年　份 Year	从业人员 Employed Persons	国有、集体、其他经济单位从业人员 Employed Persons in State-owned, Collective-owned and Other Economic Institutions	城镇个体劳动者 Urban Self-employed	农村集体和个体劳动者 Rural Collective and Self-employed Workers	其　他 Others
1993	1 043 985	788 821	18 146	237 018	
1994	1 049 985	767 146	35 696	247 143	
1995	1 079 744	798 884	38 243	242 617	
1996	1 039 692	759 936	44 516	235 240	
1997	981 826	703 890	49 878	228 058	
1998	963 211	638 707	68 252	256 252	
1999	983 401	645 583	43 284	294 534	
2000	1 040 411	636 923	61 000	316 063	26 425
2001	1 114 514	650 633	85 608	344 027	34 246
2002	1 199 864	686 637	107 590	361 881	43 756
2003	1 268 717	674 381	135 592	404 422	54 322
2004	1 302 723	643 628	162 251	436 504	60 340
2005	1 440 763	746 714	178 173	444 433	71 443
2006	1 467 145	720 105	200 638	461 395	85 007
2007	1 490 809	708 308	194 419	498 633	89 449
2008	1 507 631	749 400	232 209	440 184	85 838
2009	2 009 539	920 081		997 835	91 623
2010	2 351 115	1 004 078		1 140 203	206 834
2011	2 806 796	1 488 778		1 150 443	167 575

注：自 2009 年起从业人员数中不包括城镇个体劳动者。
Note: The number of employed persons excludes that of individual workers in towns since the year of 2009.

表 14-2 各行业从业人员数
Number of Employed Persons by Sector
(2011)

单位:人 (person)

指标	Indicators	从业人员 Employed Persons	#国有、集体、其他经济单位从业人员 Employed Persons in State-owned, Collective-owned and Other Economic Institutions	农村集体劳动者 Rural Collective Labors	其他 Others
总计	**Total**	**2 806 796**	**1 488 778**	**1 150 443**	**167 575**
按三次产业分	**By Industry**				
第一产业	Primary Industry	143 662	1 411	141 320	931
第二产业	Secondary Industry	1 473 627	689 239	664 364	120 024
第三产业	Tertiary Industry	1 189 507	798 128	344 759	46 620
按行业分	**By Sector**				
农、林、牧、渔业	Farming, Forestry, Animal Husbandry and Fishery	143 662	1 411	141 320	931
采矿业	Mining	173	173		
制造业	Manufacturing	1 203 253	518 649	602 845	81 759
电力、燃气及水的生产和供应业	Production and Supply of Electricity, Gas and Tap Water	26 458	13 171	13 287	
建筑业	Construction	243 743	157 246	48 232	38 265
交通运输、仓储和邮政业	Transportation, Warehousing and Post Service	184 177	111 653	68 541	3 983
信息传输、计算机服务和软件业	Information Transmission, Computer Service and Computer Software	54 821	45 297	6 895	2 629
#信息传输	Information Transmission	18 429	18 429		
批发和零售业	Wholesale and Retail	247 414	165 668	74 512	7 234
住宿和餐饮业	Hotel and Catering	49 603	26 354	13 990	9 259
金融业	Banking	223 432	223 242		190
房地产业	Real Estate	49 448	41 927		7 521
租赁和商务服务业	Leasing and Business Service	55 483	47 430		8 053
科学研究、技术服务和地质勘查业	Scientific Research, Technical Services and Geological Prospecting	47 419	25 127	18 959	3 333
水利、环境和公共设施管理业	Water Conservancy, Environment and Public Facilities Administration	23 413	10 014	12 570	829
#公共设施管理业	Public Facilities Administration	2 071	1 368		703
居民服务和其他服务业	Resident Service and Other Services	152 284	1 242	148 847	2 195
教育	Education	46 410	45 593		817
卫生、社会保障和社会福利业	Healthcare, Social Security and Social Welfare	26 657	25 707	410	540
文化、体育和娱乐业	Culture, Sports and Entertainment	5 226	5 154	35	37
公共管理和社会组织	Public Administration and Social Organizations	23 720	23 720		

注:1. 国有、集体、其他经济单位从业人员包括职工中的在岗职工和其他从业人员。
2. 从业人员数中不包括城镇个体劳动者。

Note: 1. Employed staff and workers in state-owned, collective-owned and other business enterprises include those who are actually working in those companies.
2. The number of employed persons excludes that of private and individual workers in towns.

表 14-3 历年职工人数
Staff and Workers in Main Years
(1993~2011)

单位:人 (person)

年份 Year	合计 Total	国有经济单位 State-owned Enterprises	集体经济单位 Collective-owned Enterprises	其他经济单位 Others	#港澳台及外商投资单位 Overseas Invested Enterprises
1993	788 821	597 417	84 811	106 593	
1994	767 146	582 477	76 023	108 646	
1995	798 884	571 398	85 955	141 531	
1996	719 634	469 966	85 030	164 638	
1997	663 163	405 349	77 072	180 742	52 405
1998	661 406	354 408	60 633	246 365	111 015
1999	677 348	355 607	56 824	264 917	126 897
2000	677 544	340 605	44 654	292 285	137 332
2001	687 694	299 186	37 756	350 752	134 732
2002	701 949	276 876	33 390	391 683	160 884
2003	671 434	249 461	25 549	396 424	136 212
2004	614 014	238 073	23 217	352 724	119 658
2005	701 553	233 350	20 431	447 772	129 890
2006	665 680	173 204	16 196	476 280	145 534
2007	631 720	188 892	16 278	426 550	186 480
2008	667 882	175 428	11 823	480 631	225 566
2009	797 302	193 246	20 408	583 648	297 093
2010	850 176	201 002	17 155	632 019	336 022
2011	1 385 342	275 135	13 728	1 096 479	627 996

表 14-4 历年在岗职工人数
Working Employees in Main Years
(1999~2011)

单位:人 (person)

年份 Year	总计 Total	国有经济单位 State-owned Enterprises	集体经济单位 Collective-owned Enterprises	其他经济单位 Others	#港澳台及外商投资单位 Overseas Invested Enterprises
1999	571 968				
2000	557 953				
2001	554 671				
2002	570 266				
2003	559 384	197 221	10 276	351 887	127 740
2004	514 941	192 574	9 142	313 225	111 531
2005	607 881	206 246	8 605	393 030	120 065
2006	592 718	209 338	7 514	375 866	113 981
2007	567 796	165 635	6 905	395 256	179 250
2008	613 835	145 198	5 692	462 945	221 795
2009	747 217	174 692	9 255	563 270	291 067
2010	805 369	181 395	8 954	615 020	330 802
2011	1 333 030	250 248	10 995	1 071 787	620 718

表 14-5　各行业职工人数
Staff and Workers by Sector
(2011)

单位:人　　　　(person)

指　标	Indicators	职工人数 Staff and Workers	#在岗职工 Working Employees	国有经济单位 State-owned Enterprises	城镇集体经济单位 Collective-owned Enterprises	其他经济单位 Others	#港澳台及外商投资单位 Overseas Invested Enterprises
总　计	**Total**	**1 385 342**	**1 333 030**	**275 135**	**13 728**	**1 096 479**	**627 996**
按三次产业分	**By Industry**						
第一产业	Primary Industry	1 410	1 377	734	153	523	89
第二产业	Secondary Industry	596 068	579 530	63 247	3 404	529 417	397 707
第三产业	Tertiary Industry	787 864	752 123	211 154	10 171	566 539	230 200
按行业分	**By Sector**						
农、林、牧、渔业	Farming, Forestry, Animal Husbandry and Fishery	1 410	1 377	734	153	523	89
采矿业	Mining	169	169			169	
制造业	Manufacturing	519 385	504 977	45 963	2 427	470 995	387 454
电力、燃气及水的生产和供应业	Production and Supply of Electricity, Gas and Tap Water	13 094	13 058	9 717	37	3 340	1 682
建筑业	Construction	63 420	61 326	7 567	940	54 913	8 571
交通运输、仓储和邮政业	Transportation, Warehousing and Post Sercice	110 813	107 113	34 674	576	75 563	10 706
信息传输、计算机服务和软件业	Information Transmission, Computer Service and Computer Software	46 460	44 372	19 034		27 426	25 431
#信息传输	Information Transmission	18 450	18 355	15 835		2 615	1 196
批发和零售业	Wholesale and Retail	163 148	158 662	5 439	3 361	154 348	107 682
住宿和餐饮业	Hotel and Catering	17 678	17 612	3 250	119	14 309	10 940
金融业	Banking	221 146	218 247	20 333	6	200 807	18 140
房地产业	Real Estate	37 572	35 801	6 533	313	30 726	17 108
租赁和商务服务业	Leasing and Business Service	61 767	43 476	21 089	1 319	39 359	24 179
科学研究、技术服务和地质勘查业	Scientific Research, Technical Services and Geological Prospecting	24 542	24 060	11 034	42	13 466	10 897
水利、环境和公共设施管理业	Water Conservancy, Environment and Publicon Facilities Administration	9 325	9 066	4 193	24	5 108	3 707
#公共设施管理业	Public Facilities Administration	1 317	1 299	451		866	
居民服务和其他服务业	Resident Service and Other Services	1 757	1 141	956		801	396
教　育	Education	41 578	41 210	38 074	529	2 975	157
卫生、社会保障和社会福利业	Healthcare, Social Security and Social Welfare	24 122	23 541	20 647	3 475		
文化、体育和娱乐业	Culture, Sports and Entertainment	4 908	4 867	3 127	130	1 651	857
公共管理和社会组织	Public Administration and Social Organizations	23 048	22 955	22 771	277		

表 14-6 工业企业从业人员与职工人数
Employed Staff and Workers in Industrial Enterprises
(2011)

单位:人 (person)

指标	Indicators	从业人员人数 Employed Persons	职工人数 Staff and Workers	#在岗职工 Working Employees
总 计	**Total**	**531 769**	**532 452**	**518 008**
按登记注册类型分	**By Type of Registration**			
国有经济单位	State-owned Enterprises	50 377	55 665	48 737
集体经济单位	Collective-owned Enterprises	2 276	2 464	1 878
其他经济单位	Others	479 116	474 323	467 393
#港澳台及外商投资单位	Overseas Invested Enterprises	394 397	389 092	385 740
按行业分	**By Sector**			
石油和天然气开采业	Industry of Petroleum and Natural Gas Exploration	173	169	169
农副食品加工业	Processing of Agricultural Side-line Food	3 323	3 261	3 234
食品制造业	Food Manufacturing	9 108	8 841	8 814
饮料制造业	Beverage Manufacturing	4 675	4 459	4 421
烟草加工业	Tobacco Processing	948	1 002	947
纺织业	Textile Industry	8 540	8 103	7 646
纺织服装，鞋，帽制造业	Textile Products, Clothes, Shoes and Hats	24 281	23 724	23 527
皮革、毛皮、羽毛(绒)及其制品业	Leather, Furs, Down and Related Products	756	685	662
木材加工及木、竹、藤、棕、草制品业	Timber Processing, Bamboo, Cane, Palm, Fiber and Straw Products	1 240	1 252	1 217
家具制造业	Furniture Manufacturing	2 981	3 001	2 921
造纸及纸制品业	Paper-making and Paper Products	4 749	4 748	4 659
印刷业和记录媒介的复制	Printing and Record Medium Reproduction	4 163	4 076	3 954
文教体育用品制造业	Stationery, Educational and Sports Good	3 949	4 145	3 697
石油加工，炼焦及核燃料加工业	Petroleum Processing and Coking Products	7 351	8 287	7 315
化学原料及化学制品制造业	Chemical Materials and Chemical Products	17 435	17 576	17 110
医药制造业	Medicine Manufacturing	19 433	19 216	18 945
化学纤维制造业	Chemical Fiber Manufacturing	69	174	55
橡胶制造业	Rubber Products	1 429	1 469	1 409
塑料制造业	Plastic Products	13 404	13 747	12 853
非金属矿物制品业	Nonmetal Mineral Products	12 367	12 912	11 645
黑色金属冶炼及压延加工业	Smelting and Pressing of Ferrous Metals	1 564	2 432	1 531
有色金属冶炼及压延加工业	Smelting and Pressing of Non-ferrous Metals	1 707	1 700	1 662
金属制品业	Metal Products	20 261	19 872	19 671
通用设备制造业	Manufacturing of Equipment for General Use	36 495	35 368	34 779
专用设备制造业	Manufacturing of Special Purpose Equipment	25 437	27 270	24 635
交通运输设备制造业	Manufacturing of Transportation Equipment	101 377	102 671	99 610
电气机械及器材制造业	Manufacturing of Electric Equipment and Machinery	33 978	33 817	33 374
通信设备、计算机及其他电子设备制造业	Telecommunications, Computer and Other Electronic Equipment Manufacturing	132 617	130 382	130 071
仪器仪表及文化、办公用机械制造业	Manufacturing of Instrument, Meter, Culture and Office Machinery	22 669	22 663	22 319
工艺品及其他制造业	Handicrafts and Other Productions	2 119	2 336	2 098
废弃资源和废旧材料回收加工业	Recycling of Abandoned Resources and Wastes			
电力、热力的生产和供应业	Production and Supply of Electricity and Heating Powe	4 197	4 145	4 142
燃气生产和供应业	Production and Supply of Gas	5 178	5 162	5 160
水的生产和供应业	Production and Supply of Tap Water	3 796	3 787	3 756

表 14-7 应届毕业生构成及就业基本情况
Composition of Fresh Graduates and Their Employment

指 标	Indicators	单 位 Unit	2005	2009	2010	2011
毕业生按性别分	**By Sex of Graduates**					
男性比重	Proportion of Male Graduates	%	48.9	45.2	46.8	46.8
女性比重	Proportion of Female Graduates	%	51.1	54.8	53.2	53.2
毕业生按学历分	**By Educational Qualifications of Graduates**					
三校毕业生比重	Proportion of Graduates from Three Kinds of Colleges	%	37.0	17.5	17.0	15.6
大专毕业生比重	Proportion of Junior College Graduates	%	38.4	41.3	40.7	39.4
本科及以上毕业生比重	Proportion of University Graduates or Those with Higher Degrees	%	24.7	41.2	42.3	45.0
毕业生总体就业率	**Overall Employment Rate of Graduates**	**%**	**65.8**	**63.4**	**64.1**	**75.1**
就业率按性别分	**Employment Rate, By Sex of Graduates**					
男性就业率	Employment Rate of Male Graduates	%	62.6	59.7	61.8	72.9
女性就业率	Employment Rate of Female Graduates	%	68.7	66.4	66.2	77.1
就业率按学历分	**Employment Rate, by Educational Qualifications**					
三校生	Graduates from Three Kinds of Colleges	%	53.3	51.9	49.2	59.6
大专生	Graduates of Junior Colleges	%	69.1	59.5	60.6	71.3
本科生及以上	Graduates of Universities or those with Higher Degrees	%	74.8	71.2	72.4	83.0
就业率按毕业院校分	**Employment Rate, by Colleges**					
重点院校就业率	Employment Rate of Graduates from Key Universities	%	79.9	75.0	75.3	84.3
普通院校就业率	Employment Rate of Graduates from Common Universities	%	70.0	63.8	65.4	78.1
民办院校就业率	Employment Rate of Graduates from Colleges Run by Private Investment	%	64.2	58.2	61.0	70.1
首份工作薪酬收入均值	**Average Monthly Salaries of First Jobs**	**元**	**1 617**	**2 125**	**2 370**	**2 724**
三校生	Graduates from Three Kinds of Colleges	元	1 101	1 563	1 773	2 012
大专生	Graduates of Junior Colleges	元	1 404	1 730	2 093	2 296
本科生及以上	Graduates of Universities or those with Higher Degrees	元	2 327	2 573	2 718	3 187

注：数据取自对新区各类应届毕业生进行的抽样调查。调查对象为常住人口口径，居住在抽中居（村）委会、应届毕业的大专院校毕业生和三校毕业生。自 2010 年起，调查抽样范围覆盖新浦东的城乡全部村居委，且调查时点改为当年 7 月 1 日零时。

Note: These data come from sample surveys to fresh graduates of different colleges and universities in PNA. The surveyed graduates are graduated from junior colleges and three kinds of colleges who are de jure population and live in the selected urban/rural residential committees. The area of survey sampling covered all of the village and neighborhood committees in new PNA since 2010 and the survey time changed to 0:00 of June 1 of that current year.

表14-8　享受居民最低生活保障人数

Number of Residents Benefiting from Guarantee of Minimum Standard of Living (2011)

单位:人　　(person)

指　标	Indicators	保障对象 Residents to be Guaranteed	城镇低保 Guarantee of Minimum Standard of Living in Urban Area	农村贫困户 Poverty Households in Rural Area
总　计	**Total**	**66 633**	**60 023**	**6 610**
潍坊新村街道	Weifangxincun Subdistrict	1 007	1 007	
陆家嘴街道	Lujiazui Subdistrict	2 205	2 205	
周家渡街道	Zhoujiadu Subdistrict	3 699	3 699	
塘桥街道	Tangqiao Subdistrict	1 299	1 299	
上钢新村街道	Shanggangxincun Subdistrict	2 601	2 601	
南码头路街道	Nanmatoulu Subdistrict	1 691	1 691	
沪东新村街道	Hudongxincun Subdistrict	2 235	2 235	
金杨新村街道	Jinyangxincun Subdistrict	1 632	1 632	
洋泾街道	Yangjing Subdistrict	1 671	1 671	
浦兴路街道	Puxinglu Subdistrict	2 882	2 882	
东明路街道	Dongminglu Subdistrict	1 847	1 847	
花木街道	Huamu Subdistrict	2 643	2 643	
申港街道	Shengang Subdistrict			
川沙新镇	Chuansha New Town	8 453	7 937	516
高桥镇	Gaoqiao Town	997	980	17
北蔡镇	Beicai Town	2 795	2 770	25
合庆镇	Heqing Town	1 165	1 045	120
唐　镇	Tangzhen Town	1 150	1 134	16

单位:人 表 14-8 续表 Continued (person)

指 标 Indicators		保障对象 Residents to be Guaranteed	城镇低保 Guarantee of Minimum Standard of Living in Urban Area	农村贫困户 Poverty Households in Rural Area
曹路镇	Caolu Town	3 281	3 208	73
金桥镇	Jinqiao Town	405	391	14
高行镇	Gaohang Town	1 466	1 466	
高东镇	Gaodong Town	1 006	955	51
张江镇	Zhangjiang Town	1 439	1 439	
三林镇	Sanlin Town	3 164	3 117	47
惠南镇	Huinan Town	2 233	1 836	397
周浦镇	Zhoupu Town	568	539	29
新场镇	Xinchang Town	1 654	1 154	500
大团镇	Datuan Town	1 606	968	638
芦潮港镇	Luchaogang Town	202	194	8
康桥镇	Kangqiao Town	465	465	
航头镇	Hangtou Town	738	498	240
六灶镇	Liuzao Town	492	110	382
祝桥镇	Zhuqiao Town	3 473	2 165	1 308
泥城镇	Nicheng Town	1 025	700	325
宣桥镇	Xuanqiao Town	941	677	264
书院镇	Shuyuan Town	1 502	366	1 136
万祥镇	Wanxiang Town	362	233	129
老港镇	Laogang Town	639	264	375

表 14-9　劳动就业及社会保障
Employment and Social Security

指　标	Indicators	单　位 Unit	2009	2010	2011
劳动就业	**Employment**				
期末城镇登记失业人数	Actual Number of Those Registered as Unemployed at Year-end	人 person	46 863	43 453	44 848
招工录用总数	Total Recruitment	人 person	234 111	287 873	265 821
征地劳动力安置	Recruitment of Those Who Have Lost Jobs Because of Requisition of Land	人 person	16 266	29 310	5 313
新增就业岗位	Number of Newly Increased Employment	人 person	123 230	140 440	153 980
社会保险	**Social Security**				
失业保险金发放人次	Unemployment Insurance Payment Distribution	人次 person-time	322 920	294 180	250 161
失业保险金发放金额	Unemployment Insurance Payment	万元 10 000 yuan	16 607	17 156	15 540
农村社会养老保险期末参保人数	Number of Persons Who Joined Endowment Insurance Program in Rural Area at Year end	人 person	92 927	91 747	227 053
农村社会养老保险期末享受人数	Number of Persons Who Benefited from Endowment Insurance Program in Rural Area at Year end	人 person	57 559	58 432	68 444
社会救助	**Social Relief**				
城镇居民低保人数	Urban Residents Who Benefit from Subsistence Allowances from the State	人 person	75 930	72 424	66 289
城镇居民低保金额	Subsistence Allowances to Urban Residents	万元 10 000 yuan	21 912	24 902	26 143
农村居民低保人数	Number of Rural Population Benefiting from Subsistence Allowance	人 person	22 713	11 119	9 140
农村居民低保金额	Amount of Subsistence Allowance for Rural Population	万元 10 000 yuan	3 257	2 285	2 348

表 14-10 收养性单位基本情况
Background of Welfare Facilities
(2011)

指标	Indicators	单位 Unit	合计 Total	社会福利院 Welfare Homes	敬老院 Homes for Senior Citizens
单位数	**Total Number**	**个 unit**	**131**	**1**	**130**
年末职工人数	**Number of Staff and Workers (Year End)**	**人 person**	**4 635**	**130**	**4 505**
#医护人员	Medical Personnel and Nurses	人 person	3 117	76	3 041
年末床位数	**Number of Beds**	**张 bed**	**22 318**	**250**	**22 068**
年末在院人数	**Persons Housed (Year End)**	**人 person**	**14 283**	**243**	**14 040**
#女 性	Female	人 person	9 190	145	9 045
#自费人员	Those at Their Own Expenses	人 person	13 685	227	13 458
在院人员按年龄分	Persons Housed by Age				
老 人	Old People	人 person	13 656	240	13 416
青壮年	Young and Middle-aged People	人 person	627	3	624
儿 童	Children	人 person			

表 14-11 残疾人事业及居家养老情况
Statistics of Disabled Persons & Life of Disabled Persons Including the Aged

指标	Indicators	单位 Unit	2009	2010	2011
残疾人事业	**Disabled Persons**				
白内障复明手术	Operations for Recovery from Cataract	例 in number	2 428	2 281	6 298
低视力配用助视器人数	Number of Bad Eyesighted Persons Equipped with Typoscope	人 person	239	153	78
低听力配用助听器人数	Number of Bad Auditioned Persons Equipped with Haudiphone	人 person	267	336	203
精神病人数	Number of Mental Patients	人 person	14 927	15 735	22 360
监护精神病人数	Number of Mental Patients Supervised	人 person	14 352	15 230	21 866
麻风畸残发放辅助用具	Auxiliary Appliances Dispensed for Persons Suffering from Leprosy, Malformation and Disability	件 piece	28	28	11
城镇残疾人就业人数	Employed Disabled Persons in Towns and Subdistricts	人 person	264	125	994
居家养老	**Life of Disabled Persons Including the Aged**				
期末养老机构床位数	Number of Beds in Old-Aged Institutions at End of Term	张 bed	16 252	22 096	22 318
居家养老护理人员数	Number of Care Workers for the Old-Aged Living at Home	人 person	3 658	3 953	3 925
居家养老服务总数	Number of Services for the Old-Aged Living at Home	人 person	41 458	47 610	49 009
#补贴数	Number of the Old Disabled Persons	人 person	40 224	41 596	37 475
新增安康通安装数	Number of New Installations for Ankangtong SIM Cards	人次 persons-time	3 600	1 776	1 627

表 14－12　红十字会基本情况
Statistics of Red Cross in PNA

指　标　Indicators		单　位　Unit	2009	2010	2011
救　灾	**Providing Disaster Relief**				
捐赠款物	Donation of Money and Clothes	万元 10 000 Yuan	337	2 790	1 765
救　助	**Salvage**				
救助款物	Salvation of Money and Clothes	万元 10 000 Yuan	1 410	1 186	1 761
受益人次	Number of Persons Benefited	人次 person-time	13 983	14 031	38 251
救　护	**Rescue**				
师资培训	Teachers Trained	人 person	15	29	5
救护员培训	Rescue Workers Trained	人 person	8 099	4 501	13 152
救护防病知识普及	Popularization of Rescue and Disease Protection	人次 person-time	127 900	59 265	21 784
预防艾滋病	Protection of AIDS	人次 person-time	58 400	31 520	21 200
遗体捐献登记	Registration of Body Donations	例 in number	165	202	255
基层组织	Grassroot Organizations	个 in number	205	281	281
社区公益服务站点	Community Public Service Stations	个 in number	382	523	833
志愿者	Volunteers	人 in number	9 645	6 491	7 431

表 14－13　廉租住房
Low Rent Housing in Main Years

指　标　Indicators		单位　Unit	2001	2005	2010	2011
廉租住房人均居住面积认定标准	Approved Standard for Living Space Per Capita in Low-Rent Housing	平方米 sq · m	5	7	< 7	< 7
廉租住房人均月收入认定标准	Approved Standard for Monthly Income Per Capita in Low-Rent Housing	元 yuan	280	300	≦ 1100	≦ 1100
受理登记	Registration					
累计受理户数	Number of Households Registered	户 household	201	1 847	6 672	7 466
累计审核登记户数	Approved Number of Households Registered	户 household	163	1 730	6 512	7 316
累计实有登记户数	Actual Number of Households Registered	户 household	159	1 678	6 456	7 266
配租户数	Number of Households Assisted	户 household	159	1 670	6 450	7 147
配租金额	Total Rent of Assisted Households	万元 10 000 yuan	37	780	12 059	15 240

注：2001 年在 159 户配租户中有 6 户为实物配租。
Note: Among the 159 households assisted in 2001, 6 households were assisted by the Government through providing of low-rent housing.

表 14 - 14 社会捐赠与帮困
Social Donations and Financial Aids

指 标 Indicators		单位 Unit	2009	2010	2011
社会捐赠	**Social Donations**				
捐赠款金额	Amount of Donations	万元 10 000 yuan	6 224	12 416	11 625
捐赠衣被	Clothes and Quilts for Donation	万件 10 000 unit	72	88	15
医疗救助	**Medical Assistance**				
医疗救助人次	Number of Medical Assistance	人次 person-time	42 796	13 096	55 571
医疗救助金额	Amount of Medical Assistance	万元 10 000 yuan	2 335	5 122	6 416
帮困助学	**Financial Aids for Study**				
帮困助学人次	Number of Financial Aids for Study	人次 person-time	25 662	18 136	29 020
帮困助学金额	Amount of Financial Aids for Study	万元 10 000 yuan	2 043	907	2 316

表 14 - 15 社会保障标准
Standard for Social Security

单位:元 (yuan)

指 标 Indicators		2009	2010	2011
职工月最低工资标准	Standard of Minimum Monthly Salary for Employees	960	1 120	1 280
城镇居民月最低生活保障标准	Standard of Minimum Monthly Living Expenses for Urban Residents	425	450	505
农村居民月最低生活保障标准	Standard of Minimum Monthly Living Expenses for Rural Residents	283	300	360
农村社会养老保险金月最低标准	Minimum Monthly Pension Insurance for Rural Residents in PNA			485

主要统计指标解释

从业人员

从业人员指从事一定社会劳动并取得劳动报酬或经营收入的人员，包括在岗职工、再就业的离退休人员、私营业主、个体户主、私营和个体从业人员、乡镇企业从业人员、农村从业人员、其他从业人员(包括民办教师、宗教职业者、现役军人等)。这一指标反映了一定时期内全部劳动力资源的实际利用情况，是研究我国基本国情国力的重要指标。

各单位的从业人员指在各级国家机关、政党机关、社会团体及企业、事业单位中工作，取得工资或其他形式的劳动报酬的全部人员。包括在岗职工、再就业的离退休人员、民办教师以及在各单位中工作的外方人员和港澳台方人员、兼职人员、借用的外单位人员和第二职业者。不包括离开本单位仍保留劳动关系的职工。各单位的就业人员反映了各单位实际参加生产或工作的全部劳动力。

职　工

职工指在国有、城镇集体、联营、股份制、外商和港、澳、台投资、其他单位及其附属机构工作，并由其支付工资的各类人员。不包括下列人员：(1)乡镇企业就业人员；(2)私营企业就业人员；(3)城镇个体劳动者；(4)离休、退休、退职人员；(5)再就业的离、退休人员；(6)民办教师；(7)在城镇单位中工作的外方及港、澳、台人员；(8)其他按有关规定不列入职工统计范围的人员。(1998 年及以后的数据均为在岗职工数据，其他相关指标如职工工资总额，职工平均工资等指标也从 1998 年按此口径进行了相应调整)。

在岗职工

指在本单位工作并由单位支付工资的人员，以及有工作岗位，但由于学习、病伤产假等原因暂未工作，仍由单位支付工资的人员。

登记注册类型

登记注册类型是以工商行政管理机关登记注册的具有法人资格的各类企业为划分对象。产业活动单位和行政机关、事业单位、社会团体及其他经济组织参照执行。

国有企业指企业全部资产归国家所有，并按《中华人民共和国企业法人登记管理条例》规定登记注册的非公司制的经济组织。不包括有限责任公司中的国有独资公司。

集体企业指企业资产归集体所有，并按《中华人民共和国企业法人登记管理条例》规定登记注册的经济组织。

股份合作企业指以合作制为基础，由企业职工共同出资入股，吸收一定比例的社会资产投资组建，实行自主经营，自负盈亏，共同劳动，民主管理，按劳动分配与按股份分红相结合的一种集体经济组织。

联营企业指两个及两个以上相同或不同所有制性质的企业法人或事业单位法人，按自愿、平等、互利的原则，共同投资组成的经济组织。联营企业包括国有联营企业、集体联营企业、国有与集体联营企业和其他联营企业。

有限责任公司指根据《中华人民共和国公司登记管理条例》规定登记注册，由 2 个以上，50 个以下的股东共同出资，每个股东以其所认缴的出资额对公司承担有限责任，公司以其全部资产对其债务承担责任的经济组织。有限责任公司包括国有独资公司以及其他有限责任公司。

股份有限公司指根据《中华人民共和国公司登记管理条例》规定登记注册，其全部注册资本由等额股份构成并通过发行股票筹集资本，股东以其认购的股份对公司承担有限责任，公司以其全部资产对其债务承担责任的经济组织。

私营企业指由自然人投资设立或由自然人控股，以雇佣劳动为基础的营利性经济组织。包括按照《公司法》、《合伙企业法》、《私营企业暂行条例》规定登记注册的私营有限责任公司、私营股份有限公司、私营合伙企业和私营独资企业。

与港澳台商投资合资经营企业指港澳台地区投资者与内地企业依照《中华人民共和国中外合资经营企业法》及有关法律的规定，按合同的比例投资设立、分享利润和分担风险的企业。

港澳台商投资合作经营企业指港澳台地区投资者与内地企业依照《中华人民共和国中外合资经营企业法》及有关法律的规定，依照合同的约定进行投资或提供条件设立、分享利润和分担风险的企业。

港澳台商独资经营企业指依照《中华人民共和国外资企业法》及有关法律的规定，在内地由港澳台商地区投资者全额投资设立的企业。港澳台商投资股份有限公司指根据国家有关规定，经外经贸部依法批准设立，其中港、澳、台商的股本占公司注册资本的比例达 25% 以上的股份有限公司。凡其中港、澳、台商的股本占公司注册资本的比例小于 25% 的，属于内资企业中股份有限公司。

中外合资经营企业指外国企业或外国人与中国内地企业依照《中华人民共和国中外合资经营企业法》及有关法律的规定，按合同规定的比例投资设立、分享利润和分担风险的企业。

中外合作经营企业指外国企业或外国人与中国内地企业依照《中华人民共和国中外合作经营企业法》及有关法律的规定，依照合作合同的约定进行投资或提供条件设立、分享利润和分担风险的企业。

外资企业指依照《中华人民共和国外资企业法》及有关法律的规定，在中国内地由外国投资者全额投资设立的企业。

外商投资股份有限公司指根据国家有关规定，经外经贸部依法批准设立，其中外资的股本占公司注册资本的比例达

25%以上的股份有限公司。凡其中外资股本占公司注册资本的比例小于25%的,属于内资企业中的股份有限公司。

国民经济行业分类

《国民经济行业分类》国家标准于1984年首次发布,1994年对其进行了第一次修订,2002年第二次修订。

本年鉴的行业分类使用2011年修订的行业分类标准。

2002年新行业分类标准按照国际通行的经济活动同质性原则划分行业,进一步打破了部门管理界限,对原标准中不符合这一原则的分类进行了调整;根据我国社会经济活动的发展状况,重点加强了第三产业的分类,新增了大量服务业方面的活动类别;对新标准的每一个行业小类,全部与国际标准产业分类的最细一层分类建立了对应关系。新修订的《国民经济行业分类》主要目的之一是与联合国的《全部经济活动的国际标准产业分类》接轨,准确反映一定时期内国民经济行业的构成状况。

失业保险

①参加保险人数:指报告期末按照国家法律、法规和有关政策规定参加了失业保险的城镇企业事业单位的职工及地方政府规定参加失业保险的其他人员的人数。

②失业保险金:指为保障失业人员的基本生活而按规定支付的失业保险金金额。

社会福利事业单位

社会福利事业单位指集中收养社会孤老、残、幼的机构。包括由民政部门管理的社会福利院、儿童福利院、精神病人福利院和城镇集体办的福利院,以及农村集体办的敬老院。

优抚对象

优抚指政府对革命烈士家庭、病故残疾工作人员以及参战负伤致残的民兵、民工的抚恤和人民群众对其的优待。优抚对象包括革命烈士家属、因公牺牲和病故军人家属、革命伤残人员、现役军属、退伍红军老战士、红军失散人员、复员军人、退伍军人、在职退役军人、在乡退役军人、带病回乡退伍军人、复退军人精神病员、孤老优抚对象等。

EXPLANATORY NOTES TO MAJOR STATISTICAL INDICATORS

Employees

Employees refer to the persons who are engaged in social working and receive remuneration payment or earn business income, including total staff and workers, re-employed retirees, employers of private enterprises, self-employ ed workers, employees in private enterprises and individual economy, employees in township enterprises, employed persons in the rural areas , and other employed persons (including teachers in the schools run by the local people, people engaged in religious profession and t he servicemen, etc.). This indicator reflects the actual utilization of total labour force during a certain period of time and is often used for the research on China's economic situation and national power.

Employees in Various Units refer to all the persons working in government agencies of various levels, political and party organizations, social organizations, enterprises and institutions, and receiving wages or other forms of payment. They include fully-employed staff and workers, re-employed retirees, teachers in schools run by the local people, foreigners and Chinese compatriots from Hong Kong, Macao, and Taiwan working in various units, part -time employees, employees of other units working temporarily at current post s, and employees holding the second job, but exclude staff and workers who have left their working units while keeping their labor contract (employment relation) unchanged. This indicator reflects the total number of laborers actually engaged in production or other operations in various units.

Staff and Workers

Staff and Workers refer to persons working in, and receive payment from units of state ownership, collective ownership, joint ownership, share holding ownership, foreign ownership, and ownership by entrepreneurs from Hong Kong, Macao, and Taiwan, and other types of ownership and their affiliated units. They do not include 1) persons employed in township enterprises, 2) persons employed in private enterprises, 3) urban self-employed persons, 4) retirees, 5) re-employed retirees, 6) teachers in the schools run by the local people, 7) foreigners and persons from Hong Kong, Macao and Taiwan who work in urban units, and 8) other persons not to be included by relevant regulations. (Data of 1998 and afterward refer to fully employed staff and workers. Other related statistics such as total wages and average wage are adjusted since 1998 accordingly).

Fully Employed Staff and Workers

Fully Employed Staff and Workers refer to persons who work in, and receive wages from their working units, as well as persons who have their work posts, but are temporarily absent from work for reasons of study or on sick, injury or maternal leave and still receive wages from their working units.

Registration Categories

Registration Categories are used to classify all kinds of enterprises that have the legal person status and have registered with the industrial and commercial administrations. The classification of business units , administrative and public institutions , social organizations and other economical bodies may refer to it.

The state-owned enterprises are economic organizations whose assets are solely owned by the state and whose registrations are made according to "Regulations of the People's Republic of China for Controlling the Registration of Enterprises as Legal Persons" excluding the state-owned liability limited companies.

The collective-owned enterprises are economic organizations

whose assets are owned by collecting and whose registration are made according to "Regulations of the People's Republic of China for Controlling the Registration of Enterprises as Legal Persons."

Share-holding cooperative enterprises are a kind of collective economic organizations based on a cooperative system. In addition to the shares bought by their workers and staff, the enterprises also absorb a certain percentage of social capital. They enjoy the autonomy in operation and are responsible for their own losses and profits. The share-holders work together, conduct democratic management, and combine labor-based distribution with share-based dividents.

Joint-owned enterprises refer to economic organizations set up with joint investment from legal persons of two or more enterprises of different ownerships or institutions according to principle of voluntary participation, equality and mutual benefit. They include state-owned joint operation enterprises, collective joint operation enterprises, state-collective joint operation enterprises and other types of joint operation enterprises.

A company with limited liability is a company registered in accordance with the "Regulations of the People's Republic of China on Administration of Company Registration." Its investment comes from more than 2 and less than 50 shareholders. Each shareholder assumes limited liability for the company according to his subscription to capital stock. The company assumes liabilities for its debts according to all its assets. Such economic organizations include solely state-invested companies and other types of companies with limited liability.

A share-holding company with limited liability refers to economic organizations registered in accordance with the "Regulations of the People's Republic of China on Administration of Company Registration." All its registered capital is composed of shares of equal value and its capital is collected through share issuing. The shareholders bear limited liability for the company according to the amount of shares they have bought from the company and the company assumes liabilities for its debts according all its assets.

A private enterprise refers to profit-making economic organizations set up with investment from natural persons or with controlling interest in the hands of natural persons who employ laborers for operation. Such enterprises include private companies with limited liability private joint stock companies limited private partnership enterprises and solely individual-invested enterprises, which are registered according to the "Company Law," "Partnership Enterprises Law" and "Interim Regulations of Private Enterprises."

The joint ventures with investment from Hong Kong, Macao and Taiwan refer to those established according to the "Law of the People's Republic of China on Chinese-foreign Joint Ventures" and regulations stipulated in relevant laws, by investors from those regions and the Chinese mainland enterprises with contracted share of investment and sharing profits and ventures between the parties.

Cooperative businesses with investment from Hong Kong, Macao and Taiwan refer to enterprises jointly set up by investors from Hong Kong, Macao and Taiwan and mainland enterprises according to the "Law of the People's Republic of China on Chinese-foreign Contractural Joint Ventures" and other relevant regulations. They invest or provide conditions for establishment, decide profit distribution, and share risks according to provisions prescribed in the cooperative venture contracts.

Solely Hong Kong, Macao and Taiwan Funded enterprises refer to enterprises set up on the mainland according to the "Law of the People's Republic of China on Foreign Capital Enterprises and solely invested by investors from Hong Kong, Macao and Taiwan."

A share-holding company with limited liability with investment from Hong Kong, Macao and Taiwan refers to any joint stock company limited that is set up according relevant state regulations and is approved by the Ministry of Foreign Economic Relations and Trade. The investment from Hong Kong, Macao and Taiwan investors must account more than 25 per-cent of the company's total capital. If such investment is less than 25 percent, it shall be classified as a joint stock company limited invested by domestic investors.

A Sino-foreign joint venture refers to any enterprise that is jointly set up by foreign enterprises or foreigners with Chinese enterprises in accordance with the "Law of the People's Republic of China on Joint Ventures with Chinese and Foreign Investment." The investors shall put in investment, share profits and risks according to the contract on the joint venture.

Sino-foreign cooperative Businesses refers to the enterprises set up by foreign enterprises or foreigners with Chinese enterprises as their partners, in line with "The Sino-foreign Cooperative Ventures Law of the People's Republic of China" and other relevant laws and regulations. The partners of the cooperative ventures will invest, take profits and share risks according to the requirements of stipulated in the contract.

A Solely Foreign-Funded enterprises refers to any enterprise that is set up on the Chinese mainland according to the "Law of the People's Republic of China on Foreign-Capital Enterprises" and with all its investment coming from foreign investors.

The foreign-invested joint stock company limited refers to any joint stock company limited that is set up according to relevant state regulations and is approved by the Ministry of Foreign Economic Relations and Trade. The foreign investment must account more than 25 per-cent of the company's total capital. If such investment is less than 25 per-cent, it shall be classified as a joint stock company limited invested by Chinese investors.

Classification of the Sectors of the National Economy

Classification of the Sectors of the National Economy was first published in 1984 and revisions were made into it in 1994 and 2002 respectively.

This Yearbook follows standards in the 2002 version of the Classification of the Sectors of the National Economy.

In the 2011 version, economic sectors are classified in accordance with the international categories of the economic activities, abolishing in definition between different administrative departments. Given the development of China's social and economic activities, more detailed classification is made of the service sector. The further breakdown of each economic sector in the latest version is geared to the most specific categorization in international practice. The latest version aims at, among others, an objective and precise presentation of the composition of the national economy in a certain period.

Unemployment Insurance

①Number of people participated in unemployment insurance program: number of staff and workers in urban enterprises or institutions and other people according to local government regulations participated in unemployment insurance program in line with national law, regulations and related policies by the end of the reference period.

②Sum of Unemployment Insurance: refer to total amount of insurance paid to un-employees to guarantee their basic lives according to related regulations.

Social Welfare Institutions

Social Welfare Institutions refer to institutions taking care of old people without children, handicapped people and orphans. They include social welfare institutions run by civil affairs departments, children's welfare institutions, welfare institutions for mental patients, and collectively-run old people's homes in rural areas.

Special Care

Special Care is offered by the government to the family member of the martyrs, disabled or demobilized servicemen or laborers who were injured on duty. Entitled to the special care are family members of the revolutionary martyrs, family members of servicemen who dies on duty or died of an illness, disabled servicemen, family members of servicemen on active service, retired veteran Red Army soldiers, scattered Red Army soldiers, demobilized servicemen, ex-servicemen, servicemen who were demobilized while on duty, ex-servicemen back to their rural homes, ex-servicemen who were demobilized because of an illness and have gone back to their rural homes, ex-servicemen who suffer from mental illness and elderly persons with no family.

第十五篇
Chapter 15

教育、文化、体育、卫生
EDUCATION, CULTURE, SPORTS AND PUBLIC HEALTH

表15-1　各级各类学校基本情况
Schools by Education Level and Type
(2011)

单位:人　　　　(person)

指　标 Indicators		学校(所) Schools (unit)	毕业生数 Graduates	招生数 Student Enrollment	在校学生数 Students Enrolled	教职员工数 Faculty and Staff	#专任教师 Full-time Faculty
总　计	**Total**	**358**	**112 065**	**135 019**	**534 374**	**40 765**	**30 923**
高等学校	Institutions of Higher Education	27	36 882	41 836	184 831	12 995	7 983
中等技术学校	Secondary Technical Schools	7	3 992	3 301	12 412	1 118	460
普通中学	High Schools	149	34 792	41 494	142 287	13 690	11 125
职业中学	Vocational Schools	7	5 434	6 295	17 747	1 094	869
小　学	Primary Schools	165	30 839	42 031	176 328	11 666	10 314
特殊教育学校	Special Education Schools	3	126	62	769	202	172

表15-2　各级各类学校占地面积和校舍建筑面积
Ground Space of Schools and Floor Space of School Buildings by Education Level and Type
(2011)

单位:万平方米　　　　(10 000 sq · m)

指　标 Indicators		学校(所) Schools (unit)	占地面积 Ground Space	校舍建筑面积 Floor Space of School Buildings
总　计	**Total**	**358**	**1 505.26**	**780.06**
高等学校	Institutions of Higher Education	27	718.13	315.66
中等技术学校	Secondary Technical Schools	7	22.59	21.15
普通中学	High Schools	149	506.98	294.86
职业中学	Vocational Schools	7	27.49	19.60
小　学	Primary Schools	165	225.37	125.41
特殊教育学校	Special Education Schools	3	4.70	3.38

表 15－3 各级各类学校女学生和女教师
Female Students and Teachers by Education Level and Type (2011)

单位：人 (person)

指 标 Indicators		女学生 Female Students		女教师 Female Faculty	
		人 数 Students	占学生总数(％) of Students(％)	人 数 Teachers	占教师总数(％) of Teachers(％)
总 计	**Total**	**253 422**	**47.4**	**20 465**	**66.2**
高等学校	Institutions of Higher Education	88 983	48.1	3 995	50.0
中等专业学校	Secondary Specialized Schools	7 019	56.6	282	61.3
普通中学	High Schools	68 718	48.3	7 431	66.8
职业中学	Vocational Schools	8 348	47.0	582	67.0
小 学	Primary Schools	80 094	45.4	8 031	77.9
特殊教育学校	Special Education Schools	260	33.8	144	83.7

表 15－4 主要年份各阶段教育实施情况
Basic Statisics of Various Phases of Education in Main Years

单位：% (％)

指 标 Indicators		2005	2009	2010	2011
小 学	**Primary School**				
小学学龄儿童净入学率	Net Enrollment Rate of School Children	100.0	100.0	100.0	100.0
初 中	**Junior School**				
初中学生净入学率	Net Enrollment Rate of Students In Junior Schools	100.0	100.0	100.0	100.0
高 中	**High School**				
初中毕业生升学率	Enrollment Quotas of Junior School Graduates	98.7	97.2	96.1	97.0

表 15-5　市、区实验性示范性中学基本情况一览
(2011)

指　标	Indicators	班级数(个) Classes (in Number)	初　中 Junior Schools	高　中 High Schools
总　计	**Total**	**795**	**129**	**666**
市实验性示范性中学	**Experimental and Demonstrative High Schools in Shanghai**	**241**	**17**	**224**
华东师范大学第二附属中学	Second High School Affiliated to Huadong Normal University	30		30
上海市建平中学	Shanghai Jianping High School	36		36
上海市进才中学	Shanghai Jincai High School	38		38
上海市洋泾中学	Shanghai Yangjing High School	43		43
上海南汇中学	Shanghai Nanhui High School	62	3	59
上海市实验学校	Shanghai Municipal Experimental High School	32	14	18
区实验性示范性中学	**Experimental and Demonstrative High Schools in Pudong**	**554**	**112**	**442**
华东师范大学附属东昌中学	Dongchang High School Affiliated to Huadong Normal University	36		36
上海市上南中学	Shanghai Shangnan High School	36		36
上海市高桥中学	Shanghai Gaoqiao High School	36		36
上海市川沙中学	Shanghai Chuansha High School	37	2	35
上海市三林中学	Shanghai Sanlin High School	30		30
上海市杨思高级中学	Shanghai Yangsi High School	24		24
上海市大团高级中学	Shanghai Datuan High School	30		30
上海市新场中学	Shanghai Xinchang High School	30		30
华东师范大学附属周浦中学	Zhoupu High School Affiliated to Huadong Normal University	36		36
上海市建平世纪中学	Shanghai Jianping Century High School	18		18
上海市新川中学	Shanghai Xinchuan High School	24		24
上海市浦东中学	Shanghai Pudong High School	18		18
上海海事大学附属北蔡高级中学	Beicai High School Affiliated to Shanghai Maritime University	12		12
上海市陆行中学	Shanghai Luhang High School	24		24
上海外国语大学附属浦东外国语学校	Pudong Foreign Languages High School Affiliated to Shanghai Foreign Languages University	44	33	11
上海市高行中学	Shanghai Gaohang High School	38	26	12
上海市香山中学	Shanghai Xiangshan High School	29	17	12
上海市南汇第一中学	Shanghai Nanhui First High School	52	34	18

Statistics of Municipal and PNA Experimenta and Demonstrative High Schools

在校学生（人）Students Enrolled (Persons)	初 中 Junior Schools	高 中 High Schools	教职员工（人）Faculty (Persons)	专任教师（人）Full-time Teachers	高 中 High Schools	初 中 Junior Schools	占地面积（平方米）Ground Space (sq. m)	运动场（馆）面积（平方米）Floor Space of Sports Grounds (Stadiums) (sq. m)	校舍建筑面积（平方米）Floor Space of School Buildings (sq. m)
30 367	**4 691**	**25 676**	**3 440**	**2 748**	**2 415**	**333**	**1 401 148**	**341 012**	**778 740**
9 260	**548**	**8 712**	**1 161**	**864**	**822**	**42**	**638 496**	**135 363**	**318 463**
1 199		1 199	168	111	111		100 000	24 949	66 179
1 467		1 467	165	135	135		39 191	7 075	31 062
1 456		1 456	194	155	155		115 294	35 504	59 536
1 593		1 593	180	142	142		55 345	15 840	42 566
2 420	117	2 303	266	207	207		254 943	34 395	90 289
1 125	431	694	188	114	72	42	73 723	17 600	28 831
21 107	**4 143**	**16 964**	**2 279**	**1 884**	**1 593**	**291**	**762 652**	**205 649**	**460 277**
1 406		1 406	142	105	105		24 664	10 384	14 267
1 407		1 407	152	124	124		18 182	9 340	16 676
1 442		1 442	153	114	114		45 643	10 995	21 683
1 468	82	1 386	165	114	114		32 503	11 400	23 399
1 295		1 295	146	118	118		35 604	13 737	19 290
931		931	112	95	95		43 355	12 312	27 978
1 177		1 177	127	110	110		63 439	19 980	26 159
1 109		1 109	130	118	118		46 220	14 572	22 378
1 427		1 427	175	152	152		90 000	8 000	36 132
646		646	75	67	67		26 488	9 699	15 672
902		902	88	86	86		23 310	8 200	13 800
623		623	75	64	64		29 687	9 847	19 593
426		426	53	44	44		26 178	11 013	17 211
828		828	99	71	71		40 766	11 410	39 216
1 707	1 319	388	160	139	44	95	71 491	21 000	70 655
1 323	908	415	126	111	50	61	37 077	12 659	17 694
1 002	526	476	111	96	56	40	19 790	7 000	16 363
1 988	1 308	680	190	156	61	95	88 255	4 101	42 111

表 15-6　普通中学和小学专任教师学历情况
Education Level of Full - Time Teachers at Junior and High Schools and Primary Schools
(2011)

单位:人　　(person)

指　标	Indicators	教师数 Faculty Contracts	大学本科毕业及以上 Graduated from University or Above	大学专科毕业 Graduated from Junior University	高中阶段毕业 Graduated from Senior High School	高中毕业以下 Below Senior High School or below
教师学历分布	**Education Level of Teachers**	**21 439**	**17 335**	**3 660**	**432**	**12**
高　中	High Schools	3 416	3 403	13		
初　中	Junior Schools	7 709	7 412	293	4	
小　学	Primary Schools	10 314	6 520	3 354	428	12
教师学历构成(%)	**Education Level Composition of Teachers (%)**	**100.0**	**80.9**	**17.0**	**2.0**	**0.1**
高　中	High Schools	100.0	99.6	0.4		
初　中	Junior Schools	100.0	96.1	3.8	0.1	
小　学	Primary Schools	100.0	63.2	32.5	4.1	0.1

表 15-7　幼儿园基本情况
Statistics of Kindergartens
(2011)

指　标	Indicators	幼儿园(所) Kindergartens (unit)	班级数(个) Classes (unit)	幼儿数(人) Children Enrolled (person)	教职员(人) Faculty and Staff (person)	#专任教师 Full-time Faculty
总　计	**Total**	**246**	**3 197**	**94 727**	**8 646**	**6 003**
教育部门办	Run by Government Education Department	169	2 507	76 672	5 749	4 552
民　办	Run by Entrepreneurs	76	685	17 900	2 873	1 439
其他部门办	Run by Other Organizations	1	5	155	24	12

表 15-8　民工子弟学校基本情况
Statistics of Schools for Children of Migrant Workers

指　标	Indicators	单　位 Unit	2005	2009	2010	2011
学校总计	**Total of Schools**	**所 in number**	**23**	**41**	**41**	**41**
小　学	Primary Schools	所 in number	6	41	41	41
混合型初中小学	Mixed Primary and Junior Schools	所 in number	17			
班级总计	**Total of Classes**	**个 in number**	**394**	**534**	**553**	**586**
小　学	Primary Schools	个 in number	339	534	553	586
初　中	Junior Schools	个 in number	55			
教职员工数	**Number of Teaching Staff**	**人 persons**	**851**	**1 647**	**1 526**	**1 646**
小　学	Primary Schools	人 persons	851	1 647	1 526	1 646
学生总计	**Total of Students**	**人 persons**	**20 520**	**25 311**	**25 768**	**28 259**
小　学	Primary Schools	人 persons	18 155	25 311	25 768	28 259
初　中	Junior Schools	人 persons	2 365			

表 15-9 文化事业
Cultural Establishments

指 标	Indicators	单 位 Unit	2010	2011
街道、镇社区文化活动中心	Culture and Activity Center for Sub-district and Town	个 unit	38	38
行政村(居委)综合文化活动室	Comprehensive Culture and Activity Room for Administrative Village (Neighborhood Committee)	个 unit	1 117	1 078
街镇图书馆藏书量	Number of Books Collected in Sub-district and Town Libraries	万册 10 000 Books	104.57	106.84
文化资源	**Cultural Resources**			
区属文化基层单位	PNA Grassroot Cultural Institutions	个 unit	16	15
公共文化设施数	Number of Public Cultural Facilities	个 unit	1 280	1 308
公益电影放映次数	Number of Welfare Films Screened	场次 in number	21 553	33 731
#外来务工人员公益电影放映	Number of Welfare Films Screened for Migrant Workers	场次 in number	225	430
业余文艺团队个数	Number of Amateur Literary and Artistic Teams	个 unit	3 261	2 996
文化交流	**Cultural Exchanges**			
赴境外演出、展览次数	Number of Performances and Exhibitions in Foreign Countries and Regions	次 time	1	4
境外艺术团来访个数	Number of Overseas Artist Teams Visited	个 unit	18	6
境外艺术团演出场次	Number of Overseas Artist Teams Performed	场次 in number	54	30
文艺创作演出情况	**Literary and Artistic Creations and Performances**			
群众文艺创作数	Number of Literary and Artistic Creations	个 unit	1 169	1 228
获奖个数	Number of Prizes	个 unit	198	181
获奖人次	Number of Person-times Who Get the Prizes	人次 person-time	2 500	2 350
获奖单位	Number of Units Who Get the Prizes	个 unit	198	181

表15-10 公共图书馆基本情况
Statistics of Public Libraries

指 标	Indicators	单 位 Unit	2000	2005	2010	2011
机构数	Number of Institutions	个 unit	5	1	3	3
职工人数	Staff and Workers	人 person	108	110	188	195
公用房屋建筑面积	Floor Space of Buildings for Public Use	平方米 sq · m	7 443	18 343	74 221	74 221
#书 库	Stack Rooms	平方米 sq · m	2 237	6 040	16 515	5 297
阅览室面积	Floor Space of Reading Rooms	平方米 sq · m	1 354	7 550	38 882	27 464
阅览室座席	Seats in Reading Rooms	个 unit	800	1 366	3 764	4 535
总藏书量	Total Book Volume	万册 10 000 volumes	80	126	290	351
#本年新购藏书	New Books Purchased in Current Year	万册 10 000 volumes	3	12	24	43
发放借书证	Library Cards Distributed	张 in number	14 579	10 524	56 598	51 962
图书流通人次	Books Circulation Persons-Time	万人次 10 000 person-times	67	150	242	324
图书外借册次	Borrowed Books-time	万册次 10 000 volume-times	80	99	177	315

表 15－11 广播电视事业基本情况
Statistics of Broadcasting and Television

指 标 Indicators		单 位 Unit	2005	2009	2010	2011
区广播电视台	PNA Radio and TV Station	座 unit	1	1	1	1
区有线网络中心	PNA Cabled Networking Center	座 unit	1	1	1	1
市属有线电视管理站	Municipal CATV Management Station	个 unit	10	10	10	10
区属有线电视管理站	PNA CATV Management Station	个 unit	3	6	7	6
镇广播电视站	Town Radio & TV Station	个 unit	13	24	24	24
广电工作从业人员	Persons Employed in Sectors of Broadcasting and Television	人 person	342		544	537
区台无线广播发射塔	Radio Broadcasting and TV Tower of PNA	座 unit	1	1	1	1
区台使用频率	Frequency Occupied by PNA	兆赫 MHz	106.5	106.5/100.1	106.5/100.1	106.5/100.1
区台无线广播覆盖率	Radio Broadcasting Coverage of PNA	%	100.0	100.0	100.0	100.0
有线广播电视专线	Cabled Broadcasting and Television Line	杆公里 pole. km	1 858	5 806	6 097	6 774
有线电视管道干线	CATV Trunk Line	公里 km	223	1 153	1 211	1 345
广播电视台播出节目时间	Broadcasting Duration of Radio and Television Stations	小时/日 hour/day		18	18	18
有线电视用户	CATV Subscribers	万户 10 000 households	73	106	131	135
村通播率	Rate of Villages Access to Broadcasting	%	100.0	100.0	100.0	100.0
区台平均日播音时间	Average Broadcasting Hours of PNA Radio Stations	套/小时 set/hour	1/14.5	1/21.0	1/21.0	2/36.0
镇广播电视站日播放时间	Airing/Broadcasting Hours of Town Radio & TV Stations	小时 hour	14.5	21.0	21.0	21.0

表 15－12　文化馆基本情况
Statistics of Cultural Centers
(2011)

指　标	Indicators	单　位 Unit	合　计 Total	浦东文化馆 Pudong Cultural Center	浦南文化馆 Punan Cultural Center	川沙文化馆 Chuansha Cultural Center	文化艺术指导中心 Art Consulting Center
机构数	Number of Centers	个 unit	4	1	1	1	1
职工人数	Staff and Workers	人 person	201	35	31	32	103
公用房屋建筑面积	Floor Space of Building for Public Use	平方米 sq · m	30 281	6 180	2 500	4 900	16 701
组织文艺活动次数	Performances Organized	次 time	1 591	100	464	241	786
举办业余文艺训练班班次	Training Course for Amateurs	班次 class-time	257	31	182		44
结业人数	Persons Graduated	人次 person-time	8 450		5 200		3 250

表 15－13　参加市级以上体育竞赛成绩情况
PNA in State-level and International-level Competitions
(2011)

单位:次　　(time)

指　标	Indicators	第 1 名 First Place Winners	第 2 名 Second Place Winners	第 3 名 Third Place Winners	第 4 名 Fourth Place Winners	第 5 名 Fifth Place Winners	第 6 名 Sixth Place Winners	第 7 名 Seventh Place Winners
合　计	**Total**	**342**	**263**	**227**	**148**	**120**	**109**	**81**
市　级	Municipal Level	288	215	203	138	112	100	77
全　国	State Level	54	48	24	10	8	9	4
团　体	**Team**	**27**	**24**	**20**	**5**	**3**	**6**	
市　级	Municipal Level	17	19	19	5	3	6	
全　国	State Level	10	5	1				
个　人	**Individual**	**315**	**239**	**207**	**143**	**117**	**103**	**81**
市　级	Municipal Level	271	196	184	133	109	94	77
全　国	State Level	44	43	23	10	8	9	4

表 15-14 举(承)办各级体育比赛情况
Sports Games of All Levels Held or Undertaken
(2011)

比赛级别	Levels	次数(次) Times (in number)	参加人次数(人次) Athletes (person-time)
总 计	**Total**	**129**	**44 343**
区级比赛	PNA Games	101	13 531
市级比赛	Shanghai Games	16	28 812
全国比赛	National Games	12	2 000

表 15-15 等级运动员和裁判员情况
Graded Athletes and Referees
(2011)

单位:人 (person)

项 目	Item	二级运动员 Grade-Ⅱ Athletes	裁判员 Referees 二级 Grade-Ⅱ	裁判员 Referees 三级 Grade-Ⅲ
合 计	**Total**	**129**	**79**	**284**
田 径	Track and Field	12		
排 球	Volleyball	3		
武 术	Martial Art	10		
篮 球	Basketball		51	152
射 击	Shooting	7		
足 球	Soccer	22		
游 泳	Swimming	28		
棒 球	Baseball	8		
散 打	Free Boxing	7		
击 剑	Fence-play	1		
围 棋	Go	3		
象 棋	Chinese Chess	2		
国际象棋	Chess	1		
乒乓球	Table Tennis	22		
举 重	Weight Lifting	2		
垒 球	Softball	1		
羽毛球	Badminton		8	36
台 球	Billiards		7	32
门 球	Croquet		11	64
健美操	Aerobics		2	

表15-16 全民健身活动设施情况
Facilities for Fitness Activities

指 标	Indicators	单 位 Unit	2009	2010	2011
农民健身家园	**Fitness Garden for Farmers**				
篮球场	Basketball Court	片 in number	182	206	227
羽毛球场	Badminton Court	片 in number	5	5	5
网球场	Tennis Court	片 in number	2	2	2
门球场	Croquet Court	片 in number	59	68	77
社区公共运动场	**Community Public Sports Ground**				
篮球场	Basketball Court	片 in number	61	69	74
门球场	Croquet Court	片 in number	23	26	34
网球场	Tennis Court	片 in number	15	16	17
足球场	Soccer Field	片 in number	1	1	1
羽毛球场	Badminton Court	片 in number	3	3	3
健身苑(点)数量	**Number of Fitness Court (Center)**	**个 in number**	**1 689**	**1 689**	**1 689**
健身苑	Fitness Court	个 in number	67	67	67
街道、镇	Subdistrict or Town	个 in number	63	63	63
体育系统	Sports System	个 in number	2	2	2
学 校	School	个 in number	2	2	2
健身点	Fitness Center	个 in number	1 622	1 622	1 622
街道、镇	Subdistrict or Town	个 in number	1 622	1 622	1 622
健身苑(点)面积	**Floor Space for Fitness Court (Center)**	**万平方米 10 000 sq. m**	**91.95**	**91.95**	**91.95**
健身苑	Fitness Court	万平方米 10 000 sq. m	15.15	15.15	15.15
街道、镇	Subdistrict or Town	万平方米 10 000 sq. m	14.00	14.00	14.00
体育系统	Sports System	万平方米 10 000 sq. m	0.60	0.60	0.60
学 校	School	万平方米 10 000 sq. m	0.55	0.55	0.55
健身点	Fitness Center	万平方米 10 000 sq. m	76.80	76.80	76.80
街道、镇	Subdistrict or Town	万平方米 10 000 sq. m	76.80	76.80	76.80
健身器材配置数	**Number of Body Fitness Apparatus**	**件 set**	**20 803**	**20 803**	**20 803**
街 道	Subdistrict	件 set	6 125	6 125	6 125
镇	Town	件 set	14 582	14 582	14 582
专业体育场馆	Professional Stadium and Gymnasium	件 set	60	60	60
学 校	School	件 set	36	36	36

表 15-17　各类卫生机构、床位及人员数

Healthcare Institutions, Hospital Beds and Professionals by Institution Type (2011)

指　标	Indicators	机构数(个) Institution (unit)	床位数(张) Beds (bed)	人员数(人) Staff (person)	#卫生技术人员 Healthcare Professional	管理人员 Administrator
总　计	**Total**	**1 074**	**17 731**	**28 024**	**23 099**	**1 351**
卫生部门合计	**Total by Healthcare Departments**	**172**	**13 841**	**22 263**	**18 534**	**972**
医院合计	Total of Hostpitals	24	10 300	15 044	12 813	670
综合性医院	Comprehensive Hospital	10	6 146	10 607	9 057	476
中医医院	Hospital of Traditional Chinese Medicine	4	1 495	2 058	1 756	111
专科医院	Special Hospital	8	2 351	1 908	1 579	79
妇幼保健院	Maternity and Pediatric Hospital	2	308	471	421	4
社区卫生服务中心	Community Health Service Center	141	3 541	6 196	5 102	248
妇幼保健所	Maternity and Pediatric Clinic	1		69	59	1
眼病牙病防治所	Visual and Dental Clinic	1		24	12	12
疾病预防控制中心	Disease Prevention and Control Center	1		282	242	3
卫监监督所	Health Supervision Institutite	1		144	129	2
急救中心	First-Aid Center	1		340	82	11
采供血机构	Blood Sampling and Supply Institute	1		75	46	12
其　他	Others	1		89	49	13
工业及其他部门合计	**Those of Industry and Other Organizations**	**902**	**3 890**	**5 761**	**4 565**	**379**
医院合计	Total of Hospitals	35	3 890	3 738	2 773	310
工业医院	Industrial Hospital	5	2 100	1 263	902	188
综合性医院	Comprehensive Hospital	3	673	773	501	161
专科医院	Special Hospital	1	420	131	77	14
护理院	Nursing Home	1	1 007	359	324	13
民办医院	Private Hospitals	30	1 790	2 475	1 871	122
#护理院	Nursing Home	1	83	50	25	3
门诊部、疗养院	Clinic and Sanitarium	96		1 192	964	69
诊所(含内设医疗机构)	Clinic (medical establishments inside)	450		831	828	
村卫生室	Village Health Rooms	321				

注：以上含浦东区域内市属三级医院及分院数据

Note: The above-mentioned data include those of municipal Grade III hospitals and their affiliated hospitals located in Pudong.

表15-18 各类卫生技术人员数
Number of Healthcare Professionals
(2011)

单位:人　　　　(person)

指标	Indicators	合计 Total	执业医师 Medical Practitioners	执业助理医师 Assistant Medical Practitioners	注册护士 Registered Nurses	药师(士) Pharmacist	检验技师(士) Inspect technician	摄像技师(士) Video technician	其他卫生技术人员 Other Healthcare Professionals
总计	**Total**	**23 099**	**8 477**	**387**	**9 631**	**1 307**	**996**	**318**	**1 983**
卫生部门合计	**Total by Healthcare Departments**	**18 534**	**6 513**	**297**	**7 858**	**1 102**	**830**	**283**	**1 651**
医院合计	Hostpitals	12 813	4 196	30	6 208	622	492	222	1 043
综合性医院	Comprehensive Hospital	9 057	3 042	13	4 317	390	329	151	815
中医医院	Hospital of Traditional Chinese Medicine	1 756	607	7	809	140	70	39	84
专科医院	Special Hospital	1 579	410	9	838	82	75	32	133
妇幼保健院	Maternity and Pediatric Hospital	421	137	1	244	10	18		11
社区卫生服务中心(站)	Community Healthcare Service Center (Station)	5 102	2 077	259	1 608	475	237	60	386
妇幼保健所	Maternity and Pediatric Clinic	59	38		11	3	3	1	3
眼病牙病防治所	Visual and Dental Clinic	12	6		4	1	1		
疾病预防控制中心	Disease Prevention and Control Center	242	144		5	1	36		56
卫监监督所	Health Supervision Institutite	129							129
急救中心	First-Aid Center	82	47	7					28
采供血机构	Blood Sampling and Supply Institute	46	5	1	22		16		2
其他	Others	49					45		4
工业及其他部门合计	**Total by Industry and other Departments**	**4 565**	**1 964**	**90**	**1 773**	**205**	**166**	**35**	**332**
医院合计	Hospitals	2 773	939	23	1 252	160	116	25	258
工业医院	Industrial Hospital	902	211	7	429	47	49	10	149
综合性医院	Comprehensive Hospital	501	162	6	206	32	39	6	50
专科医院	Special Hospital	77	15	1	54	4	2	1	
护理院	Nursing Home	324	34		169	11	8	3	99
民办医院	Private Hospital	1 871	728	16	823	113	67	15	109
#护理院	Nursing Home	25	4		12		1		8
门诊部、疗养院	Clinic and Sanitarium	964	457	16	340	35	46	10	60
诊所(含内设医疗机构)	Clinic (medical establishments inside)	828	568	51	181	10	4		14

注:以上含浦东区域内市属三级医院及分院数据

Note: The above-mentioned data include those of municipal Grade III hospitals and their affiliated hospitals located in Pudong.

表 15-19 区级医院基本情况
Statistics of PNA-level Hospitals
(2011)

指 标	Indicators	人员数（人） Staff (person)	#卫生技术人员 Healthcare Professionals	建筑面积（平方米） Floor Space (sq·m)	#业务用房 Floor Space for Treatment	床位数（张） Beds (bed)	全年诊疗人次（万人次） Annual Patients Treated (10 000 person-times)
总 计	**Total**	**10 291**	**8 765**	**490 509**	**382 838**	**7 486**	**1 037.04**
综合医院	**Comprehensive Hospitals**	**8 324**	**7 125**	**367 030**	**279 284**	**4 760**	**824.75**
东方医院	Oriental Hospital	1 838	1 624	65 788	54 363	802	167.00
第七人民医院	No. 7 People's Hospital	1 167	1 036	43 798	36 184	642	107.69
华山医院南汇分院	Nanhui Branch of Huashan Hospital	1 051	934	87 599	64 104	930	117.30
浦东新区人民医院	PNA People's Hospital	1 271	1 097	91 561	56 998	808	127.24
浦东新区公利医院	PNA Gongli Hospital	1 248	1 048	22 383	17 842	577	141.08
第九人民医院周浦分院	Zhoupu Branch of Shanghai No. 9 People's Hospital	776	618	23 441	17 333	390	84.02
浦南医院	Punan Hospital	973	768	32 460	32 460	611	80.42
专科医院	**Specialized Hospitals**	**1 967**	**1 640**	**123 479**	**103 554**	**2 726**	**212.29**
传染病院	Infectious Disease Control Hospital	85	65	7 380	4 500	100	4.07
浦东新区中医医院	Hospital of Traditional Chinese Medicine, PNA	466	384	24 331	22 531	300	80.44
妇幼保健院	Maternity and Pediatric Hospital	382	334	20 031	17 455	250	36.74
光明中医医院	Guangming Chinese Medicine Hospital	432	378	16 000	13 800	318	71.69
南汇精神卫生中心	Nanhui Mental Health Center	81	67	12 500	10 725	320	1.99
浦东新区精神卫生中心	Mental Health Centre, PNA	194	161	21 771	17 634	775	7.49
南华医院	Nanhua Hospital	120	101	7 398	6 101	153	7.16
老年医院	Laonian Hospital	122	82	7 800	6 600	350	1.40
肺科医院	Pulmonary Disease Hospital	85	68	6 268	4 208	160	1.30

表 15－20　综合医院工作质量情况
Workload in Comprehensive Hospitals

指　标 Indicators		手术人数(人次) Operations (person-time)		入院病人数(人次) Inpatients(person-time)		出院病人数(人次) Inpatients Leaving for Home(person-time)	
		2010	2011	2010	2011	2010	2011
总　计	**Total**	**55 065**	**77 411**	**149 515**	**156 899**	**149 588**	**156 846**
东方医院	Oriental Hospital	11 050	18 625	26 172	30 926	26 164	30 948
第七人民医院	No. 7 People's Hospital	6 504	7 455	16 215	16 671	16 227	16 671
华山医院南汇分院	Nanhui Branch of Huashan Hospital	11 089	13 638	32 329	32 306	32 316	32 350
浦东新区人民医院	PNA People's Hospital	7 899	11 941	23 295	24 899	23 282	24 807
浦东新区公利医院	PNA Gongli Hospital	8 446	11 940	18 738	20 601	18 805	20 564
第九人民医院周浦分院	Zhoupu Branch of Shanghai No. 9 People's Hospital	4 099	7 503	15 513	14 852	15 592	14 857
浦南医院	Punan Hospital	5 978	6 309	17 253	16 644	17 202	16 649

表 15－20　续表　Continued

指　标 Indicators		出院者平均住院日数(日) Average Days of Inpatients at Hospital(day)		平均病床工作日(日) Average Beds Exploitation(day)		病床使用率(%) Rate of Beds Exploitation(%)	
		2010	2011	2010	2011	2010	2011
总　计	**Total**	**11.88**	**10.36**	**348.27**	**355.37**	**95.42**	**97.36**
东方医院	Oriental Hospital	11.21	9.85	367.77	368.49	100.76	100.96
第七人民医院	No. 7 People's Hospital	13.36	13.12	329.98	337.21	90.40	92.39
华山医院南汇分院	Nanhui Branch of Huashan Hospital	9.93	9.72	337.40	386.82	92.44	105.98
浦东新区人民医院	PNA People's Hospital	9.56	9.59	371.90	338.08	101.89	92.63
浦东新区公利医院	PNA Gongli Hospital	9.65	9.26	314.57	328.41	86.18	89.97
第九人民医院周浦分院	Zhoupu Branch of Shanghai No. 9 People's Hospital	9.87	9.87	392.46	375.59	107.52	102.90
浦南医院	Punan Hospital	12.71	12.73	353.65	347.49	96.89	95.20

注：老年医院 2011 年起调整为专科医院

Note: Laonian Hopsital was readjusted as one of special hospitals in 2011.

表15-21 医院诊疗人次和入院人数
Outpatients and Inpatients Treated
(2011)

指 标	Indicators	诊疗人次（万人次）Total Patients Treated (10 000 person-times)	#门、急诊 Outpatients or Emergency Treatment	入院人数（万人次）Inpatients (10 000 person-times)	每百诊次的入院人数（人）Inpatients Per 100 Total Patient/time (person)	出院人数（万人次）Inpatients Leaving for Home (10 000 person-times)
总　计	**Total**	**3 489.44**	**3 444.40**	**29.13**	**0.83**	**38.88**
卫生部门合计	**Total by Healthcare Departments**	**3 073.35**	**3 040.16**	**25.06**	**0.82**	**34.91**
医院合计	Hostpitals	1 486.81	1 472.06	20.03	1.35	29.46
综合性医院	Comprehensive Hospital	1 038.18	1 023.43	15.79	1.52	21.66
中医医院	Hospital of Traditional Chinese Medicine	296.15	296.15	1.63	0.55	4.85
专科医院	Special Hospital	152.49	152.49	2.61	1.71	2.95
社区卫生服务中心(站)	Community Healthcare Service Center (Station)	1 539.08	1 520.64	3.37	0.22	3.39
妇幼保健所	Maternity and Pediatric Clinic	46.02	46.02	1.66	3.60	2.06
眼病牙病防治所	Visual and Dental Clinic	1.44	1.44			
工业及其他部门合计	**Total by Industry and other Departments**	**416.09**	**404.24**	**4.07**	**0.98**	**3.97**
医院合计	Hospitals	351.87	340.01	4.07	1.16	3.97
工业医院	Industrial Hospital	49.01	49.01	1.15	2.35	1.08
综合性医院	Comprehensive Hospital	46.98	46.98	0.72	1.54	0.72
专科医院	Special Hospital			…		…
护理院	Nursing Home	2.03	2.03	0.42	20.83	0.36
民办医院	Private Hospitals	302.86	291.00	2.92	0.96	2.89
#护理院	Nursing Home			0.05		0.05
门诊部、疗养院	Clinics and Sanitariums	64.23	64.23			

注：1、业务指标不包括诊所(含内设机构)、村卫生室
2、以上数据除入院人数指标外均包含浦东地域市属三级医院分院数据

Note: 1、Business indicators exclude those of clinics (medical establishments inside) and village health rooms.
2、Except the number of inpatients, the above-mentioned data include those of municipal Grade III hospitals and their affiliated hospitals located in Pudong.

表 15-22　医疗业务效益指标
Indicators of Medical Results

指　标 Indicators		单　位 Unit	2005	2009	2010	2011
医院(卫生部门)	**Hospitals (Healthcare Departments)**					
手术人次数	Operation Person-times	人次 person-time	32 404	61 213	69 354	93 519
病床周转率	Turnover of Beds	次/床 time/bed	26.77	26.74	24.95	26.71
病床平均工作日	Average Bed in Service	日/床 day/bed	374.72	356.71	344.26	355.15
病床使用率	Rate of Bed Exploitation	%	102.66	97.73	94.32	97.30
出院者平均住院日	Average Days of Inpatient at Hospital	日 day	13.37	12.61	13.06	12.17
平均每张处方费用	**Average Fee for Each Prescription**	**元 yuan**	**93.66**			
#综合医院	Comprehensive Hospitals	元 yuan	106.56			
专科医院	Specialized Hospitals	元 yuan	101.84			
街道、镇医院	Subdistrict/Town Hospitals	元 yuan	85.77			
其他部门医院	Other Hospitals	元 yuan	110.23			
综合医院出院病人平均医疗费	**Average Medical Fee of Inpatients at Comprehensive Hospitals**	**元/人 yuan/person**	**7 499.06**	**9 212.29**	**10 362.34**	**10 983.72**

注：1、2009 年始，平均每张处方费用不作统计。
2、本表不含浦东区域内市属三级医院分院数据

Note：1、The average expense of every medical prescription has not been put into statistics since 2009.
2. Data in this table exclude those of municipal Grade III hospitals and their affiliated hospitals located in Pudong.

表 15-23　公民义务献血、用血情况
Voluntary Blood Donation and Blood Transfusion

指　标 Indicators		单　位 Unit	2009	2010	2011
献血人次	Number of Person-times Who Voluntarily Donate Their Blood	人份 in number	46 975	49 902	47 959
无偿献血占献血人次比重	Ratio of Person-times Who Voluntarily Donate Their Blood in Total Number of Blood Donations	%	100.0	93.0	96.0
用血量	Amount of Blood Transfusion				
#全　血	Whole Blood	人次 person-time	195	96	52
红细胞	Red Blood Cell	人次 person-time	14 913	41 729	41 666
血　浆	Blood Plasma	人次 person-time	13 854	37 740	45 739

表 15-24 主要年份前十五位疾病死亡原因及构成
Death Causes of 15 Major Diseases and Their Composition in Main Years

单位:% (%)

疾病死亡原因 Cause of Death		构成比 Composition Rate					
		1997	2000	2005	2009	2010	2011
循环系统病	Circulatory System Disease	35.85	32.40	34.55	33.50	34.24	34.25
肿 瘤	Tumor	26.87	30.40	31.04	31.96	32.52	32.65
呼吸系病	Respiratory Disease	16.11	13.80	11.00	10.29	9.66	10.05
损伤和中毒	Trauma & Toxicosis	5.86	6.30	5.48	5.65	5.73	5.42
消化系病	Digestive Disease	2.57	2.90	2.70	2.95	2.78	2.84
内分泌代谢免疫病	Internal Secretion, Metabolic & Immunity Diseases	2.64	2.70	4.10	4.03	4.03	4.16
传染病寄生虫病	Infectious Disease and Pardsitic Disease	1.94	2.10	1.52	1.45	1.19	1.2
精神病	Mental Disease	1.66	1.90	0.97	0.91	0.65	0.45
泌尿生殖系病	Genitourinary Disease	1.10	1.11	0.93	0.78	0.85	0.95
神经系病	Neuro Disease	0.66	0.62	0.78	1.21	1.05	1.07
先天异常	Congenital Anomaly	0.48	0.35	0.27			
血液造血器官疾病	Haematopoietic Tissue Disease	0.24	0.29	0.34			
新生儿病	Disease of the New-borns	0.22	0.11	0.10			
妊娠分娩产褥症	Pregnancy/Childbirth/ Puerperium Disease	0.01					
其他疾病	Others Diseases	3.79	5.02	6.22			

表15-25 家庭病床情况
Patients Staying in Family Ward Beds

指 标 Indicators		单 位 Unit	2000	2005	2010	2011
中西医师(士)赴家庭病床诊疗总人次	Total Number of Doctors of Traditional Chinese Medicine and of Western Medicine Treating Patients in Family Ward Beds	人次 person-time	102 539	109 579	162 608	139 092
期初原有家庭病床数	Number of Family Ward Beds at Beginning of Term	张 bed	1 817	2 097	2 555	2 604
期内新建家庭病床数	Number of New Established Family Ward Beds During the Term	张 bed	3 779	4 340	5 005	4 732
期内撤床病人数	Number of Patients Leaving Family Ward Beds During the Term	人 person	3 861	4 260	4 928	4 859
治 愈	Patients Cured	人 person	34	1	2	8
好 转	Patients Getting Better	人 person	484	149	264	163
稳 定	Patients Turning Stablized	人 person	2 798	3 452	3 711	3 582
转 院	Patients Turning to Another Hospital	人 person	293	419	618	696
要求撤床	Patients Asking to Cancel the Ward Beds	人 person	152	204	279	339
死 亡	Dead Patients	人 person	100	35	54	71
期末实有家庭病床数	Acutual Number of Family Ward Beds at End of Term	张 bed	1 735	2 177	2 632	2 477
期内家庭病床病人住床总床日数	Total Bed-days of Patients Staying in Familiy Ward Beds During the Term	天 day	663 099	777 590	1 042 073	1 100 242
期内撤床病人住床总床日数	Total Bed-days of Patients Who Have Stayed in Ward Beds Asking to Cancel Ward Beds During the Term	天 day	48 716	610 522	589 302	557 883
期内撤床病人诊疗总人次数	Total Person-times of Patients Who Have Taken Medical Care Asking to Cancel Ward Beds During the Term	人次 person-time	61 482	90 942	100 068	84 545

主要统计指标解释

学　校

指按国家规定的设置标准和审批程序批准设立的，招收适龄人口实施各级各类教育活动的教育机构。

普通高等学校

指按照国家规定的设置标准和审批程序批准举办的，通过全国普通高等学校统一招生考试，招收高中毕业生为主要培养对象，实施高等教育的全日制大学、独立设置的学院和高等专科学校、高等职业学校和其他机构。

大学、独立设置的学院主要实施本科层次以上教育，高等专科学校、高等职业学校实施专科层次教育，其他机构是承担国家普通招生计划任务不计校数的机构。包括普通高等学校分校和批准筹建的普通高等学校等。

成人高等学校

指按国家规定的设置标准和审批程序举办的，通过全国成人高等教育统一招生考试，招收高中毕业或同等学历的人员为主要培养对象，利用函授、业余、脱产的多种形式对其实施高等学历教育的学校。包括：职工高等学校、农民高等学校、管理干部学院、教育学院、独立函授学院、广播电视大学、其他机构等。

民办的其他高等教育机构

指经省、自治区、直辖市教育行政部门审批并颁发办学许可证，但不具有颁发学历文凭资格的实施高等教育的单位。学历文凭考试机构是指民办的经教育行政部门专门批准，进行全日制高等教育的其他高等教育机构。

中等专业学校

指经县或县以上教育行政部门批准设立，招收初中毕业生实施中等专业课程教育的教学机构。

职业中学（职业高中、职业初中）

指经县或县以上教育行政部门批准设立，招收小学或初中毕业生实施中等职业技术教育的教学机构。按学校性质类别可分为：独立设置的职业中学（包括：职业初中、职业高中、职业初高中合设学校）；附设有普通中学班的职业中学。

普通中学（普通高中、普通初中）

普通中学分为普通高级中学和普通初级中学两个阶段。普通初级中学是指独立设置的招收小学毕业的适龄人口进行初级中等基础教育的机构；普通高级中学是指独立设置的招收初中毕业的适龄人口进行高级中等基础教育的机构；完全中学是指普通初、高中合设的教育机构；一贯制学校是指在一所学校连续实施中小学教育的机构。其中包括实施九年义务教育的九年一贯制学校和实施高中教育的十二年一贯制学校。（说明：一贯制学校的办学条件如能划分为小学、初中、高中，则分开填报；如不能划分清楚，可按就高不就低的方法填入初中、高中报表中，不能重复填写。）

普通小学

指由区或区以上教育行政部门批准，招收学龄儿童实施初等教育的教学机构。

幼儿园

指招收三周岁以上（含三周岁）学龄前幼儿，对其进行保育和教育的单位。

特殊教育学校

指本市独立设置的招收盲聋哑和智残儿童，以及其他特殊需要的儿童、青少年进行普通或职业初、中等教育的教学机构。

文化机构

是指专门从事文化工作具有法人资格，独立核算的事业，企业单位，以及单独核算，附属于事业单位的经营性专业文化活动单位。包括从事艺术、图书馆、档案馆、群众文化、文物保护、艺术教育、艺术研究、文化娱乐、新闻出版等机构，以及其他文化机构。

等级运动员人数

指经考核正式批准授予等级运动员称号的人数。运动员等级分为国际级运动健将、运动健将、一级运动员、二级运动员、三级运动员、少年级运动员。该指标主要反映运动员队伍的技术质量水平。

等级裁判员人数

指经考核正式批准授予等级裁判员称号的人数。裁判员等级分为国际裁判、国家级裁判、一级裁判、二级裁判、三级裁判。该指标主要反映裁判员队伍的技术质量水平。

卫生机构

卫生机构是指从卫生行政部门取得《医疗机构执业许可证》，或从民政、工商行政、机构编制管理部门取得法人单位登记证书，为社会提供医疗保健、疾病控制、卫生监督服务或从事医学研究、医学教育等卫生单位和卫生社会团体。

医疗机构

医疗机构是指根据《医疗机构管理条例》的规定，经登记取得《医疗机构执业许可证》的机构。包括医院、社区卫生服务中心(站)、卫生院、门诊部、诊疗所、医务室、村卫生室、妇幼保健院(所、站)、专科疾病防治院(所、站)、急救中心、临床检验中心。

医　院

医院指设有固定床位,能收容病人住院并能为病人提供医疗、护理服务的医疗机构,包括县及县以上医院、农村乡卫生院和其他医院三部分。县及县以上医院按业务性质不同分为综合医院和专科医院。

卫生技术人员

卫生技术人员指从事卫生技术工作并在卫生事业机构领取劳动报酬的专业人员。包括中医师、西医师、中西医结合高级医师、护师、中药师、西药师、检验师、其他技师、中医士、西医士、护士、助产士、中药剂士、西药剂士、检验士、其他技士、其他中医、护理员、中药剂员、西药剂员、检验员、其他初级卫生技术人员。

医　生

医生指在医疗、预防保健机构工作且取得《执业医师证书》的执业医师和执业助理医师。

EXPLANATORY NOTES TO MAJOR STATISTICAL INDICATORS

School Institutions

School Institutions refer to education establishment set up according to the government evaluation and approval procedures, enrolling population of the right age, providing various phase education activity.

Regular Institutions of Higher Education

Regular Institutions of Higher Learning refer to educational establishments set up according to the government evaluation and approval procedures, enrolling graduates from senior secondary schools and providing higher education courses and training for senior professionals. They include full-time universities, colleges, high professional schools, high professional vocational schools and others.

Universities and colleges are mainly providing undergraduate courses; those high professional schools and high professional vocational schools are mainly providing professional trainings; and others refer to educational establishments, which are responsible for enrolling students but not covered in the total number of schools, including: branch schools of universities and colleges, and universities and colleges that have been proved and prepared to construct.

Institutions of Higher Education for Adults

Institution of Higher Learning for Adults refer to educational establishments, set up in line with relevant rules approved by the government, enrolling personnel with senior secondary schools or equivalent education, and providing higher education courses in many forms of correspondence, spare time, or full time for adults. Institutions of higher schools for adults include schools of higher educations for staff and workers, schools of higher education for peasants, colleges for management cadres, pedagogical colleges, independent correspondence colleges, Radio and TV universities and other educational establishment, etc.

Civil Other Institution of Higher Education

Civil Other Institution of Higher Education refer to educational establishment set up according to rules approved and permitted by educational administration department of municipal government and not be provided with qualification to awarding diploma.

Specialized Secondary schools

Specialized Secondary schools refer to educational establishment set up according to approval and permission by educational administration department of district and above government, enrolling graduates from junior secondary schools and providing secondary professional education courses.

Vocational Secondary Schools (senior secondary schools and junior secondary schools)

Vocational Secondary Schools (senior secondary schools and junior secondary schools) refer to educational establishment set up according to approval and permission by educational administration department of district and above government, enrolling graduates from primary schools and junior secondary schools and providing secondary vocational education courses.

Regular Secondary Schools (senior secondary schools and junior secondary schools)

Regular Secondary Schools (senior secondary schools and junior secondary schools) are classified as senior secondary schools and junior secondary schools. Junior Secondary Schools refer to educational establishment enrolling graduates from primary schools and providing junior secondary educational courses. Senior Secondary Schools refer to educational establishment enrolling graduates from junior secondary schools and providing higher secondary educational courses.

Regular Primary Schools

Regular Primary Schools refer to educational establishment set up according to approval and permission by educational administration department of district and above government, enrolling graduates from children of school age and providing primary educational courses.

Kindergartens

Kindergartens refer to nursery and education establishment, enrolling children in 3 years old and above.

Special Education Schools

Special Education Schools refer to educational establishments set up independently, enrolling blind, deaf, dumb, amentia or other special children, and educational establishment, providing regular or vocational junior and senior secondary education for hobbledehoy.

Cultural Institutions

Cultural Institution refers to undertaking and business institutions which specialize in cultural work and have legal personality and independent accounting system, and those professional cultural institutions attached to undertaking institutions and have independent accounting system. It includes institutions specialize in art, library, archives, mass culture, historical relic protection, art education, art research, entertainment, news and publication and other cultural institutions.

Number of Athletes in Grades

Number of Athletes in Grades refers to the number of athletes who have been given titles through examination. The titles of athletes include international masters of sports, masters of sports, first-grade, second-grade and third-grade sportsmen and young athletes. This indicator reflects skill of the athletes.

Number of Referees in Grades

Number of Referees in Grades refers to the number of referees who have been given titles after examination. They are classified as international referees, national referees and referees of the first, second and third grades. This indicator reflects the skill of referees.

Health Care Institutions

Health Care Institution refers to medical institutions and corporations providing health care, disease control and medical supervision service or engaged in medical research and medical education, which obtain Medical Institution Practice License from Medical Administration or Corporative Registration Certificate from Civil Administration, Commercial Administration or Organizational Management Administration.

Medical Organizations

Medical Institution refers to institutions which register Medical Institution Practice License according to Medical Institution Management Regulation, including hospitals, community medical service centers, medical house, clinics, dispensaries, medicine rooms, village medicine rooms, hospitals for maternity and kids care, special disease cure hospitals, first-aid center, clinical inspection centers.

Hospitals

Hospitals refer to medical institutions with permanent hospital beds, which are able to take in patients and provide them with medical and nursing services. Hospitals are classified into three categories: hospitals at or above the county level, hospitals of rural townships, and other hospitals. Hospitals at or above county level are divided into comprehensive and specialized hospitals.

Medical Professionals

Medical Professionals refers to those professionals engaged in medical work and receive salaries from medical institutions, including doctors of Chinese and Western medicine, senior doctors of integrated Chinese-Western medicine, head nurses, pharmacists of Chinese and Western medicine, laboratory specialists , other specialists, junior doctors of Chinese and Western medicine, nurses, midwives, druggists of Chinese and Western medicine, laboratory technicians, other technicians, other practitioners of Chinese medicine, nursing attendants, pharmacological workers of Chinese and Western medicine, laboratory workers and other primary medical personnel.

Doctors

Doctors refer to certified physicians and certified assistant physicians with certifications working in medical and health care and prevention agencies.

第十六篇

Chapter 16

法律、社会治安及其他

LAWS, PUBLIC ORDER AND OTHERS

表16-1　主要年份律师、公证及调解工作基本情况
Lawyers, Notaries and Mediations in Main Years

指　标　Indicators		单 位 Unit	2009	2010	2011
律师事务所	**Law and Lawyers' Offices**	**个 unit**	**202**	**214**	**217**
合伙所	Partner Offices	个 unit	165	172	171
个人所	Individual Offices	个 unit	37	42	46
律师工作人员	**Lawyer Staff**	**人 person**	2 528	2 958	3 269
#专职律师	Full-time Lawyers	人 person	2 334	2 842	3 144
兼职律师	Part-time Lawyers	人 person	111	116	125
律师办理各类法律事务	**All Kinds of Legal Affairs Handled by Lawyers**				
担任法律顾问	Legal Advisers	家 unit	9 034	9 170	9 252
刑事诉讼辩护及代理	Litigation Defense and Legal Representation in Criminal Cases	件 unit	2 783	2 392	3 077
民事案件诉讼代理	Legal Representation in Civil Cases	件 unit	5 714	6 152	6 193
行政案件诉讼代理	Legal Representation in Administrative Cases	件 unit	110	98	90
非诉讼法律事务	Non-Litigation Legal Affairs	件 unit	5 601	5 741	5 814
公证工作	**Notarization**				
公证处	Notary Offices	个 unit	2	1	1
公证人员	Notarization	人 person	40	40	52
#公证员	Notaries	人 person	26	26	36
办理各类公证文件	All Kinds of Notarial Documents Conducted	件 unit	31 283	27 535	25 233
国内公证	Notarization for Domestic Affairs	件 unit	18 845	13 205	10 228
涉外公证	Notarization Concerning Foreign Affairs	件 unit	11 777	13 447	14 270
涉港澳台公证	Notarization Concerning Affairs in Macao, Hong Kong and TaiWan	件 unit	661	883	735
人民调解工作	**Mediation Work**				
专职司法助理员	Full-time Judicial Assistants	人 person	115	124	124
人民调解委员会	People's Mediation Commission	个 person	1 132	1 142	1 142
调解员	Mediators	人 person	5 660	5 386	6 066
调解民间纠纷	Mediation for Disputes among the People	件 unit	35 144	41 622	46 971

表 16-2 道路交通事故
Road Traffic Accidents

指 标	Indicators	单 位 Unit	2009	2010	2011
次 数	Number of Traffic Accidents	起 in number	915	726	838
死亡人数	Death Toll	人 person	250	242	215
伤残人数	Number of Wounded and Disabled	人 person	893	633	755
损失折款	Amount Converted from the Losses	万元 10 000 yuan	432	240	251

表 16-3 火灾事故
Fire Accidents

指 标	Indicators	单 位 Unit	2009	2010	2011
次 数	Number	起 in number	1 111	1 274	1 305
#纵 火	Arson	起 in number	13	19	12
电 气	Electric	起 in number	413	500	544
违章操作	False Operations	起 in number	72	59	60
吸 烟	Cigarette Smoking	起 in number	52	38	51
生活用火不慎	Careless Use of Fire in Daily Life	起 in number	282	218	245
玩 火	Playing with Fire	起 in number	27	33	32
自 燃	Spontaneous Ignition	起 in number	21	8	24
死亡人数	Death Toll	人 person	18	8	8
伤残人数	Number of Wounded and Disabled	人 person	14	6	14
损失折款	Amount Converted from the Losses	万元 10 000 yuan	677	1 083	1 729

表 16-4 社会治安
Public Order

指 标	Indicators	单 位 Unit	2009	2010	2011
刑事案件立案数	Number of Registered Criminal Cases	件 piece	25 664	23 517	26 070
行政(治安)案件查处	Investigation and Prosecution of Administrative (Public Order) Cases	件 piece	1 241 064	622 580	958 881
治安案件查处数	Number of Investigation and Prosecution of Public Order Cases	件 piece	92 168	95 669	104 609

表 16-5 档案管理
Archives Management

指 标 Indicators		单 位 Unit	2009	2010	2011
机构数	**Number of Institutions**	**个 unit**	**1**	**1**	**1**
档案局(馆)	Archives Bureaus (Chanceries)	个 unit	1	1	1
从业人员	**Employees**	**人 person**	**87**	**93**	**88**
专 职	Full-time Employees	人 person	87	93	88
馆藏档案	**Collected Files**				
全 宗	Whole File	个 unit	357	359	360
案 卷	Rolls	万卷 10 000 rolls	215	235	239
录音、录像、影片档案	Archives of Records, Videos and Films	万盘 10 000 discs	0.14	0.16	0.16
照片档案	Photo Archives	万张 10 000 pieces	10.74	12.91	13.07
底 图	Base Maps	万张 10 000 pieces	1.20	0.21	0.21
电子档案	**Electric Archives**				
磁 盘	Discs	万盘 10 000 discs	0.03	0.03	0.03
光 盘	Compact Discs	万盘 10 000 discs	0.36	0.43	0.43
微缩胶片	**Microfiches**				
平 片	Plain Films	万张 10 000 pieces	0.20	0.20	0.20
卷 片	Coiled Films	万米 10 000 meters	12.86	12.93	12.93
档案利用情况	**Utilization of Archives**				
利用卷次	Number of Roll-times Utilized	万卷次 10 000 roll-times	5.91	6.89	6.20
利用人次	Number of Person-times Utilized	万人次 10 000 person-times	6.45	5.71	6.23
综合档案开放利用情况	**Open and Utilization of Comprehensive Archives**				
建国前案卷	Rolls Archived Before Liberation	卷 roll	401	425	425
建国后案卷	Rolls Archived After Liberation	万卷 10 000 rolls	5.88	5.88	5.88
建筑面积	**Floor Space**	**平方米 sq·m**	**17 524**	**17 524**	**17 524**
#库 房	Storeroom	平方米 sq·m	8 200	8 200	8 200

表16-6 信访情况
Complaint Letters and Visits

指 标	Indicators	单位 Unit	2009	2010	2011
信访办受理人民来信、来访	**People's Letters and Visits Handled by Offices of Complaint Letters and Visits**	**件(批) piece (batch)**	**28 497**	**27 741**	**26 786**
来信数	Number of People's Letters	件(批) piece (batch)	14 239	12 453	8 981
#电子邮件	E-mails	件(批) piece (batch)	7 847	9 452	12 318
来访数	Number of Visits	件(批) piece (batch)	2 721	1 893	2 377
#来电数	Number of Calls	件(批) piece (batch)	3 690	3 943	3 110
进京非正常上访人次数	Number of Person-times Visiting Beijing in Secret	人次 person-times			242
到市政府集体上访批次	Number of Patch-times Visiting Municipal Government	批次 batch-times	174	145	231
到市政府集体上访人次数	Number of Person-times with three and more persons Visiting Municipal Government	人次 person-times	3 156	2 947	4 875

表 16-7 法院收、结案情况
Cases Accepted and Ended by Courts

指 标	Indicators	单 位 Unit	2009	2010	2011
法院收案数	Number of Cases Accepted by Courts	件 piece	70 313	76 028	83 897
#刑 事	Criminal	件 piece	3 503	3 406	3 571
民 事	Civil	件 piece	46 324	52 356	57 106
#经 济	Economic	件 piece	9 277	11 091	9 645
婚姻家庭类	Marriage and Family	件 piece	6 594	6 746	6 419
行 政	Administrative	件 piece	476	381	350
法院结案数	Number of Cases Ended by Courts	件 piece	69 483	75 899	84 077
法院未结案数	Number of Cases Not Ended by Courts	件 piece	8 395	8 556	8 378
法院结案率	Rate of Cases Ended by Courts	%	89.1	89.8	90.9
法院上诉率	Rate of Appeals by Courts	%	22.7	23.4	21.1
法院实际执行率	Rate of Actual Executions by Courts	%	56.9	82.5	87.4
法院审限内结案率	Rate of Cases Ended by Courts Within Time Limit	%	97.3	98.3	98.5

表 16-8 外事活动情况
Activities in Foreign Affairs

指标	Indicators	2010 批数(批) Delegations (in number)	2010 人数(人) Visitors (person)	2011 批数(批) Delegations (in number)	2011 人数(人) Visitors (person)
接待外国人来访总计	**Foreigners Received**	**343**	**2 909**	**219**	**2 247**
#副总理以上国宾团	Deputy Prime Ministers and Above	3	39	2	24
部长级(含副部长)团	Ministers (Including Deputy Ministers)	6	93	4	60
其他政界人士团	Persons of Political/Government Circles	42	503	50	1 249
经贸界团	Businessmen	112	525	128	611
新闻界团	Newsreporters	7	104	15	120
其他团	Others	51	1 066	20	183
邀请外国人来访总计	**Foreigners Invited**	**26 343**	**30 958**	**9 732**	**10 382**
按签证性质分	By Type of Visa				
多次签证	Multi-Entry	2 579	2 624	1 931	2 015
一次性签证	One-Entry	23 756	28 326	6 679	7 428
按国别(地区)分	By Country/Region				
#美　国	United States of America		3 471		1 193
德　国	Germany		3 003		745
日　本	Japan		2 086		2 179
审批因公出国访问总计	**Approved Overseas Visits on State Missions**	**864**	**2 930**	**1 190**	**3 884**
按出国性质分	By Purpose				
经　贸	Business	842	2 774	973	3 083
非经贸	Non-Business	22	156	42	247
按出访国家(地区)分	By Country/Region				
#美　国	United States of America	85		153	
日　本	Japan	50		41	
中国香港	Hong Kong, China	28		49	

表16-9　主要年份人大情况
Statistics of Deputies to the People's Congress in Main Years

指　标	Indicators	单　位 Unit	2000	2005	2010	2011
全国人大代表人数	Number of Deputies to the National People's Congress	人 person	2	1		
全国人大代表提出议案	Proposals Suggested by Deputies to NPC	件 piece	4	5		
市人大代表人数	Number of Deputies to the Municipal People's Congress	人 person	70	80	118	116
#女　性	Female	人 person	13	19	37	37
市人大常委人数	Number of Standing Committee Members in MPC	人 person	4	4	6	6
市人大代表提出议案	Proposals Suggested by Deputies to MPC	件 piece	5	4	8	6
新区人大代表人数	Number of Deputies to PNA People's Congress	人 person	380	436	443	444
#女　性	Female	人 person	109	158	136	143
新区人大常委人数	Number of Standing Committee Members in PPC	人 person	27	28	34	31
#女　性	Female	人 person	4	4	11	9
新区人大代表提出议案	Proposals Suggested by Deputies to PPC	件 piece		9	4	7

注：2000年新区人大常委会成立之初，未设议案组。

Note: Since the standing committee of PNA People's Congress was established in 2000, the proposal group was not formed.

表16-10　主要年份政协情况
Statistics of Political Consultative Conference Affairs in Main Years

指　标	Indicators	单　位 Unit	2000	2005	2010	2011
全国政协委员人数	National Political Consultative Conference Commissioners	人 person		7	10	10
市政协委员人数	Municipal Political Consultative Conference Commissioners	人 person		58	66	63
#女　性	Female	人 person		6	8	7
新区政协委员人数	PNA Political Consultative Conference Commissioners	人 person	270	379	645	644
#女　性	Female	人 person	47	84	161	161
新区政协常委人数	Standing Commissioners of PNA Political Consultative Conference	人 person	38	55	93	93
#女　性	Female	人 person	7	8	13	13
新区政协委员提案	Proposals Submitted by PNA Political Consultative Conference Commissioners	件 piece	82	205	528	302
#被采纳提案	Proposals Accepted	件 piece	53	165	467	274

注："全国政协委员人数"和"市政协委员人数"均指在浦东工作的政协委员人数。

Note: Both the item of National Political Consultative Conference Commissioners and that of Municipal Political Consultative Conference Commissioners refer to those who work in Pudong New Area.

表 16-11 主要年份精神文明建设情况

Construction of Role Models in Main Years

单位:个 (unit)

指 标	Indicators	2000	2005	2010	2011
市级文明社区	Model Communities at Municipal Level	6	6	12	10
市级文明镇	Model Towns at Municipal Level	4	6	16	16
文明小区	Model Quarters	298	393	908	908
# 市 级	Municipal-level	119	208	414	414
文明村	Model Villages	102	101	254	254
# 市 级	Municipal-level	27	53	112	112
文明开发园区	Model Development Parks	27	6	11	11
文明大厦	Model Mansions		22	45	45
文明单位	PNA Model Institutions	469	484	1 081	1 081
# 市 级	Municipal-level	52	113	245	245
军民共建先进集体(对)	Model Collectives of Army-civilian (pair)	56	76	97	97
# 市 级	Municipal-level	20	24	22	22
五好文明家庭(户)	Model Families (household)	199	203	241	480
"三八"红旗手(人)	Female Models (person)	252	306	192	
# 国 家	State Level			1	
市 级	Municipal-level	33	32	41	
"三八"红旗集体	Female Model Groups	83	99	88	
# 国 家	State Level			3	
市 级	Municipal-level	8	11	10	
文明班组	Model Crews	136	338	479	478
# 市 级	Municipal-level	12	12		4
区文明岗位	PNA-level Model Posts	66	202	227	232
市级文明岗	Municipal Model Posts				129

注：1. 除"文明班组"和"红旗文明岗"外,表列各项均为每两年评选一次。
2. 为规范"三八"红旗手和红旗集体的评选标准,2011 年新区未举行该类活动评选。

Note: 1. Except "Model Grew" and "Model Post", all the items in the listed table are choosen through public appraisal every two years.
2. To normalize the stardards for choosing female models and model groups, we did not organize these activities in 2011.

主要统计指标解释

律　师

指依法取得律师执业证书，担任法律顾问，民事（刑事、行政）案件代理人、刑事案件辩护人、办理非诉讼业务，解答法律询问，代写法律事务文书等，为社会提供法律服务的人员。

公证人员

指在国家机关依法办理公证事务的司法人员。包括公证员、助理公证员和在公证处工作的其他人员。

公证文书

指公证处根据当事人申请，依照事实和法律，按照法定程序制作的，具有法律效力的司法证明文书。根据公证书用途和使用地，公证书分为国内公证书、国内经济公证书、涉外民事公证书、涉外经济公证书四类。

调解民间纠纷

指调解委员会按照法律规定，根据自愿原则，用说服教育的方法调解民间发生的有关民事权利和义务争执的件数，包括调解成功数和调解未成功数。该指标主要反映人民调解委员会的工作量。

立　案

指人民检察院对受理的报案、控告、举报或自首及自行发现的犯罪线索、犯罪嫌疑人进行初步调查后，认为存在职务犯罪事实和应追究刑事责任，并决定作为刑事案件进行侦查的诉讼活动，是追究犯罪的开始。该指标主要反映人民检察院依法将职务犯罪线索作为刑事案件进行侦查的诉讼活动。

EXPLANATORY NOTES TO MAJOR STATISTICAL INDICATORS

Lawyers

Lawyers are certified legal workers according to law, and who are employed by legal counseling firms to act as legal advisers, agents in criminal or civil lawsuits, or defenders in criminal lawsuits, or to handle non-litigious legal affairs, to advise on matters of law or to write legal papers for others, and provide service to the public.

Notary Personnel

Notary Personnel are judicial workers of the state notary organs handling notarization work according to law. They include notaries, assistant notaries, and other people working in notary firms.

Notary Documents

Notary Documents refer to the judicatory notary documents drawn up by the request of the party and are in accordance with facts and laws and following certain legal proceedings. According to usage and locality, the notary documents are divided into following 4 types: domestic notary documents, domestic economic notary documents, foreign-related civil notary documents and foreign-related economic notary documents.

Mediation of Civil Disputes

Mediation of Civil Disputes refers to number of cases made by mediation committees in mediating in civil disputes concerning civil rights and duties through persuasion and education in accordance with the provisions of law on a voluntary basis, so as to solve disputes by helping the parties involved come to an agreement and understanding, including those unsuccessful ones. This indicator reflects the workload of the mediation committees.

Acceptance of Case

Acceptance of Case refers to the decision made by the people's procuratorate office on reported cases, prosecution, impeachment, surrender, self-found criminal clues or suspects after initial investigation to confirm the act of crime and to start legal proceedings of the case as criminal case.

第十七篇

Chapter 17

城市建设和环境保护

URBAN CONSTRUCTION AND ENVIRONMENTAL PROTECTION

表 17-1 历年各类房屋构成情况
Composition of all Kinds of Buildings in Main Years
(2006～2011)

单位:万平方米 (10 000 sq·m)

指标 Indicators		2006	2007	2008	2009	2010	2011
总计	**Total**	**11 150.90**	**11 504.03**	**12 567.85**	**17 399.80**	**18 760.72**	**19 600.71**
居住房屋	**Residential Buildings**	**6 883.96**	**7 147.99**	**7 835.57**	**11 039.96**	**11 971.31**	**12 544.30**
花园住宅	Garden Residence	306.66	333.67	357.77	459.02	518.00	534.83
公寓	Apartments	19.62	19.62	19.62	20.81	23.81	1 1371.36
新公房	Public Housing	6 516.55	6 747.57	7 411.05	10 150.56	10 982.28	
联列住宅	Terrace Housing						137.09
新式里弄	New-styled Lanes	2.25	2.25	2.25	162.32	165.90	165.90
旧式里弄	Old-styled Lanes	37.45	37.45	37.45	237.70	142.20	142.20
低标住宅	Low-standard Housing						53.80
简屋	Simple Housing	1.37	7.37	7.37	7.98	8.30	8.30
其他	Others	0.06	0.06	0.06	1.57	130.82	130.82
非居住房屋	**Non-Residential Buildings**	**4 266.94**	**4 356.04**	**4 732.28**	**6 359.84**	**6 789.41**	**7 056.41**
工厂	Factories	695.14	724.14	786.25	1 448.45	1 458.00	1 547.00
学校	Schools	272.35	278.94	297.94	470.70	463.19	532.44
仓库堆栈	Warehouses	92.78	92.78	108.58	125.70	130.14	78.00
办公建筑	Office Buildings	1 486.68	1 517.69	1 599.39	1 825.14	1 781.05	1 858.19
商场店铺	Emporiums and Shops	1 201.25	1 212.75	1 379.53	1 707.29	1 760.50	1 760.50
医院	Hospitals	73.27	73.27	86.68	126.93	117.09	128.90
旅馆	Hotels	141.02	141.02	151.22	165.89	203.22	203.22
影剧院	Theatres and Cinemas	12.80	12.80	12.80	17.24	18.16	18.02
其他	Others	291.65	302.65	309.89	472.50	858.06	930.14

表 17-2 八层以上房屋分布(至 2011 年累计)
Distribution of 8-storey and Above Buildings (Total by the End of 2011)

单位:万平方米 (10 000 sq·m)

指 标 Indicators		总 计 Total	8~10 层 8~10 Storeys	11~15 层 11~15 Storeys	16~19 层 16~19 Storeys	20~29 层 20~29 Storeys	30 层以上 30 Storeys and Above
幢	In number	5 203	527	3 110	852	534	180
面 积	Area	8 593	300	5 415	897	1 166	814

表 17-3 市政工程设施
Public Utilities

指 标	Indicators	单 位 Unit	2000	2005	2010	2011
城市道路长度	Length of Urban Roads	公里 km	835	960	1 224	1 255
城市道路面积	Area of Urban Roads	万平方米 10 000 sq·m	1 180	1 704	2 463	2 666
城市桥梁	Urban Bridges	座 unit	121	169	370	495
雨水、污水泵站	Pump Stations for Rain/Sewage	座 unit	102	148	176	176
雨水、污水管长度	Length of Rain/Sewage Pipe	公里 km	1 196	1 858	2 805	2 805
公路里程	Length of Rural Highways	公里 km	511	905	1 937	1 983
公路面积	Area of Rural Highways	万平方米 10 000 sq·m	849	1 360	3 173	3 285
公路桥梁	Highway Bridges	座 unit	355	635	1 533	1 616

注：1. 2007 年起道路长度和道路面积统计口径改变。
2. 雨水、污水泵站数据不包含南片,因南片排水所已撤销;公路里程、面积、桥梁包括农村在内。

Note：1. The statistical approach has changed for the length and coverage of roads since 2007.
2. The data of pump stations for rain water and sewage exclude those of the southern part because the discharge stations in the southern part have been cancelled. The data of the length and coverage of roads, and the bridges include those in the rural area.

表 17－4　环境保护
Environmental Protection

指　标	Indicators	单　位 Unit	2000	2005	2010	2011
工业固体废物产生量	Amount of Industrial Solid Waste	万吨/年 10 000 tons/year	144	250	268	268
工业固体废物综合利用量	Comprehensive Utilization of Industrial Solid Waste	万吨 /年 10 000 tons/year	137	242	243	248
工业废水排放量	Discharge of Industrial Waste Water	万吨/年 10 000 tons/year	12 520	7 103	6 679	6 895
#符合排放标准	Up to the Standards	万吨/年 10 000 tons/year	11 826	6 900	6 560	5 896
工业废气排放总量	Industrial Waste Gas Emission	亿标立方米/年 100 million cu・m/year	734	1 112	1 696	1 865
二氧化硫日平均值	Daily Average Amount of Sulphur Dioxide	毫克/立方米 milligram / cu・m	0.010	0.056	0.035	0.030
二氧化氮日平均值	Daily Average Amount of Nitrogen Dioxide	毫克/立方米 milligram / cu・m	0.018	0.046	0.041	0.039
可吸入颗粒物日平均值	Average Daily Amount of Inhaleable Particles	毫克/立方米 milligram / cu・m	0.116	0.081	0.071	0.069
区域环境噪声平均值	Average Value of Regional Ambient Noise	分贝 decibel	55.8	57.4	54.8	55.6
空气质量优良率	Rate of Fine Air Quality	%		89.3	92.6	94.2
污水纳管率	Rate of Sewage Piping	%		70.4	81.9	82.5

表 17-5 城市环境卫生
Urban Environmental Sanitation

指标 Indicators		单位 Unit	2000	2005	2010	2011
清运垃圾	**Garbage Disposal**	**万吨 10 000 tons**	**101.50**	**104.22**	**169.86**	**168.92**
生活垃圾	Domestic Waste	万吨 10 000 tons	69.85	103.10	168.98	158.86
建筑垃圾	Construction Refuse	万吨 10 000 tons	31.65	1.12	0.88	10.06
清运粪便	**Night Soil Disposal**	**万吨 10 000 tons**	**27.69**	**31.45**	**35.31**	**31.82**
环境卫生设施	**Facilities of Environmental Sanitation**					
公共厕所	Public Restrooms	所 unit	123	219	900	934
垃圾箱	Garbage Bins/Cans	只 unit	8 516	9 216	4 013	3 962
废物箱	Litterbins	只 unit	3 989	8 317	19 384	22 183
倒粪站	Manure-Dumping Stations	个 unit	130	89	102	104
化粪池	Septic Tanks	个 unit	3 987	4 711	5 855	5 850
垃圾处理	**Trash Disposal**					
垃圾焚烧	Trash Burning	万吨 10 000 tons		44.49	44.40	44.14
焚烧垃圾发电量	Power Output by Trash Burning	万千瓦·时 10 000 kw·h		10 841	12 619	13 217
环卫机械总数	**Machineries Used in Environmental Sanitation**	**辆 vehicle**		**598**	**1 191**	**1 211**

注：2009 年起，垃圾箱统计口径作调整。
Note: The statistical approach for garbage bins has been readjusted since 2009.

表17-6　园林绿化
Parks,Gardens and Green Space

指　标 Indicators		单　位 Unit	2000	2005	2010	2011
园林绿地面积	Total Area of Parks, Gardens and Green Space	万平方米 10 000 sq·m	3 830.15	8 439.52	12 019.49	12 518.60
#公共绿地	Public Green Space	万平方米 10 000 sq·m	1 465.08	4 154.71	5 565.51	5 951.40
单位附属绿地	Green Space of Organizations	万平方米 10 000 sq·m	1 332.11	1 508.15	2 479.00	2 519.78
居住区绿地	Residential Green Space	万平方米 10 000 sq·m	891.26	1 139.81	2 834.12	2 893.34
建成区绿化覆盖面积	Green Coverage of Built Area	万平方米 10 000 sq·m	3 074.47	6 426.88	12 283.46	12 923.80
建成区绿化覆盖率	Coverage Rate of Urban Green Area in PNA	%	30.2	37.8	36.1	36.1
新辟、扩大各类绿地	New and Extended Green Space	万平方米 10 000 sq·m		199.50	516.76	344.78
#公共绿地	Public Green Space	万平方米 10 000 sq·m		78.97	294.71	244.76
公园个数	Parks	个 unit	12	17	20	24
#免费公园	Ticket-free Parks	个 unit		15	17	20
公园面积	Area of Parks	万平方米 10 000 sq·m	162.62	214.25	486.27	493.42
#免费公园	Ticket-free Parks	万平方米 10 000 sq·m		68.88	78.31	113.06
人均公共绿地	Public Green Space Per Capita	平方米/人 sq·m/person	11.00	24.42	22.71	23.94
行道树年末累计数	Accumulated Trees on Streets	万株 10 000 pcs	30.40	36.79	23.20	31.67

表 17-7 水、电、煤气供应
Supply of Tap Water, Electricity and Gas

指 标 Indicators		单 位 Unit	2000	2005	2010	2011
自来水	**Tap Water**					
水厂生产能力	Capacity of Tap Water Plants	万立方米/日 10 000 cu·m/day	171.98	171.20	241.00	234.00
供水管道总长度	Length of Water Supply Pipes	公里 km	2 635	3 100	8 471	9 597
全年售水总量	Total Annual Volume of Water Sold	万立方米 10 000 cu·m	33 014	41 926	60 088	59 418
#工业用水	Industrial Water	万立方米 10 000 cu·m	14 678	10 526	14 541	12 063
生活用水	Domestic Water	万立方米 10 000 cu·m	17 655	21 749	21 876	20 710
每日平均售水量	Daily Average Tap Water Consumption	万立方米 10 000 cu·m	90	115	165	163
电 力	**Electricity**					
用电最高日负荷	Maximum Daily Load of Electricity	万千瓦 10 000 kw	146.70	285.70	553.00	556.00
全年售电量	Annual Electricity Sold	亿千瓦·时 100 million kwh	69.75	128.19	229.71	239.00
各类用电户数	Various Electricity Users	万户 10 000 households	82.14	117.91	190.03	193.70
天然气	**Natural Gas**					
管线长度	Length of Gas Pipes	公里 km	1 927	3 574	6 463	6 766
全年销售量	Annual Volume of Gas Sold	万立方米 10 000 cu·m	11 107	44 300	64 200	66 800
#生活用气	Domestic Use	万立方米 10 000 cu·m	4 540	18 700	23 926	25 900
家庭用天然气户数	Natural Gas-Using Household	万户 10 000 households	38.00	75.50	121.25	127.42
液化石油气	**Liquified Petroleum Gas (LPG)**					
全年销售量	Annual Volume of Gas Sold	吨 ton	35 790	52 000	66 700	57 400
#生活用气	Domestic Use	吨 ton	28 043	50 000	54 000	44 100
家庭用液化气户数	LPG-Using Households	万户 10 000 households	45.55	45.90	69.11	73.39

表 17-8 交通运输
Transportation

指 标	Indicators	单 位 Unit	2000	2005	2010	2011
公共交通	**Public Transport**					
年末实有公交线路条数	Routes of Public Transport at year-end	条 route	97	108	232	252
年末运营线路长度	Length of Public Transport Routes at year-end	公里 km	1 783	2 125	4 770	5 019
年末运营公共车辆	Buses in Operation at year-end	辆 vehicle	1 817	2 041	3 450	3 550
全年运客量	Annual Passengers Carried	万人次 10 000 person-times	29 802	34 894	60 317	57 591
专线客运	**Public Feeder Bus System**					
专线客运线路条数	Routes of Public Feeder Buses	条 route	72	68	43	43
年末营运线路长度	Length of Routes in Operation at year end	公里 km	2 191	2 069	1 623	1 647
运营专线车辆	Public Feeder Buses in Operation	辆 vehicle	1 136	1 575	1 023	1 377
全年运客量	Annual Passengers Carried	万人次 10 000 person-times	20 094	28 293	14 879	22 252
隧道大桥	**Tunnels and Bridges**					
越江隧道条数	Tunnels across the Huangpu River	条 route	2	6	12	12
越江大桥座数	Bridges across the Huangpu River	座 in number	3	4	4	4
越江桥隧道车道数	Number of Lanes on Tunnels and Bridges across the Huangpu River	条 lane	26	54	84	84
轨 道	**City Railways**					
运营条数	Number of Railways in Operation	条 route			7	7
运营线路里程	Length of Routes in Operation	公里 km			109	109
站点数	Number of City Railway Stations	个 Unit			73	73
港 口	**Ports**					
港口货物吞吐量	Volume of Cargo Handled at Ports	万吨 10 000tons			22 470	26 332
外高桥港区货物吞吐量	Volume of Cargo Handled at Waigaoqiao Port	万吨 10 000 tons			13 570	14 596
洋山港货物吞吐量	Volume of Cargo Handled at Yangshan Port	万吨 10 000 tons			8 900	11 736
集装箱吞吐量	Volume of Containers Handled	万标箱 10 000 TEUs			2 510	2 881
外高桥港区集装箱吐量	Volume of Containers Handled at Waigaoqiao Port	万标箱 10 000 TEUs			1 499	1 571
洋山港集装箱吞吐量	Volume of Containers Handled at Yangshan Port	万标箱 10 000 TEUs			1 011	1 310
民用航空	**Civil Aviation**					
浦东机场旅客吞吐量	Passenger Capacity at Pudong International Airport	万人次 10 000 person-times		2 358	4 041	4 144
浦东机场货邮吞吐量	Volume of Cargo and Post Handled at Pudong International Airport	万吨 10 000 tons		185	322	311

表 17-9 邮电通信设施和邮电业务量
Post and Telecommunications Facilities and the Volume of Business

指 标	Indicators	单 位 Unit	2000	2005	2010	2011
邮政设施	**Postal Facilities**					
邮电局、所	Post Office	个 unit	74	93	136	124
信筒、信箱	Mailbox	处 unit	591	624	641	1 076
报刊发行站	Newpaper and Magazine Distributors	个 unit	1 224	728	392	1 049
邮路单程长度	Length of Single-Way Post	公里 km	3 577	3 282	822	902
农村投递路线总长度	Total Length of Postal Routes	公里 km	3 514	3 691	6 688	9 373
邮运汽车	Postal Vehicle	辆 vehicle	132	108	144	205
邮政业务总量	**Business Value of Postal Service**					
邮政业务收入	Postal Service Income	万元 10 000 yuan		35 300	43 990	52 288
函 件	Mails	万件 10 000 pieces	4 514	5 409	15 112	20 201
包 件	Parcels	万件 10 000 pieces	37	94	93	90
汇 票	Drafts	万张 10 000 pieces	107	98	162	173
订销报刊累计数	Accumulated Circulation of Newspapers and Magazines	万份 10 000 pieces	12 493	11 750	7 326	18 050
特快专递	Special Express	万份 10 000 pieces	86	281	618	87
集邮业务	Stamp-Collecting Business	万枚 10 000 pieces	1 549	354	663	863
邮政储蓄年末收储余额	Postal Savings Balance at Year End	万元 10 000 yuan	129 865	235 230	1 008 020	1 171 274
电讯设施、用户及业务收入	**Telecommunication Facilities, Subscribers and Operating Income**					
本地电话局用交换机容量	Urban Switchboard Capacity	万门 10 000 units	110	146	218	222
本地电话用户数	Local Telephone Users	万户 10 000 households	77	118	161	158
电信宽带用户数	Subscribers of Telecommunication Broad-Band	门 unit		281 408	806 341	900 796
电信业务收入	Telecommunication Income	万元 10 000 yuan		119 250	353 092	363 919
网络互动电视(IPTV)	Internet Interactive TV Network	线 Line			263 280	299 216
“我的 e 家”用户	“My e-Home” Subscribers	户 Household			625 799	627 829
光纤入户(FTTH)	Fiber To The Home(FTTH)	户 Household			53 731	271 913

注：电信业务收入，不包括移动通信和中国联通以及与其结算的业务量。报刊发行站、邮路单程长度、订销报刊不包括邮政投递的业务量。

Note: The business value of China Mobile and China Unicom as well as the related business is not included in the Telecommunication Income. Fields of newspaper distribution stations, one-way length of postal routes, subscriptions and unsubscriptions of newspapers and magazines exclude the postal delivery volume.

表 17－10　房屋拆迁情况
Housing Demolition and Resettlement

指　标　Indicators		单　位　Unit	2000	2005	2010	2011
房屋完成拆迁总户数	**Total Resettlement**	**户 household**	**13 311**	**23 294**	**3 725**	**2 011**
重大项目拆迁	Resettlement Because of Key Investment Projects	户 household		18 288	1 175	1 474
企事业单位	Resettlement of Enterprises and Institutions	户 household		351	77	128
公　房	Resettlement of Public Housing Residents	户 household		4 487		
私　房	Resettlement of Private Housing Residents	户 household		13 361	1 085	1 346
个体工商	Resettlement of Individuals Engaged in Industry and Commerce	户 household		89	13	
旧城改造拆迁	Resettlement Because of Renovation of Old Towns	户 household	5 720	211		
其　他	Others	户 household	7 591	4 795	2 550	537
完成拆迁总面积	**Tota Area of Resettlement**	**万平方米 10 000 sq·m**	**184.34**	**474.63**	**139.78**	**101.83**
重大项目拆迁	Resettlement Because of Key Investment Projects	万平方米 10 000 sq·m		363.14	26.79	68.18
企事业单位	Resettlement of Enterprises and Institutions	万平方米 10 000 sq·m		59.67	5.06	41.06
公　房	Resettlement of Public Housing Residents	万平方米 10 000 sq·m		22.34		
私　房	Resettlement of Private Housing Residents	万平方米 10 000 sq·m		277.46	18.83	27.12
个体工商	Resettlement of Individuals Engaged in Industry and Commerce	万平方米 10 000 sq·m		3.67	2.90	
旧城改造拆迁	Resettlement Because of Renovation of Old Towns	万平方米 10 000 sq·m	31.85	5.83		
# 企事业单位	Resettlement of Enterprises and Institutions	万平方米 10 000 sq·m	7.61	3.81		
其　他	Others	万平方米 10 000 sq·m	152.49	105.66	112.99	33.65

主要统计指标解释

城市基础设施

城市基础设施包括电力建设、交通运输、邮电通信、市内公共交通、自来水、煤气、市政建设、园林绿化、环境卫生等。

道路长度

道路长度指除土路外，路面经过铺装宽度在3.5米以上的道路，包括高级、次高级道路和普通道路。

城市园林绿地面积

指报告期末用作园林和绿化的各种绿地面积。包括公共绿地、居住区绿地、单位附属绿地、防护绿地、生产绿地、道路绿地和风景林地面积。

不包括：

(1)屋顶绿化、垂直绿化、阳台绿化和室内绿化。

(2)以物质生产为主的林地、耕地、牧草地、果园和竹园等。

(3) 城市总体规划中不列入绿地的水域。

公共绿地

公共绿地指向公众开放的市级、区级、居住区级各类公园、街旁游园，包括其范围内的水域。其中居住区级公园应不小于1万平方米，街旁游园的宽度不小于8米，面积不小于400平方米。

供水管道长度

指从送水泵至用户水表之间所有管道的长度。不包括新安装尚未使用的管道。

生活用水

生活用水包括公共服务用水和居民家庭用水。公共服务用水指为城市社会公共生活服务的用水。包括行政事业单位、部队营区和公共设施服务、社会服务业、批发零售贸易业、旅馆饮食业以及其他公共服务业等单位的用水。居民家庭用水指城市范围内所有居民家庭的日常生活用水。包括城市居民、农民家庭、公共供水站用水。

工业固体废弃物产生量

指报告期内企业在生产过程中产生的固体状、半固体状和高浓度液体状废弃物的总量，包括危险废物、冶炼废渣、粉煤灰、炉渣、煤矸石、尾矿、放射性废物和其他废物等；不包括矿山开采的剥离废石和掘进废石（煤矸石和呈酸性或碱性的废石除外）。酸性或碱性废石指采掘的废石其流经水、雨淋水的pH值小于4或pH值大于10.5者。

工业固体废物综合利用量

指通过回收、加工、循环、交换等方式，从固体废物中提取或者使其转化为可以利用的资源、能源和其他原材料的固体废物量（包括当年利用往年的工业固体废物累计贮存量），如用作农业肥料、生产建筑材料、筑路等。综合利用量由原产生固体废物的单位统计。

工业废水排放量

工业废水排放量指经过企业厂区所有排放口排到企业外部的工业废水量。包括生产废水、外排的直接冷却水、超标排放的矿井地下水和与工业废水混排的厂区生活污水，不包括外排的间接冷却水（清污不分流的间接冷却水应计算在内）。

工业废水排放达标量

指报告期内废水中各项污染物指标都达到国家或地方排放标准的外排工业废水量，包括未经处理外排达标的，经废水处理设施处理后达标排放的，以及经污水处理厂处理后达标排放的。

工业废气排放量

工业废气排放量指企业厂区内燃料燃烧和生产工艺过程中产生的各种排入空气的含有污染物的气体总量，按标准状态〔273K,101 325Pa〕计算。测算公式为：

工业废气排放量 ＝ 燃料燃烧过程中废气排放量 ＋ 生产工艺过程中废气排放量

生活垃圾清运量

指报告期内收集和运送到垃圾处理厂（场）的生活垃圾数量。生活垃圾指城市日常生活或为城市日常生活提供服务的活动中产生的固体废物以及法律行政规定的视为城市生活垃圾的固体废物。包括：居民生活垃圾、商业垃圾、集市贸易市场垃圾、街道清扫垃圾、公共场所垃圾和机关、学校、厂矿等单位的生活垃圾。

运营公交车辆数

指年末公交企业（单位）用于运营业务的全部车辆数。以企业（单位）固定资产台帐中已投入运营的车辆数为准。

邮政业务总量

指以货币表现的邮政部门用于邮政服务的总数量。它综合反映了一定时期邮政工作的总成果,是研究邮政业务量构成和发展趋势的重要指标。它用各种邮政分类业务量,如函件件数、电报份数、订销报刊累计份数等,分别乘以相应的平均单位(不变价),加总后再加上其他业务收入求得。

局用交换机容量

指安装在电信企业用于接续本地固定电话的电话交换机容量。

住宅电话用户

指安装在居民住宅或农民家里并按照住宅电话用户登记注册和收费的电话用户。包括私人付费、单位付费和按规定免费安装的住宅电话用户。

EXPLANATORY NOTES TO MAJOR STATISTICAL INDICATORS

Urban Infrastructure Facilities

Urban Infrastructure Facilities include facilities for power generating, transportation, post and telecommunication, urban public transportation, supply of tap water and gas, development of municipal engineering, city landscaping and sanitation.

Length of Roads

Length of Roads refers to the roads with a paved surface, and with a width of more than 3 – 5 meters, including high quality, medium quality and ordinary roads.

Area of Urban Gardens and Green Areas

Area of Urban Gardens and Green Areas refers to the total area occupied for green projects at the end of the reference period, including public green land, green land in residential quarters, green land attached to institutions, protection green land, production green land, roadside green land and forest in scenic spots. It does not include the following:

(1) Greenery and plants on roofs, balconies, indoors and vertical green areas;

(2) Forest, cultivated land grassland, orchards and bamboo grooves that are for production purpose and etc.;

(3) Water areas that are not included in urban master plan as green land.

Public Green Area

Public Green Area refers to green areas open to the public such as municipal, community and neighborhood parks and roadside parks, including waters within parks. Neighborhood parks should occupy an area larger than 10,000 square meters, and the width of roadside parks should occupy an area larger than 400 square meters, with a width of more that 8 meters.

Length of Water Supply Pipelines

Length of Water Supply Pipelines refers to the total length of all the pipelines between the water pumps and the user's water meters, excluding pipelines newly installed but not used yet.

Consumption of Water for Residential Use

Consumption of Water for Residential Use refers to the water consumption of households for daily life and the water consumption of public service facilities. The latter refers to water consumption for urban public services, including the consumption of government agencies and public institutions, military barracks, public facilities, wholesale and retail outlets, restaurants, hotels, and other units providing public services. Household water consumption refers to consumption of water for daily life of all households in the boundary of cities, including households of urban residents and farmers, and public water supply stations.

Industrial Solid Wastes Produced

Industrial Solid Wastes Produced refers to total volume of solid, semi-solid and high concentration liquid residues produced by industrial enterprises from production process in a given period of time, including hazardous wastes, slag, coal ash, gangue, tailings, radioactive residues and other wastes, but excluding stones stripped or dug out in mining (gangue and acid or alkaline stones not included). A stone is acid or alkaline depending on the pH value of the water below 4 or above 10.5 when the stone is in, or soaked by, the water.

Volume of Industrial Solid Wastes Utilized in a Comprehensive Way

Volume of Industrial Solid Wastes Utilized in a Comprehensive Way refers to the volume of solid wastes from which useful materials can be extracted or which can be changed into utilizable resources, energy or other materials, including the volume of industrial solid wastes stored up in previous years and utilized in the current year, such as the solid wastes utilized as fertilizers, building materials, for making roads or for other purposes. Statistical data on utilization of industrial solid wastes are collected by solid wastes producing units.

Volume of Industrial Waste Water Discharged

Volume of Industrial Waste Water Discharged refers to the volume of industrial waste water discharged, through all outlets, to the outside of industrial enterprises, including waste water produced, direct-cooling water, underground water from mines that does not meet the standard of discharge, and the domestic sewage mixed up with industrial waste water when discharged, but excluding discharged indirect-cooling water.

Industrial Waste Water Meeting Discharge Standards

Industrial Waste Water Meeting Discharge Standards refers to volume of industrial waste water discharge which, with or without treatment, reaches national or local standards with regard to all pollutants.

Volume of Waste Industrial Gas Emission

Industrial Waste Air Emission refers to discharge into atmosphere of waste air containing pollutants generated from fuel burning and production process in enterprises within a given period of time. It is calculated at standard status (273K, 101325Pa) as:

Industrial waste air emission = emission through fuel burning + emission through production process

Consumption Wastes Transported

Consumption Wastes Transported refers to volume of consumption wastes collected and transported to disposal factories or sites. Consumption Wastes are solid wastes produced from urban households or from seryice activities for urban households , and solid wastes regarded by laws and regulations as urban consumption wastes, including those from households, commercial activities, markets cleaning of streets, public sites, offices, schools, factories, mining units and other sources.

Number of Vehicles under Operation

Number of Vehicles under Operation refers to the total number of vehicles under operation by public transport enterprises (units) at the end of the year, based on the records of operational vehicles by the enterprises (units).

Volume of Post Business

Volume of Post Business refers to the total amount of post services provided by the post department, which reflects the total achievements by the post departments during a given period of time in a comprehensive way, and is an important indicator to study the composition and development of the post business. It is arrived by first multiplying the business volume of different types, such as number of letters, telegrams and accumulated number of newspaper and journals subscribed and sold, etc. by their respective average unit price (fixed price) and then adding these products together, plus the income from other business revenues.

Capacity of Office Telephone Exchanges

Capacity of Office Telephone Exchanges refers to the capacity of telephone exchanges installed in the office of telecommunication service providers for communication between fixed telephones.

Household Telephone Subscribers

Household Telephone Subscribers refer to telephone sets installed in the dwelling units of urban or rural residents, and registered as residence subscribers for payment, including 3 types of payment for the service: private payment, public payment and free service.

第十八篇

Chapter 18

重点开发区和镇

KEY DEVELOPMENT ZONES AND TOWN

表 18-1　陆家嘴金融贸易区主要经济指标
Major Economic Indicators in Lujiazui Finance and Trade Zone

指　标	Indicators	单　位 Unit	2010	2011
税收总额(税务部门口径)	Total Amount of Tax Revenues (from the Tax Departments)	亿元 100 million yuan	344.37	380.87
地方财政收入	Local Fiscal Revenue	亿元 100 million yuan	112.12	122.84
固定资产投资额	Investment in Fixed Assets	亿元 100 million yuan	171.06	177.57
#房地产开发投资额	Investment in Real Estate	亿元 100 million yuan	113.95	120.71
#办公楼及商业营业用房	Office and Commercial Buildings	亿元 100 million yuan	80.98	70.73
房地产新开工面积	Floor Space of New Construction of Buildings	万平方米 10 000 sq·m	20.83	83.87
房地产竣工面积	Floor Space of Completed Buildings	万平方米 10 000 sq·m	42.22	93.14
外商直接投资项目	Projects of Foreign Direct Investment	个 unit	257	294
外商直接投资合同金额	Contracted Amount of Foreign Direct Investment	亿美元 USD 100 million	15.70	28.74
外商直接投资实际到位金额	Actual Paid Amount of Foreign Direct Investment	亿美元 USD 100 million	9.83	24.10
新增内资企业注册户数	Number of New Domestic Enterprises Registered	个 unit	1 288	1 442
新增内资企业注册资本	Capital of New Domestic Enterprises Registered	亿元 100 million yuan	105.07	247.51
金融业增加值	Added Value of Finance Industry	亿元 100 million yuan	687.77	845.12
期末金融机构数	Number of Financial Institutions at End of Term	个 unit	592	630
#外资银行法人行	Foreign Banks and Corporate Banks	个 unit	18	18
基金总公司	Head Office of Funds	个 unit	29	30
期末认定跨国公司地区总部个数	Number of Approved Regional Headquarters of Transnational Companies at End of Term	个 unit	65	71
举办展览(博览)次数	Number of Exhibitions (Fairs) Hosted	次 time	120	119
商品销售总额(限额以上)	Gross Sales of Commodities (Above Quota)	亿元 100 million yuan	5 239.72	8 166.82
社会消费品零售总额(限额以上)	Total Volume of Retail Sales for Social Consumer Goods (Above Quota)	亿元 100 million yuan	235.50	292.35
期末星级宾馆个数	Number of Star Hotels at End of Term	个 unit	27	32
主要景点接待人次	Person-times Received by Main Sight Spots	万人次 10 000 persom-times	2 414.18	1 554.99
商办楼宇数	Number of Office Buildings	幢 in number	197	201
商办楼宇建筑面积	Floor Space of Office Buildings	万平方米 10 000 sq·m	1 158.70	1 196.85
商办楼宇平均入驻率	Average Occupancy Rate of Office Buildings	%	86.0	94.4

注：地方财政收入即为原“地方税收”口径,后续相关指标口径相同。
Note: The local fiscal revenue is the former local tax approach. The relevant indicators hereinafter have the same statistical approach.

表 18-2 金桥出口加工区主要经济指标
Major Economic Indicators in Jinqiao Export Processing Zone

指 标	Indicators	单 位 Unit	2010	2011
税收总额(税务部门口径)	Total Amount of Tax Revenues (from the Tax Departments)	亿元 100 million yuan	77.00	79.45
地方财政收入	Local Fiscal Revenue	亿元 100 million yuan	19.26	18.83
固定资产投资额	Investment in Fixed Assets	亿元 100 million yuan	60.48	62.85
#房地产开发投资额	Investment in Real Estate	亿元 100 million yuan	8.80	10.96
工业投资额	Investment in Industries	亿元 100 million yuan	48.05	47.04
房地产新开工面积	Floor Space of New Construction of Buildings	万平方米 10 000 sq·m	14.16	73.69
房地产竣工面积	Floor Space of Completed Buildings	万平方米 10 000 sq·m	7.57	12.93
外商直接投资项目	Projects of Foreign Direct Investment	个 unit	35	26
外商直接投资合同金额	Contracted Amount of Foreign Direct Investment	亿美元 USD 100 million	6.35	3.05
外商直接投资实际到位金额	Actual Paid Amount of Foreign Direct Investment	亿美元 USD 100 million	3.35	2.20
新增内资企业注册户数	Number of New Domestic Enterprises Registered	个 unit	168	227
新增内资企业注册资本	Capital of New Domestic Enterprises Registered	亿元 100 million yuan	10.85	19.81
工业总产值	Gross Value of Industrial Output	亿元 100 million yuan	2 095.30	2 275.66
#高技术产业产值	Output Value of High-tech Industries	亿元 100 million yuan	663.45	734.15
#新产品产值	Output Value of New Products	亿元 100 million yuan	1 198.53	
工业重点发展行业产值	Output Value of Key Industrial Sectors for Development	亿元 100 million yuan	1 740.73	1 859.65
#电子信息产品制造业	Manufacturing of Electronic and Information Products	亿元 100 million yuan	603.28	683.32
汽车制造业	Automobile Industry	亿元 100 million yuan	864.34	909.67
成套设备制造业	Manufacturing of Complete Equipment	亿元 100 million yuan	165.99	143.52
生物医药制造业	Manufacturing of Biological Medicine	亿元 100 million yuan	29.69	26.71
工业出口交货值	Delivery Value of Industrial Exports	亿元 100 million yuan	392.18	422.61
新产品产值率	Production Value Rate of New Products	%	57.2	
经认定高新技术企业数	Number of Approved High-tech Enterprises	个 unit	85	
生产性服务业经营收入	Operating Income of Productive Services	亿元 100 million yuan	367.99	415.51
期末从业人员数	Number of Employed Persons at End of Term	万人 10 000 persoms	12.50	

注：工业总产值为规模以上口径。后续相关指标口径相同。
Note: The gross value of industrial output has the approach for enterprises with above-certain scales. The relevant indicators hereinafter have the same statistical approach.

表 18-3 南汇工业园区主要经济指标
Main Economic Indicators in Nanhui Industrial Park

指 标 Indicators		单 位 Unit	2010	2011
税收总额（税务部门口径）	Total Amount of Tax Revenues (from the Tax Departments)	亿元 100 million yuan	6.80	7.22
地方财政收入	Local Fiscal Revenue	亿元 100 million yuan	1.89	1.92
固定资产投资额	Investment in Fixed Assets	亿元 100 million yuan	15.21	18.04
#工业投资额	Investment in Industries	亿元 100 million yuan	13.26	16.11
外商直接投资项目	Projects of Foreign Direct Investment	个 unit	7	7
外商直接投资合同金额	Contracted Amount of Foreign Direct Investment	亿美元 USD 100 million	1.02	0.80
外商直接投资实际到位金额	Actual Paid Amount of Foreign Direct Investment	亿美元 USD 100 million	0.51	0.47
新增内资企业注册户数	Number of New Domestic Enterprises Registered	个 unit	217	161
新增内资企业注册资本	Capital of New Domestic Enterprises Registered	亿元 100 million yuan	5.59	5.09
工业总产值	Gross Value of Industrial Output	亿元 100 million yuan	108.62	132.18
#高技术产业产值	Output Value of High-tech Industries	亿元 100 million yuan	20.29	32.84
工业重点发展行业产值	Output Value of Key Industrial Sectors for Development	亿元 100 million yuan	67.16	84.94
#电子信息产品制造	Manufacturing of Electronic and Information Products	亿元 100 million yuan	30.38	46.72
汽车制造业	Automobile Industry	亿元 100 million yuan	12.26	12.12
成套设备制造业	Manufacturing of Complete Equipment	亿元 100 million yuan	19.34	21.20
生物医药制造业	Manufacturing of Biological Medicine	亿元 100 million yuan	3.65	3.68
工业出口交货值	Delivery Value of Industrial Exports	亿元 100 million yuan	26.51	30.79
工业利润总额	Total Amount of Industrial Profits	亿元 100 million yuan	9.12	6.51

表 18－4　张江高科技园区主要经济指标
Major Economic Indicators in Zhangjiang High-tech Park

指　标　Indicators		单　位　Unit	2010	2011
税收总额(税务部门口径)	Total Amount of Tax Revenues (from the Tax Departments)	亿元 100 million yuan	109.87	132.72
地方财政收入	Local Fiscal Revenue	亿元 100 million yuan	34.22	37.98
固定资产投资额	Investment in Fixed Assets	亿元 100 million yuan	131.60	146.83
#房地产开发投资额	Investment in Real Estate	亿元 100 million yuan	4.11	15.68
工业投资额	Investment in Industries	亿元 100 million yuan	93.81	100.45
外商直接投资项目	Projects of Foreign Direct Investment	个 unit	97	93
外商直接投资合同金额	Contracted Amount of Foreign Direct Investment	亿美元 USD 100 million	10.48	9.27
外商直接投资实际到位金额	Actual Paid Amount of Foreign Direct Investment	亿美元 USD 100 million	7.21	8.36
新增内资企业注册户数	Number of New Domestic Enterprises Registered	个 unit	564	683
新增内资企业注册资本	Capital of New Domestic Enterprises Registered	亿元 100 million yuan	87.43	174.97
工业总产值	Gross Value of Industrial Output	亿元 100 million yuan	608.09	555.70
#高技术产业产值	Output Value of High-tech Industries	亿元 100 million yuan	388.01	339.55
工业重点发展行业产值	Output Value of Key Industrial Sectors for Development	亿元 100 million yuan	566.90	505.68
#电子信息产品制造业	Manufacturing of Electronic and Information Products	亿元 100 million yuan	257.89	203.58
汽车制造业	Automobile Industry	亿元 100 million yuan	152.93	137.09
生物医药制造业	Manufacturing of Biological Medicine	亿元 100 million yuan	129.90	134.67
工业出口交货值	Delivery Value of Industrial Exports	亿元 100 million yuan	235.72	210.81
信息传输、计算机服务和软件业营业收入	Operating Income of Information Transmission, Computer Services and Software Industry	亿元 100 million yuan	436.98	475.58
文化产业营业收入	Operating Income of Cultural Industry	亿元 100 million yuan	553.58	595.43
知识产权授权数	Number of Authorizations for Intellectual Property	件 item	2 443	3 753
#专利授权数	Number of Patent Authorizations	件 item	1 806	2 823
技术交易数量	Number of Technology Transfers	件 item	1 014	1 298
技术合同金额	Contracted Value of Technologies	亿元 100 million yuan	57.53	50.80
经认定高新技术企业数	Number of Approved High-tech Enterprises	个 unit	333	366
在孵企业数	Number of Enterprises Being Incubated	个 unit	702	
经认定研发机构数	Number of Approved Research and Development Institutions	个 unit	128	
公共服务平台服务企业次数	Number of Enterprises Served by Public Service Platforms	次 time	264 400	
期末从业人员数	Number of Employed Persons at End of Term	万人 10 000 persons	17.35	18.95

表18-5 康桥工业开发区主要经济指标
Main Economic Indicators in Kangqiao Industrial Development Zone

指 标 Indicators		单 位 Unit	2010	2011
税收总额(税务部门口径)	Total Amount of Tax Revenues (from the Tax Departments)	亿元 100 million yuan	18.65	24.71
地方财政收入	Local Fiscal Revenue	亿元 100 million yuan	5.48	6.79
固定资产投资额	Investment in Fixed Assets	亿元 100 million yuan	72.66	67.04
#工业投资额	Investment in Industries	亿元 100 million yuan	15.17	22.55
外商直接投资项目	Projects of Foreign Direct Investment	个 unit	14	8
外商直接投资合同金额	Contracted Amount of Foreign Direct Investment	亿美元 USD 100 million	0.70	0.86
外商直接投资实际到位金额	Actual Paid Amount of Foreign Direct Investment	亿美元 USD 100 million	0.61	0.75
新增内资企业注册户数	Number of New Domestic Enterprises Registered	个 unit	466	407
新增内资企业注册资本	Capital of New Domestic Enterprises Registered	亿元 100 million yuan	6.68	6.69
工业总产值	Gross Value of Industrial Output	亿元 100 million yuan	987.63	1 372.58
#高技术产业产值	Output Value of High-tech Industries	亿元 100 million yuan	552.57	882.10
#新产品产值	Output Value of New Products	亿元 100 million yuan	78.69	
工业重点发展行业产值	Output Value of Key Industrial Sectors for Development	亿元 100 million yuan	758.60	1 115.63
#电子信息产品制造	Manufacturing of Electronic and Information Products	亿元 100 million yuan	573.48	897.35
汽车制造业	Automobile Industry	亿元 100 million yuan	82.54	91.52
成套设备制造业	Manufacturing of Complete Equipment	亿元 100 million yuan	82.75	104.67
工业出口交货值	Delivery Value of Industrial Exports	亿元 100 million yuan	617.41	881.30
工业利润总额	Total Amount of Industrial Profits	亿元 100 million yuan	62.11	70.88

表 18-6 国际医学园区主要经济指标
Main Economic Indicators in International Medical Park

指 标 Indicators		单 位 Unit	2010	2011
税收总额(税务部门口径)	Total Amount of Tax Revenues (from the Tax Departments)	亿元 100 million yuan	1.57	2.30
地方财政收入	Local Fiscal Revenue	亿元 100 million yuan	0.44	0.65
固定资产投资额	Investment in Fixed Assets	亿元 100 million yuan	9.98	20.59
#工业投资额	Investment in Industries	亿元 100 million yuan	3.51	4.53
#医疗仪器设备及器械投资额	Investment in Medical Equipment, Apparatus and Appliances	亿元 100 million yuan	3.51	4.53
外商直接投资项目	Projects of Foreign Direct Investment	个 unit	7	2
外商直接投资合同金额	Contracted Amount of Foreign Direct Investment	亿美元 USD 100 million	0.41	0.36
外商直接投资实际到位金额	Actual Paid Amount of Foreign Direct Investment	亿美元 USD 100 million	0.23	0.25
新增内资企业注册户数	Number of New Domestic Enterprises Registered	个 unit	40	37
新增内资企业注册资本	Capital of New Domestic Enterprises Registered	亿元 100 million yuan	4.90	4.80
工业总产值	Gross Value of Industrial Output	亿元 100 million yuan	25.50	26.97
#高技术产业产值	Output Value of High-tech Industries	亿元 100 million yuan	23.15	24.85
工业重点发展行业产值	Output Value of Key Industrial Sectors for Development	亿元 100 million yuan	25.20	26.76
#生物医药制造业	Manufacturing of Biological Medicine	亿元 100 million yuan	21.34	23.55
工业出口交货值	Delivery Value of Industrial Exports	亿元 100 million yuan	13.04	13.53
生物医药产业营业收入	Operating Income of Bio-medicine Industry	亿元 100 million yuan	22.08	54.33
期末生物医药企业签约个数	Number of Contracted Bio-medicine Enterprises at End of Term	个 unit	61	67
期末医院签约个数	Number of Contracted Hospitals at End of Term	个 unit	8	8
期末在建医院个数	Number of Hospitals under Construction at End of Term	个 unit	1	2

表 18-7　外高桥保税区主要经济指标

Major Economic Indicators in Waigaoqiao Free Trade Zone

指　标　Indicators		单　位　Unit	2010	2011
税收总额(税务部门口径)	Total Amount of Tax Revenues (from the Tax Departments)	亿元 100 million yuan	294.44	351.81
地方财政收入	Local Fiscal Revenue	亿元 100 million yuan	68.16	77.28
海关部门税收	Tax Revenues by Customs Departments	亿元 100 million yuan	444.30	587.20
固定资产投资额	Investment in Fixed Assets	亿元 100 million yuan	30.40	25.35
外商直接投资项目	Projects of Foreign Direct Investment	个 unit	103	127
外商直接投资合同金额	Contracted Amount of Foreign Direct Investment	亿美元 USD 100 million	6.77	7.36
外商直接投资实际到位金额	Actual Paid Amount of Foreign Direct Investment	亿美元 USD 100 million	4.39	5.83
新增内资企业注册户数	Number of New Domestic Enterprises Registered	个 unit	162	222
新增内资企业注册资本	Capital of New Domestic Enterprises Registered	亿元 100 million yuan	4.91	9.35
港口货物吞吐量	Cargo Handling Capacity	万吨 10 000 tons	13 570	14 596
集装箱吞吐量	Container Handling Capacity	万标箱 10 000 TEUs	1 499	1 571
商品销售总额(限额以上)	Gross Sales of Commodities (Above Quota)	亿元 100 million yuan	862.79	923.53
商品销售总额(注册地口径)	Gross Sales of Commodities (Approach of Registered Place)	亿元 100 million yuan	7 805.00	9 690.00
保税市场交易额	Volume of Transactions in Free Trade Markets	亿美元 USD 100 million	902.90	1 152.20
交通运输业营业收入(注册地口径)	Operating Income of Transportation Industry (Approach of Registered Place)	亿元 100 million yuan	103.00	96.00
仓储业营业收入(注册地口径)	Operating Income of Storage Industry (Approach of Registered Place)	亿元 100 million yuan	57.00	63.00
工业总产值	Gross Value of Industrial Output	亿元 100 million yuan	707.64	731.47
#高技术产业产值	Output Value of High-tech Industries	亿元 100 million yuan	453.86	491.28
工业重点发展行业产值	Output Value of Key Industrial Sectors for Development	亿元 100 million yuan	603.19	642.03
#电子信息产品制造业	Manufacturing of Electronic and Information Products	亿元 100 million yuan	467.73	506.00
汽车制造业	Automobile Industry	亿元 100 million yuan	43.11	38.20
石化及精细化工制造业	Manufacturing of Petrochemical Industry and Refined Industry	亿元 100 million yuan	51.39	47.67
工业出口交货值	Delivery Value of Industrial Exports	亿元 100 million yuan	164.87	149.40
进出口总额	Total Volume of Foreign Trade	亿美元 USD 100 million	770.20	915.00
出口额	Amount of Exports	亿美元 USD 100 million	178.00	200.00
进口额	Amount of Imports	亿美元 USD 100 million	592.20	715.00
期末从业人员数(注册地口径)	Number of Employed Persons at End of Term (Approach of Registered Place)	万人 10 000 persoms	23.20	23.70
期末历年累计竣工房屋面积	Floor Space of Accumulated Completed Buildings in Main Years at End of Term	万平方米 10 000 sq · m	812.19	824.84

表18-8 洋山保税港区主要经济指标
Major Economic Indicators in Yangshan Bonded Area Port

指标	Indicators	单位 Unit	2010	2011
税收总额(税务部门口径)	Total Amount of Tax Revenues (from the Tax Departments)	亿元 100 million yuan		
地方财政收入	Local Fiscal Revenue	亿元 100 million yuan		0.12
海关部门税收	Tax Revenues by Customs Departments	亿元 100 million yuan	236.10	332.70
固定资产投资额	Investment in Fixed Assets	亿元 100 million yuan	0.20	0.77
外商直接投资项目	Projects of Foreign Direct Investment	个 unit		19
外商直接投资合同金额	Contracted Amount of Foreign Direct Investment	亿美元 USD 100 million		1.01
外商直接投资实际到位金额	Actual Paid Amount of Foreign Direct Investment	亿美元 USD 100 million		
新增内资企业注册户数	Number of Actual Registered Domestic Enterprises at End of Term	个 unit	90	103
新增内资企业注册资本	Registered Capital of Actual Domestic Enterprises at End of Term	亿元 100 million yuan	11.84	19.93
港口货物吞吐量	Cargo Handling Capacity at Port	万吨 10 000 tons	8 900	11 736
集装箱吞吐量	Container Handling Capacity	万标箱 10 000 TEUs	1 010.80	1 309.90
#洋山港国际中转量	International Transferring Amount at Yangshan Port	万标箱 10 000 TEUs	83.60	93.00
#洋山港水水中转	Ship-to-ship Transferring Amount at Yangshan Port	万标箱 10 000 TEUs	435.30	601.50
进出口总额	Total Volume of Foreign Trade	亿美元 USD 100 million	35.60	59.00
出口额	Amount of Exports	亿美元 USD 100 million	11.80	30.00
进口额	Amount of Imports	亿美元 USD 100 million	23.80	29.00

表18-9 临港产业区主要经济指标
Main Economic Indicators in Lingang Industrial Park

指　标　Indicators		单　位　Unit	2010	2011
税收总额(税务部门口径)	Total Amount of Tax Revenues (from the Tax Departments)	亿元 100 million yuan	7.52	6.22
地方财政收入	Local Fiscal Revenue	亿元 100 million yuan	1.99	1.58
固定资产投资额	Investment in Fixed Assets	亿元 100 million yuan	58.52	44.88
#工业投资额	Investment in Industries	亿元 100 million yuan	34.59	35.60
外商直接投资项目	Projects of Foreign Direct Investment	个 unit		2
外商直接投资合同金额	Contracted Amount of Foreign Direct Investment	亿美元 USD 100 million	0.02	0.80
外商直接投资实际到位金额	Actual Paid Amount of Foreign Direct Investment	亿美元 USD 100 million		0.34
新增内资企业注册户数	Number of New Domestic Enterprises Registered	个 unit		55
新增内资企业注册资本	Capital of New Domestic Enterprises Registered	亿元 100 million yuan		5.69
工业总产值	Gross Value of Industrial Output	亿元 100 million yuan	172.19	204.89
#高技术产业产值	Output Value of High-tech Industries	亿元 100 million yuan	0.83	1.58
工业重点发展行业产值	Output Value of Key Industrial Sectors for Development	亿元 100 million yuan	79.17	95.20
#汽车制造业	Automobile Industry	亿元 100 million yuan	7.17	7.77
成套设备制造业	Manufacturing of Complete Equipment	亿元 100 million yuan	68.61	82.88
工业出口交货值	Delivery Value of Industrial Exports	亿元 100 million yuan	36.40	46.60
工业利润总额	Total Amount of Industrial Profits	亿元 100 million yuan	13.11	14.79

表18-10 各镇财政收入及工业总产值
Financial Revenue and Gross Output Value of Industry in Towns

单位:亿元 | 100 million yuan

镇 Town		财政收入 Financial Revenue			工业总产值 Gross Output Value of Industry		
		2009	2010	2011	2009	2010	2011
总 计	**Total**	**254.14**	**302.16**	**334.08**	**1 985.10**	**2 261.09**	**2 193.86**
川沙新镇	Chuansha New Town	16.07	23.19	24.90	159.62	172.53	160.66
高桥镇	Gaoqiao Town	15.38	18.71	17.78	96.53	122.12	126.89
北蔡镇	Beicai Town	33.50	19.08	27.70	58.02	67.89	64.52
合庆镇	Heqing Town	8.74	10.52	12.08	149.74	177.77	174.61
唐　镇	Tangzhen Town	11.22	14.41	17.60	55.35	63.52	63.42
曹路镇	Caolu Town	16.05	21.19	21.74	159.25	180.49	182.99
金桥镇	Jinqiao Town	16.77	25.01	25.32	20.93	24.87	20.42
高行镇	Gaohang Town	19.02	24.36	22.26	142.37	181.17	193.84
高东镇	Gaodong Town	15.35	16.54	17.07	355.34	346.95	363.27
张江镇	Zhangjiang Town	12.87	14.25	17.25	39.61	46.11	43.62
三林镇	Sanlin Town	16.48	18.18	18.08	53.34	57.28	43.27
惠南镇	Huinan Town	7.00	9.53	9.44	16.85	19.00	15.38
周浦镇	Zhoupu Town	9.04	13.18	13.87	76.98	89.33	85.91
新场镇	Xinchang Town	3.91	4.76	5.93	85.38	91.71	82.85
大团镇	Datuan Town	2.36	2.93	3.36	18.09	19.57	13.45
芦潮港镇	Luchaogang Town	4.79	6.31	7.25	10.69	13.11	14.53
康桥镇	Kangqiao Town	12.33	17.19	21.44	151.55	199.88	211.56
航头镇	Hangtou Town	7.14	10.24	11.31	81.22	92.71	79.37
六灶镇	Liuzao Town	2.26	3.16	4.24	26.09	31.29	25.75
祝桥镇	Zhuqiao Town	7.37	8.01	10.64	98.32	110.09	90.10
泥城镇	Nicheng Town	4.80	5.79	8.32	16.70	18.75	12.43
宣桥镇	Xuanqiao Town	3.96	6.10	5.21	47.57	53.85	49.54
书院镇	Shuyuan Town	3.18	4.23	5.18	23.01	26.21	22.10
万祥镇	Wanxiang Town	2.07	2.73	3.60	13.04	18.66	20.31
老港镇	Laogang Town	2.48	2.56	2.49	29.51	36.23	33.06

主要统计指标解释

货物流量包括货物运输总量和货物进出仓量

货物运输总量

指在报告期内，以重量单位吨位计算的各种运输工具实际完成运输过程的货物数量，公路和水路的货运量按报告期到达货物数量统计，即报告期内已送达目的地并投卸完的货物数量为该报告期的货物运输总量。

货物进仓量

指在报告期内进入本企业仓库和堆放场地的各种货物的重量。按来源分为来自国外、来自国内一般地区和来自国内特殊监管区域（即保税区、出口加工区、保税物流园区等海关特殊监管区域）。

货物出仓量

指在报告期内运出本企业仓库和堆放场地的各种货物的重量。按流向分为流向国外、流向国内一般地区和流向国内特殊监管区域（即保税区，出口加工区、保税物流园区等海关特殊监管区域）。

上海市高新技术企业认定条件

（一）在本市注册的企业，近三年内通过自主研发、受让、受赠、并购等方式，或通过在全球范围内 5 年以上的独占许可方式，对其主要产品（服务）的核心技术拥有在中国内地得到中国法律保护的自主知识产权；

（二）产品（服务）属于高新技术企业认定管理办法的附件《国家重点支持的高新技术领域》规定的范围；

（三）具有大学专科以上学历的科技人员占企业当年职工总数的 30% 以上，其中研发人员占企业当年职工总数的 10% 以上；

（四）企业为获得科学技术（不包括人文、社会科学）新知识，创造性运用科学技术新知识，或实质性改进技术、产品（服务）而持续进行了研究开发活动，且近三个会计年度的研究开发费用总额占销售收入总额的比例符合如下要求：

1、最近一年销售收入小于 5000 万元的企业，比例不低于 8%；

2、最近一年销售收入在 5000 万元至 20000 万元的企业，比例不低于 4%；

3、最近一年销售收人在 20000 万元以上的企业，比例不低于 3%。

其中，企业在中国内地发生的研究开发费用总额占全部研究开发费用总额的比例不低于 60 %。企业注册成立时间满一年但不足三年的，按实际经营年限计算；

（五）高新技术产品（服务）收入占企业当年总收入的 60% 以上；

（六）企业研究开发组织管理水平、科技成果转化能力、自主知识产权数量、销售与总资产成长性等指标符合《高新技术企业认定管理工作指引》的要求。

EXPLANATORY NOTES TO MAJOR STATISTICAL INDICATORS

The Flow of Goods Includes the Total of Goods and the Amount of Goods Entered and Left the Warehouse

Total of Cargo Transport

Refers to the number of cargoes that have been completely finished by all kinds of transportation means that are calculated by weight with the unit of ton during the reference period. The transport volume by road and that by water are calculated by the number of cargoes that have actually arrived during the reference period, namely the volume of goods that has been transported to its destination and discharged during the reference period is the total of cargo transport during the reference period.

Amount of Goods Entered the Warehouse

Refers to the weight of all kinds of goods that have entered the warehouse and storage space of this enterprise during the reference period. Grouped by its sources, they are from the overseas, ordinary domestic regions and specially-supervised domestic regions (namely special regions supervised by the Customs House such as bonded zones, export processing zones, bonded logistics parks).

Amount of Goods Left the Warehouse

Refers to the weight of all kinds of goods that have left the warehouse and storage space of this enterprise during the reference period. Grouped by its flows, they are to the overseas, ordinary domestic regions and specially-supervised domestic regions (namely special regions supervised by the Customs House such as bonded zones, export processing zones, bonded logistics parks).

Conditions for Ldentification of High-tech Enterprises in Shanghai

(I) Enterprises, which have registered in Shanghai, possess independent intellectual property rights protected by Chinese laws in China for the core technology of their main products or services, by means of independent research and development, transferring, donation and purchasing, or in possession of exclusive licenses for over five years all over the world.

(Ⅱ) Their products or services belong to the scope specified in the Appendix: High-tech Fields Key Supported by the State of Identification and Management Methods of High-tech Enterprises.

(Ⅲ) High-tech employees with education levels of college degrees or above occupy over 30% of the total number of employees in that year, in which R&D persons are over 10%.

(Ⅳ) In order to obtain the new knowledge of science and technology (excluding human studies), take advantage of the new knowledge of science and technology in a creative way, or improve their products or services in a substantial way, enterprises have continued to conduct R&D activities and the ratios of the sum of expenses for research and development in the total sales revenue during the current three fiscal years should accord with the following requirements:

1. This ratio is not less than 8% for enterprises with its sales revenue of the previous year less than RMB 50 million.

2. This ratio is not less than 4% for enterprises with its sales revenue of the previous year between RMB 50 million and RMB 200 million.

3. This ratio is not less than 3% for enterprises with its sales revenue of the previous year over RMB 200 million.

Which the sum expenses for research and development in domestic regions of China of the enterprise should account for more than 60% of the total R&D expenses. If the enterprise has registered for more than one year and less than three years, we will calculate its actual operation period.

(Ⅴ) The revenue of high-tech products or services accounts for over 60% of the total income of the enterprise at the year.

(Ⅵ) Indicators such as the level of R&D organization and management, the transferring capability of scientific and technical achievements, the number of independent intellectual property rights, and sales and total assets growth accord with the requirements of the Working Guidance of Identification and Management for High-tech Enterprises.

第十九篇

Chapter 19

上海市统计资料

STATISTICS OF SHANGHAI MUNICIPALITY

SHANGHAI PUDONG NEW AREA STATISTICAL YEARBOOK

表 19-1　主要年份人口、从业人员、工资和婚姻情况
Population, Employment, Wages and Marriage in Main Years

指　标	Indicators	1990	2000	2005	2010	2011
年末总人口（万人）	**Year-end Population (10 000 persons)**	**1 283.35**	**1 321.63**	**1 360.26**	**1 412.32**	**1 419.36**
按性别分	Grouped by Sex					
男	Male	647.13	665.51	683.51	703.57	706.37
女	Female	636.22	656.12	676.75	708.75	712.99
按农业、非农业分	Grouped by Agriculture and Non-agriculture					
农业人口	Agriculture	418.89	335.47	211.32	157.37	151.60
非农业人口	Non-agriculture	864.46	986.16	1 148.94	1 254.95	1 267.76
常住人口(万人)	Year-end Resident Population(10 000 persons)	1 334.00	1 608.60	1 890.26	2 302.66	2 347.46
人口密度(人/平方公里)	Density of Population (persons/sq. km)	2 104	2 537	2 981	3 632	3 702
总户数(万户)	Total Households (10 000 household)	415.28	475.73	496.69	519.27	522.01
每户平均人口(人)	Average Persons Per Household (persons)	3.1	2.8	2.7	2.7	2.7
人口自然变动	**Natural Change**					
出生人口(万人)	Number of Birth (10 000 persons)	13.12	6.95	8.25	10.02	10.15
出生率(‰)	Birth Rate (‰)	10.20	5.30	6.10	7.13	7.17
死亡人口(万人)	Number of Death (10 000 persons)	8.63	9.45	10.23	10.87	11.11
死亡率(‰)	Death Rate (‰)	6.70	7.20	7.50	7.73	7.85
自然增长率(‰)	Natural Growth Rate (‰)	3.51	-2.50	-1.46	-0.60	-0.68
人口迁徙变动	**Migration Change**					
迁入人口(万人)	Inflows (10 000 persons)	12.18	15.16	12.96	17.22	13.15
迁入率(‰)	Rate of Inflows (‰)	9.52	11.51	9.55	12.24	9.29
迁出人口(万人)	Outflows (10 000 persons)	10.72	5.32	3.46	4.97	5.33
迁出率(‰)	Rate of Outflows (‰)	8.38	4.04	2.55	3.53	3.76
从业人员(万人)	**Employment (10 000 persons)**	**787.72**	**828.35**	**863.32**	**1 090.76**	**1 104.33**
职工人数(万人)	Staff and Workers (10 000 persons)	508.10	390.14	420.12	648.49	868.42
职工工资总额(亿元)	Wages of Staff and Workers (100 million yuan)	146.78	614.53	1 146.95	3 018.55	4 505.57
职工年平均工资(元)	Average Annual Wages of Staff and Workers (yuan)	2 917	15 420	26 823	46 757	51 968
婚姻登记	**Registered Marriage**					
准予登记结婚(万对)	Marriage Registration Permitted(10 000 couples)	10.77	9.31	10.27	13.03	14.89
初婚(万人)	First Marriage (10 000 persons)	19.49	15.08	16.44	20.10	23.94
再婚(万人)	Remarriage (10 000 persons)	2.04	2.89	4.09	5.96	5.84
离婚登记(万人)	Divorce (10 000 persons)	3.27	6.36	7.86	9.34	9.57

表 19-2 主要年份上海市生产总值和指数
Value Added And Indices in Main Years

指 标	Indicators	1990	2000	2005	2010	2011
上海市生产总值(亿元)	**Gross Domestic Product (100 million yuan)**	**781.66**	**4 771.17**	**9 247.66**	**17 165.98**	**19 195.69**
第一产业	Primary Industry	34.24	76.68	90.26	114.15	124.94
第二产业	Secondary Industry	505.60	2 207.63	4 381.20	7 218.32	7 927.89
工 业	Industry	469.83	1 998.96	4 036.85	6 536.21	7 208.59
建筑业	Construction	35.77	208.67	344.35	682.11	719.30
第三产业	Tertiary Industry	241.82	2 486.86	4 776.20	9 833.51	11 142.86
构 成(%)	**Composition (%)**					
第一产业	Primary Industry	4.3	1.8	1.0	0.7	0.7
第二产业	Secondary Industry	63.8	47.6	47.4	42.0	41.3
工 业	Industry	59.1	43.0	43.7	38.0	37.6
建筑业	Construction	4.7	4.6	3.7	4.0	3.7
第三产业	Tertiary Industry	31.9	50.6	51.6	57.3	58.0
人均生产总值(元)	**Average GDP Per Capita (yuan)**	**5 911**	**30 047**	**49 648**	**76 074**	**82 560**
上海市生产总值指数(以1990年为100)	Indices of GDP (1990 = 100)	100.0	319.1	560.7	953.0	1 031.1
第一产业	Primary Industry	100.0	126.8	118.0	112.8	112.0
第二产业	Secondary Industry	100.0	305.0	564.5	915.8	975.3
第三产业	Tertiary Industry	100.0	375.9	639.7	1 143.6	1 252.2
上海市生产总值指数(以上年为100)	**Indices of GDP (preceding year = 100)**	**103.5**	**111.0**	**111.4**	**110.3**	**108.2**
第一产业	Primary Industry	104.3	103.4	90.3	93.4	99.3
第二产业	Secondary Industry	102.8	109.8	110.5	116.8	106.3
第三产业	Tertiary Industry	105.3	113.5	112.8	105.7	109.6

表19-3 主要年份全社会固定资产投资主要指标
Major Indicators Of Total Investment in Fixed Assets in Main Years

指标	Indicators	1990	2000	2005	2010	2011
投资总额(亿元)	**Total Investment (100 million yuan)**	**227.08**	**1 869.67**	**3 542.55**	**5 317.67**	**5 067.09**
#房地产	Real Estate	8.16	566.17	1 246.86	1 980.68	2 170.31
在投资总额中按构成分	In Total Investment Grouped by Use of Funds					
#建筑安装工程	Construction and Installation	127.63	882.91	2 079.04	2 820.17	2 991.95
设备、工具、器具购置	Purchase of Equipment, Tools and Instrument	79.51	482.47	610.38	991.10	834.17
按建设性质分	Grouped by Type of Construction					
#新 建	New Construction	78.01	730.76	1 604.58	2 052.69	1 764.74
改建和技改	Reconstruction and Technical Renovation	70.48	216.40	231.15	513.80	413.81
扩 建	Expansion	47.50	216.71	306.00	368.07	348.73
按三次产业分	Grouped by Type of Industry					
第一产业	Primary Industry	3.20	7.87	5.58	16.40	18.62
第二产业	Secondary Industry	133.00	615.94	1 082.10	1 435.37	1 295.83
第三产业	Tertiary Industry	90.88	1 245.86	2 454.87	3 865.90	3 752.64
按经济类型分	Grouped by Economic Types					
#国有经济	State-owned	192.24	829.98	1 240.27	2 234.12	1 875.48
集体经济	Collective-owned	18.29	156.34	131.07	183.07	133.33
联营经济	Joint Owned		41.20	21.53	11.52	10.62
股份制经济	Share-holding		421.53	916.27	1 200.26	1 349.65
外商投资经济	Foreign Funded		222.86	504.16	439.28	473.28
港澳台投资经济	Hong Kong, Macao and Taiwan Funded		96.19	136.15	247.67	253.29
房屋建筑面积(万平方米)	**Floor Space of Buildings (10 000 sq. m)**					
施工面积	Floor Space Under Construction	3 801.46	8 636.31	14 477.85	15 020.76	16 572.36
#住 宅	Residential Housing	2 269.06	4 804.12	8 267.24	7 344.07	8 441.61
竣工面积	Floor Space Completed	2 138.44	3 266.52	4 873.82	2 776.21	2 926.28
#住 宅	Residential Housing	1 339.02	1 724.02	2 819.35	1 415.44	1 581.03
房屋建筑面积竣工率(%)	Rate of Floor Space of Buildings Completed (%)	56.3	37.8	33.7	18.5	17.7
资金来源合计(亿元)	**Total Capital Source (100 million yuan)**	**261.46**	**2 061.66**	**5 108.34**	**7 997.62**	**7 969.18**
上年末结余资金	A Balance at End of Previous Year	28.85	241.05	860.75	1 440.57	1 679.64
当年资金来源小计	Sub-total Capital Source of the Year	232.61	1 820.61	4 247.59	6 557.05	6 289.54
国家预算内资金	Capital Within the State Budget	14.39	48.30	46.42	116.71	75.89
国内贷款	Domestic Loans	62.52	379.21	955.29	1 568.79	1 330.99
债 券	State Treasury Bond		4.85	2.00	10.06	3.47
利用外资	Foreign Capital Absorbed	35.46	161.83	235.61	239.18	158.31
自筹资金	Self-raised Capital	94.13	905.46	1 976.72	3 273.11	3 352.48
其他资金	Other Capital	26.11	320.96	1 031.55	1 349.21	1 368.40

表 19-4 主要年份城市基础设施投资额和公用事业
Investment in Urban Infrastructure And Public Utilities in Main Years

指 标	Indicators	1990	2000	2005	2010	2011
城市基础设施投资额（亿元）	**Investment in Urban Infrastructure (100 million yuan)**	**47.22**	**449.90**	**885.74**	**1 497.46**	**1 157.34**
电力建设	Electric Construction	17.53	64.61	124.22	148.50	118.81
交通邮电	Traffic and Post	10.06	117.52	443.90	866.20	668.52
公用设施	Public Facilities	19.63	267.77	317.62	482.76	370.01
公用事业	Public Utilities	10.83	104.43	41.33	86.58	54.22
自来水	Tap Water	1.06	5.35	29.66	61.63	41.85
燃 气	Gas	1.81	6.88	11.67	24.95	12.37
市政建设	Municipal Construction	8.80	163.34	276.28	396.18	315.80
#园林建设	Parks, Gardens and Green Areas	0.11	38.76	13.88	35.87	44.71
环境卫生	Environment Sanitation	0.37	19.34	15.36	10.80	23.91
市政工程	Urban Municipal Engineering	8.31	102.36	246.58	349.27	247.15
自来水	**Tap Water**					
自来水管道长度(公里)	Length of Tap Water Pipelines (km)	3 483	15 943	23 718	31 182	32 217
自来水供应能力（万立方米/日）	Tap Water Supply (10 000 cu · m/day)	462	1 048	1 096	1 131	1 150
售水量(亿立方米)	Sales of Tap Water (100 milion cu · m)	12.25	19.75	22.81	24.44	24.41
#生产用水	Industrial Use	5.90	5.49	6.42	5.80	5.60
生活用水	Residential Use	6.11	11.88	16.39	18.64	18.81
燃气、液化气	**Gas and Liquefied Gas**					
管道燃气	Pipeline Gas					
管线长度(公里)	Length of Gas Pipelines (km)	2 700	6 606	8 468	5 517	4 710
燃气销售量(亿立方米)	Sales of Coal Gas (100 million cu · m)	12.15	20.56	37.47	55.51	62.29
#家庭用	Family Use	7.63	16.22	18.88	14.07	13.95
家庭用液化气户数(万户)	Household of Family Use Petroleum Gas (10 000 household)	113.19	255.89	236.54	316.37	310.62
道 路	**Road**					
铺装道路长度(公里)	Length of Road Paved (km)	1 631	6 641	12 227	16 687	16 792
铺装道路面积(万平方米)	Area of Road Paved (10 000 sq. m)	1 787	8 147	20 942	25 607	26 176
交 通	**Traffic**					
年末实有公交线路条数(条)	Lines of Public Traffic (year-end) (route)	390	978	940	1 165	1 202
年末实有公交线路长度(公里)	Lines of Public Traffic Routes (year-end) (km)	18 593	23 260	21 794	23 131	22 906
年末运营公交车辆(辆)	Public Transportation Vehicles(year-end) (vehicle)	6 264	17 939	17 985	17 455	16 589
客运总量(亿人次)	Passengers Carried (100 million person-times)	54.37	26.49	27.81	28.08	28.11
出租汽车运营车辆数(辆)	Taxi in Operation (vehicle)	11 298	42 943	47 794	50 007	50 438
隧 道	**Tunnels**					
越江隧道条数(条)	Routes of Tunnels Across the Huangpu River (route)	2	2	6	12	13
越江大桥座数(座)	Number of Bridges Across the Huangpu River (unit)	1	5	6	10	10
城市绿化	**Urban Greenbelt**					
城市绿地面积(公顷)	Area of Parks, Garden and Green Areas (hectare)	3 570	12 601	28 865	120 148	122 283
人均公共绿地面积（平方米/人）	Public Green Area Per Capita (sq · m/person)	1.02	4.60	11.01	13.00	13.10
绿化覆盖率(%)	Green Area Coverage (%)	12.4	22.2	37.0	38.2	38.2
公园数(个)	Number of Parks (unit)	83	122	144	148	153

注：2009 年原园林绿地面积改为城市绿地面积，统计分类作了调整。
Note: As the field of green-land area was changed into that of urban green space in 2009, the classification has been readjusted thereafter.

表19-5 主要年份农业主要指标
Major Indicators of Agriculture in Main Years

指 标 Indicators		1990	2000	2005	2010	2011
农业总产值(亿元)	**Gross Output Value of Agriculture (100 million yuan)**	**68.16**	**216.50**	**233.39**	**287.03**	**314.58**
#种植业	Planting	29.09	89.82	111.25	155.27	165.07
林 业	Forestry	0.37	1.41	11.11	7.53	7.62
牧 业	Animal Husbandry	30.25	87.35	54.34	62.90	77.44
渔 业	Fishery	8.04	37.92	51.64	52.62	54.72
主要农副产品产量	**Output of Major Farm and Sideline Products**					
粮 食(万吨)	Grain (10 000 tons)	244.36	174.00	105.36	118.40	121.95
油菜籽(万吨)	Rapeseed (10 000 tons)	18.17	15.71	6.51	2.04	1.64
蔬 菜(万吨)	Vegetables (10 000 tons)	186.79	377.00	409.03	398.08	408.24
水 果(万吨)	Fruit (10 000 tons)	9.42	22.54	33.63	44.16	40.22
年末圈存量(万头)	Hogs at year-end (10 000 in number)	237.53	241.60	153.16	171.87	180.65
猪肉产量(万吨)	Pork (10 000 tons)	23.32	25.96	18.02	17.87	19.12
牛奶产量(万吨)	Cow Milk (10 000 tons)	22.68	25.95	23.76	24.71	29.08
鲜蛋上市量(万吨)	Poulty Eggs (10 000 tons)	15.07	16.64	8.40	6.28	6.30
水产品(万吨)	Aquatic Products (10 000 tons)	27.36	28.87	35.35	28.97	28.37
淡水产品	Freshwater Aquatic Products	10.32	16.64	20.32	16.82	16.57
海水产品	Seawater Aquatic Products	17.04	12.23	15.03	12.15	11.80
农业机械总动力(万千瓦)	**Total Power of Agricultural Machinery (10 000 kw)**	**276.50**	**142.50**	**96.46**	**28.97**	**105.58**

表 19-6 规模以上工业企业主要指标

Major Indicators of the City's Above-Certain-Scale Industrial Enterprises (2011)

指 标	Indicators	单位数（个）Number of Enterprises (unit)	从业人员（万人）Employees (10 000 persons)	工业总产值（亿元）Gross Output Value of Industry (100 million yuan)	年末资产总计（亿元）Total Assets (year-end) (100 million yuan)	利润总额（亿元）Total After-tax Profits (100 million yuan)	税金总额（亿元）Total Tax and Duties (100 million yuan)
总　计	**Total**	**9 962**	**264.11**	**32 445.15**	**29 454.30**	**2 253.82**	**1 561.86**
按隶属关系分	**Grouped by Subordination**						
#中央工业	Central Government	169	15.78	7 054.79	7 825.47	331.92	792.97
市(局)属工业	Municipality	671	38.56	6 733.75	7 232.07	932.91	393.71
区属工业	District	490	10.87	979.09	848.18	52.91	22.85
镇属工业	Town	1 031	25.56	1 543.01	1 394.01	88.22	40.11
乡属工业	Township	74	1.96	204.12	129.71	10.60	4.10
村委会属工业	Village Committee	327	5.64	401.38	264.68	20.07	9.47
按登记注册类型分	**Grouped by Registration Categories**						
内　资	Domestic	5 419	107.34	12 595.81	14 687.53	867.40	908.10
国　有	State-owned	191	8.44	1 285.13	2 193.32	28.34	48.77
集　体	Collective-owned	172	3.30	205.46	126.56	8.58	5.68
股份合作	Share-holding Coorperation	115	1.40	71.03	49.05	3.95	2.17
联　营	Joint Owned	55	1.12	83.72	55.43	4.26	2.50
有限责任公司	Companies with Limited Liabilities	837	27.91	4 291.63	5 037.24	338.89	599.93
股份有限公司	Share-holding Companies with Limited Liabilities	144	9.96	3 103.86	4 275.16	292.66	156.00
私　营	Private	3 875	54.69	3 478.83	2 894.96	186.99	91.45
其　他	Others	30	0.53	76.17	55.82	3.73	1.59
港澳台商投资	Hong Kong, Macao and Taiwan Funded	1 276	42.56	5 473.20	3 512.73	230.58	148.48
外商投资	Foreign Funded	3 267	114.21	14 376.13	11 254.03	1 155.84	505.28
按轻、重工业分	**Grouped by Light and Heavy Industry**						
轻工业	Light Industry	3 589	89.54	6 788.15	6 457.74	589.36	717.15
重工业	Heavy Industry	6 373	174.57	25 656.99	22 996.55	1 664.47	844.71
按企业规模分	**Grouped by Size of Enterprises**						
大型企业	Large	319	89.25	17 526.78	15 678.77	1 305.39	1 156.10
中型企业	Medium	1 589	85.52	7 219.83	6 446.62	462.99	208.17
小型企业	Small	8 054	89.34	7 698.54	7 328.90	485.44	197.59

注：本表为国有企业及销售收入在500万元以上的非国有企业。
Note: Data in this table is collected from state-owned enterprises and non-state-owned enterprises with revenue of sales more than 5 million yuan.

表19-7 主要年份国内外贸易主要指标
Major Indicators of Domestic and Foreign Trade in Main Years

指标	Indicators	1990	2000	2005	2010	2011
社会消费品零售总额(亿元)	**Total Retail Sales Value of Consumer Goods (100 million yuan)**	**333.86**	**1 865.28**	**2 979.50**	**6 070.50**	**6 814.80**
按用途分	Grouped by Type of Goods					
吃的商品	Food	142.15	743.31	1 026.70	1 830.64	2 036.14
穿的商品	Clothing	52.33	248.94	335.30	686.15	760.31
用的商品	Articles	137.23	858.33	1 563.15	3 197.85	3 590.39
烧的商品	Fuels	2.15	14.70	54.35	355.86	427.96
按行业分	Grouped by Sector					
#批发零售贸易业	Wholesale and Retail Trade	265.67	1 493.13	2 637.29	5 391.59	6 100.99
餐饮业	Catering Trade	17.08	134.12	342.21	678.91	713.81
外贸出口商品总额(亿美元)	**Total Value of Exports (USD 100 million)**	**53.21**	**253.54**	**907.42**	**1 807.84**	**2 097.89**
外贸进口商品总额(亿美元)	Total Value of Imports (USD 100 million)	21.10	293.56	956.23	1 880.85	2 276.47
外商直接投资签约项目数(个)	Projects of Foreign Direct Investment (unit)	203	1 814	4 091	3 906	4 329
#中外合资	Joint Venture	161	441	601	445	511
中外合作	Cooperative Operation	12	226	44	14	13
外商独资	Foreign Enterprise	30	1 146	3 442	3 443	3 801
外商直接投资合同金额(亿美元)	Contracted Foreign Capital of Foreign Direct Investment (USD 100 million)	3.75	63.90	138.33	153.07	201.03
#中外合资	Joint Venture	1.98	13.86	19.62	21.54	23.85
中外合作	Cooperative Operation	0.40	5.86	2.66	1.11	14.85
外商独资	Foreign Enterprise	1.36	44.14	109.47	128.17	160.22

表 19-8　主要年份口岸进出口商品总额
Total Export and Import at Port in Main Years

单位:亿美元　　　　(USD 100 million)

指　标	Indicators	1990	2000	2005	2010	2011
口岸进出口总额	**Total Value of Import and Export**	**172.89**	**1 093.11**	**3 506.78**	**6 846.45**	**8 123.14**
出口总额	**Total Value of Export**	**86.62**	**615.72**	**2 124.30**	**4 233.40**	**4 999.64**
#一般贸易	Original Trade	51.39	341.02	1 057.68	2 183.98	2 691.93
来料加工装配贸易	Processing and Assembly Trade	3.20	64.21	195.83	178.52	151.78
进料加工贸易	Processing Trade of Imported Material	30.67	205.13	813.26	1 639.70	1 846.59
对外承包工程货物	Constracted Projects in Foreign Countries	0.41	1.25	6.37	60.55	77.70
进口总额	**Total Value of Import**	**86.27**	**477.39**	**1 382.48**	**2 613.05**	**3 123.50**
#一般贸易	Original Trade	51.79	212.65	502.49	1 209.42	1 558.35
来料加工装配贸易	Processing and Assembly Trade of Import	2.40	44.87	133.69	169.36	135.68
进料加工贸易	Processing Trade of Imported Material	19.70	125.13	409.30	552.83	610.32
租赁贸易	International Leasing		2.47	7.85	18.56	13.69
外商投资进口设备	Imported Equipment of Foreign Funded Enterprise	6.11	40.26	74.76	43.81	51.18

表 19-9　主要年份财政和保险

Major Indicators of Finance, Cash Balance and Insurance in Main Years

单位:亿元　　(100 million yuan)

指　标	Indicators	1990	2000	2005	2010	2011
全市财政收入	**Financial Revenue**	**284.36**	**1 752.70**	**4 095.81**		
#中央财政收入	Central Financial Revenue	114.33	1 246.47	2 661.91		
地方财政收入	Local Government Revenue	170.03	497.96	1 433.90	2 873.58	3 429.83
#增值税	Value-added Tax		93.55	226.12	388.62	416.70
营业税	Sales Tax		153.81	512.93	933.91	1 041.49
企业所得税	Enterprise Income Tax		103.03	249.15	606.05	731.05
个人所得税	Individual Income Tax		60.24	111.92	261.20	314.95
#市级财政收入	Financial Revenue at Prefectural Level		215.81	553.33	1 393.23	1 675.79
区县级财政收入	Financial Revenue at District (Country) Level		282.15	880.57	1 480.35	1 754.05
地方财政支出	**Local Government Expenditure**	**75.56**	**622.84**	**1 660.32**	**3 302.89**	**3 914.88**
保险费收入	**Premium Income**	**8.99**	**127.23**	**333.62**	**883.86**	**753.11**
赔款及给付	Indemnity Expenditure and Payment	2.23	36.20	87.46	194.54	260.71
赔款率(%)	Indemnity and Premium Ratio(%)	24.7	28.5	26.2	22.0	34.6

表 19-10 主要年份交通运输
Transportaion in Main Years

指 标	Indicators	1990	2000	2005	2010	2011
铁路运输	**By Railway**					
运营里程(公里)	Operations in Length (km)	259	257	269	414	453
正线延展里程(公里)	Extension of Main Tracks in Length (km)	356	397	406	697	774
旅客发送量(万人次)	Volume of Passengers Carried (10 000 person-times)	2 476	2 980	4 313	6 095	6 198
旅客周转量(亿人·公里)	Volume of Passengers Circulated (100 million persons · km)	26.85	35.40	48.86	60.16	63.11
货物运输量(万吨)	Volume of Goods Transported (10 000 tons)	1 257	1 055	1 278	959	888
货物周转量(亿吨·公里)	Volume of Goods Circulated (100 million tons · km)	111	122	47	26	21
公路运输	**By Road**					
通车里程(公里)	Available for Traffic in Length (km)	3 050	6 078	8 110	11 974	12 084
#高速公路	Expressway	36	98	560	775	806
货运汽车每车吨年产量(万吨·公里)	Yearly Output per Truck · Ton (10 000 tons · km)	1.72	1.50	1.64	2.01	1.93
汽油车耗油(升/百吨·公里)	Oil Consumption of Gasoline Vehicles (L/100 tons · km)	6.50	6.87	8.85	5.50	5.57
柴油车耗油(升/百吨·公里)	Oil Consumption of Diesel Vehicles (L/100 tons · km)	4.00	4.77	4.51	6.07	5.01
旅客发送量(万人次)	Volume of Passengers Carried (10 000 person-times)	605	2 482	2 468	3 634	3 477
旅客周转量(亿人·公里)	Volume of Passengers Circulated (100 million persons · km)	8.42	16.44	75.06	115.44	106.74
货物运输量(万吨)	Volume of Goods Transported (10 000 tons)	605	2 482	2 468	40 890	42 685
货物周转量(亿吨·公里)	Volume of Goods Circulated (100 million · km)	11	56	73	266	284
水路运输	**By Water**					
旅客周转量(亿人·公里)	Volume of Passengers Circulated (100 million persons · km)	40.84	6.77	4.52	3.69	1.02
货物运输量(万吨)	Volume of Goods Transported (10 000 tons)	12 864	18 442	34 557	38 803	49 389
#远洋运输(万吨)	Ocean Transportation (10 000 tons)	2 246	7 022	10 091	15 172	16 044
货物周转量(亿吨·公里)	Volume of Goods Circulated (100 million tons · km)	3 236	6 430	11 986	15 818	20 005
#远洋运输(亿吨·公里)	Ocean Transportation (100 million tons · km)	1 957	5 285	9 285	14 535	15 654
港 口	**Ports**					
港口旅客发送量(万人次)	Volume of Passengers Carried at Ports (10 000 person-times)	555	539	626	85	78
民用航空	**Civil Aviation**					
旅客发送量(万人次)	Volume of Passengers Carried (10 000 person-times)	199	892	2 080	3 642	3 766
旅客周转量(亿人·公里)	Volume of Passengers Circulated (100 million persons · km)	37.84	176.11	535.48	1 034.96	1 136.69
货物运输量(万吨)	Volume of Goods Transported (10 000 tons)	13	88	222	371	356
货物周转量(亿吨·公里)	Volume of Goods Circulated (100 million tons · km)	1	12	27	63	57

注：港口旅客发送量从2006年起不包含海港到内河部分。
Note: The volume of Passenger Departures excludes those from seaports to freshwater since 2006.

表19-11　主要年份教育、卫生事业情况
Statistics of Education and Healthcare in Main Years

指　标	Indicators	1990	2000	2005	2010	2011
学　校(所)	**School (unit)**					
高等学校	Institutions of Higher Education	50	37	60	66	66
中等专业学校	Special Secondary Schools	110	84	81	65	64
职业中学	Vocational Middle Schools	80	60	37	26	28
普通中学	Regular Secondary Schools	712	861	807	755	754
小　学	Primary Schools	2 630	1 021	640	766	764
特殊教育学校	Special Schools	29	34	28	29	29
在校学生数(万人)	**Student Enrollment (10 000 persons)**					
高等学校	Institutions of Higher Education	12.13	22.68	44.26	51.57	51.13
中等专业学校	Special Secondary Schools	6.17	11.89	13.67	10.91	10.22
职业中学	Vocational Middle Schools	3.66	8.48	5.76	3.77	3.52
普通中学	Regular Secondary Schools	48.31	79.54	77.02	59.44	59.17
小　学	Primary Schools	110.19	78.86	53.50	70.16	73.11
特殊教育学校	Special Schools	0.33	0.54	0.52	0.50	0.49
教职员工(万人)	**Staff and Workers (10 000 persons)**					
高等学校	Institutions of Higher Education	7.06	6.08	7.09	7.42	7.41
中等专业学校	Special Secondary Schools	1.49	1.27	1.09	0.91	0.89
职业中学	Vocational Middle Schools	0.53	0.66	0.51	0.43	0.42
普通中学	Regular Secondary Schools	6.62	7.66	7.46	6.73	7.53
小　学	Primary Schools	7.48	6.13	4.94	5.58	4.82
特殊教育学校	Special Schools	0.11	0.16	0.16	0.16	0.16
卫生机构数(个)	**Health Care Institutions (unit)**	**7 690**	**4 400**	**2 527**	**3 270**	**3 358**
#医　院	Hospital	462	459	487	306	308
医院床位数(张)	**Hospital Beds (bed)**	**69 636**	**75 334**	**90 800**	**105 083**	**107 130**
卫生技术人员(万人)	**Medical Technical Personnel (10 000 persons)**	**15.85**	**10.71**	**10.35**	**13.54**	**13.91**
#执业医生	Medical Parctitioners	5.82	4.99	4.40	5.13	5.21
护师、护士	Senior and Junior Nurses	3.27	3.68	3.94	5.59	5.89
医院治疗人次(万人次)	**Total Patients Treated (10 000 person-times)**	**8 395.00**	**8 631.67**	**9 455.71**	**21 002.46**	**20 205.30**
#门、急诊	Out-patients and Emergency Patients		8 432.29	9 277.79	20 676.24	19 964.97
医院入院人数(万人次)	**In Patients (10 000 person-times)**	**95.28**	**122.79**	**147.91**	**285.68**	**268.28**
医院每百诊次的入院人数(人)	**In Patients Per 100 Patient-times (person)**	**1.10**	**1.40**	**1.56**	**1.40**	**1.33**

表 19-12 居民消费价格指数(以上年价格为 100)
Consumer Price Indices of Residents(Preceding Year = 100)

指 标	Indicators	2011
居民消费价格指数	**Overall Residents Consumer Price Index**	**105.2**
食 品	**Food**	**110.8**
粮 食	Grain	113.5
淀粉及制品	Starch and Related products	106.6
干豆类及豆制品	Dry Beans and Bean Products	114.7
油 脂	Oil and Fat	117.5
肉禽及其制品	Meat Poultry and Their Products	119.9
蛋	Eggs	113.5
水产品	Aquatic Products	113.7
菜	Vegetables	99.8
#鲜 菜	Fresh Vegetables	98.3
调味品	Flavoring	107.7
糖	Sugar	104.8
茶及饮料	Tea and Beverages	105.1
干鲜瓜果	Dried and Fresh Fruits	114.5
#鲜 果	Fresh Fruits	117.5
糕点饼干面包	Cakes,Biscuits and Bread	108.8
奶及奶制品	Milk and Its Products	108.2
在外用膳食品	Out-of-home food	107.9
其他食品及食品加工服务	Other Food and Food Processing Service	107.4
烟酒及用品	**Tobacco, Alcohol and Related Products**	**101.3**
烟 草	Tobacco	100.3
酒	Liquor	103.9
吸烟饮酒用品	Related Products for Smoking and Driking	
衣 着	**Clothing**	**104.3**
服 装	Garments	105.4
男式服装	Men's Wear	103.7
女式服装	Women's Wear	107.4
儿童服装	Children's Wear	100.3
衣着材料	Clothing Materials	119.8
鞋袜帽	Shoes,Socks and Hats	99.0
#鞋	Shoes	98.5
衣着加工服务	Garment Processing Service	119.1

指 标	Indicators	2011
家庭设备用品及维修服务	**Home Appliances and Required Service**	**107.1**
耐用消费品	Durable Consumer Goods	102.8
室内装饰品	Interior Decorations	101.5
床上用品	Bed Articles	116.4
家庭日用杂志	Daily Use Household Articles	107.6
家庭服务及加工维修服务	Other Daily Use Articles	118.0
医疗保健和个人用品	**Medicine,Medical Services and Personal Articles**	**104.1**
医疗保健	Medicine and Medical Services	100.6
#中药材及中成药	Chinese Medicinal Crop And Patent Medicine	105.8
西 药	Western Medicine	94.6
保健器具及用品	Healthcare and Equipment	104.9
医疗保健服务	Medical and Healthcare Service	103.1
个人用品及服务	Personal Articles and Service	107.4
交通和通信	**Means of Transportation and Communication**	**100.2**
交 通	Transport	101.8
#交通工具	Transport Tools	101.6
通 信	Communications	96.3
通信工具	Communications tools	79.9
通信服务	Communications Service	99.7
娱乐教育文化用品及服务	**Recreation,Education and Culture Articles**	**99.2**
文娱用耐用消费品及服务	Durable Consumer Goods for Recreational Use	89.7
教 育	Education	101.8
文化娱乐用品	Recreation and Culture Articles	102.8
旅游及外出	Tourism	99.9
居 住	**Residence**	**105.4**
建房及装修材料	Housing Construction And Finishing Materials	103.3
租 房	House Leasing	105.6
自有住房	Self-owned House	107.1
水电燃料	Water,Electricity and Fuels	101.8
#水	Water	111.4
电	Electricity	100.0
液化石油气	LPG	106.0
管道燃气	Gas	100.0

表19-13　主要年份商品零售价格指数（以上年价格为100）
Classified Retail Price Index in Main Years (Preceding Year = 100)

指　标	Indicators	2001	2003	2004	2005	2010	2011
商品零售价格指数	**Overall Retail Price Index**	**98.6**	**99.0**	**100.9**	**99.4**	**101.7**	**104.1**
食品类	Food	98.4	101.5	108.6	104.7	107.6	111.0
粮　食	Grain	100.1	100.5	128.8	102.1	112.0	113.3
淀粉及制品	Starch and Related Products	100.4	109.2	107.2	105.2	95.5	106.6
干豆类及豆制品	Dry Beans and Bean Products	111.3	102.7	124.8	103.6	108.7	114.7
油　脂	Oil or Fat	81.4	106.8	114.4	91.2	105.6	117.3
肉禽及其制品	Meat Poultry and Their Products	100.4	101.7	117.6	105.5	104.2	119.9
蛋	Eggs	110.7	101.0	118.6	105.8	106.1	113.5
水产品	Aquatic Products	90.1	103.9	107.7	114.4	116.1	113.7
菜	Vegetables	107.1	101.5	95.5	103.4	111.0	99.8
调味品	Flavoring	99.5	98.4	103.0	102.1	106.5	107.5
糖	Sugar	104.4	98.9	103.1	103.8	103.8	104.8
干鲜瓜果	Dried and Fresh Fruits	107.3	97.6	118.3	99.4	112.1	114.5
糕点饼干面包	Cakes, Biscuits and Bread	99.8	101.4	100.9	98.4	100.5	108.8
奶及奶制品	Milk and Its Products	99.8	101.4	99.6	100.8	102.3	108.2
在外用膳食品	Out-of-home Food	100.7	100.7	103.1	104.4	105.6	107.9
其它食品	Other Food	99.5	101.5	96.9	101.1	105.0	107.4
饮料、烟酒	Beverages, Tobacco and Liquor	98.4	99.5	98.8	99.6	101.9	102.3
服装、鞋帽类	Garments, Shoes and Hats	107.7	96.7	93.9	92.6	98.4	103.9
纺织品类	Textiles	98.8	99.8	102.2	99.4	103.9	117.6
家用电器及音像器材	Household Appliances and Audio-video Appliances	95.0	95.8	93.4	93.1	92.4	96
文化办公用品	Cultural and Office Articies	98.7	93.7	91.9	91.6	97.7	94.7
日用品	Daily Use Articles	99.0	99.1	98.4	100.5	100.3	106.2
体育娱乐用品	Sports and Recreation Goods	99.1	97.4	96.8	94.7	95.9	103.8
交通、通信用品	Transportation and Communication Goods	97.4	91.2	90.2	88.5	94.0	98.3
家　具	Furniture	90.4	99.5	98.2	100.1	101.1	104.2
化妆品类	Cosmetics	100.7	100.4	99.0	96.1	101.0	104.8
金银珠宝类	Jewelry	87.2	106.5	107.9	107.3	111.7	107.9
中西药品及医疗保健用品类	Traditional Chinese and Western Medicines	98.7	98.3	95.6	97.7	99.8	99.4
书报杂志及电子出版物类	Books, Newspapers, Magazines and Electronic Publications	99.5	98.3	99.6	98.0	103.2	102.1
燃料类	Fuels	111.4	108.6	107.0	109.1	112.8	107.2
建筑材料及五金电料类	Building Materials and Hardwares	101.8	100.8	104.7	104.0	103.3	104.2

主要统计指标解释

居民消费价格指数

居民消费价格指数是度量一组代表性消费商品及服务项目价格水平随着时间而变动的相对数,反映居民家庭购买的消费品及服务价格水平的变动情况。它是宏观经济分析和决策、价格总水平监测和调控以及国民经济核算的重要指标。其按年度计算的变动率通常被用来作为反映通货膨胀或紧缩程度的指标。

现行的居民消费价格指数按用途分为八个大类,包括食品、烟酒及用品、衣着、家庭设备用品及维修服务、医疗保健和个人用品、交通和通信、娱乐教育文化用品及服务、居住。

商品零售价格指数

商品零售价格指数是反映一定时期内城乡商品零售价格变动趋势和程度的相对数。商品零售价格的变动直接影响城乡居民的生活支出和国家的财政收入,影响居民购买力和市场供需的平衡,影响消费与积累的比例关系。因此,该指数可以从一个侧面对上述经济活动进行观察和分析。

EXPLANATORY NOTES TO MAJOR STATISTICAL INDICATORS

Consumer Price Index

The Consumer Price Index is an index that reflects the time-based change of prices of a group of representative consumption commodities and services. It is an important reference factor for macro-economic analysis and strategy, monitoring and adjustment of overall price level and the national economic budgeting. The year-on-year change of the index is often a norm reflecting the inflation or deflation.

The current CPI covers eight categories of goods and services: food; tobacco, liquor and related articles; garments; household facilities, articles and repair services; medical and health care and personal items; traffic and telecommunications; education, culture and recreation articles and services and residence.

Retail Price Indices

Retail Price Indices reflect the trend and degree of change in retail prices of commodities during a given period. The change in retail prices of commodities directly affect the living expenditure of urban and rural residents, government revenue, purchasing power of residents and the equilibrium of market supply and demand, and the ratio of consumption to accumulation. Therefore, the retail price indices are useful to analyze the changes of the above economic activities.

(京)新登字041号

图书在版编目(CIP)数据

上海浦东新区统计年鉴.2012/上海市浦东新区统计局
国家统计局浦东调查队编.
——北京：中国统计出版社，2012.8
ISBN 978-7-5037-6629-9/C.2703

Ⅰ.①上…
Ⅱ.①上… ②国…
Ⅲ.①统计资料-浦东新区-2012-年鉴
Ⅳ.①C832.513-54

中国版本图书馆CIP数据核字(2012)第181776号

上海浦东新区统计年鉴—2012

作　　者/上海市浦东新区统计局　国家统计局浦东调查队
责任编辑/陈越月
执行编辑/肖现平　施湘君　计勤敏
封面设计/蔡旭洲
出版发行/中国统计出版社
通信地址/北京市西城区月坛南街57号
邮　　编/100826
办公地址/北京市丰台区西三环南路甲6号
电　　话/(010)63376907
网　　址/http://csp.stats.gov.cn
印　　刷/上海万卷印刷有限公司
经　　销/新华书店
开　　本/890×1240毫米1/16
字　　数/95.68万字
印　　张/23
印　　数/1～1500册
版　　别/2012年8月第1版
版　　次/2012年8月第1次印刷
书　　号/ISBN 978-7-5037-6629-9/C.2703
定　　价/320.00元